About the Author

Dr John Hilley is a political scientist who was educated at the University of Sydney, Australia, and the University of Glasgow, Scotland. This is his first book.

Malaysia: Mahathirism, Hegemony and the New Opposition

John Hilley

Zed Books
LONDON · NEW YORK

Malaysia: Mahathirism, Hegemony and the New Opposition was first published by Zed Books Ltd, 7 Cynthia Street, London, N1 9JF, UK and Room 400, 175 Fifth Avenue, New York, NY 10010, USA in 2001.

Distributed in the USA exclusively by Palgrave, a division of St Martin's Press, LLC, 175 Fifth Avenue, New York, NY 10010, USA.

Cover designed by Andrew Corbett
Set in Monotype Ehrhardt and Franklin Gothic by Ewan Smith
Printed and bound in Thailand

A catalogue record for this book is available from the British Library

Library of Congress Cataloging-in-Publication Data: available

ISBN 1 85649 917 0 cased
ISBN 1 85649 918 9 limp

Second impression, 2002

Contents

Tables

Acknowledgements

A number of people and institutions have given me valuable assistance in researching and writing this book.

My thanks to the University of Glasgow and the Carnegie Trust for supporting the PhD study on which the text is based. I would like to thank Mark Thompson, Richard Crook, David Stansfield, Chris Berry, Jane Duckett and others at the Department of Politics, Glasgow, for their guidance and debate. My appreciations also to Stephen Herbert, Wallace McNeish, Donna McKinnon, Ricardo Gomez and the other Glasgow postgraduates for their friendship and stimulation.

My warmest thanks to the Dean and academic community at the Social Sciences Faculty, Universiti Sains Malaysia, for their help, discussion and kindness, particularly Latif Kamaluddin, Mustafa K. Anuar, Francis Loh Kok Wah, Mohamad Abdad Mohamad Zain, Zaharom Nain, Mahamad Hakimi Ibrahim, Rohana Ariffin and the staff at USM library. My special thanks to Khoo Boo Teik for his valued insights and support.

I would like to record my debt to the many and varied people across Malaysia who provided me with information, material and opinion. My fond regards also to many others in Penang for their discursive interest, social insights and friendship, particularly Haresh K. Chhabra at Kolej Antarabangsa, Felix Partrikeeff, Michael and Carolyn van Langenberg, Maura Crowley and Hai Long. My thanks also to the Centre for Southeast Asian Studies, University of Hull, John Sidel at SOAS, Peter Preston at the University of Birmingham and Robert Molteno at Zed Books for their helpful direction.

Finally, thanks and love to my children Caroline and Paul for 'looking after me', my mum, sisters and brothers for their good hearts and humour, my extended family and friends for their moral support, and, most of all, my wife Jacqui for her love and understanding.

All views, interpretations and faults within the text belong, of course, to the present author.

Abbreviations and Organisations

ABIM	Angkatan Belia Islam Malaysia (Malaysian Islamic Youth Movement)
ACA	Anti Corruption Agency
ADB	Asian Development Bank
Adil	Pergerakan Keadilan Sosial (Movement for Social Justice)
AFP	Agence France Presse
Aliran	Aliran Kesedaran Negara (National Consciousness Movement)
AMCJA	All Malaya Council of Joint Action
ANC	African National Congress
APEC	Asia Pacific Economic Co-operation
APU	Angkatan Perpaduan Ummah (Muslim Unity Force)
ARF	ASEAN Regional Forum
Arqam	Darul Arqam (House of Arqam)
ASEAN	Association of Southeast Asian Nations
ASTRO	All Asia Television and Radio Company
Bank Negara	National Bank (central bank)
Bhd	Berhad (limited company)
BN	Barisan Nasional (National Front)
BOT	Build-Operate Transfer
CAP	Consumers Association Penang
CCC	Chinese Consultative Committee
CDRC	Corporate Debt Restructuring Committee
CM	Chief Minister
Dakwah Foundation	Revival Foundation
DAP	Democratic Action Party
Dewan Rakyat	People's Parliament
DJZ	Dongjiaozong (Chinese Education Movement)
EAEC	East Asian Economic Caucus

EPF	Employers Provident Fund
EPSM	Environmental Protection Society of Malaysia
EPU	Economic Planning Unit
EU	European Union
FDI	Foreign Direct Investment
FEER	*Far Eastern Economic Review*
FELDA	Federal Land Development Authority
FOMCA	Federation of Malaysian Consumers Association
FTZ	Free Trade Zone
G7/G8	Group of 7/Group of 8 (leading industrialised countries)
Gagasan	Coalition for People's Democracy
Gagasan Rakyat Malaysia	Malaysian People's Front
Gerak	Malaysian People's Movement for Justice
Gerakan	Parti Gerakan Rakyat Malaysia (People's Movement Party Malaysia)
HAKAM	Kebangsaan Hak Asasi Manusia Malaysia (National Human Rights Society Malaysia)
HICOM	Heavy Industries Corporation of Malaysia
IADC	Islamic Affairs Development Committee
ICA	Industrial Coordination Act
ICB	Islamic Consultative Body
IEF	Islamic Economic Foundation
IFC	International Finance Corporation
IKIM	Institute for Islamic Understanding Malaysia
IMP	Independence of Malaya Party
IMTGT	Indonesia, Malaysia, Thailand Growth Triangle
IPR	Institute for Policy Research
IRAD	Islamic Religious Affairs Department
ISA	Internal Security Act
ISIS	Institute of Strategic International Studies
IPR	Institute of Policy Research
IT	Information Technology
JIM	Jemmah Islah Malaysia (Congregation of Peace Malaysia – formerly Islamic Representative Council)
JKKK	Jawatankuasa Kemajuan dan Keselamatan Kampung (Village Security and Development Committee)
JPP	Jabatan Pembangunan Persekutuan (Federal Development Department)
JUST	International Movement for a Just World

KeADILan/PKN	Parti Keadilan Nasional (National Justice Party)
KLSE	Kuala Lumpur Stock Exchange
MAI	Multilateral Agreement on Investment
MAS	Malaysian Airlines Service
MB	Menteri Besar (Chief Minister)
MBC	Malysian Business Council
MBF	Malaysia Borneo Finance (Bhd)
MCA	Malaysian Chinese Association
MCCC	Malaysian Chinese Chamber of Commerce
MCP	Malayan Communist Party
MDC	Multimedia Development Corporation
MIC	Malaysian Indian Congress
MIER	Malaysian Institute for Economic Research
MITI	Ministry of International Trade and Industry
MNC/TNC	multinational/transnational corporation
MNPA	Malaysian Newspaper Publishers Association
MPH	Multi Purpose Holdings
MSC	Mutimedia Super Corridor
MSRC	Malaysian Strategic Research Centre
NAFTA	North American Free Trade Agreement
NATO	North Atlantic Treaty Organisation
NCP	National Cultural Policy
NDP	New Development Policy
NEAC	National Economic Action Committee
NECC	National Economic Consultative Council
NEP	New Economic Policy
NERP	National Economic Recovery Plan
NGO	non-governmental organisation
NIC	newly industrialising country
NII	National Information Infrastructure
NITA	National IT Agenda
NITC	National Information Technology Council
NOP	National Operations Council
NSMs	new social movements
NSTP	New Straits Times Press
NTV7	Natseven TV station
OECD	Organisation for Economic Cooperation and Development
OPP	Outline Perspective Plan
PAP	People's Action Party (Singapore)

PAS	Parti Islam SeMalaysia (Islamic Party of Malaysia)
PBB	Parti Pesaka Bumiputera Bersatu (United Bumiputera Party) (Sarawak)
PBS	Parti Bersatu Sabah (United Sabah Party)
PCCC	Penang Chinese Chamber of Commerce
PKMM	Malay Nationalist Party
PKPIM	National Association of Muslim Students Malaysia
PNB	Permodalan Nasional Berhad (National Equity Corporation)
PPP	People's Progressive Party
PRM	Parti Rakyat Malaysia (Malaysian People's Party – formerly Parti Sosialis Rakyat Malaysia, Malaysian People's Socialist Party)
Pusat Islam	Islamic Centre
PUTERA	Central Force of the Malay People
RTM	Radio Televisyen Malaysia
S46	Parti Melayu Semangat '46 (Spirit of '46)
SAPs	structural adjustment programmes
SB	Special Branch
SDRs	Special Drawing Rights
SERI	Socio-Economic & Environmental Research Institute
SLORC	State Law and Order Restoration Council (Burma)
SMIs	small–medium industries
STMB	Sistem Televisyen Malaysia Bhd
SUARAM	Voice of the Malaysian People
Tenaganita	Women's Force
UEM	United Engineers (M) (Bhd)
UM	University of Malaya
UMNO	United Malays National Organisation
UMNO Baru	New UMNO
USM	Universiti Sains Malaysia (Science University Malaysia)
Wanita MCA	Women's MCA
Wanita UMNO	Women's UMNO
Wawasan 2020	Vision 2020
WTO	World Trade Organisation
Yang di Pertuan Agong	The King

Introduction: The New Orientalism

Malaysia offers intriguing images for the Western observer, many of them rooted in colonial romanticism: the enigma of the East, the adventurism of Empire, the allure of alternative races, religions and cultures. From the sixteenth century until the eve of independence in the 1950s, European histories of Southeast Asia record an idealised story of colonial development and Christian mission, with indigenous peoples and cultures assumed as passive appendages.[1] Through the observations, studies and writings of ethnographers, travellers, traders and colonial administrators, the dissemination of popular imperialist discourse became an intrinsic part of colonial legitimation.[2] Thus, alongside military conquest, ethnocentric representations of such societies helped convey and sustain a particular *language* of domination. When Captain Francis Light proclaimed Penang a British possession in 1786, opening a route to the Straits Settlements of Malacca and Singapore, the extending order assembled its authority around an incorporated aristocracy and a racial division of labour. But it also relied on constructed ideas of ethnicity to create an ideology of separateness. Hence, at Merdeka (Independence) in 1957, Malaya had reached a settlement structured around ethnic parties and communal politics, a system of control designed to maintain domestic class interests and neo-colonial dependency.

At the turn of the millennium, representations of Malaysian society appear rather more enlightened, though still conditioned by such symbols. Through what may be termed the language of 'new Orientalism', Asia-Pacific observers adopted a rather different view of Malaysia throughout the 1980s and 1990s: that of heroic achiever; in many ways, the model of assertiveness for aspirant states to follow on the road to economic development. In contrast to colonial images, here was a more admiring set of evaluations from the West and the key institutions of global capitalism. As the economy forged ahead during this period, the Malaysian prime minister, Dr Mahathir Mohamad, could claim that the challenges of harnessing a Malay business class and reconciling Malay privileges within a fragile ethnic order had now given way to new and more ambitious national goals. Malay, Chinese and foreign enterprise was being used to steer the country towards a new age of high-tech development, a process of information-led economic adjustment, signified by the 'intelligent' Multimedia Super Corridor (MSC), which would take Malaysia into the twenty-first century as a key player in the new global marketplace. For Mahathir, such projects were a statement of the new spirit of national confidence, a harbinger of growth, cooperation and social prosperity to come.

Yet by mid-1997 all such euphoria and Western admiration appeared rather more conditional as financial panic spread contagion-like through the region. Unable to resist the onslaught of global market forces, Malaysia felt the shock of currency and stock-market collapse, social dislocation and political upheaval, culminating in the crisis of Deputy Prime Minister Anwar Ibrahim's dismissal, trial and sentencing by April 1999. As pressure from the International Monetary Fund (IMF), foreign capital and Western political classes mounted, the calls for economic liberalisation and political transparency became a critical test for the Barisan Nasional (BN) (National Front) government, notably its ruling party, the United Malays National Organisation (UMNO). (The BN also comprises the Malaysian Chinese Association (MCA), the Malaysian Indian Congress (MIC) and a range of smaller component parties.[3])

Internal to the conflict was Anwar's own complex relationships with Mahathir on the one hand and an amalgam of Western/neo-liberal agencies – what we might term the 'IMF nexus' – on the other. Although Mahathir's anti-Western diatribes had long been a source of irritation to Western diplomats and foreign capital, this had undermined neither Western/US geopolitical interests in the region nor, despite the contradictions of his 'free-market' agenda, Mahathir's attempts to attract foreign investors. Nevertheless, Anwar's less strident language and close association with leading IMF, World Bank and Western figures had gained him a position of considerable favour within such circles. Thus, as Mahathir's 'heir apparent', here was a key minister to be cultivated. By 1997, however, the economic crisis had brought that whole set of relationships into critical focus. Now, in the biggest challenge of his 16-year rule, Mahathir, the veteran statesman and fixer, was facing not only the hostility of Western institutions, but the spectre of popular unrest, dissenting elements within UMNO and the emerging problem of Anwar himself.

The tension had become apparent by October 1997 as Mahathir clashed with the maverick investor George Soros. For many Malaysia watchers, it was vintage Mahathir. Yet, while his 'resistant crusade' against anomic capitalism and predatory speculators had not impressed the international fund-managers or many panic-stricken Malaysian businesses, it did signal the paradox of Mahathir's relations with the West. For he had not only coveted the 'modernist' imagery of growth as a sign of 'approval' from the West – thus providing a stimulus for inward investment, technological advancement and wealth creation – but used it also as a post-colonial lingua franca to challenge Western norms and posit Malaysia's achievement as a specific product of the 'Asian way'.

As a defining symbol of such, Mahathir had invoked the spectre of the record-breaking Petronas twin towers in Kuala Lumpur as a celebratory statement of national achievement – perhaps even a two-fingered gesture to the old colonial order. Yet, if one were to search for an alternative metaphor for the towers, it might reflect, more appropriately, the sense of duality with the West: a separation of identities standing together in tense proximity, a representation of the continuous convergence and conflict of ideas. At the same time, Asia-Pacific observers and Western capitalist institutions had also indulged in euphoric metaphors for the region: the new global epicentre, the Japanese miracle, tiger economies, the new dawn of Chinese growth, Japan Inc., and other *Zeitgeist* notions of the 'Pacific Century'. Yet, as the new realities began to dawn by mid-1997, signalling global market crises, all that imagery now seemed *passé*.

As the implications of the crisis unfolded on capital markets beyond the region, those in the West who had lauded the 'Asian miracle' now took their distance. The IMF, Western academics and parts of the business media took refuge in scapegoating 'Asian crony capitalists', chiding profligate state managers and warning sternly of the need for financial penitence and political reform. But, as Walden Bello, pointing to the permissive role of hedge funds, had noted, the issue of transparency could not disguise the structural role played by speculative global capital in the crisis. Nor was that *frisson* of market panic unconnected with the influence of the business media itself:

> Business publications and wire services proliferated in the region beginning in the mid-1980s. These news agents became critical interpreters of the news in Asia to investors all over the world and served as a vital supplement to the electronic linkages that made real-time transactions possible among the key stock exchanges ... For the most part, these media highlighted the boom, glorified the high growth rates and reported uncritically on so-called success stories ... Their advice ... was dispensed to readers as gospel truth.[4]

This euphoria had also been given 'authority' by Western academia:

> Indeed, it was economists and political scientists in the West who were primarily responsible for the idea of the 'Asian miracle'. There was a remarkable consensus between the Left and Right in academe that Asian growth was exceptional.[5]

Here, notes Bello, the World Bank, arbitrating between these poles (the 'left' playing up, *viz.* Korea and Taiwan, the interventionist state, the right, *viz.* Hong Kong and Singapore, the spectre of free-marketism), had declared the economic fundamentals of the Asian tiger economies favourable for continued prosperity. Thus, its 1993 book *The East Asian Miracle*:

> became a kind of bible, not only in the academic world but in financial and corporate circles ... In short, a global network of investors, journalists, investment analysts and academics was locked into a psychology of boom, where growth rates, expectations, analysis, advice and reporting interacted in a mutually reinforcing inflationary fashion. What has crashed ... has not only been Asia's economies, but the Asian *miracle establishment*.[6]

However, domestic elites in the region had also played their part in reproducing such ideology, thus forming an integral part of the miracle establishment – at least, until the collapse of the 'miracle' itself. Significantly, by the time of the Anwar crisis in late 1998, this had become crystallised around a conflict of ideology between the mainstream Malaysian media and key parts of the Western media.

Meanwhile, political legitimacy in the region had begun to unravel. In Thailand, South Korea and Indonesia, regimes became as fragile as the symbols of growth and prosperity that had surrounded them. All were to fall victim to, or be seriously weakened by, the crisis. Even Suharto's eventual removal and Habibie's temporary attempt to hold up the Golkar regime could not stem the social upheaval and demand for political reform in Indonesia. In Japan, the situation lurched towards financial crisis, recession, increased suicides and the fall of the Liberal Party under Hashimoto. In Malaysia, however, where the symbolism of growth had been, perhaps, most intense, Mahathir prepared for a more concerted defence of the system, a task that would be 'realised' in the BN's renewed mandate at the November 1999 general election, though now within a vitally changed political landscape.

Central to Mahathir's iconography of power has been the project of Vision 2020: a millennial symbol of growth, wealth-creation and nation-building on an unprecedented scale. In seeking to achieve economic maturity and NIC (newly industrialised country) status by that year, Mahathir has sought to galvanise the public imagination through ideas of a shared vision of prosperity. The Vision represents not only the challenge of economic development, but the very idealisation of national–popular unity: a concept captured in the Vision ideal of Bangsa (one nation) Malaysia. By the late 1990s, the Vision also encompassed previous icons such as Mahathir's Look East and Malaysia Inc. And, just as these contrived to turn away from the West towards Japan, so too had Mahathir integrated another such symbol in his role as 'man-of-the-South': the modern anti-imperialist figure leading the oppressed periphery against the promiscuous power of the North.[7]

To understand the Vision as hegemonic discourse, it is important to recognise its significance in macro-economic planning. Announced by Mahathir in February 1991, the Vision statement set out a series of policy objectives for growth and social development to be realised through policy measures beginning under the Sixth Malaysia Plan (1991–95), the New Development Policy (NDP) (1991) and the Second Outline Perspective Plan (OPP2) (1991–2000). In effect, OPP2, NDP and the Sixth Malaysia Plan all form part of a complementary set of policy documents linked into Vision 2020.[8]

In *Malaysia's Vision 2020: Understanding the Concept, Implications and Challenges*,[9] we find the connecting themes and policy features of these documents *vis-à-vis* Malaysia Inc., public–private sector relations, industrial targets, science and technology, education and training, moral values in business, and human resource development. Underlying all these policy aims has been the push for an average per annum growth rate of 7 per cent in real terms over the OPP2 period,[10] a ten-year growth schedule setting the country on track for sustained industrial development by 2020.

The related message within the Vision, however, concerns the set of aims posed by the Vision's *Nine Challenges Facing All Malaysians*, a charter for economic development, national integration and social community:

The first is the challenge of establishing a united Malaysian nation, with a sense of common and shared destiny. This must be a nation at peace with itself, territorially and ethnically integrated, living in harmony and full and fair partnership, made of one 'Bangsa Malaysia' with political loyalty and dedication to the nation.

The second is the challenge of creating a psychologically liberated, secure and developed Malaysian society with faith and confidence in itself, justifiably proud of what it is, of what it has accomplished, robust enough to face all manner of adversity. The Malaysian society must be distinguished by the pursuit of excellence, fully aware of its potentials, psychologically subservient to none and respected by the peoples of other nations.

The third challenge we have always faced is that of fostering and developing mature democratic society, practising a form of mature consensual, community-oriented Malaysian democracy that can be a model for many developing countries.

The fourth is the challenge of establishing a fully moral and ethical society, whose citizens are strong in religious and spiritual values and imbued with the highest of ethical standards.

The fifth is the challenge of establishing a mature, liberal and tolerant society in which Malaysians of all colours and creeds are free to practise and profess their customs, cultures and religious beliefs and yet feel that they belong to one nation.

The sixth is the challenge of establishing a scientific and progressive society, a society that is innovative and forward-looking, one that is not only a consumer of technology but also a contributor to scientific and technological civilisation of the future.

The seventh is the challenge of establishing a fully caring society and a caring culture, a social system in which society will come before self, in which the welfare of the people will revolve not around the state or the individual but around a strong and resilient family system.

The eighth is the challenge of ensuring an economically-just society. This is a society in which there is a fair and equitable distribution of the wealth of the nation, in which there is full partnership in economic progress. Such a society cannot be in place as long as there is the identification of race with economic function, and the identification of economic backwardness with race.

The ninth is the challenge of establishing a prosperous society, with an economy that is fully competitive, dynamic, robust and resilient. [11]

We need not look too hard here for the rhetorical flourishes or 'Asian values' that, apparently, 'define' this endeavour. So, why should Vision 2020 be held up as any more of a nation-building construct than, say, Malaysia's Rukunegara, or Pancasila in Indonesia?[12] Certainly, Mahathir's initial announcement of the Vision was received with muted public enthusiasm. But what came to distinguish the ideal more readily by the mid-1990s was the general perception of actual benefits to be realised in the new growth-driven landscape and the potential prospects of economic, social and cultural advancement across the ethnic spectrum. While, perhaps, people were not conversant with the minutiae of Vision objectives, there appeared to exist, at least before the crisis, a strong popular association between the *idea* of 'collective economic development' and Vision 2020 as a signifier of future rewards. Significantly, even as the crisis dawned by 1997, this sense of Vision development as an *eventual* provider of prosperity was not entirely extinguished. What therefore has to be explained is how these associations had come to assume such popular resonance and to what extent the crisis had affected those perceptions.[13]

Following this line of enquiry, it can be argued that Mahathirism had come to depend upon a more complex set of class-based, political and intellectual dynamics by the 1990s. Cultural production, the delineation of social values and the filtering of consensual ideas became an increasingly crucial part of the legitimation process. The objective interests of the Malay bourgeoisie, based since the early 1970s around a tightly ordered ethnic-class reward structure, became situated around not only processes of state patronage, but also more multi-faceted forms of civil persuasion. While continued economic growth, following the mid-1980s' recession, had helped Mahathir retain a substantive middle-class support base, as illustrated by his convincing mandate at the 1995 general election,[14] Malaysian civil society became an increasingly *contested* site requiring new and more subtle forms of populist consensus, political co-optation and intellectual enterprise.

Why was this occurring? It is the basic contention of this study that as a condition of the rapid economic transition and 'accommodation' of globally ascendant neo-liberal practices in Malaysia from the early 1980s, a newly evolving set of state–class relations had begun to unfold, setting in motion social tensions that came to require a more *hegemonic* form of authority with which to sustain it. Thus, what had been emerging, albeit tentatively, was a reward structure and political order based on the culti-vation of *consent* within the arena of civil society, as opposed to *coercion* via the strong arm of the state. This does not mean that the latter had been abandoned as a response mechanism. As continuous use of the Internal Security Act (ISA) and other emergency powers before and during the crisis has shown, coercive instruments remain readily available. However, within the context of Vision development, the use, or threat, of such also now revealed the limitations of that option as a legitimation strategy. For, while sustained by the immediate benefits of the the reward structure, acceptance of the prevailing order is also conditioned by the consensual appeal and ongoing promise of wealth creation, expanded opportunities and longer-term rewards. Thus it is not argued that the Vision will, or ever intended to, deliver any of this. The key issue, rather, concerns the way in which the project helps *contextualise* popular understandings of modernisation, social mobility and cross-ethnic prosperity as part of an 'inclusive' national framework. Neither does this require specific adherence to Mahathir and UMNO/BN. What matters is a basic endorsement of the Vision as an assumed motif for growth and development, an acceptance serving a system-reinforcing purpose, even if it takes expression as the 'TINA effect'.[15]

In this regard, the Vision has been used to consolidate the new state–class arrangements built in the 1980s, a progression of Mahathir's challenge to entrenched state elites. The political initiatives of the New Economic Policy (NEP), introduced in response to deep-rooted tensions and riots in 1969, were designed to lift the indigenous Malays, or *Bumiputeras* (sons of the soil), into an enhanced socio-economic position relative to the Chinese.

However, political control has also involved harmonisation of Malay, Chinese and Indian (respectively, 62%, 28% and 8% of the 22 million population[16]) claims through the ethnic party construct of the Barisan Nasional. The principles of the NEP (though altered to the NDP after 1990) have remained a constant facet of the reward structure. But as Mahathir came to address the 'imposed' conditions *and* the political opportunities of the new neo-liberal/deregulatory agenda from the early 1980s, the nature of the state began to change. These changes involved not only a restructuring and dispersal of bureaucratic sinecures, small Malay capital and *Bumiputera* interests, but also the need to engage more consciously in refashioning social consensus.

The cultivation of social perceptions has meant an increasingly significant role for cultural production in Malaysia. Media organisations, information agencies and popular entertainment have, thus, become ever more crucial means of legitimation. As part of this shift, the 'great debate' between 'Asian values' and 'liberal democracy' has also assumed new potency. The new circumstances of economic prosperity, wealth restructuring and social dislocation have not only compelled the political class to contest the civil terrain more assertively, hence the promotion of 'Asian values,' but have also given rise to a more intensive set of intellectual debates over the validity of Western liberal democracy, not least in relation to the codes and practices of Islam.

The importance of these underlying issues, and their bearing on the crisis from mid-1997, are evident in a perhaps prescient essay written by Anwar prior to his sacking and arrest. Among other telling observations, he asserted that:

> Only the fostering of a genuine civil society, of which democracy is a crucial component, can assure the path of sustained growth – economically, socially and politically ... Asian societies and governments have acquired a fondness for the free market of goods and services. But increasingly they will have to deal with the free market of ideas. Some will vehemently oppose this Babel even though the alternative is a sterile and sanitised uniformity.[17]

This view of civil society as a *contested site* is important in two senses. First, it offers a context for identifying the emerging tensions within the power structure. While Mahathir's idea of civil development took its cue from ideas of nation-building, economic prosperity and social values encoded in the Nine Challenges, Anwar's was more about civil reconstruction 'from below', including reform of institutions such as the legal system and the practices of Islamic jurisprudence. Complementing this view, a more detailed exposition of the case for civil reform had appeared in Anwar's 1996 book *The Asian Renaissance*. In an environment of 'Vision prosperity', such offerings posed more of a discomfort than a threat to conservative elements within UMNO. However, the extension of Anwar's views through a Western prism of liberalisation and recovery now threatened to expose not only the deficits of Malaysian civil institutions but the more specific nature of power relations within the political–corporate hierarchy. Hence the showdown with Mahathir.

Second, the idea of a contested civil space allows for a more qualitative way of thinking about alternative intellectual discourse and the potential for new forms of democratic expression within Malaysian society. However, this aspect of the analysis specifically rejects orthodox modernisation readings, or variants thereof, that seek to make linear connections between economic development, the opening up of civil society and consequent pressures for liberal democracy. Such pressures are, indeed, likely to surface, as they have in Malaysia, but they may be seen as forming part of a far more contingent process than that suggested by this type of liberal-developmentalist framework.

It may also be noted, in this regard, that while Mahathir and UMNO were being riven by allegations of cronyism amid the Anwar situation, serious corruption scandals and money politics were being unearthed within Western parties and institutions.[18] In contrast to UMNO's activities, such dealings have been subject to greater 'parliamentary scrutiny' and media insight. Yet each situation helps illustrate the more specific interface between *state–class* actors, wherein political elites, as holders of state office, provide access for given corporate interests, while the latter offer wealth, connections and support for the project in hand. Alongside the management of civil consciousness, this provides a basis for locating the key relationships and tensions within Mahathirism and the Vision project.

Here, three main Gramscian themes can be noted as central to our discussion. (See also Appendix for a synopsis of their meaning and application.)

The Power Bloc, Hegemony and the Intellectual

The power bloc Gramsci's idea of a 'historical bloc' provides a useful illustration of how power relations develop. However, the power bloc (as we shall term it here) cannot be reduced to a mere set of political coalitions or corporatist alliances. Rather, it represents a more integrated set of state–class accommodations and ideological mediations over a historical phase.[19] This allows us to consider, more comprehensively, the evolving framework of power from the colonial period in Malaya, through the changing configurations of state–class relations under the Alliance, NEP and Vision projects.

Hegemony Intrinsic to the bloc, and in contrast to liberal and neo-realist readings, the Gramscian meaning of hegemony involves a more qualitative dimension of power, involving two main elements for the leading class: first, the building of strategic alignments and concessions to subsidiary groups; second, a more conscious cultivation of the leading group's interests, ideas and values through civil, moral and intellectual processes. While the former may be more instrumental in practice, the latter is vital in serving to articulate such values as *national–popular* constructs, allowing the leading group to assume the mantle of the national interest. This also denotes the sense in which power is formed along a continuum between *domination* and *hegemony* – that is, through state coercion and/or civil consent. In short, the leading class's recourse to coercive means in order to maintain power (domination) is inversely related to the quality of its consensual legitimacy (hegemony).

This is not to suggest an inexorable shift towards the latter pole, but, rather, to understand the tensions and contradictions within that development. Thus, it is not (*viz.* liberal readings) the extent of 'democracy' in Malaysia that is at issue here, but the extent of *hegemony* in terms of Mahathir's problematic movement along this spectrum at different points in the project – *a conceptually different issue from that posed by liberal analyses*. Thus, as will be argued, the crisis from mid-1997, the removal of Anwar and the civil clampdown have thrown that process into sharp relief, testing the project's consensual claims.

For present purposes, Anne Munro-Kua comes closest to this type of hegemonic/state–class approach in *Authoritarian Populism in Malaysia*. In this view, the Malay state-class has internalised power through repressive functions and populist policies, while allowing competing class fractions to shape political and ethnic relations.[20] However, while Munro-Kua, correctly, sees this populism as a legitimating function of the coercive state, the orientation of the present study places more emphasis on how Mahathir has sought to create legitimacy by consent through the Vision.

The intellectual This suggests an ethical-moral challenge for the leading class in building an ideology of developmentalism. Here, notes Gramsci, the state is: 'ethical in as much as one of its most important functions is to raise the great mass of the population to a particular cultural and moral level … which corresponds to the needs of the productive forces for development, and hence to the interests of the ruling classes'.[21] As such, this requires us to consider not only the economic and political components of any hegemonic order, but also the integrated role of the intellectual within that process. Transcending liberal distinctions between state and civil society, this allows us to situate the intellectual as an *organiser* of hegemony within and between these sites of power. Here, Gramsci provides a new theoretical understanding of intellectual activity as *structural* enterprise, a key aspect being the construction of national-popular discourse. Following this conception, the intellectual may be viewed as rather more than an academic, social analyst or purveyor of knowledge. Such a departure does not, of course, exclude or dismiss such roles; far from it. Rather, it takes us towards a more considered view of how 'specialised' intellectuals and 'intellectual communities' may comprise part of a power order by helping to design, reproduce and filter dominant or 'common-sense' ideas through key institutions. The university, in this sense, is not a neutral domain for 'autonomous' intellectuals. As Bourdieu also argues, it is a protean site for the construction of ideologies, a space that power elites seek to influence, organise and control.[22] However, this does not mean that intellectuals are passive instruments of the prevailing order. Again, what we have to consider is the *contested* nature of this space. Here, four aspects concerning 'intellectual enterprise' are of salience.

Organic intellectuals and the UMNO network   Gramsci's conception of the *organic intellectual* gives practical meaning to the interactive process of legitimation conducted around what we might term the 'UMNO network'. This helps convey the sense in which individuals and institutions, both within and beyond the party, help sustain hegemony through the reification of dominant interests and social meaning. Here, key intellectual agencies linked to the UMNO network help create a *shared understanding* of policy ideas, social development and cultural values. Alongside UMNO's extensive corporate links, these would include government-sponsored think-tanks such as the Institute for Policy Research, the Malaysian Business Council, whose inaugural meeting had brought key politicians and captains of industry together to launch the Vision,[23] and 'independent' bodies such as the Malaysian Institute for Economic Research (MIER). Reflecting the government's 'Islamisation policy' from the 1980s, UMNO also extends its influence through religious institutes such as the Islamic Economic Foundation, the Dakwah Foundation (both set up by Mahathir),[24] the Asia Pacific Mosque Council,[25] Pusat Islam (Islamic Centre) and the Institute for Islamic Understanding Malaysia (IKIM). Here, for example, IKIM's objectives, detailed in *An Inspiration for the Future of Islam*, offers a complementary course for 'Vision-Islam', from its approving foreword on Dr Mahathir to its research priorities and seminar activities – as in 'Islam's Contribution Towards Achieving the Objectives of Vision 2020'.[26] Alongside extensive sponsorship of Islamic conferences, Vision ideas have also been promoted through broader cultural forums such as the Congress of Malay Intellectuals.[27]

Traditional intellectuals: Islam and organic assimilation Gramsci also presents us with a category of *traditional* intellectuals whose historical significance and social identity represent potential constraints upon the organic order. As a paradigm for the present case, Mahathir and influential parts of the UMNO network have engaged in a concerted elaboration of modernist Islamic principles in an attempt to 'win over' traditional elements to Vision development. In this sense, the conflict between UMNO and Parti Islam SeMalaysia (PAS) represents not just an immediate political contest, but an *intellectual* struggle. Here, the network has sought to mediate, control and harness the icons, symbols and images of Islam. But with political support for PAS in Kelantan and the rural hinterlands rooted in particularised feelings of Islamic identity and economic isolation, the Vision model has been highly contested. In turn, attempts by Nik Aziz, Kelantan's PAS *menteri besar* (chief minister), to entrench *shariah* law and initiate Islamic codes have been strongly resisted as a threat to Barisan hegemony. Responding to the Islamic resurgence in Malaysia from the early 1980s, UMNO's co-optation of Anwar as leader of Angkatan Belia Islam Malaysia (Malaysian Islamic Youth Movement; ABIM), and other *dakwah* (Islamic revival) groups also denotes an ongoing effort to 'assimilate' traditional intellectuals.

Intellectual filters: agenda-setting and the media As intimated, the reproduction of *agenda-setting* discourse forms another crucial aspect of intellectual enterprise. Reflecting, for example, a range of contemporary publications by Pelanduk,[28] Vision ideas have become part of mainstream policy literature, offering a policy-type language consistent with Vision 'liberalisation'. However, as with IKIM's output, such discourse also encompasses other bodies with a 'shared view' on issues of social and religious development. For example, in *Hudud in Malaysia*, a critical treatise on PAS's proposals for *hudud* law (notably the Kelantan *Syariah* Criminal Enactment), Rose Ismail and the Sisters of Islam Forum express a 'common interest' in the promotion of Islamic modernity based on ideas of Wawasan 2020.[29] Thus, while having its own independent aims, the *encouragement* of such ideas suggests another form of 'intellectual assimilation', helping to internalise Vision-Islam through academic and populist discourse.

In this regard, the main agenda-setting agency in Malaysia, as elsewhere, is the mass media. Linking state and corporate elites, media institutions represent a vital part of the UMNO network, helping to filter information, entertainment and civil values. Yet, while an overt platform for BN messages, the Malaysian media also became more attentive to the nuances of market segmentation and the promotion of 'new middle-classness' from the 1980s, encouraging a form of safe 'role model' media discourse based on lifestyle images and social concerns. This appeal to 'responsible' middle-class sensibilities has provided a context for managed 'media debate', helping to keep dissent distanced from any meaningful critique of the power structure. However, with a more critical response to biased press and TV output emerging during the crisis, media managers were now engaged in a process of internal reappraisal and adjustment to the new political and social mood.

Critical intellectuals and counter-hegemony In Malaysia, there is limited space for the critical intellectual. This, of course, is evident elsewhere. But, as suggested, the process of intellectual incorporation in Malaysia has a number of 'idiosyncratic' features centred around what might be termed 'insiderism'. In Malaysia, to be on the outside is to be not only oppositional, but dysfunctional. And this culture permeates all parts of the social order, from the inclusion of academics in 'national advisory' boards to the 'problem-sharing' discourse taken up by 'media intellectuals' during the crisis. Potential dissent in Malaysian universities has also been mediated through subtle forms of social incorporation, including the characterisation of student radicalism as socially deviant. Thus, when the government talks of the need for debate or consultation, it means *within* the Barisan. And when NGOs address social issues, they are encouraged to do so from *within* a 'problem-solving' mode of analysis.

Insiderism also informs the *context* of opposition party politics. For example, while the Democratic Action Party (DAP) has consistently opposed UMNO/BN, its 'Malaysian Malaysia' manifesto illustrates the sense in which standard Vision concepts have been adopted as agenda-setting motifs and internalised as mainstream political discourse. Thus the marginalisation of opposition is not only about electoral controls and the centralisation of executive functions. It is also about the more subtle filtering of dominant national values.

Despite this, Malaysia has seen the steady growth of a critical 'intellectual community' connecting PAS, DAP and the more left-leaning Parti Rakyat Malaysia (PRM) with a range of NGOs such as Aliran, Suaram, Tenaganita and Hakam. Together, this grouping had come to play a central role alongside the nascent *reformasi* bodies by the time of the crisis. This new 'networking' also reflects the growing strength of NGOs, *viz.* New Social Movements, as an alternative *form* of political opposition, a view reflected in Hewison and Rodan's analysis of 'the left' in the region and the increasing roles of liberals and social reformers in contesting the civil space.[30] These shifts, therefore, allow us to consider the political and intellectual capacities of the broad opposition in building an alternative project.

Towards an Application

As a preparatory task, the opening discussion in Chapter 1 will review and critique some of the main literature concerning issues of class, state and legitimacy in Malaysia. This will set out the main historical background to the study, with particular emphasis on the evolving configuration of state–class relations and the construction of ethnic ideology. The chapter will also highlight some of the ideological assumptions underlying liberal-developmentalist readings on democracy and growth in the region.

This takes us to the first substantive part of the study. Adopting the typology of economic, political and ideological forms, the next three chapters will consider the respective components of the Malaysian power bloc through this three-fronted view of hegemony.

Chapter 2 will assess the *economic* basis of the bloc in relation to the reward system and organisation of capital. The principal claim here is that, conditioned by extraneous neo-liberal forces, important structural changes have occurred from the 1980s, allowing Mahathir a set of 'hegemonic opportunities' to reshape state–class relations through the new circumstances of privatisation, deregulation and the remodification of Bumiputeraism. Taking up these issues, the chapter proceeds towards an assessment of the economic crisis from mid-1997 and the class/economic issues surrounding the Anwar affair.

Chapter 3 then considers the *political* component of the bloc. Mahathir's attempts to alter the rationale of NEP rewards, particularly in the transfer to the NDP, required a consolidation of legitimacy at the political level. It is argued that the 1987/88 UMNO split was connected with this and other policy/class tensions, rather than conventional political factionalism within the party, the reformulation of UMNO after the split reflecting a realignment within the bloc itself. The chapter is also concerned with Mahathir's attempts to synthesise a new type of political consensus from neo-liberal and neo-corporatist elements. It goes on to assess Mahathir's consolidation of the political bloc after 1990 and the implications of the Anwar purge for UMNO/BN.

Chapter 4 turns more specifically to the *ideological* component of the project. This section considers the reproductive capacities of the UMNO network through its engagement and control of intellectual discourse and cultural output. With reference to the Vision project, the chapter argues that new responses to social pressures were becoming evident by the mid-1990s as Mahathir tried to negotiate a new shift towards civil consensus. Here, the crisis will be used to illustrate the nature of ideological enterprise, the attempted management of the situation through constructed media imagery and the contradictions within this process. Attention is given to the messages and forms of presentation within news and popular output over this period. This takes us, in Chapter 5, to a more specific analysis of the media *vis-à-vis* the Anwar affair. Here, particular attention is paid to the 'competing agendas' of the domestic and foreign media and their respective coverage of the crisis.

Bearing in mind our view of civil society as a *contested* site, the remaining chapters consider the meaning and effectiveness of intellectual enterprise in relation to counter-hegemonic forces. Chapter 6 adopts Gramsci's organic/ traditional typology to illustrate the task for UMNO in managing the challenge from PAS. While the purge on sects such as Al Arqam denotes the ready use of coercion to control Islamic agencies, the tension between UMNO and PAS has required Mahathir to seek a more consensual basis for Vision-Islam. Rejecting various forms of *assabiyah* (narrow chauvinism), which it associates with the Vision, PAS has sought to build an alternative discourse. Here, the chapter examines some of the paradoxes within the PAS project, its struggle for 'organicity' and its attempts to fuse Islamic civil codes and social collectivist ideas into a cross-racial agenda. Continuing this theme, Chapter 7 looks in more detail at PAS's role during the crisis, its relationship with Anwar and the prospects of a new PAS politics emerging out of the *reformasi* situation.

As another part of the 'traditional intellectual community', Chapter 8 considers the counter-hegemonic role of 'the left' in Malaysia. In tracing the status of 'left ideas' and their place within the *reformasi*, the discussion reflects on how Islam and other cultural sensitivities have informed and constrained 'radical agendas' in Malaysia. The proliferation of new middle-class strata, encroaching values of Western liberalism *and* the spectre of Islamisation have also created more complex forms of *embourgeoisement* and political cultural identity. Here, UMNO has sought to keep 'dissent' contained within a received framework of ideas. However, with the crisis stimulating new forms of cooperation between parties, NGOs and *ad hoc* reform groups, fresh opportunities for meaningful counter-hegemony could now be discerned.

Finally, Chapter 9 offers a *résumé* of the Vision project, an assessment of the 1999 General Election and some comments on the opposition alignment by early 2000. Noting some of the immediate post-election fallout, it is argued that the new construction of oppositional forces are now better placed to mount a serious *intellectual*, as well as political, challenge to the Barisan and the wider power bloc.

Notes

1. McCloud (1995), pp. 2–3.

2. Said (1993).

3. The Barisan Nasional comprises mainly (late 1999): Peninsular Malaysia, UMNO, the MCA, the MIC and the Parti Gerakan; in Sabah, UMNO Sabah, Parti Demokratik Sabah (PDS), the Sabah People's Party (SAPP) and the Liberal Democratic Party (LDP); in Sarawak, the Sarawak United People's Party (SUPP), the Sarawak National Party (SNAP) and the Parti Bansa Dayak Sarawak. The Parti Bersatu Sabah (PBS) left the BN coalition in 1990. The BN has won all general elections since 1974.

4. 'Caveat investors', *Far Eastern Economic Review (FEER)*, 31 December 1998 and 7 January 1999.

5. Ibid.

6. Ibid. Emphasis added.

7. Jeshurun (1993), pp. 214–15.

8. Vision 2020 was announced by Dr Mahathir on 28 February 1991 at the inaugural gathering of the Malaysian Business Council. *The Second Outline Perspective Plan (OPP2) (1991–2000)* (1991) reviews the achievements of OPP1 and the New Economic Policy, which ended in 1990, and sets out the objectives of the New Development Policy to run from 1991 to 2000. The Sixth Malaysia Plan specified the medium-term programmes to be implemented as part of OPP2.

9. First published in 1993, this text is based on papers and discussions drawn from the first major seminar on Vision 2020 led by Dr Mahathir.

10. The editor of the text, Ahmad Sarji Abdul Hamid, sets out this target figure in his Introduction (1993), p. xvi.

11. Reproduced from *Malaysia: The Way Forward*, a working paper launching Vision 2020, presented by Dr Mahathir at the inaugural meeting of the Malaysian Business Council, 28 February 1991.

12. The respective official codes of national identity in Malaysia and Indonesia.

13. The economic crisis, beginning in 1997, is hereafter referred to as 'the crisis'.

14. The Barisan Nasional took 162 of the 192 seats in the national parliament, the Dewan Rakyat, at the April 1995 General Election. It took 10 of the 11 states, the exception being Kelantan, which is controlled by the Parti Islam SeMalaysia.

15. 'There Is No Alternative' – the rubric of Thatcherism's economic shake-out in the early 1980s.

16. Malaysia (1998) *Yearbook of Statistics*, p. 35. The figures (for mid-1998) denote (approx.) percentage of total Malaysian citizens (20,625,500). Males and females account for close to 50% each of the total population (22,179,500).

17. Anwar Ibrahim, *FEER* (50th Anniversary edn), October 1996.

18. For example, in Britain, key New Labour figure Peter Mandelson's resignation in December 1998 for having obtained a 'preferential' loan from millionaire cabinet colleague Geoffrey Robinson. In Germany, by late 1999, former Chancellor Helmut Kohl had also been exposed for accepting large 'financial donations' while in government. State-crony processes were also evident at the supranational level with the damning report on corruption and resignation of the entire EU commission in March 1999

19. Showstack Sassoon (1980), p. 121. See also Gill and Law (1989).

20. See also Munro-Kua (1996), 'Appendix: theoretical considerations', pp. 154–63.

21. Gramsci (1971), p. 258.

22. For a discussion of Bourdieu's critique of the university system and intellectuals, see Clammer (1996), pp. 183–4.

23. Khoo Boo Teik (1995), p. 327.

24. See Mutalib (1993), p. 31.

25. See Esposito and Voll (1996), p. 138.

26. Syed Othman Alhabshi (1994), pp. 42, 46.

27. In response here to concerns about the erosion of the Malay language, Mahathir defended the increased use of English as a teaching medium in universities. *New Straits Times*, 23 January 1994.

28. See, for example, Ahmad Sarji (ed.) (1993) *Malaysia's Vision 2020: Understanding the Concept, Implications and Challenges* (Pelanduk); Ahmad Sarji, (1996) *Civil Service Reforms: Towards Malaysia's Vision 2020* (Pelanduk); and Aziz Zariza (1997) *Mahathir's Paradigm Shift* (Firma).

29. Ismail (1995), p. 9.

30. Hewison and Rodan (1996), p. 43. See also Bagguley (1993) for a critical account of how this type of political identification has come to transcend orthodox political expression.

1

The Construction of Legitimacy: Vision 2020 and the Language of Control

The main purpose here is to offer a historical background against which to locate Vision 2020 as an emergent hegemonic framework. Integral to this discussion will be a review and critique of literature concerned with state, class and legitimacy in Malaysia. This is linked to an examination of certain liberal discourses and 'assumed' language within mainstream political science with regard to Southeast Asia. This concerns, most notably, liberal representations of 'democratic transition', 'Asian values' and civil society. Although the literature is varied and instructive, it is suggested that much of it invokes a certain *mode* of analysis – a received *idiom* of thought that, in taking 'dysfunctional' obstacles to 'liberal development' within these societies as a starting point, constitutes a form of subtextual ideology *sui generis*. However, it is also suggested that the legitimacy of domestic elites is also built around a *contestation* of these discourses. Thus Mahathir may employ the idea of 'Asian values' or 'Asian democracy' as a language of populist legitimation. But the language itself has to be 'negotiated' as an *intellectual* construct against other dominant agendas. It is in this sense that the propagation of class-based *ethnic ideology* has been used in varying historical forms.

Vision 2020: Development, Society and Post-ethnicity

The populist message of Vision 2020 lies in its base sentiment of common national development. It plays upon constructed symbols of national unity, invoking a *vox populi* of social belonging and common purpose: 'Malaysia boleh' (Malaysia can), as the media message puts it. In this sense, the Vision represents much more than an industrial plan for advanced economic development. It is an attempt to stimulate a new social context for the emergence of an alternative social order. As such, it projects challenging messages of economic cooperation, ethnic integration and communal partnership as signifiers of a more *inclusive* nationalism, reward structure and social community.

But the Vision is also an expression of class-based interests and the particular composition of the Malaysian state. Hence it is important to recognise the *evolution* of state–class ideology in Malaya/Malaysia and the sense in which Vision 2020 constitutes a new hegemonic framework. In particular, this allows us to address Vision language as a nascent discourse and form of what may be termed 'post-ethnic nationalism': that is, a gathering shift away from NEP ideology, ethnic balancing and the old 'politics of consociationalism' – class constructions and state forms variously designed to reproduce the ideas and interests of the dominant class fractions across ethnic lines. Although these ethnic cleavages remain a perennial part of social and political consciousness, a new type of state–class construction has been emerging, more relevant to the prevailing economic climate of global markets, deregulation and the expanded opportunities of capital accumulation. Thus the social changes effected by rapid economic development and neo-liberal demands have required a more inclusive, 'cross-ethnic' conception of the national interest.

Class, State and the Ideology of Ethnicity

Attempts within mainstream political science to understand the nature of political legitimacy in 'developing' countries such as Malaysia have involved two principal approaches. One has been to view the task as an analytical 'problem' of 'democratic transition' by considering the use of 'qualified' forms of democracy as particular to given state forms and political systems. As will be argued, the problem with this approach is that it is both quantitatively artificial and premised on certain Freedom House-type assumptions of what democracy actually is. The second approach is to isolate a particular aspect of the social order, such as racial or ethnic cleavages, and to build an explanation of the broader political system around it. In some cases, a convergence of these approaches is used. For example, in Diamond, Linz and Lipset (eds), *Democracy in Developing Countries: Asia*, Zakaria takes up the theme of ethnic polarities, and their 'central significance' within the political structure, to describe Malaysia as a 'Quasi democracy in a divided society'.[1] A further variation of Zakaria's communal theme can be seen in Morley (ed.), *Driven by Growth: Political Change in the Asia Pacific Region*, a complement to the Lipset-type literature, taking, as the title suggests, a similar developmentalist view. Here, under the concluding subheading of 'Race, growth and politics', Zakaria has this to say about Malaysia:

the conclusion seems inescapable that communalism remains and will continue for some time to remain the key to Malaysian politics ... Thus, in

Malaysia the all-enveloping cloud of communal rivalry obscures the political direction in which economic growth may be driving, whether primarily democratic or authoritarian.[2]

Issues of growth and state legitimacy in Malaysia are thus commonly situated around the 'dysfunctional' politics of ethnicity. Ethnic loyalties, racial tensions and the balancing of communal rewards are seen as pivotal features of the overall political and social order – a sort of main gravitational force setting the motion of political events and pulling the connecting elements together into a kind of revolving orbit. It is, of course, necessary to recognise here the particular salience of communal identity within this process. One must also be sensitive to the deeper seam of culture, custom and belief that, quite simply, undercuts class as a form of social identity. But this need not involve us in a primordialist view of culture and communal identity as determinant forms of analyses. For while racial affiliations and ethnic loyalties often supersede those of class identity, it is also necessary to show how class interests underlie communal divisions and ethnic ideology.

For Said, this suggests ideas of 'the other' as a signifier of power. In *Orientalism*, Said shows how the West gave coherence to an ideology of distinctiveness by reproducing its own dominant identity through the denigration of another. Thus could Disraeli find both meaning and purpose in the idea of the East, seeing it as no less than 'a *career*, one in which one could remake and restore not only the Orient, but oneself'.[3] In *Culture and Imperialism*,[4] Said illustrates the importance of popular narrative as a medium of colonial ideology, showing how the classic nineteenth-century novel and related forms helped give expression to an ascendant politics and culture of Empire. Colonial power depended not only upon the assertion of economic and political authority, but also upon the legitimation of that authority through a popularised colonial language. At the same time, Said is also at pains to specify the idea of *resistance to power*. Thus, in the colonial context, he points to the struggle of committed writers such as Frantz Fanon and C. L. R. James, in contrast to the imperialist imagery of Kipling's 'white man's burden', or *Heart of Darkness*, where, despite Conrad's implicit empathy for subjugated natives, there is little acknowledgement of indigenous cultural resources as an *engagement* of ideas:

> to ignore or otherwise discount the overlapping experience of Westerners and Orientals, the interdependence of cultural terrains in which coloniser and colonised co-existed and battled each other through projections as well as rival geographies, narratives and histories is to miss what is essential about the world in the past century.[5]

Thus, for Said, this is a contested process, albeit one 'negotiated' within a particular context of power. As Preston also notes, European constructions of the East as mystical, irrational and backward not only sustained an ideology of Western superiority, but obscured the complex ways in which such societies emerged as the product of multiple cultural exchanges and capitalist expansion.[6] In a similar vein, Maaruf has noted the failure of contemporary mainstream discourse to recognise the specificity of history and tradition in shaping political and economic development in the region. Thus, for the Malays:

> consciousness of tradition as well as the emotional and philosophical attachments to it, is an existential problem and not merely a surface feature. It is this single fact which has gone a long way in moulding their culture, thought and character, and in conditioning their response to the challenges of social change, development and modernisation ... [T]here has been ... a lack of appreciation that tradition is a living force moulding the world view of the Malays.[7]

As historical biography, Khoo Boo Teik's *Paradoxes of Mahathirism* offers a particularly nuanced view of Mahathir's own negotiation of this ideological terrain. Taking its core components – nationalism, capitalism, Islam, populism and authoritarianism – Khoo sees the complex and contradictory nature of Mahathirism as an evolving ideology. For example, Mahathir's consistent, and often zealous, support for Malay rights from the post-war colonial period never involved any straightforward endorsement of 'Malayness', an identity he has regarded as regressive and detrimental to Malay development. The tensions between consensual and coercive statecraft are also explored in the paradox of Mahathir as both populist and authoritarian,[8] another base issue for the present study.

Complementing this, Munro-Kua's *Authoritarian Populism in Malaysia* offers a key study of Mahathirism as a form of state authority arising out of the constructed circumstances of class and communalism in the colonial period. Again, this approach has a special resonance here given its view of authoritarian populism and the state's simultaneous use of repressive and consensual strategies. However, perhaps more problematically, it also suggests a view of Mahathirism as an ongoing *Malay* nationalist strategy:

> [Mahathir's] rule has seen an extensive expansion of executive power and consequent blocking of various mediations while strengthening his own direct link to the populist base. While nationalism has been an important strand of populism, this is essentially a 'Malay' nationalism, which seeks to mobilize support for the Malay bourgeois class project through communal appeal.[9]

While, again, recognising the centrality of Malay nationalism as a 'founding project' for UMNO *and* Mahathir, the Vision indicates a gathering strategy of *post-ethnic* nationalism. How, then, might we address the tensions between the two? In seeking an historical context for this shift, let us consider the evolving nature of the state and its sponsorship of ethnic ideologies through the following phases: Colonialism to Merdeka (circa 1786–1957), Alliance consociationalism (1957–69), and NEP Bumi-puteraism (1971–91).

The Colonial Phase

In 1956, a year before Merdeka, J. S. Furnivall used his classic conception of 'the plural society' to describe the process of ethnic differentiation in colonial Malaya. Following his previous studies of Indonesia and Burma, Furnivall argued in *Colonial Policy and Practice* that ethnic migration to Malaya, in response to the demands of the colonial economy, had given rise to a social order segmented by race and custom:

> They mix but do not combine. Each group holds by its own religion, its own culture and language, its own ideas and ways. As individuals they meet, but only in the market place, in buying and selling. There is a plural society, with different sections of the community living side by side, but separately within the same political unit. Even in the economic sphere there is a division of labour along racial lines.[10]

Pluralism, as understood by Furnivall, has since been discarded for its *a priori* view of ethnic relations. In effect, it took communal divisions as given phenomena, rather than social cleavages requiring critical explanation.[11] Nevertheless, its importance as a discursive model, even by the late 1970s, as exemplified in texts such as *Pluralism in Malaysia*,[12] illustrates the way in which colonial representations of the ethnic factor helped shape mainstream analyses of the state and social system in Malaysia. Alongside an ambivalent view of the colonial legacy, this has helped maintain basic conceptions of ethnic division and communal politics as 'primordially given' rather than products of the colonial state itself.

Through the colonial office, the British and other commercial interests had sought to restructure the domestic economy, turning it from subsistence agriculture into a key producer of primary products and raw materials for the British and European markets. As capitalist appropriation became fully organised around the abundant resources of tin and rubber, the British encouraged a policy of ethnic immigration and stratified labour relations as part of an export-led strategy. With the consequent growth of Indian and Chinese immigrants to Malaya as indentured labour, most notably through the credit-ticket system, an ethnic division of labour had begun to form by the early nineteenth century.[13] Following the development of the Straits Settlements as key trading centres, the rising demand for tin by the 1850s saw the expansion of Chinese mining settlements into Perak and Selangor. With world demand for rubber also growing, the British continued to sponsor the importation of Indian labour to work on European-owned plantations.[14] Thus, with the integration of each ethnic grouping into different sectors of the colonial economy and distinct social milieux, colonial representations of racial attributes began to find popular resonance.

Indians, mainly Tamils, were regarded as compliant and efficient, suited to routine agriculture and the administrative conditions of British colonial office. The Chinese, bound together through the complex networks of the *kongsi* clan system and *Kapitan* labour pools, were viewed by the British as a particularly industrious race, evidenced by their ready access to capital and productive activity in mining and plantation agriculture. This did not, however, protect the Chinese coolie from exploitation at the hands of British or Chinese capitalists – the plentiful supply of opium helping to maintain labour dependency, while providing valuable revenue for the colonial office.[15] Meanwhile, the Chinese and Indian communities remained excluded from political office, a 'pro-Malay' privilege retained for a select class of Malay civil servants as a means of co-opting the feudal aristocracy.

In contrast, the native Malay peasant came to be portrayed as a dysfunctional part of the colonial mode of production: detached from commercial activity, unwilling to participate in waged labour and unreliable as a racial type. It is important to note that this view derives from an 'objective' and sympathetic conception of the Malay. Sir Thomas Stamford Raffles, founder of Singapore, saw in the Malay a sense of predicament, his 'negative traits' the product of sensitivities to insult and previous colonial subjugation. Similar sentiments were offered by other colonial observers such as Hugh Clifford and Sir Frank Swettenham, who both deplored the general 'lack of understanding' towards Malay society. Yet despite this empathy, a colonial genre of travel stories and ethnographic caveats came to reflect an idealised picture of the 'real Malay' as indolent, lazy and untrustworthy, establishing a popular cultural stereotype and a rationale for 'benevolent' intervention.[16] Thus, at the height of Empire, could Swettenham, as colonial Governor, offer a 'definitive' image of a people in his claim that the 'leading characteristic of the Malay of every class is a disinclination to work'.[17]

As Alatas has shown, most definitively in *The Myth of the Lazy Native*, this was not only an essential part of colonial ideology, but was later to become part of the ideological context of Mahathir's NEP nationalism (see Chapter 2).

Other recent state-based analyses have also helped illuminate the colonial legacy and the ways in which ethnic, religious and other cultural forms are used as ongoing legitimation strategies. For example, Jesudason, employing a state-centred model derived from Skocpol, views the construction of the Malaysian state as 'syncretic' in form, namely because it is:

> a product of a particular historical-structural configuration that has allowed the power holders to combine a broad array of economic, ideological and coercive elements in managing the society, including limiting the effectiveness of the opposition as a democratising force ... The syncretic state operates at a multidimensional level, mixing coercive elements with electoral and democratic procedures; it propagates religion in society as it pursues secular economic goals; it engages in ethnic mobilisation while inculcating national feeling; and it pursues a combination of economic practices ranging from liberal capitalism, state economic intervention, to rentier arrangements. These features are in important ways a product of the externally implanted nature of the colonial state and the colonial capitalist economy.[18]

Although Jesudason correctly notes the colonial context of the Malaysian state, the hybrid nature of its legitimacy and the particular way in which it 'trades off' these various elements, there is a tendency here to view class as something of an adjunct to state-centrism. By implication, class becomes a by-product, albeit an important one, of the state, a dependent element of the state's omnipotence. Jesudason does insist that the Malaysian state's propagation of syncretic measures is neither static nor uninfluenced by potential pressures from within civil society and the middle class. However, he sees any real crisis of legitimacy emerging, more probably, as a loss of coherence within the state itself as it confronts the problems of social stability generated by economic change.[19] He also notes how the state constrains particular forms of class mobilisation while lurching precariously towards contradiction as it tries to manage the social outcomes of sustained development.

Yet, bearing in mind the importance of the state in articulating class interests, as well as this potential for internal state crises, what has to be specified more clearly here is the idea of a state–class nexus: that is, a more dynamic conception of state–class interactions premised upon the historical, contingent relationship between competing state elites, class elements and fractions of capital, structural relations that, in turn, influence and condition class formation at the broader social level. Moreover, civil society is more significant than Jesudason perhaps allows, given its increasing relevance as an arena of legitimation and medium for offsetting the propensity to state crises itself – hence, as suggested, the greater contestation of civil institutions in an attempt to build populist consensus.

As with Munro-Kua, K. S. Jomo and Hua Wu Yin come closer to the idea of a state–class nexus. Again, both point to the historical implications of colonialism, citing, for example, the incorporation of the Malay middle classes into the administrative apparatus of the state and the extent to which this served to limit the formation of a Malay bourgeoisie. This, in turn, helps us understand better the consequent nature of the NEP state in seeking to redress this 'anomaly'. Jomo also notes how the later ascendancy of 'Malay statist capitalists' and the 'onus of capital accumulation on the state' gave rise to: 'new contradictions with other capitalist fractions ... [Hence] ... the more pronounced forms of class contention in contemporary Malaysia are outcomes of class contradictions generated by the rise of the statist bourgeoisie'.[20]

For Hua Wu Yin, communal division within Malaysian society is, again, rooted in the colonial experience. The legacy is a *dependent* capitalism in Malaysia and a ruling class that must rely upon the exploitation of communal division as a source of class domination.[21] Rejecting pluralist explanations of the communal factor, he points to the 'institutionalisation of communalism' by the Malay bourgeoisie under the NEP as the 'cardinal mechanism by which the Malaysian ruling class ... maintain[s] the loyalty of the Malay masses'.[22]

Brennan argues, further, that the Malay bourgeoisie's pragmatic alliance with international capital after Merdeka not only reflected its dependent integration into the global economy, but also helped generate new hostilities by displacing sections of the non–Malay bourgeoisie from that process. In other words, class conflict has been the engine of communal conflict, stoking ethnic tensions and maintaining communal divisions, the traditional support bases for UMNO, the MCA and the MIC.[23]

In this regard, Brown shows how ethnic politics in Malaysia is located within a more holistic context of state forms, class relations and the particular construction of *ethnic ideology*. Again, this distinctive class approach sees ethnic affiliations and communal divisions as state–class arrangements arising out of the prevailing economic structure. Brown's analysis moves beyond both core Marxist state theory and later 'relative autonomy' models – as well as Jesudason/Skocpol state-centred views – to a position that recognises, more incisively, the dynamics of contending class interests and balancing processes within the state. Applying these insights to the development of the state from the colonial period to the NEP, Brown notes how: 'One such available ideological theme, and that which predominated, was *the ideology of ethnicity*.'[24]

It is also necessary to set these ethnic ideologies against the particular circumstances of the decolonisation process itself. The first element here concerns the *form* of colonial rule between 1946 and Merdeka. The British had employed a form of indirect rule, by adhering to 'pro-Malay' policies and recognising the Malay Sultans as 'natural rulers', thus avoiding unnecessary conflict. This included the setting up of State Legislative and Executive Councils as advisory bodies appointed by, and respondent to, the colonial government, allowing state functions to remain in the hands of the Sultans, leaving little scope for any opposition. Despite the tensions of the Japanese occupation, these arrangements remained largely intact throughout the war years.[25] However, the attempt to move towards a more uniform structure in 1946 through the Malayan Union scheme was seen as a betrayal by the Malay aristocracy.

It was from here and other conservative Malay institutions that the UMNO political class emerged in that year to oppose the scheme, giving rise to a conservative Malay nationalist coalition. The Malayan Union had been introduced by the British as an initial attempt to bring the nine Malay states of Perlis, Kedah, Kelantan, Terengganu, Pahang, Perak, Selangor, Negri Sembilan and Johore, plus the two (Crown) Straits Settlements of Penang and Malacca under the ambit of a stable central governing body for the first time. Under the scheme, administrative powers were to be organised on a cross-ethnic basis, an arrangement presented, ostensibly, as a democratic reform of the political system and precursor to eventual self-government,[26] but one that reflected, more acutely, Britain's evolved relations with the multi-ethnic bourgeoisie and the need to protect British foreign interests.[27] However, UMNO successfully opposed the scheme over its provisions to restrict the Sultans' powers and the threat to Malay rights. The scheme was replaced in 1948 by the Federation of Malaya Agreement, drawn up by British and Malay leaders, amid protests from the non-Malays.[28] Under this arrangement, the Sultans' position and other Malay rights with regard to indigenous status were secured. Despite some concessions over immigration, non-Malays did not get the full citizenship rights proposed in the 1946 plan. Moreover, the principle of federalism, enshrined in the agreement, offered Malays security that, while legislative control moved towards the centre, this would not create a monolithic Union with no recognition of the states and traditional forms of Malay government. Later, influenced by British interests and calculations of how to curb the threat of Chinese radicalism in Singapore, Tunku Abdul Rahman backed Singaporean entry into the Federation, despite Malay fears of Chinese dominance. Balanced by the other Bumiputera states of Sabah and Sarawak, Singapore's merger brought Malaysia into existence in 1963. However, ongoing tensions, reflected by an increasingly militant challenge to the Alliance from the People's Action Party (PAP) for expanded citizenship rights, saw Singapore expelled from the Federation in 1965.

The Federation agreement had, thus, given rise to a second key element here, that of communally located political parties. As the main bourgeois elements came to consider their place and role within the emerging political structure, the 'communal agenda' of the Federation negotiations became the prevailing context for the political mobilisation of the subordinate classes. It was out of this process that the communal positions of UMNO, the MCA and the MIC would emerge as class patrons of each ethnic grouping. Indeed, it was within this context that Dato Onn bin Jaafar, the founder of UMNO, was forced to relinquish his post as president in 1951 for seeking the entry of non-Malays into the party. The Independence of Malaya Party (IMP), which he subsequently set up in 1951, was not to prove a significant force. Again, for Zakaria this was, and remains, proof that the 'failure of noncommunal political parties is simply a consequence of the nature of the polity in which political mobilization has greatest success when it appeals to race'.[29] However, this view again understates the vital sense in which particular class interests were being established through the Federation process and the consociational framework to follow.

Against this, the non-communal All Malay Council of Joint Action (AMCJA), representing Chinese, Malays, Indians and others, had opposed the Federation, calling instead for independence and a new structure based on universal citizenship, power-sharing arrangements with inbuilt Malay rights and retention of the Malay monarchy, though deprived of pre-rogative powers. Alongside its radical Malay nationalist coalition partner PUTERA (Central Force of the Malay People), it represented an alterna-tive, if weak, counterpoint to UMNO's conservative nationalism. However, it was through the latter political medium that the colonial government chose to negotiate.

And this ties into the third important factor of the decolonisation process: the Malayan Emergency (1948–60). In effect, this was a class-based war fought between the Malaysian Communist Party (MCP) and the British and multi-ethnic bourgeois coalition. One of the principal reasons for the British coming to favour the Federation plan by 1948, rather than the Union scheme, was the need to develop the ethnic divide-and-rule strategy in the face of class pressures and communist insurrection. By seeking to portray the MCP as an avowedly Chinese nationalist body, rather than a broad-based, anti-colonial class movement, the British hoped to stifle Malay support for any form of class politics or radical nationalism. Despite its mainly Chinese base, the MCP had built a considerable level of support among Malays and Indians by 1948.[30] Under its leader, Chin Peng, it had fought a major military campaign alongside the British to defeat the Japan-ese. Decorated after the war, Chin led the MCP from a position of passive struggle for independence to one of armed conflict following the Federation agreement in 1948. The party's mobilisation of working-class unrest after the war, notably through the Pan Malayan Federation of Trade Unions, had threatened the very basis of the colonial order. Thus, while seeking to portray labour dissent as MCP subversion, the British moved towards a clearer recognition of UMNO and conservative Malay nationalism as the main vehicle of political reform. (Although the MCP was beaten before Merdeka, the Emergency remained in force until 1960. Banned under the Constitution, the MCP signed a formal 'peace deal' in 1989.[31]) Nevertheless, while consolidating this relationship through the Federation agreement, the British still sought a cross-ethnic independence arrangement that would ensure political, economic and social stability.

The legacy of the colonial state can thus be seen as significant in three main respects. First, it helped draw the Malayan economy into the world capitalist system, thus setting the basis of metropole-domestic class relations. Second, as a central feature of this process, it created an ethnic division of labour in which racial attributes became synonymous with class position. And, third, it provided the nucleus of a pragmatic alliance between the Malay aristocracy/state bureaucracy, the main Chinese commercial bourgeoisie and Indian *petite bourgeoisie*, setting the framework of class accommodations, consociational politics and ethnic ideology to follow.

The Alliance Phase

Following Independence, Malaya was governed by the Alliance, a communal party-based coalition that held UMNO, the MCA and the MIC together till 1969. UMNO and the MCA had, together, successfully contested the 1952 municipal elections in Kuala Lumpur. Joined by the MIC to form the Alliance, they followed this by winning the 1955 general election, establishing a political coalition that allowed Tunku Abdul Rahman, the country's first leader, to negotiate the Merdeka settlement in 1957. Under the Tunku, the colonial settlement – following the Reid Commission's report[32] – had secured the formal powers of the Yang di Pertuan Agong (King), the Sultans and a privileged niche for a Malay administrative elite. A constitutional system had been agreed, based upon British parliamentary structures and Crown prerogatives while retaining the federalist principle. The British also saw in the Tunku a stable figurehead for the coalition, someone who would retain a *laisser-faire* approach to foreign capital, favour British interests and, in the gathering Cold War climate, maintain opposition to communism in the region.

In contrast to the Malay elite, the economic position of ordinary Malays had not been substantially improved by decolonisation. The colonial labour structure, racial segmentation and hierarchical social codes, based on deferential emotions of *adat* (custom), had kept Bumiputeras, more generally, tied either to *kampong* (village) subsistence or conditions of urban poverty. Yet, like their Malay counterparts, large sections of Chinese labour also remained locked into a situation of class exploitation and social deprivation. Following the defeat of the Japanese, major restructuring of the country's primary sector, given impetus by the large demand for rubber and tin during the Korean War, had seen a major enhancement of the country's export base and sustained accumulation opportunities for domestic and metropolitan capital. Again, it had been the attempted mobilisation of both ethnic groups against such exploitation after 1948 that had formed the basis of the MCP's efforts to wage a class war of independence. But with Independence secured and organised around the consociational arrangements of the Malay state and Chinese business interests, class politics became subordinate to ethnic politics.

The essence of Alliance power lay in the 'bargain' struck between the Malay landowning aristocracy, who held *political* authority through UMNO and control of the civil service, and the Chinese commercial bourgeoisie, who were allowed to protect their economic interests through the MCA. During the 1969 election, the Tunku, acknowledging the discrete political and economic powers of the Malays and Chinese, restated how the 'blending of the two ... ha[d] brought about peace and harmony, coupled with prosperity to the country'.[33] As such, Alliance ideology had helped institutionalise an exclusive 'partnership of understanding' between ethnic patrons who between them claimed the necessary abilities to manage racial tensions and promote social prosperity.[34]

Yet, even as economic production grew during the 1950s, giving apparent credence to the Alliance formula, new class pressures signified the gathering crisis of Alliance consociationalism. Under the 1958 Pioneer Industries Ordinance policy and the First and Second Malaya Plans (1955–65), import-substitution manufacturing had been encouraged through credit incentives, infrastructure investment and tariff protection, a process that, given the government's ongoing *laisser-faire* commitment, saw foreign, rather than domestic, investment grow. Despite the shift towards export-oriented industrialisation under the First Malaysia Plan (1966–70) and diversification into palm oil and other primary products by the late 1960s, these incentives to foreign capital remained largely intact.[35] Thus, as Khoo notes, the accruing problems for the Alliance had a number of interacting facets, not all exclusively linked to ethnic demands. First, the Alliance state's low-capital support for the rural sector, reliance upon primary commodity production and general *laisser-faire* orientation saw it exposed to the 'familiar neo-colonial mode of underdevelopment' by the late 1960s, and thus unable to meet gathering expectations of 'economic democracy' to accompany the aspirations of political independence.[36] Second, marginalised sections of the Malay peasantry began to tie their interests more specifically to the social ideas of the PAS, which, at that point, had linked its Islamic agenda to a Malay nationalist idiom. Third, concern was being expressed by middle- and working-class non-Malays that the special Malay rights guaranteed under the constitution would undermine their access to social provisions, such as education. Finally, and perhaps most significantly, a key section of Malay bureaucrats, middle-class intelligentsia and politicians within UMNO began to question the Alliance's *laisser-faire* policies and relationship with Chinese capital, demanding a greater level of state intervention and share of wealth for the Malays.[37]

In this latter regard, the enterprise and social mobility of a nominal Chinese business community, tightly organised around ties of kinship and with privileged links to the Malay political class, had given rise to increasing anti-Chinese resentment at the broader social level. At the same time, mainstream Chinese support for the MCA and its role as communal patron within the Alliance began to erode. Again, this reflected a certain search within each ethnic group for alternative parties to represent their economic and cultural interests. But the rejection of the Alliance structure, particularly by the Chinese, can also be seen as coincident with the flowering of a more vibrant 'class politics' at that point. Although mainly regarded as Chinese parties, the DAP, the Gerakan and the People's Progressive Party (PPP), unlike the Alliance, had campaigned on broad socio-economic rather than racial issues. In the general election of 1969, the three 'Chinese' opposition parties took 56.4% of the non-Malay vote as opposed to 40.4% for the Alliance. Together with the movement of many rural Malays from UMNO to PAS, giving PAS 40% of the Malay vote, this shift saw electoral support for the Alliance fall from a high of 79.6% in 1955 to 48.5% in 1969.[38]

Disenchantment with the Alliance formula was thus being expressed across racial lines. For the Chinese, it was fostered by the need to find new ways of articulating their socio-economic and cultural interests. On the Malay side, it was motivated by perceptions of increasing Chinese economic dominance and fears that the 1969 election outcome threatened their political position and constitutional rights. Thereafter, social enmities, stoked in large part by ethnic chauvinism and fratricidal language during the election campaign, erupted into ethnic riots on 13 May 1969, most notably in Kuala Lumpur. Yet, as Khoo notes, this, again, should be seen within the context of wider class pressures and the contradiction of consociationalism:

> The inability of the Alliance's *laissez-faire* capitalism to satisfy these demands accentuated the ethnic dimensions of Malaysia's decolonization and laid the

conditions for the violence of 13 May 1969 ... In that sense, the 13 May incident, which has often been taken to mean the breakdown of Malaysia's multi-ethnic consociationalism exclusively, also brought about a rupture in the balance between the Malay state, domestic non-Malay capital and foreign capital. That is to say, the 'Merdeka compromise' was not simply the casualty of ethnic polarization and extreme communalism. It was also the victim of 'class' onslaught mounted by an immiserated Malay peasantry, an urban non-Malay working class suffering from unemployment, a non-Malay middle class clamouring for political and cultural liberalization ... and a Malay *petit bourgeois* demand for economic regulation (of non-Malay capital) and state intervention.[39]

The structural instability and ultimate crisis of Alliance consociationalism by the late 1960s thus reflected two class-based contradictions within the state: first, the dependent development of the economy under neo-colonialism involving *laisser-faire* forms of surplus appropriation and gathering economic stagnation; second, the emergence of tensions between competing bourgeois fractions seeking enhanced access to state resources as economic conditions contracted.[40] These contradictions, in turn, helped fuel the ethnic animosities, fear and suspicions that became the hallmark of the 1969 riots. This is not to deny the 'primal' nature of Malay and Chinese reaction during that crisis. But it is necessary to distinguish between the popular motivation of that reaction and the structural roots of such consciousness. In effect, the practice and ideology of consociational politics had allowed political and social identity to become situated around ethnic polarities, thus providing the basis for a groundswell of ethnic fears to emerge at a key point of economic dislocation.

The NEP Phase

The NEP is considered more fully in Chapter 2 *vis-à-vis* Mahathirism. However, it is necessary here to sketch some of the background circumstances of emerging class pressures and ethnic ideologies within the state by the late 1960s. Since Merdeka, the Chinese had harboured fears that their language, educational traditions and culture were under threat from an increasingly dominant Malay political class. It is within this context that the DAP, offering a more egalitarian and universalist political agenda, found itself the main repository of Chinese disenchantment with the Alliance throughout the 1960s, culminating in the erosion of the Alliance vote in 1969. For the Malays, in turn, this rise of Chinese opposition represented a dangerous challenge to their constitutional rights. Moreover, it fed into more pressing concerns across Malay bourgeois, middle-class and peasant groups that the 'Malay share' of national wealth and incomes had declined relative to Chinese incomes. Certainly, statistical evidence does show Malay incomes, relative to Chinese, falling from a ratio of 1:2 to 1:2.5 between 1958 and 1967.[41] However, the more significant disparities of wealth under the Alliance had been *intra*-racial rather than inter-racial in composition. Between 1957 and 1970, intra-racial disparities grew by 36.2% among Malays and by 21.6% among the Chinese. In the same period, the wealthiest 20% of Malays saw their share of national wealth increase from 42.5% to 52.5%, while the poorest 40% of Malays' share fell from 19.5% to 12.7%. For the Chinese, the respective shares were 45.8% to 52.6% and 18% to 13.9%.[42] Nevertheless, Malay grievances and the crisis of 1969 had allowed inter-ethnic rather than intra-ethnic disparities to take centre-stage, thus providing a new set of Malay 'priorities' within the state.

Reflecting this rupture in state–class relations, the Tunku handed over the premiership to Tun Abdul Razak in 1970, giving way to a new generation of UMNO leaders from mainly bureaucratic backgrounds. In February 1971, following a period of emergency rule, imposed under the National Operations Council (NOC), the Alliance coalition (later reformed as the Barisan Nasional for the 1974 general election) proceeded to address Malay inequalities through the interventionist strategies of the NEP. But while offering socio-economic redress and employment guarantees for upwardly mobile Malays within the public sector, the new ethnic ideology of Bumi-puteraism on which it was predicated also allowed the emergent 'NEP class' privileged use of the state as a new accumulation site. Here, in essence, was a 'state bureaucratic bourgeoisie' in the making.

It is necessary to locate the class basis of this group for two reasons. First, it helps illustrate the sense in which consociationalism was re-formulated and rationalised as an amended political system and ideology by the new bureaucratic–bourgeois alliance. Second, it helps set the context for the subsequent evolution of Mahathirism itself from a position of overt NEP nationalism to that of post-ethnic nationalism via the Vision.

As noted, this amalgam of Malay bureaucrat and middle-class elements had begun to assert its influence by the late 1960s in response to the Alliance's *laisser-faire* policies and relationship with Chinese capital. But their rise also indicated an increasing class challenge *within* UMNO itself. This was partly motivated by a gathering disdain for the Malay aristocracy, whose conservatism and feudal orientations were coming to be seen as increasingly anachronistic by bureaucrats, teachers and other professionals within UMNO. Such perceptions were also linked, more specifically, to the sectoral interests of this class fraction within the state. The rapid expansion of the state bureaucracy over the 1960s, prompted by decolonisation, had seen the sizeable recruitment of lower middle-class Malays into the civil service.[43] Not only did this class set the scene for the emergence of an 'ultra' political faction within UMNO, it also acted as a new cohesive force within the public sector, pushing for economic restructuring and controls over Chinese capital, pressures that were to provide the impetus for state interventionism after 1969.

This, in turn, signified a shift in the form of ethnic ideology employed by the state. The Alliance variant had defended Bumiputera political rights as a key part of the consociational construct, but *not* at the expense of cross-racial bourgeois interests or the free role of metropolitan capital. In contrast, the new state-class placed Bumiputeraism at the core of both its political *and* economic agenda. The outcome was a set of state institutions more amenable to the mutual interests of small indigenous capital and state bureaucrats. But the need to legitimate these relations through state interventionism also required a fuller articulation of Bumiputeraism as an ethnic ideology. Thus, by appearing to promote expanded economic rights for *all* Malays, the new state-class was able to establish a populist rationale for selective direction of the economy, privileged access to state resources and control over the distribution of wealth.

Mahathir's own development through decolonisation to 1969 and the emergence of the NEP state suggests some contradictory elements here. Mahathir had been closely associated with both the anti-Union movement from 1946 and the Malay nationalist agenda of 1969. Yet he occupied a somewhat paradoxical position with regard to both. He fought for the Malay Federation cause in 1948 without being specifically wedded either to conservative or to radical nationalist wings. In particular, he harboured a deep resentment towards the Malay aristocracy, seeing in them a feudal, rentier class indifferent to the subsistence existence of poor rural Malays, hardships that Mahathir had himself partly experienced during his study years and then witnessed first-hand as a young medical doctor in Alor Setar.[44] As doctor-politician, Mahathir had campaigned vociferously as a Malay nationalist in the 1965 election, attacking, in particular, the PAP's 'Chinese chauvinism' and 'socialistic doctrines', thus making his mark against the PAP's vibrant young leader Lee Kuan Yew. Mahathir's most notable statement as an 'adopted ultra' came in his letter to the Tunku after the 1969 riots. Denouncing his 'placatory' gestures to the Chinese and 'betrayal' of the Malays, he called for the Tunku's resignation, an act that resulted in his own expulsion from UMNO, but secured his place as a symbol of Malay nationalism amongst the ultra faction.[45] As we shall see in Chapter 2, Mahathir was to develop the case for Malay nationalism during the 1970s via the arguments of *The Malay Dilemma*. Yet he did so without being closely identified with the new NEP bureaucratic elite, an element he gradually came to regard, after coming to office in 1981, as an impediment to 'modernisation', economic reform and Malay development itself.

A more focused analysis of nationalism as ethnic ideology is taken up in the discussion of the NEP to follow. However, following the theme of constructed ideology, we need to consider how representations of 'democracy', 'development' and 'Asian values' have also been used as contested discourse.

Democracy, Asian Values and the Ideology of Growth

It is instructive to note how the interests of Western capitalism *and* the Mahathir project have been underwritten by an *ideology of growth*. For Mahathir, this has involved the selective use of neo-liberal language to promote privatisation, initiate state reforms and assuage foreign capital. For the key capitalist institutions, the ideology of growth suggests an ongoing attempt to 'remake' the region in its own image – a kind of 'Disraelian task', cf. Said in *Orientalism* – through the propagation of liberal capitalist business practices. The main feature of this has been the long-term promotion of the liberal developmentalist state: in essence, a set of growth-led arguments for the minimalist (or 'facilitative') state, wholesale deregulation and open-market policies. Here, the shared neo-liberal ideas of finance ministers and transnational capital have come to inform the very framework within which such economies and societies may act.[46]

This is not an argument *against* growth – even though the idea of *sustainable* growth has been largely ignored or marginalised by governments and capitalist institutions. Neither can we overlook the 'push for growth' as part of the intrinsic struggle for global capitalist competitiveness. However, it is also necessary to see how liberal discourse has helped *reify* the *language* of growth. With the shift towards a global neo-liberal agenda from the late 1970s, 'growth-led' became the intellectual *leitmotif* of key agencies such as the IMF, World Bank and Trilateral Commission. Thus the 'imperative of growth' has become hegemonic code for free-market arrangements and private-sector accumulation. As mainstream Asia-Pacific texts such as *Driven by Growth* more than imply, capitalist development constitutes the essential progenitor for liberal democracy in developing countries – or, in more complementary form, the liberal market promotes the emergence of democracy, while, *vice versa*, democratic structures help stimulate investment, growth and capitalist development.

As the Southeast Asian economies faced the reality of structural weaknesses, global over-capacity and the anarchy of financial markets by

1997, such assumptions of growth-led development looked rather exposed, while the supposed correlation between growth and democracy looked even more problematic. During the boom years, the populist appeal of growth-driven development had helped sustain Mahathirism as a project, placating the middle class and offsetting demands for democratic reform. The irony was that it had taken an actual *crisis* of growth by 1997 to stimulate pressures for democratic change.

As demands for greater transparency and political reform were articulated on behalf of foreign capital by the IMF, finance ministers and influential sections of the Western media, Mahathirism found itself under serious attack. The consequent denunciations of George Soros can, of course, be seen as part of a populist diversionary strategy. Yet it also signified a more specific aspect of the legitimation process in Malaysia: the sense in which Mahathir, unlike Suharto, was prepared to contest the issues on more purely ideological grounds. Thus, for Mahathir, the Vision involves the *positive* assertion of Western growth-led images as statements of Malaysian modernity. But it also involves a *negative*, or reactive, response to the assumptions of Western liberal development.

The prevailing tendency within mainstream political science towards growth-led models of democratic transition has its genealogy in modernisation theory.[47] Early modernisation literature, typified by Huntington's 'Great Dichotomy' between 'traditional' and 'modern' societies – an 'imitation' of Weber's traditional/rational 'ideal-types' – is now in disrepute, its view of 'inexorable' social transition criticised for its linearity and ethnocentricity.[48] Yet the privileged academic position given to such ideas in the USA during the 1950s and 1960s remains remarkably intact.[49] Seeking a rationale for nuclear strategies and Cold War geopolitics, the USA utilised 'realist' academics from across the disciplinary spectrum, with scientists, technologists and political scientists adopting the role of 'policy-planners'.[50] Integral to Soviet containment was the view that free-market capitalism led to modernity and Western-style democracy. Hence, notes Preston, modernisation theory took the role of a 'descriptive general policy science' seeking to show how 'dysfunctional' practices in 'traditional' societies impeded 'modern development'.[51]

In *Rethinking Development: Essays on Development and Southeast Asia*, Preston shows how orthodox social science has come, via modernisation theory and its present variants, to inherit this policy-oriented view – one that 'clearly "arguing on behalf of the planners" can hardly be called "value-neutral"'.[52] Such discourse thus retains a certain policy-planner understanding of what development goals should mean. Typical examples within the Asia-Pacific genre would include Mohamed Ariff's *The Malaysian Economy: Pacific Connections* and Jong S. Jun (ed.), *Development in the Asia*

Pacific.[53] Effectively negating state–class relations and ideological production, such texts have tended to reconstitute issues of social development as generic 'policy issues'.

Other accounts have taken up the issue as 'flawed' capitalist development in the region. For example, in *Behind the Myth: Business, Money and Power in Southeast Asia* Clad, linking money politics and state largess to the late retention of patrimonial capitalism and the subversion of bourgeois innovation, has argued for large-scale privatisation and state disengagement in order 'to give marketplace economics a real chance'.[54] This complements Yoshihara's portrayal of Southeast Asian capitalism as 'ersatz' in type, built around rent-seeking activity inimical to productive development.[55]

Of course, much of this 'fits' the Malaysian case. Yet it is also an apt description of the City of London, the whole edifice of which is built precisely around speculation, short-term dealing and rentier accumulation.[56] More instructively, Gomez and Jomo show in *Malaysia's Political Economy: Politics, Patronage and Profits* how the allocation of rents through state licences, concessions and subsidies is linked into a more class-based assemblage of party politics and corporate networks across the Barisan. Yet, while valid, this attack on internal corruption was, again, being used by 1997 to reinforce the rather conceited claims of Western agencies that 'dysfunctional' 'crony capitalism', rather than the anarchic practices of global markets, was mainly responsible for the Southeast Asian crises.[57]

Despite a revised 'developmentalist literature', precipitated by the 'new wave' of 'democratisations' in Latin America and East Asia in the 1980s and 1990s (Case, Pye, Lipset, Diamond and others), there remains here a taken-for-granted view of democratic development as an analytical premise. In *Political Oppositions in Industrialising Asia*, Rodan notes how this forms part of a dual distortion:

> two very powerful themes are discernible in this vast body of literature on political change in late industrialising countries of East and Southeast Asia. The first of these is a propensity to equate the challenge to, or demise of, authoritarian rule with the advance of 'democracy'. This concept is generally employed unproblematically, but implicitly endorses a liberal democratic or formalistic definition of the term ... [and] remains the point of reference for these analyses ... A second theme ... is a not unrelated romanticisation of civil society ... depicted as the natural domain of personal and group freedoms ... [a] tendency [which] downplays the significance of gross inequalities of power and resources [therein].[58]

The broad assumption here is that economic development and the expansion of democratic freedoms are mutually evolving forces. Another is the implicit use of liberal *capitalist* democracy as a synonym for democracy.

But is 'democracy', in the *liberal capitalist* meaning of the term, the most likely outcome of, or necessary framework for, growth and development? The received liberal wisdom has been to regard democracy, the free market and growth as mutual concepts. The corollary is that an expanding, educated middle class, the product of that process, comes to demand individual rights and freedoms, thus posing an inevitable threat to authoritarian regimes. Yet, as Vatikiotis clinically puts it:

> The problem with this well-worn conceptual framework is that it is based on a simplistic and even subjective interpretation of actual events. Southeast Asia has not been kind to the neat predictions of Western social science ... Political reality in Southeast Asia is amorphous and often defies categorisation.[59]

The varying experiences of the Asian NICs makes assumptions of growth-driven democracy highly questionable. Taiwan and South Korea, although now nominally 'democratic', achieved NIC status under authoritarian regimes. Yet this does not mean that development was dependent on either this regime type *or* that of liberal democracy. What we have to consider, rather, is the particular set of historical circumstances in which these countries found themselves in the post-war period: namely, global economic reconstruction, US aid and intervention, the expansion of Japanese capital and sensitive geopolitical factors in the region. In this sense, 'democracy' in Japan was shaped by a particular conjuncture of US security imperatives and the consolidation of internal conservative alliances in the post-war period. Thus, for Friedman:

> what is assumed about the West's imperatives for democratisation is dangerously misleading Western mythology ... Contrary to the conventional Western misperception, East Asia's paths to democracy are as diverse as is any other region's ... Consequently, the binary of tradition versus modernity, understood as a way of stigmatizing and marginalizing non-European civilization as backward, should be critically re-examined to ferret out parochial misconceptions.[60]

Beyond 'authoritarian developmentalism' and variations of the 'anomalous democratisation' argument, Friedman sees the potential for democracy in all cultures, with political actors as key agents in that struggle. Yet even this universal/human agency view rather understates the more dynamic sense in which political, economic and cultural factors *together* condition that process. Moreover, it lacks insight into how particular constructs of democracy and development represent ideological discourse *within* that process.

Upholding the link between liberal democracy and 'economic freedom', the *Economist* view also rejects any necessary correlation between authoritarianism and growth:

> It is absurd to conclude from East Asia's success, and from that fact alone, that non-democratic government is best for development ... [If one observes the political map,] it remains true that nearly all of the world's richest countries are free and nearly all of the poorest countries are not.[61]

Citing empirical and econometric studies of the link between democracy and growth,[62] a three-way typology of political systems is shown here classifying countries as 'free, partly free, or not free' according to such indices as free elections, civil liberties, multi-party legislatures and an unfettered press. Malaysia is categorised as partly free, with the USA and Iraq at opposite ends of the continuum. The main claim here is that economic freedom is not the only stimulus to growth:

> civil and political freedoms do the same ... [P]olitical freedom adds to the economic benefits already secured by economic freedom [because] it encourages firms and people to behave as if those freedoms will endure ... Here lies the decisive advantage conferred by political freedom – meaning democracy, and the dispersion of political power that goes with it.[63]

This analysis is persuasive in that 'authoritarian development' is *not* an *essential* condition for economic expansion. On the other hand, we have to recognise the particular free-market logic informing this view. Reflecting Lockean property ideals, it constitutes not only a liberal (or neo-liberal) paradigm for development, but an entrenched set of criteria and value judgements against which countries are accorded democratic status.

Case's portrayal of Malaysia as a 'semi-democracy' is indicative of that set of assumptions. Case accepts Huntington's definition here, arguing that 'democratic content can be ... measured along two lines: liberal participation and electoral contestation'.[64] While open, competitive elections and political opposition are permitted in Malaysia, electoral contestation remains circumscribed by gerrymandering (giving weighted priority to the mainly Malay rural constituencies[65]) and a broad array of underhand strategies designed to marginalise the opposition, such as bans on outdoor opposition rallies. Thus, for Case, in 'bracket[ing] liberal participation and electoral contestation with semi-democratic controls ... the government in Malaysia has been able to perpetuate its semi-democracy'.[66]

As we shall see, the repressive apparatus of the state does, indeed, act as a serious constraint on political opposition in Malaysia. For example, the Societies Act has been used to proscribe 'seditious' groups, the Internal Security Act (ISA) to imprison dissidents, the Printing Press Act to control the media and the Universities and University Colleges Act (UUCA) to limit student dissent. However, the problem with Case's view is twofold. First, it assumes, *viz.* the liberal separation between state and civil society, that the Western state does not resort to coercion. Second, in using quantitative liberal criteria to 'measure' democracy, it helps internalise liberal democracy as ideological discourse in itself; in effect, the language employed becomes not only the premise of the study, but part of a more incorporated vocabulary. The result is the proliferation of categorisation-based enquiry and the artificial arrangement of countries into neat compartments: 'semi-democratic', 'quasi-democratic', 'pseudo-democratic', and so on.

This narrow definition of 'representative democracy'[67] and preoccupation with quantitative categorisation affirms, for Chomsky, the sense in which liberal-capitalist institutions have specifically sought to 'deter democracy' by limiting its definition and participation.[68] As such, 'minimalist democracy' has been absorbed and filtered as 'Free-World' discourse across the centre-liberal and right-wing spectrum, informing both liberal academia and the labyrinth of conservative institutions, notably in the USA.

One of these, Freedom House, a major compiler of 'democratic country ratings' is frequently cited in mainstream political science literature.[69] For example, both Means's standard reader, *Malaysian Politics: The Second Generation*,[70] and Jesudason's more critical account of the Malaysian 'syncretic state' take Freedom House's ranking of political rights in Malaysia as an assumed reference.[71] Thus, the idea of minimal democracy, an axiom of the Western capitalist state,[72] has been adopted as a 'definitive' point of reference for academic enquiry.

This exercise in 'democratic ranking' can still, of course, offer informative insights. For example, Crouch shows how the political elite in Malaysia oscillates between positions of liberal relaxation and repression in response to social pressures from below.[73] In this sense, the polity exhibits both democratic *and* authoritarian tendencies simultaneously, granting, for example, greater middle-class freedoms, while suppressing working-class labour power. Similarly, citing Malaysia as 'semi-democratic', Thompson offers four valid reasons for the 'limitation of democratisation' in the region: the fostering of economic growth and limited wealth inequality; the persuasive elite claim that these polities are founded on alternative forms of democracy; the successful cultivation of ethnic balancing; and the popular receptiveness of nationalist anti-Western rhetoric.[74]

Such factors do, indeed, help illustrate patterns of control and regime legitimation. The more nuanced point, however, concerns the analytical *context* within which they are addressed. The methodological task of ranking countries according to liberal democratic criteria (for Crouch, a set of conditions derived from Schumpeter and Dahl)[75] helps reproduce an idealised *mode* of analysis; allowing, in effect, the *terms of debate* to be set around the liberal-determined 'problem' of 'democratic dysfunctions' within 'the *other* society'. This not only helps cloak liberal language as 'neutral policy science', it also 'conceals' the sense in which it represents hegemonic discourse in itself.

At the same time, we need to recognise how such discourse is 'traded' as 'Asian values' by *domestic* interests. The problem here is that with loaded meaning and pejorative associations now surrounding 'Asian values', their relevance tends to be obscured. Thus the 'value of Asian values' has been overshadowed by an agenda-setting debate between two competing hegemonies. As will be noted in relation to the Anwar affair, there *are* such things as Asian values, conventions, codes and ways of seeing society that are 'indigenous' to, though not homogeneous within, Asia. These include complex interactions of the extended family, tight business practices (derived from the Chinese clan system), Malay custom (*adat*), social deference, *kampong* collectivity and, of course, communitarian concepts of Islam. However, as the rise of consumer individualism in Malaysia shows, this does not preclude receptiveness to other values and aspirations. The key point to note is the way in which 'Asian values' have been *appropriated* both as domestic ideology *and* as liberal 'anti-discourse'.

The further twist here is the sense in which liberal discourse and Asian values have assumed both contested *and* convergent forms. Thus we find both discourses promoting the same ideology of growth in pursuit of capital accumulation. Here, some Western academics have sought lessons from the 'Asian way' to growth while upholding liberal values, while others have flirted with 'Asian values' as a mirror to social disorder in Western societies. On the other hand, having almost *invented* itself as a free-market *entrepôt* economy, Goh Chok Tong in Singapore seeks to maintain Confucian values. Thus, having created a capitalist hub, the avuncular Lee Kuan Yew can attribute the success of Singapore to its very rejection of liberal democracy:

> I do not believe that democracy necessarily leads to development. I believe that what a country needs to develop is discipline more than democracy. The exuberance of democracy leads to indiscipline and disorderly conduct which are inimical to development.[76]

Mahathirism has defended a similar 'Asian Way' to development. Thus, rather than leading to greater 'democracy', Mahathir's modernising endeavours have been used to limit and redefine the *meaning* of democratic participation. Aware of the potentialities of an expanding civil society, Anwar had also argued, pre-crisis, for a more 'particularised' democracy, rather than the Western liberal model:

The Western media deride us for failing to emulate their model of democracy. But Malaysia is guided by the cultural and value systems and the
religious beliefs of its people ... [W]e have to choose between responsible
democracy and destructive democracy ... for our race, religion and nation.[77]

Thus the issue of democracy here is rationalised not only in terms of
whether it complements growth, but also in relation to wider issues of
civil, cultural and 'moral development'. Again, notes Vatikiotis, this forms
part of a negotiated complex of ideas:

All the modern political ideologies espoused by contemporary Southeast
Asian states draw on tradition but present themselves as modern, forward
thinking creeds. Indonesia's *Pancasila* state ideology, Singapore's 'Core
Principles', and Malaysia's *Rukunegara*, all espouse Western civil society
principles such as freedom, justice and human dignity. They also emphasise
the traditional, and for the most part collective, foundations of society: the
need for tolerance, a strong sense of community, collective discipline, respect
for leadership, and spirituality.[78]

At this point, however, the distinction between an 'ethical' state paternalism and latent authoritarianism becomes blurred. The notion of a 'limited
democracy' becomes reified as an ideological statement of political cultural
identity; a *necessarily* 'different form of democracy' for a 'different set of
cultural values'. This interplay of indigenous values and constructed ideology involves, in turn, an appeal to anti-Western populism. Thus any
criticism of Mahathir by foreign politicians or the Western media can be
counterposed as an attack not merely upon Mahathir himself, but upon the
integrity of the nation. For example, in imposing a ban on British trade
and imports (February–August 1994) in response to the *Sunday Times*
Pergau Dam 'aid for arms' allegations,[79] Mahathir charged the British with
having a 'colonial brain', and of portraying Malaysia, gratuitously, as a 'tin-
pot country or banana republic'.[80] In *Hidden Agenda*, a propagandist tract
written by Mahathir acolytes during the crisis, the Prime Minister has this
to say about the West:

Some in Asia believe that the West engineered the currency crisis to forcibly
open the Tiger markets that were closed to it. Some think it is to stop East
Asia in its development track, preventing it from becoming a potent rival
and competitor ... Until recently, it seemed the East Asian train was unstoppable and would have smashed into the 21st century, long designated
the Asia-Pacific Era, and snatched from the West the window of global
opportunities ... Then came the unrelenting currency attacks that brought
down the value of local currencies and the share markets, throwing the
region into turmoil ... To this, add the relentless Western media attacks on

East Asia with reports that are negative, damaging and destructive, further eroding confidence.[81]

The anti-colonial soundbite is none too gracefully deployed here. But the use of nationalist polemic for political consumption should not disguise Mahathir's willingness to contest the issues of development and democracy as ideological constructs. Nor should it disguise the wider debate taking place among Malaysian intellectuals over the nature of democracy and its application within civil society. In effect, some ask, can a polity incorporating the ideals of *qualitative* participation and human rights be formed around the conventional norms of liberal capitalist democracy?[82] Again, while identifying the expedient motives underlying the Mahathir rhetoric, Vatikiotis notes both its popular persuasiveness and the sense in which it complements a wider ambivalence about the West:

> Mahathir's rhetorical view that the West is distorting democracy may not sway the urbane Western-educated minority already sold on the materialistic ephemera of Western culture, but it is potentially persuasive in less privileged, less worldly-wise strata of society. Ironically enough, exposure to Western media considered as a measure of openness in Southeast Asia is allowing ordinary people of the region to witness some of the very problems with Western society their leaders would have them reject.[83]

Thus, taking these elements together, we see how liberal democracy, Asian values and the ideology of growth have been contested, contextualised and filtered as *intellectual constructs*. Labelling and ranking of countries' democratic status have also allowed an artificial discourse to proliferate, disguising the more particular sense in which dominant institutions define and, ultimately, limit democracy through their ability to *set the terms* of debate. In these regards, the dissemination of language, images and ideology forms a critical element in the process of hegemonic legitimation.

Notes

1. Zakaria Haji Ahmad (1989), p. 347.
2. Zakaria Haji Ahmad (1993), pp. 159–60.
3. Said (1978), p. 166.
4. Said (1993).
5. Ibid., p. xx.
6. Preston (1998), p. 226.
7. Maaruf (1992), p. 251.
8. Khoo Boo Teik (1995), pp. 261, 333.
9. Munro-Kua (1996), p. 8.

10. Furnivall (1956), p. 304.

11. See Hua Wu Yin (1983).

12. Nagata (1975).

13. Under this arrangement, the migrant bound himself to the Chinese employer, who held the rights to his wages and services until the debt had been repaid. See Andaya and Andaya (1982), p. 136.

14. Brown (1994), p. 216.

15. Andaya and Andaya (1982), pp. 138–9.

16. Ibid., pp. 175–9.

17. Cited in Alatas (1977a), p. 44; see also pp. 39–47.

18. Jesudason (1996), pp. 129, 131.

19. Ibid., p. 130.

20. Jomo (1986), pp. 271, 272.

21. Hua Wu Yin (1983).

22. Ibid., pp. 2, 6, 150, 193.

23. Brennan (1985), p. 95.

24. Brown (1944), pp. 211–13. Italics added.

25. See Means (1976), pp. 43–8.

26. Ibid., p. 51.

27. Brown (1994), p. 220.

28. See Munro-Kua (1996), pp. 18–19.

29. Zakaria (1993), p. 356.

30. Khoo Boo Teik (1997), p. 51. Brown (1994), p. 222.

31. Chin Peng has lived in exile in Thailand since Independence.

32. See Shafruddin (1987), pp. 2–13, for an account of the Reid Commission's remit and report of 1957.

33. Cited in Brown (1994), p. 239.

34. Ibid., p. 214.

35. Gomez and Jomo (1997), pp. 16–17.

36. Khoo Boo Teik (1997), p. 53.

37. Ibid.

38. Brown (1994), pp. 234–5.

39. Khoo Boo Teik (1997), pp. 53–4.

40. Brown (1994), p. 230.

41. Cited in ibid., p. 231.

42. Ibid., p. 233.

43. The total number of Malays within the civil service by 1970 was 48,946, or 64.5% of Malays. This represented a quadrupling of Malay recruitment between 1950 and 1957 and a further doubling between 1957 and 1970. While Malays comprised 86.6% of the elite ranks, 53.4% of the total civil service now came from poorer, rural backgrounds by this point. Brown (1994), p. 239.

44. Khoo Boo Teik (1995), pp. 87, 198–200, 294–5.

45. Ibid., pp. 22–3.

46. See Gill (1990a), (1990b), (1995); see also Gill and Law (1988), (1989).

47. While modernisation theory drew upon ideal types of 'traditional' and 'legal-rational' authority (Weber 1978), it can be mainly traced to positivist-functionalist ideas within US academia from the 1940s.

48. Preston (1986), pp. 93–4.

49. As in Project Camelot, where US academics liaised with the military in counter-insurgency studies.

50. See Lawrence (1996), p. 46: Lawrence also notes how Walt Rostow assumed a key role within the State Department's policy planning staff, thereafter securing CIA money to establish the MIT Center for International Studies; p. 54.

51. Preston (1986), p. 70.

52. Preston (1987), p. 43.

53. Ariff (1991); Jun (1994).

54. Clad (1989), pp. 247, 256–9. Clad was a former *FEER* journalist and ISA detainee.

55. Yoshihara (1988), pp. 4, 68, 80.

56. See, for example, Harris (1988).

57. A good example of this view in the West was offered by Peter Sutherland, director-general of the WTO (1995), former Tory Chancellor Norman Lamont and Sumantra Ghoshal of the London Business School on the TV discussion forum *Weekly Planet* (UK, Channel 4), 29 July 1998.

58. Rodan (1996), pp. 3–4.

59. Vatikiotis (1996), p. 5.

60. Friedman (1994), pp. 20, 21, 25, 28, 29.

61. 'Democracy and growth: why voting is good for you', *The Economist*, 27 August 1994.

62. Notably the study by ex-World Bank analyst Surjit Bhalla, 'Free societies, free markets and social welfare'; see ibid.

63. *The Economist*, 27 August 1994.

64. Case (1993), p. 76.

65. The priority weighing of rural over urban constituencies is entrenched in the 1957 Constitution. Although amended several times, the principle, allowing greater representation to Malays, gives the government a substantial majority in the Dewan Rakyat.

66. Case (1993), pp. 77, 82.

67. See Pateman (1970). American academia provides the main intellectual milieu for this narrow approach in the work of Dahl, Parsons, Nye, Verba, Gilpin, and, more lately, Fukuyama. Huntington's 1975 report *The Crisis of Democracy* argued that there was too much democracy in Western societies and that the education system and other key institutions should control this 'democratic distemper'. Cited in Kellner (1990), p. xiii.

68. MacPherson (1973). See Chomsky (1991) on how Western political institutions serve to restrict democratic participation.

69. One may note here Freedom House's links to the World Anticommunist League, Resistance International, Accuracy in Media, Radio Free Europe and the Central Intelligence Agency, and its proxy role as electoral monitor for the USA. E. Herman and N. Chomsky (1994), p. 28.

70. Means (1991).

71. Jesudason (1996), p. 128.

72. For a discussion of the extensive democratic deficits in Britain, for example, see Hutton (1995).

73. Crouch (1996).

74. Thompson (1993), p. 471.

75. Crouch (1996), p. 3.

76. 'Democracy and growth', *The Economist*, 27 August 1994.

77. *New Straits Times*, 26 September 1994.

78. Vatikiotis (1996), p. 29.

79. See *Sunday Times*, 23 January 1994, 20 February 1994. The issue was initially featured by the *Sunday Times*, 20 February 1994.

80. Cited in *FEER*, 17 March 1994. Invoking the principle of democratic accountability against the Western media, he also retorted: 'Nobody elects the press. Andrew Neil [then *Sunday Times* editor] can stay there because there is a contract with Murdoch ... But there is no such guarantee for elected people like us.' 'Nobody elects the press: Mahathir speaks out on media, culture and trade', *FEER*, 7 April 1994. The controversy was also clouded by Murdoch's attempt to buy Star TV in Hong Kong, a move opposed by Mahathir.

81. Cited in 'Read it and weep', *FEER*, 21 May 1998.

82. See Vatikiotis, 1996, p. 83.

83. Ibid., p. 89.

2

Constructing the Vision: State–Class Relations, the Power Bloc and the Origins of Crisis

This section considers the economic basis of the power bloc from the early 1980s to the unfolding crisis of 1997. The main purpose is to illustrate the new configuration of state–class relations taking shape during this period and the impact of such at the social level. Here, Mahathir's project is considered in relation to three main reference points: the 'Malay dilemma', NEP distribution and the spectre of privatisation. The contradictions and tensions noted within each provide, in turn, a basis for addressing the crisis and the Anwar affair.

The Malay Dilemma and the Challenge of Modernity

In *The Malay Dilemma*, Mahathir cites hereditary and cultural influences as key causal impediments to Malay development. Initially banned on publication in 1970, following the riots of 1969, this book came to crystallise Bumiputera grievances at a critical period, becoming, effectively, the intellectual rationale for the NEP.

The essence of the dilemma can be traced to Mahathir's portrayal of Malay political culture as a deep-rooted predicament. While highlighting disparities of wealth and opportunity, Mahathir sought to probe deeper, arguing that the Malays suffered, inter-generationally, from a subservient inner psyche. In seeking reasons for the absence of bourgeois motivation – loosely akin to a Calvinist work ethic – Mahathir adopted an eclectic mix of genetic, psychological and socio-cultural argument to illustrate the inherent weaknesses of Malay codes. Certain Malay qualities were portrayed as obstacles to progress, most notably, a concern with *form*, and a tendency towards *fatalism*. Here:

> adherence to form as prescribed by *adat* [custom/convention] … is so important that it is preferred to the actual substance. Thus, the formality of official status is regarded as more important than the authority which should go with it … [Then there is] the fatalism which characterises the Malay

attitude to life ... It makes acceptance of everything, whether good or bad, possible with unprotesting tolerance and resignation.[1]

For Mahathir, such passivity, alongside a misconstrued understanding of Malay politeness, interpreted by foreigners as deference, precluded the development of a dynamic business culture. Symptomatic of this was the Malay conception of property:

> For most Malays property and land are synonymous [and] ... attachments to the land are deeply ingrained, ... [while] money is a convenience to the Malays. [It is this] inability to understand the potential capacity of money [which] makes the Malays poor businessmen.[2]

In short, Malay underachievement was rooted in an absent, or dysfunctional, business culture, stunting the development of a Malay bourgeoisie and Malay society.

While Mahathir's *Dilemma* saw the relevance of cultural conditioning, there was little explanation of the historical class context within which it occurred. Alongside many speculative assertions about inherent racial traits, it relied on a discourse of cultural determinism to explain the Malays' subservient place within the capitalist order of the early 1970s and the measures needed to correct that imbalance. As regards the prognosis itself, Khoo observes that while claiming to highlight intrinsic Malay traits as impediments to development, though avoiding claims to scientific objectivity, 'Mahathir plunged into a Social Darwinism all of his own'.[3] Yet, for all its intellectual shortcomings, *The Malay Dilemma* had become a potent narrative and source of reflection for Malays. And it provided Mahathir with an immediate backdrop against which to launch a reformist project.

In seeking to usher in this new agenda, Mahathir was aware of the need to balance the drive for prosperity with a sense of social consciousness. More specifically, any promotion of a materialist ethic had to be measured against Islamic social codes. For Mahathir, this reflected the need for a reassertion of Malay/Islamic values. Here, he argued, the values of Malay community were being profaned by an obsessive individualism. Yet, invoking the tenets of the Quran and other sacred texts, the indictment was not of accumulation and wealth generation *per se*, but of materialism. In his 1986 book *The Challenge*, a further exposition of Malaysian society, Mahathir considers the seductive influence of materialism and the need for a transcendent modernism:

> In recent times, the ideology and logic of materialism have all too easily influenced human society. This is the direct result of the impact of Western thought and system of values, which fanatically focus on the material as the basis of life ... [I]n a situation where materialism holds sway, it is hardly

surprising that materialist values are used to control the movements and activities of society.[4]

Reflecting the PAP's calls in Singapore for a reassertion of traditional authority,[5] Mahathir was now offering a redefined Malay/Islamic identity as a counterpoint to Western individualism. At the same time, material acquisition was denounced as the basis of non-spiritual socialism, with its 'obsessive' redistributive ideologies, rather than a necessary product of capitalism. This was not to 'excuse' capitalism, which also had the capacity to corrupt social consciousness. Rather, the task was to harness its productive qualities.[6]

Thus, while Mahathir equates socialism, communism and capitalism as devoid of spirituality, the latter's redemptive qualities lie in its ability to generate economic well-being through wealth creation. The central message, therefore, is that acquisition and inequality of wealth do not necessarily undermine individual spirituality. For Mahathir, the key problem in socialist doctrine is that it fetishises materialism in its 'fixation' with wealth and redistribution:

> Based upon these materialistic concepts and values, a slogan has been concocted to influence the minds and hearts of the people: it goes: 'the poor are poorer, the rich richer'. Created by socialists in the West, the slogan has spread and infected the rest of the world. Among the communities caught in its trap are the Malays of Malaysia.[7]

Mahathir's view of socialism rather misses its deeper moral and humanist meaning. The more immediate question here, however, concerns the extent to which a modern Malay-Islamic value system could be reconciled with an evolving capitalist culture. For Mahathir this involved the need for measured assimilation:

> The East is now going through a phase in which independence in the physical sense has been achieved, but the influence of Western imperialism is still pervasive ... This makes it difficult to screen such influence so that only the good aspects are assimilated. [At the same time, there is] no reason why the influence of the ex-colonialists, or more accurately, Western influence, cannot be analysed and systematically and judiciously assimilated by a nation or group.[8]

Thus Mahathir's treatise on imperialism and the West did not spring from any fundamental objection to, or radical critique of, capitalism itself. As Khoo notes:

> At heart it was a condemnation of Western motives, machinations and manipulations ... But intemperate as the language sometimes sounded by

diplomatic standards, it was not the anti-imperialist language of radical Asian, African, or Latin American nationalists. Mahathir would be unrecognizable among Ho Chi Minh, Frantz Fanon ... or Fidel Castro ... He was only against 'imperialism' as protectionism but would have hardly conceived of imperialism in the form of 'foreign investments'.[9]

Here, Mahathir saw not only the unstoppable momentum of Western capitalist culture, but also the potent symbolism of modernity in crafting popular consciousness. *The Challenge* thus invoked the need for a new understanding of Malay development as a *specific issue* of Islamic modernity, providing, in turn, a new nationalist-popular direction for the Islamic resurgence in Malaysia:

> To Mahathir's mind ... what Islam most urgently required of the Malays was for them to attain 'a balance between this world (*dunia*) and the next (*akhirat*)' ... or ... 'worldly wealth' and 'worldly knowledge' ... [thus offering] ... a reading of Islam which came not from an Islamic theologian but a Malay nationalist. The result was that the Malay dilemma was recast as a Muslim dilemma.[10]

Hence, from the 'discourse of dilemma' in the 1970s to the 'challenge of modernity' in the 1980s, Mahathir had sought to promote a reformist, growth-driven agenda conducive to modern Islamic thinking; one that would give impetus to Bumiputera competitiveness and lift Malays out of their 'dependent' socio-economic condition.

Yet out of one contradiction another had unfolded. The main vehicle for Malay development from the early 1970s had been the NEP. Having institutionalised Bumiputera rewards and state patronage, however, the modernist rubric of economic growth was now being constrained by the reluctance of Malays and Malay capital to compete in a more open-market environment. As a framework for social redistribution *vis-à-vis* the Chinese and Indians, the NEP had created not only new brooding ethnic resentments, but a concentration of middle-class interests within the public sector, an entrenched bureaucracy and an increasingly inflexible relationship between the state and domestic capital.

The NEP: Class Formation and Contradictions

Precipitating a fundamental realignment of state–class relations, the key outcome of the 1969 conflict had been the implementation of the NEP. Its dual aims, contained within the Outline Perspective Plan (1971–90) (OPP1), were: 'to achieve national unity through the two-pronged objectives of eradicating poverty irrespective of race, and restructuring society to eliminate the identification of race with economic function'.[11] Underlying this set of objectives, enshrined in the Second Malaysian Plan (1971–75), were positive discrimination policies designed to achieve a 30% target of Bumiputera commercial ownership by 1990. Allied to this was a series of interventions to promote a new state-sponsored bourgeoisie protected from the predatory impulses of international and other domestic (namely, Chinese) capital. A notable statement of intent here, also, was the Malaysian government's City of London 'raid' on British-owned Guthrie stock in 1971.[12] Accompanied by complementary forms of preferential treatment for Malays in education, jobs and other key areas, the state appeared set to resolve the contradiction of its own subordinate bourgeoisie.[13]

Under Mahathir, the imperatives of ethnic redistribution were to be linked more specifically to a drive for NIC status. However, limiting the heavy industrialisation strategy envisaged by Mahathir was his view that the Malay entrepreneurs created by the NEP were not yet able to function as an independent capitalist class. In response, domestic capital's weaknesses were being met with a heavy programme of state investment (through the Heavy Industries Corporation of Malaysia – HICOM) and protection of infant industries. But it also involved an easing of the state's relationship with non-Malay capital, though one in which, through the framework of Malaysia Inc.,[14] Malay capital still played the decisive role.

This was still 'statist economic development',[15] a top-down model of capitalist transformation that kept the domestic bourgeoisie politically dependent. While aware of its necessity as a keystone of the reward system, Mahathir was, however, under no illusions about its long-term effects in harbouring complacency.[16] While facilitating Malay entrepreneurship through the selective provision of business contracts, licences, financing

TABLE 2.1 Malaysia: ownership of share capital (%)[19]

	1970	1990	1995
Bumiputera	2.4	19.3	20.6
Bumiputera individuals and institutions	1.6	14.2	18.6
Trust agencies	0.8	5.1	2.0
Non-Bumiputera	28.3	46.8	43.4
Chinese	27.2	45.5	40.9
Indians	1.1	1.0	1.5
Others	–	0.3	1.0
Nominee companies	6.0	8.5	8.3
Foreigners	63.4	25.5	27.7

TABLE 2.2 Occupation and income by ethnic group (1995/96) (%)[23]

	Bumiputera	Chinese	Indian	Other
Occupation (1995)				
Professional and technical	64.3	26.2	7.3	2.2
Teachers and nurses	72.3	20.5	6.6	0.6
Administrative and managerial	36.1	54.7	5.1	4.1
Clerical workers	57.2	34.4	7.7	0.7
Sales workers	36.2	51.9	6.5	5.4
Service workers	58.2	22.8	8.7	10.3
Agriculture workers	63.1	12.9	7.5	16.5
Production workers	44.8	35.0	10.3	9.9
Professionals (selected) (1996)				
Architects	28.1	70.3	1.4	0.2
Accountants	14.4	78.8	5.7	1.1
Engineers	36.5	56.6	6.8	0.1
Dentists	32.1	45.1	21.1	1.7
Doctors	34.4	31.6	31.1	2.9
Veterinary surgeons	40.2	24.2	33.2	2.4
Surveyors	46.3	48.9	3.9	0.9
Lawyers	28.8	46.6	23.2	1.2
Mean monthly gross household income (RM) (1995)	1,600	2,895	2,153	1,274

and other forms of state assistance, the 30% NEP target had also proved an untenable aim. Nevertheless, between 1970 and 1990 Malay ownership of domestic corporate equity rose from 2.4% to an impressive 19.3%. The bulk of this (14.2%) was owned directly by individual Bumiputeras and institutions,[17] the rest being controlled through state-based trusts such as Permodalan Nasional Berhad (PNB – National Equity Corporation), a structure designed to attract and utilise small-scale Malay investment. Reflecting the traditional presence of the Chinese diaspora and its capital networks in Southeast Asia, the 29% ethnic Chinese community in Malaysia continued to represent the largest share (44.5%) by 1990.[18] However, the Malay state had secured control of the more significant corporate, industrial and financial sectors of the economy by this point, notably in petroleum, plantations, mineral extraction and banking. Gomez, Jomo and others also note that the actual size of the Bumiputera share of corporate wealth has been considerably underestimated.[20]

Coincident with the state's leading role in generating Bumiputera wealth, through equity investment agencies and state-based development corpora-

TABLE 2.3 Employment by sector (1997) (%)[24]

Manufacturing	27.7
Other sectors	21.0
Wholesale and retail trade, hotels and restaurants	16.5
Agriculture, forestry, livestock and fishing	15.2
Government services	10.5
Construction	9.1

tions, there emerged a rapidly expanded Malay middle/service class. In the NEP years, 1970–90, the proportion of the Malay workforce employed in middle-class jobs rose from 12.9% to 27%, an increase from 33.6% to 48.1% of total share of the main middle-class occupational categories. In the same period, the number of Chinese and Indian middle-class jobs held (as a proportion of their respective workforces) also rose, from 28.6% to 43.2%, and from 23.4% to 27.3%.[21] The key point here is that while continued growth provided more upward social mobility for all three ethnic groups, the Chinese and Indian share declined relative to Malay middle-class employment. In particular, Bumiputeras became predominant in government services.[22]

The importance of middle-class support must also be seen in relation to the ethnic divisions within the working class and the control of labour power in Malaysia. Again, class-based ethnic ideology has featured prominently here, serving to fragment class alliances, thus allowing working-class political consciousness and dissent to remain communally focused and channelled through the various MCA, MIC and UMNO party machineries.

This, in turn, has made it easier to marginalise labour power and implement anti-trade union legislation. From the early 1980s, Mahathir promoted Japanese-based employer–labour relations, principally through the encouragement of 'in-house' trade unions. By 1998, only 12% of the 8.5 million workforce in Malaysia was unionised.[27] The strategy here has been to marginalise national unions by promoting 'enterprise union'

TABLE 2.4 Total labour force (1998)[25] and unemployment rate (1985–98)

	1985	1992	1995	1996	1997	1998
Unemployment rate (%)[26]	6.9	3.7	2.8	2.6	2.6	4.9
Total labour force						9,006,500
Employed						8,563,300

practices, where union leadership is specifically geared to the needs of the company, productivity and corporate investment.[28]

The labour model being pursued here also bears comparison with Singapore. Under the PAP, the Singaporean state-class sought a conspicuously international environment for capital accumulation. While projecting ideals of state paternalism, it did so within a context of social co-optation and pragmatic alliance with those sections of capital (foreign *and* domestic) most amenable to an open-door *entrepôt* economy. This, required a compliant, low-cost labour base as a stimulus to mass manufacturing and export-led growth.[29]

The structural base of the Singaporean economy has largely shifted from industrial manufacturing to specialised technology and services, with much of its manual labour pool situated in the neighbouring Malaysian state of Johore. From the 1970s, Malaysia's shift from agriculture to services and manufacturing, high GDP output and positive balance of payments situation had placed it in a favourable position to follow Singapore in the more capital-intensive and technology-based sectors.[31] Steady growth rates of around 8% following the 1985 recession to 1996 had given further impetus to this process.[32] Of course, despite NEP nationalisation, the Malaysian state has always sought a close relationship with international capital. One reason for this was that the domestic-led industrialisation models suggested by Taiwan and South Korea would have been undesirable for Malaysia, since this might have allowed Chinese capital even more power over Malay capital.[33] However, in following the Singaporean model,

TABLE 2.5 Malaysia: export structure (1970–98) (%)[30]

	1970*	1993	1998
Electrical and electronic products	–	45.5	54
Other manufactured goods	–	24.0	23.3
Palm oil	6.0	4.8	5.8
Other exports	–	3.4	4.8
Textiles, clothing and footwear	–	4.5	3.2
Liquefied natural gas (LNG)	–	0.4	2.9
Crude oil	–	6.6	2.6
Timber	5.9	6.2	1.5
Rubber	39.6	1.7	1.1
Tin	24.1	2.2	0.2
Other commodities	19.0	0.7	0.6

* Selected 1970 figures are for West Malaysia.

concessions to international capital had left the Malaysian economy exposed to the insecurities of FDI and the volatility of world markets. Accordingly, between 1980 and 1989, Malaysia's share of foreign investment fell from 2.3 to 0.7%, as a percentage of global FDI,[34] a situation exacerbated by the emergence of Laos, Vietnam, and, most notably, China as more lucrative accumulation sites in the region. Intensified by recession and budget crises, these new forms of dependency had become particularly evident by the mid-1980s.[35]

A further aspect of this dependency was Mahathir's courting of Japanese TNCs in a bid to build a globally competitive electronics sector. Outwith the OECD states, Malaysia and the other 'second-tier' Southeast Asian NICs (Thailand, Indonesia and the Philippines) became major recipients of Japanese FDI by the late 1980s, with the Southeast Asian region comprising Japan's largest investment area outside the US market.[36] Reflecting Japan's burgeoning trade surpluses and the appreciating yen (*endaka*), initiated under the Plaza Agreement of 1985, a new wave of investment saw the concentration of off-shore branch-assembly production and the utilisation of cheap labour. This restructuring – or 'global localisation' – of Japanese TNCs saw top companies such as Sony and Hitachi opt for new forms of off-shore activity based on the location needs of middle-range contractors.[37] Production of quality goods was controlled by foreign firms' own subcontractors located in the host country, with local companies confined to supplying basic materials.[38] With Japanese conglomerates maintaining ownership of the production process, this allowed limited scope for technology transfer to Malaysian franchises.[39] Thus Malaysia has been used as a low-cost production site, with hi-tech research and development (R&D) concentrated in Europe and North America.[40] Yet, despite these limitations, acquired technology and low-priced labour had become the new orthodoxy of development for countries such as Malaysia by the 1980s.[41]

This new dependence also saw the removal of investment controls, the provision of tax incentives and assurances over capital repatriation to foreign, particularly Japanese, investors, measures beginning under the Fourth Malaysian Plan, 1981–85.[42] At the same time, Malaysia's growing concentration on electronics exposed it to large-scale retrenchment of labour in the wake of the mid-1980s downturn in semiconductors,[43] a situation exacerbated by Malaysian/ASEAN export dependence on Japan and its long-standing failure to penetrate Japanese protectionist markets.[44]

An associated trend here was the widening regional disparities in manufacturing and growth between states in Malaysia itself, with concentrations of investment and wealth in the Free Trade Zones (FTZs) of Penang, Selangor (the Klang Valley) and Johore, contrasting with slower industrial development in, for example, Kelantan, Perlis and Terengganu.[46]

TABLE 2:6 Gross domestic product by sector (1995–98) (%)[45]

	1995	1997	1998
Growth	9.4	7.7	-4.8
Services	44.2	44.9	48.1
Manufacturing	33.1	35.7	35.4
Agriculture, forestry and fishing	13.6	11.9	11.8
Mining	7.4	6.7	7.0
Construction	4.4	4.8	4.1
Less: imputed bank service charges	–	8.2	9.2
Plus: import duties	–	4.1	2.8
	100.0	100.0	100.0

Another key factor here has been the steady influx of foreign labour. The government claims that around 1.2 million workers in Malaysia are foreign migrants, although varying NGO estimates put the figure at 3 million, half of them undocumented.[47] The use of foreign workers has served the dual purpose of filling unskilled labour shortages, notably in the low-paid service and manufacturing sectors, while helping to control labour power by keeping unit labour costs low. This has been especially important in view of increasing competition within and between these sectors and with regard to Malaysia's regional competitiveness.

The traditional source of Malaysia's cheap labour pool has been Indonesian migrants – mostly concentrated in the domestic service, agricultural and transportation sectors.[48] However, many more form part of the black economy, notably in the construction sector. By the early 1990s, the pattern of foreign labour had come to comprise, more particularly, young Bangladeshi workers, many brought in by unscrupulous agents, to fill severe labour shortages in the low-paid textile industries and sweatshops, for example in and around the Penang FTZs.[49] They are victimised and socially isolated, and this has added another tier of ethnic–class division, further altering the ethnic composition of the labour force, although the low-paid sectors still depend on Malaysian women from across the ethnic spectrum.

Shaping the NEP Society: Ethnicity, Poverty and the New Middle Class

While major disparities remain, there is little doubt that two decades of growth and NEP redistribution have given rise to a new Malay middle class. Reflecting the experience of black people and other socially marginalised groups in the USA, affirmative action in Malaysia can be defended as a progressive ideal. However, mainstream discussion of the NEP tends to obscure the point that Bumiputera policies arose as crisis responses to the contradictions of capitalist development under the Alliance state.

But the NEP also bred a new sense of uncertainty among many Malays themselves. In an openly searching reference to the moral ambiguities of the NEP, the writer Rehman Rashid offers the following vignette in *A Malaysian Journey*:

> In 1971 there was designed a new five part Code of Conduct called the *Rukunegara*, the 'National Credo', which was patterned after Indonesia's *Pancasila*. Belief in God, Loyalty to the King and Country, Good Behaviour and Morality, that sort of thing. There was a nationwide school essay competition to popularise the concept, and I won first prize in my age group. A reporter came to take my picture, and soon I received a cheque for RM 250 ... Later I was brought down to Kuala Lumpur with the other prize winners for the ceremony. We were given certificates [and] taken on a tour of the *New Straits Times* which had sponsored the competition. They made a fuss over us, calling us fine young Malaysians and the like. It was winning the *Rukunegara Essay* Competition that made me first think that under this New Economic Policy, no Bumiputra could ever be sure that such 'victories' as came his way were fully deserved. Certainly, I hadn't thought that my essay ... was markedly better than those that received the lesser prize. And the second prize winner had been a Chinese, and the third prize winner Indian! Happenstance? I didn't think so.[50]

As with the Alliance state, NEP class interests had fostered new communal tensions. The affirmative benefits of the NEP had also stimulated a greater tendency towards Islam as a source of communal status among the newly educated Malay middle classes, primarily those in the public sector. With Islamic codes becoming more fully institutionalised in key areas such as education, commerce and civil law,[51] Chinese and Indian fears of cultural marginalisation intensified during the 1980s.

The focus on ethnic redistribution had also led to an effective diminution of the other NEP policy objective, that of poverty eradication.[52] The sense in which the 'poverty problem' became an issue of NEP development is evident in Fong Chan Onn's *The Malaysian Economic Challenge*, a policy-planner view by the Barisan deputy education minister that sought to link poverty solutions to various 'ethnic twinning' arrangements and the promotion of a Malay commercial class.[53] However, despite this imbalance in priorities and the unreliability of the government's statistical calculations (and other sensitive data),[54] there is little doubt that poverty has been significantly reduced across all ethnic groups. During the NEP period,

1970–90, the poverty rate fell from 49.3% to 13.5%.[55] On the other hand, key disparities were still evident in the gaps between the urban and rural populations in Peninsular Malaysia (with respective sectoral poverty rates of 8.1% and 17.3% in 1987).[56] In the rural sector, the NEP also provided expanded opportunities, but this benefited business, in the main, rather than low-paid workers. Here, notes Halim Salleh, the Federal Land Development Authority (FELDA) schemes had merely created new forms of indebtedness for the settlers while offering new accumulation sites for Malay, Chinese and foreign capital.[57]

Nevertheless, the selective sponsorsip of Bumiputera interests and the rise of a Malay capitalist class had become a new expression of the Malay dilemma. In effect, the 'subsidy mentality' and ethnic chauvinisms created by the NEP were now inconsistent with Mahathir's modernity project.[58] This also reflected fears of Malay disaffection emerging from the forthcoming New Development Policy (1991), modifications to the NEP that would offer relatively fewer guarantees to Malays in an effort to generate competition.[59] Likewise, Mahathir was aware of the need to avoid alienating rural Malays dependent on NEP infrastructure. However, by the early 1990s, a more assertive language was emerging, giving cautionary notice of a scaled-down system of Malay privileges. As Anwar, taking up Mahathir's concerns, had warned: 'If you flunk your exams, we won't keep passing you just because you are a Malay. If you cannot perform on a contract, you won't get another one.'[60] And the significance of contracts and rewards can be seen as vital in this regard. For it was through the new opportunities of privatisation that Mahathir had sought, and found, a 'resolution' of the NEP dilemma.

Privatisation: The New Hegemonic Opportunity

The immediate question here was how Mahathir would structure any domestic privatisation programme, and its attendant ideals of a 'hands-off' state, with Look East and Malaysia Inc., which required – Japanese-style – a neo-corporatist 'hands-on' approach. Moreover, there was no clear explanation of how NEP interventionism and the security of Malay investment was to be balanced against the *laisser-faire* ideals of privatisation. The profile broadly adopted by Mahathir was to cast the state as 'facilitating' private sector development, while emphasising the values of cooperation with the business community as a stimulus to growth.[61]

It is, of course, the case that all modern capitalist economies involve some form of state intervention. There is no fundamental contradiction, in this sense, between the NEP, on the one hand, and privatisation, on the other. Privatisation under Thatcher also allowed top Tory political elites greater access to the new corporate sector – 'crony capitalism' differentiated only by the veil of multi-directorships and respectable boardroom practices. What made privatisation so significant in Malaysia, though, was the fact that UMNO had become a key player as a *party* through corporate ownership and holding companies such as the Hatibudi Group and Fleet Holdings. Privatisation and financial deregulation were, in this sense, closely identified from the mid-1980s with the expansion and modernisation of the Kuala Lumpur Stock Exchange (KLSE), a project directly overseen by Mahathir. Here, noted *The Economist*:

> the stockbrokers dealing in Kuala Lumpur's booming market have little doubt that politics and business are deeply interlocked in Malaysia. The brokers have noticed that the hottest properties are often 'UMNO stocks', meaning those thought to be tied to the political fortunes of rising stars within the party ... Other companies become hot tips when they are taken over by politically well connected people who stand to benefit from public contracts.[62]

The more critical point about privatisation, however, was that it offered a new means of reconfiguring the NEP state through the transfer of wealth and resources to selectively designated political–corporate elites. The 'contradiction' of privatisation in Malaysia thus lay in the particular use of deregulated state resources to strengthen UMNO/proxy corporate control. By shifting the dispensation of projects and services from the site of NEP sinecures to the Economic Planning Unit (EPU), part of the Prime Minister's Department, rentiers – Bumiputeras and non-Bumiputeras – became more closely dependent on the UMNO hierarchy, allowing Mahathir and Finance Minister Daim Zainuddin more effective control over the patronage process.[63] As a milestone policy of economic modernisation, privatisation thus offered a more flexible set of arrangements for altering the class base of the power bloc, checking elements hitherto protected by the state, while promising new forms of wealth and political access for large-scale capital. Thus privatisation: 'found its logical supporters among the captains of Malaysian industry and commerce who sensed the opening of new business opportunities in the impending transfer of state enterprises and services to private capital'.[64]

The new opportunities of privatisation can be identified, in particular, with the rise of Daim Zainuddin. From 1984, and with no prior experience of political office, Daim, close friend and confidant of Mahathir, used the Finance portfolio to distribute privatised assets, while enhancing his own personal wealth base.[65] Reflecting the ethos, if not the practice, of the Thatcherite 'enterprise culture', Daim's tenure coincided with the expansion of a *nouveau riche* political culture in Malaysia.[66] Yet, while this parvenu represented a challenge to 'old money' and traditional elites, privatisation itself was more carefully projected by Mahathir as a radical challenge, an opportunity to assert the new independent stature of a Malay business class.

However, Mahathir's 'endorsement' of privatisation also reflected the ascendant neo-liberal/monetarist orthodoxy that had taken a grip in the West. Adopted first in the USA by Carter in the late 1970s,[67] and by Thatcher in the early 1980s, the demise of Keynesian corporatism,[68] coupled with the greater mobility and volatility of financial flows, notably through the new Eurocurrency markets, had created a sharper disjunction between national and transnational forms of capital, allowing the latter a more autonomous role in shaping the global business climate.[69] A monetarist network had crystallised around the US Treasury, investment banks, Friedmanite academics and assorted political elites in the US Congress; a collective influence signifying 'the triumph of the American banking complex and of monetarist ideas in the United States'.[70] Related policy constructs based on deflation, tight public spending, deregulated markets and the privatisation of state assets thus became standard doctrine in Western countries.[71]

In seeking FDI-led development, countries such as Malaysia became increasingly subject to this agenda from the 1980s. But rather than greater productive investment in sectors such as manufacturing, this allowed for the rapid emergence of shorter-term capital inflows and portfolio-type investment composed mainly of stocks and shares. Indeed, as Jomo has argued, the ascendance of *finance* capital, neo-liberal reforms and the proliferation of portfolio-based FDI from the 1980s – rather than 'crony capitalism' – can be viewed as the key structural factors behind the emergent crisis in Malaysia by 1997. In this regard, financial liberalisation has been the 'centrepiece' of IMF stabilisation and World Bank structural adjustment programmes (SAPs), with agencies such as the International Finance Corporation (IFC), an arm of the latter, imposing 'conformist behaviour' on the South.[72] As another observer notes, in the context of IMF and World Bank debt and aid programmes:

> the role of these institutions cannot be reduced to their budgets. They help create and maintain *the rules* for the global economy. They sustain its momentum and make sure that any alternative vision proves impractical and unworkable.[73]

And through this process, the possible parameters of state action are, effectively, set out:

> What may have been crucial in the adoption of monetarist policies was the

growing acceptance of a policy outlook among political leaders, as well as central and private bankers ... Where such policies are adopted with little ... belief in the credibility of possible alternatives, *the power of capital attains hegemonic status*[74]

It is against this shift that changes in the domestic bloc may be understood. For Mahathir, it offered an opportune moment to redefine the state's relationship with foreign capital and those sections of domestic capital linked to the public sector. While augmented by other brooding factionalisms, Mahathir's use of privatisation to assuage foreign investors and transform Malay rentiers into an internationally competitive business group had helped expose critical fissures within UMNO by 1988. (See Chapter 3.)

The 'new rules' of neo-liberalism also posed the problem of how to allow a more open market while preserving UMNO's political-corporate control. Two basic situations remain inimical to foreign investment: one is political instability; the other is the over-entanglement of the state in market processes, particularly where this involves state control over key economic enterprises and selective monopolisation of rewards to state-sponsored groups. Pointing to the latter impediment, *vis-à-vis* NEP restrictions on foreign investment, the World Bank's 1986 report on the Malaysian economy had called for the 'unshackling' of state–Bumiputera interests.[75] Moreover, while the Malaysian media pointed to 'political stability' as the top reason for continued foreign investment,[76] international business remained sensitive to UMNO's concentration of executive control. Of course, foreign capital is not averse to dealing with repressive regimes: risk, after all, is an intrinsic feature of the market, with fund managers thriving on market uncertainty – and often creating political instability in the process. However, despite Mahathir's promise of greater guarantees to foreign capital, a special report on the Malaysian economy in 1988 by financial consultants Merril Lynch expressed serious concern over 'the government's over-extended and inefficient intervention in business', while noting that 'political uncertainty is the single largest risk to sustained recovery'.[77]

The Malaysian economy was also exposed to other problems by the mid-1980s: a massive increase in foreign debt; the halving of oil prices in 1982; the collapse of the tin market (caused, partly, by the Malaysian government's failed attempt to influence the price through cartel activity on the London Exchange); and the plummeting of rubber and palm oil prices in 1984.[78] On top of this, the state's NEP obligations had led to major fiscal overstretch.

Thus, with the new monetarist climate offering a rationale for reform, an effectively imposed set of policy adjustments from without could be presented as a new set of political initiatives from within. Hence, between 1984 and 1987, public spending was drastically reduced, borrowing restrained, and other austerity measures such as job and wage freezes introduced. The budget deficit in this period fell from 20% to 7% of GNP, this being accompanied by a relaxation of NEP constraints on foreign investment and a change in the Industrial Coordination Act (ICA) which had set limitations on foreign participation and equity holdings. Unemployment also rose from under 5% to 8.6% in this period.[79] Deflationary measures and deregulatory initiatives had, thus, been used to keep the IMF at bay, placate the international money markets and maintain financial stability.[80] In this sense, notes Saravanamuttu, 'denationalisation' offered a key moment for structural adjustment.[81]

Meanwhile, as Mahathir proclaimed privatisation as a new means of weaning Bumiputeras away from state dependency, Daim's transfer of resources to strategic elites helped secure a new corporate support base. This involved the flow of wealth not only to UMNO patrons, but also to key clientele within the MCA and MIC. Indeed, in 1986, Samy Vellu, president of the MIC, indicated his approval by publicly defending such political–corporate relationships.[82] By appearing to transfer the burden of state services to the private sector – a process facilitated by the absence of any open tender system – UMNO had brought all the key public-sector assets under closer party control.[83]

Thus, between 1983 and 1990, 37 privatisation projects had been completed, with another 93 in preparation by 1992–93. The main instruments used under the Privatisation Master Plan (1991) were Sales of Equity and Build-Operate Transfer (BOT) licences, the former to sell off, for example, Malaysia Airlines (1985), Sports Toto (M) Bhd Gaming (1985), Syarikat Telekom (M) Bhd (1990) and Perusahaan Otomobil Nasional (Proton) Bhd (1991), the latter to grant licences/contracts for the operating/building of Sistem Televisyen (M) (TV3) (1983), the Kuala Lumpur Interchange (1987) and the North–South Highway (1988).[84] In addition, around forty government services were transferred to UMNO's PNB and other trust agencies, and another 120 companies hived off to the private sector.[85] By 1990 equity sales had raised RM1.18 billion, RM8.2 billion had been saved through the BOT schemes, and RM7.45 billion of state debt had been off-loaded to the private sector. By 1992, the sale of key utilities, such as telephone, postal and electricity services, had saved the government RM3.2 billion in operating costs, with combined equity revenue by 1992 amounting to RM6.7 billion.[86] With further divestments, such as Petronas Gas Bhd (1995), completed by the mid-1990s, the government claimed that it had saved around RM40.6 billion in operating expenditure, with 92,700 public-sector jobs rationalised.[87]

With Malaysians facing the market realities of profit-oriented services,[88] political-corporate largess was being cloaked in the language of 'state efficiency'. For example, when Mahathir declared the North–South Highway open in September 1994, the media, in congratulatory tones, emphasised its early completion rather than the scandal of the RM3.4 billion contract awarded to United Engineers Bhd (UEM), a low-prestige subsidiary of UMNO's investment company Hatibudi.[89] The sale of key public assets such as Tenaga Nasional Bhd (National Electricity) also replaced state monopolies with private ones, offering vast opportunities for selected corporate elites.

Privatisation was, thus, creating a whole new patronage network. For example, in granting the licence for a privatised broadcasting channel to TV3, the major shareholding interests emerged as UMNO's Fleet Holding Group, Daim Zainuddin and the MIC's Maika Holdings, bringing all the major broadcasting media and press in Malaysia under UMNO control.[90] A select cohort of (mainly Bumiputera) business elites with key stakes in the newly privatised public assets had also established themselves around Anwar by the early 1990s, helping him to defeat Ghafar Baba for the post of UMNO deputy president in 1993. Many of these were part of a younger, more ambitious corporate circle frustrated at Daim's control of the patronage apparatus.[91] Indeed, the key conflict to come between Anwar and Daim can be traced in large part to tensions over the dispensation of contracts.

Other privatised concessions indicated a new alignment between UMNO and well-connected Chinese business.[92] Reflecting UMNO's near-successful takeover of the MCA's principal investment arm Multi Purpose Holdings (MPH), the 1980s saw a new stream of Chinese tycoons moving away from the traditional MCA nexus in an effort to establish fuller links with UMNO.[93] An indication of such was the awarding of 70% of Sports Toto, the state gaming concern, to Vincent Tan Chee Yioun, a sale directed by Daim via the Ministry of Finance Inc., a state-based holding company under his control. Tan and other key Chinese capitalists are understood to have developed close ties with the UMNO leadership, including the likelihood of acting as nominal business proxies for top UMNO figures.[94] Thus, while small to medium Chinese firms use nominal Malay directors and other 'Ali-Baba' arrangements to circumvent NEP licences, top Chinese capitalists now have greater access to state elites, suggesting an increasingly sophisticated network of reciprocal links:

> Accepting the fact of Malay political dominance and seeing the need to establish their own lines of communication with prominent UMNO leaders, ... the successful Chinese businessmen have carefully chosen their Malay

partners and allies ... [Thus,] the orientation of the individual tycoons is away from the Chinese community in a quest for Malay patronage and overseas business opportunities.[95]

Thus, while social resentment lingered among non-Malays, notably in the managerial and professional sectors,[97] privatisation was now being used *inter alia* with Vision policies to nurture social accommodation *across* the ethnic spectrum. The period 1991–93, notes Jomo, had seen 'the most rapid expansion and transformation in Malaysian history', with, for example, the balance of payments at a peak of RM16.7 billion in 1992 (RM5.3 billion in 1990) and exports and capital inflows at record levels,[98] a surge in economic activity offering new scope for an expanded reward structure:

> The confirmation of the change in policy direction came with the adoption of Vision 2020, seen to favour growth, modernisation and industrialisation over the NEP's emphasis on inter-ethnic redistribution. While foreign investors continued to be courted, the government has also started to allow local Chinese capital more room to move. Chinese capital has also been encouraged by various other reforms, e.g. easier access to listing on the stock

TABLE 2.7 State–class relations: key corporate elites closely linked to UMNO[96]

Main holding company	Selected corporate interests
Bumiputeras	
Wan Azmi Wan Hamzah	Land & General, R.J. Reynolds
Halim Saad	(Renong), United Engineers (M) Bhd
Samsudin Abu Hassan	Aokam Perdana Bhd, Landmarks Bhd
Tajudin Ramli	Technology Resources Ind., Malaysia Airlines (MAS)
Yahya Ahmad	(HICOM Holdings Bhd), Gadek Bhd
Ahmad Sebi Abu Bakar	Advance Synergy Bhd
Azman Hashim	(Arab Malaysian Group)
Ibrahim Mohamed	(Unipheonix Corp. Bhd)
Non-Bumiputeras	
Vincent Tan Chee Yioun	(Berjaya Group), Sports Toto (M) Sdn Bhd
T. Ananda Krishnan	(Pacific States Investments), MAI Holdings, Usaha Tegas,Tanjong
Dick Chan	Metroplex Bhd
T.K. Lim	Kamunting Bhd
Ting Pek Khiing	Ekran Bhd
Quek Leng Chan	(Hong Leong Group)
Loy Hean Heong	(Malayan Borneo Finance Bhd)

market, greater official encouragement of small and medium industries (SMIs) as well as other government efforts.[99]

Thus, at the high point of 'late Mahathirism' (circa 1991 to early 1997), the Vision had provided incentives and rewards sufficient to realise a considerable degree of consent: 'Most Malaysians could not remember a time of greater prosperity or lesser inter-ethnic recrimination ... Economic indicators alone would not have captured the pride that Malaysians had discovered, perhaps for first time, in being Malaysian.'[100] Yet the privatisation ideals used to effect this shift did not constitute a volte-face on the NEP state, but a modified reward structure repositioned around new political–corporate accommodations. And, as the crisis loomed, the fragility of these relations and Mahathir's 'liberalisation' project now became apparent.

The Emerging Crisis: 1997

The economic implications of the crisis following Anwar's removal will be developed in subsequent chapters. For the moment, let us consider the more structural dimensions of the crisis *vis-à-vis* the power bloc and state–class relations.

The volatile fluctuations within the financial markets across the region by mid-1997 offered a stark illustration of how external forces could critically undermine domestic policy. But they also exposed a new crisis point in domestic state–class relations and the contradictions of Mahathir's deregulatory agenda. The rout itself had started in Thailand, but spread rapidly through the region. As in Mexico in the 1980s, fund managers had poured capital into Thailand, allowing domestic bankers easy access to international money markets and the means with which to fuel a massive credit boom. When the international banks, fearful of overheating and burgeoning trade imbalances, took fright, the exposure of an economy built on services and lavish consumption became all too apparent. The knock-on effect saw the calling in of domestic loans, the freezing of credit to property developers, a collapse of the construction industry, the shedding of labour and major social dislocation. Intensifying the crisis, the value of the Thai baht came under severe fire from international speculators, leaving the government – and treasury elites who had hidden the extent of the state's debt – effectively helpless to contain the mounting panic. And just as international capital had helped direct the Thai economic boom, so too was it now able to set the remedial agenda through the medicine of an IMF austerity package.

Investors who had enjoyed years of rapid growth in Malaysia while turning a blind eye to its underlying structural problems now expressed serious concern. For example, in June 1997, Malaysia had registered a RM2.8 billion trade shortfall, triggering a 22-month low on the KLSE.[101] Alongside skilled labour shortages and rising wage costs, the continued appreciation of the yen was also driving up the import cost of key Japanese capital goods. As the baht crisis gathered momentum, the ringgit fell to its lowest point against the US dollar for 26 years, a signal of intense downward pressure on the currency in the months to come.[102]

Meanwhile, an environmental disaster of immense proportions was unfolding as the effects of slash-and-burn forest clearance in Kalimantan and Sumutra, exacerbated by the freak El Niño weather phenomenon, began to spread a dense cocktail of poisonous smog fumes over the entire region. Together with the omnipotence of international capital, here in stark reality were the actual effects of globalisation and the virtual irrelevance of state borders and governments to control such processes.[103]

Denouncing the international speculators, and George Soros in particular, as 'racists' intent on undermining Malaysia's economy, Mahathir 'intervened' with a vaguely defined RM60 billion rescue fund to prevent short-term share-trading in key blue-chip companies, while threatening other punitive measures, including arrest, for those helping foreign dealers to 'sell short'.[104] With fund managers unable to sell their stock freely, the US Securities Exchange Commission stood poised to declare Malaysia a controlled market, obliging US pension funds to withdraw their investment interests in the country. The uncertainty within government circles and *ad hoc* announcement of these measures were interpreted as further signs of instability by edgy fund managers, leading to an increased state of panic. As the pressure mounted, Mahathir, realising the scale of the crisis and the negative signals from the markets, abandoned the curbs. The damage limitation exercise which followed also saw the postponement of key 'megaprojects' such as the Bakun Dam and the proposed new international airport at Kedah, developments now subject to higher external currency costs. However, determined to protect the flagship Cyberjaya project, Mahathir, slating the IMF's unhelpful intervention in Thailand, denounced external calls for their cancellation as an attempt to 'subvert' Malaysian growth.

As tensions rose, Mahathir and Soros engaged in an acrimonious exchange at the IMF/World Bank gathering in Hong Kong. Responding to Mahathir's calls for an end to the unwarranted attacks on the economy, Soros counselled the PM to look first at Malaysia's own internal problems, labelling him 'a menace to his country'.[105] Reflecting their opposing perceptions of 'Asian values', Mahathir had accused Soros and other fund managers of working to an 'agenda' by selling the ringgit and seeking to undermine the KLSE. However, this conveniently overlooked the Bank Negara's own record as one of the most zealous players in the currency markets throughout the 1990s, evidenced by its attack on sterling during the UK's ERM crisis in 1992.[106] Moreover, it was apparent that, as with domestic trusts and pension funds, many other regional speculators had contributed to this latest bout.

With the choking smog enveloping the whole country by September, a gloomy mood descended, intensifying the economic crisis. A further closeted issue here was that many Malaysian logging companies, with links to Mahathir, were also involved in the slash-and-burn disaster in Indonesia – hence Malaysia's softly, softly dealings with Suharto over the problem. While Anwar's measured interventions had helped heal the rift at the IMF, enhancing his own standing in the process, deep unease over the continued viability of Malaysia's banking and credit institutions began to emerge. The international credit rating agency Standard and Poor revised Malaysia's rating from 'stable' to 'negative', while panic withdrawals by investors at the country's biggest finance house Malaysia Borneo Finance Bhd (MBF) continued, despite assurances from its senior managers and the Bank Negara.[107]

As noted, a key aspect of Malaysia's exposure to the crisis lay in the particular type of foreign capital investment it was attracting by the 1990s. Throughout the 1980s, the major element of FDI was directed towards the industrial and manufacturing sectors. Despite an increasing level of foreign ownership and outflow of profits, this form of FDI had been relatively 'rooted' as physical investment, contributing to the rapid growth in industrial output during the 1980s. By the 1990s, however, the predominant basis of capital inflow had shifted to that of portfolio investment.

Vigorously promoted by Mahathir, the KLSE's market capitalisation had grown rapidly between 1990 and 1996 through a rush of short-term bonds, shares and other speculative instruments. Thus the relatively easier process of capital withdrawal associated with portfolio investment had,

TABLE 2.8 Kuala Lumpur Stock Exchange: selected indices (1990–98)[108]

	Composite index	Number of listed companies	Market capitalisation (RM billion)
1990	505.92	285	131.66
1996	1,237.96	621	806.77
1997	594.44	708	375.80
1998	389.08	734	255.00

unlike the mid-1980s downturn, led to a quicker, sharper and more debilitating shock to the Malaysian financial system, as noted in the figures for 1997.[109] Another important factor here was that most of the Southeast Asian economies had sought to maintain a *de facto* currency peg against the US dollar – again, as Jomo notes, reflecting the priorities of finance capital in the region rather than domestic, particularly export-based, capital.[110]

Meanwhile, the confidence of international fund managers continued to erode. Mahathir had championed the KLSE as a new financial centre to rival Singapore and Hong Kong. Within the proclaimed new era of deregulated, open trading, selective intervention on behalf of given companies would severely undermine such claims. Mahathir's belligerent interventions and measures to defend domestic stocks had already been interpreted as inept interference and a serious impediment to future market activity. As one analyst from the Political and Economic Risk Consultancy concluded, it had 'damaged Malaysia's credibility' and 'cast doubts on its ability to regulate and maintain the sophisticated financial system needed to make Malaysia into a regional financial centre'.[111]

With the crisis threatening to wipe out the wealth base of corporations tied to UMNO, the special assistance granted to such companies was now revealing the contradiction of deregulation. For example, by late 1997, the privatised Tenaga Nasional, Malaysia's second biggest company, was touting for assistance, warning of a fall in demand for electricity and impending RM2 billion losses in its forex-based loan repayments.[112] Meanwhile, the government were forced into taking over the Bakun Dam project from Ekran Bhd following contractual problems arising from the crisis.[113]

More crucial still was the selective bail-out of the giant Renong conglomerate, controlled by UMNO through Halim Saad. Renong had been at the forefront of Mahathir's Cyberjaya and Putrajaya projects. As concern over the company's viability mounted, foreign investors began to voice serious misgivings about corporate transparency and the government's commitment to open financial practices. This followed Anwar's decision to allow a special waiver to Renong's subsidiary UEM in the rescue buy-out of its parent company. Malaysian stock market rules for takeovers specify that where the purchasing group acquires a holding of over 33%, it must also make a general offer, at optimum rates, to the remaining minority shareholders, a process that would have proved extremely difficult for UEM to finance.[114]

In effect, it was a critical test of the government's regulatory credentials, watched closely by the broader business community. Deeply suspicious of the circumstances surrounding the deal, investors dumped Renong and UEM stock, halving the share value of both companies and wiping almost 25% off the value of the KLSE.[115] Although temporarily withdrawn due to the critical response of the markets and plunge in share prices,[116] the waiver was finally reaffirmed by Anwar in January 1998, a dispensation read by the markets as confirmation of special protection for politically linked clients, producing a further collapse in market confidence and a run on the ringgit.[117] By mid-1998, favourable low-interest loans were being directed to struggling corporations from the national Employees Provident Fund (EPF) (investment assets in 1997: RM129 billion), including a deal to rescue the shipping operations and liquefied gas interests of Mahathir's son Mizran through a Petronas buy-out.[118]

The Renong bail-out and use of EPF assets now indicated emergency attempts to hold the patronage network together. But, despite ongoing overtures to foreign investors, Mahathir was now regarded as a serious liability, a fear reflected in the editorial positions and content of key business journals such as *The Economist*, *Asiaweek*, *Far Eastern Economic Review*, *Newsweek* and *Time*. The foreign media's view of the crisis will be dealt with more closely in subsequent chapters. However, it is worth noting here how these organs provided intellectual support for foreign capital at this point by 'advising' Mahathir to heed IMF help, undertake financial reforms, allow greater deregulation and refrain from intemperate language.[119]

And, perhaps for the first time, this reaction began to find serious resonance among the domestic business class. The underlying sentiment was that, despite recognised problems, the fundamentals of the Malaysian economy were good – in contrast to Thailand – and that neither the KLSE's rating nor the ringgit's true value merited the extent of the fall brought about by speculators. Nor did they see Mahathir as unjustified in pointing this out. The deeper, if more quietly spoken, feeling was that without Mahathir's acerbic interventions, both could have been prevented from sliding as far and as fast as they did. Moreover, despite the public show of solidarity for Mahathir from big Chinese business and agencies such as the Malaysian Chinese Chamber of Commerce, similar concerns were being expressed privately in these quarters over Mahathir's tirades. To some extent, this unease reflected the relative exposure of different parts of Chinese business to the crisis. For example, those involved in rent-seeking such as property development could expect to be hit harder than the domestic export sector, the latter hoping for a boost in overseas markets due to the low value of the ringgit.[120]

Anwar's Interventions

As the crisis deepened, the broad business community looked to Anwar to produce a more comprehensive set of confidence-building measures. As noted, small business had not been averse to showing its displeasure at the power of big corporations, seeing the denial of bail-outs as necessary to recovery.[121]

The first big opportunity came in the October 1997 budget. But while directed at business generally, the budget also offered Anwar the space in which to address the concerns of particular components of capital. In the preface to the accompanying *Economic Report 1997/98*, Anwar noted that: 'The immediate challenge we now face is to restore investors' confidence and stability in the markets.'[122] Again, while generally applicable, this suggested an urgent need to send reassuring signals to *foreign* capital. At the same time, the government needed to correct the internal economic structure, and, thus, its relationship with domestic capital. The flawed calculation here seems to have been that by demonstrating a willingness to take hard decisions in relation to the latter, the former would read it as an appropriate signal of intent, paving the way for a return of foreign investor confidence. Hence the principal budget message to the domestic business class was that it must use the circumstances of the slowdown and the weak ringgit to restructure, improve productivity and help boost the country's export competitiveness.

However, Anwar's initiatives also indicated the need to maintain the support of small business, most notably, perhaps, domestic Chinese capital, as in the special budget allocation of RM1 billion to small–medium industries (SMIs). Accounting for 84% of all manufacturing in Malaysia,[123] SMIs represent the mainstream area of Chinese business activity. Suggesting a certain shift in state–class relations 'in favour' of domestic capital, Anwar's measures were therefore broadly welcomed at this level. The main elements included:

- measures to curb imports through increased duties on a range of capital and consumer goods, most notably luxury cars;
- a 10–15% range of tax incentives for high-performing exporters;
- the removal of levies and raising of quotas on foreigners' property purchases;
- a 2% reduction in corporate tax to 28%; and
- the deferment of more mega-projects.

Alongside a broad austerity package, a relative tightening of monetary policy and control on credit, the recovery strategy thus comprised incentives to assist lagging sectors of the economy, stimulate demand for domestic products (notably electronics and cars), boost exports, hold up the construction industry and alleviate the threat of inflation.[124] Other emergency initiatives included the discouraging of foreign travel (including the doubling of passport costs), cutbacks on overseas study, and plans to repatriate foreign workers, notably Bangladeshi and Indonesian service sector employees.[125] Denying gathering reports of harsh treatment of migrant workers in detention camps,[126] this latter aspect was both a political overture to fearful Malaysians and an attempt to prop up the currency by stemming the outflow of migrant earnings. Mahathir also announced the creation of a National Economic Action Council (NEAC), a body of 'independent' advisers charged with formulating recovery measures.[127]

From the perspective of foreign capital, things looked less optimistic. Anticipating many of the measures, the markets remained unimpressed by the budget, expressing scepticism about the up-beat nature of the government's economic forecasts, notably the projected GDP growth rate of 7%.[128] As the ringgit and KLSE continued to fall, the more immediate message from foreign investors and fund managers was the need for much greater transparency and financial deregulation. And underlying this disenchantment lay a further implication: the need for political reform, even a change of leader.

Thus difficult policy choices remained: a recovery programme tailored to foreign capital or an internally driven one with an enhanced role for domestic capital. Perhaps realising that, in any event, confidence would not return to the region for some time, Mahathir and Anwar still leaned towards the latter, seeking to demonstrate a capacity for tough economic management. But as negative responses from both foreign and domestic investors began to grow,[129] the key task became that of maintaining economic stability.

Signalling his appointment as head of the NEAC, it is also significant to note the emerging role played by Daim at this point (see also next chapter) in trying to discount rumours of a gathering crisis in the banking sector.[130] Related measures now included plans for the merger of big bank and finance companies such as Hong Leong Finance and Arab-Malaysian Finance.[131] Nevertheless, withdrawals of deposits from domestic banks were now intensifying as investment funds continued to flow out, putting pressure on the Bank Negara to hike up base rates, a move resisted by Mahathir, who feared that this would stunt borrowing, investment and growth. Urging people to resist shifting their accounts to foreign banks, Mahathir warned that the capital shortages caused by such withdrawals were forcing further borrowing from foreign banks and higher interest rates.[132] Again, highlighting the dependence of the Malaysian economy on short-term funds, a RM13.9 billion net outflow of 'hot money' had contributed to the RM19 billion services account deficit and an overall balance of payments deficit of RM8.2 billion.[133]

Thus, as capital flight and the ringgit's slide continued, Anwar was forced in December 1997 into a further set of emergency 'post-budget' measures. Recognising the markets' deep reservations over the government's budget forecasts:

- The growth projection for 1998 was revised downwards from 7% to 4–5%.
- A further 18% was to be trimmed from Federal expenditure.
- The current account deficit was to be reduced from 5% to a new target of 3% of GNP.
- Ministerial salaries were to be cut by 10%.
- All proposed megaprojects were to be deferred.
- Fuller corporate regulation and transparency (no more Renong-type bail-outs) were to be initiated.[134]

As the markets reacted favourably to the revisions and perceptions that Anwar might be poised to check the privileges of UMNO business clients, Lim Kit Siang, who had called for further measures, urged Anwar to convene a 'third 1998 budget' to develop the package and 'show the world that the Malaysian Government and its people have completely purged the "denial syndrome"'.[135]

More critically, this set of policy initiatives now signalled rising tensions between Anwar and his Bank Negara allies on the one hand and Mahathir and Daim on the other. Although Mahathir had chaired and approved the cabinet austerity plan, it was broadly seen as Anwar's strategy, enhancing his international standing, even though it represented a tacit admission of the government's own, partial, culpability for the crisis. Seeking to counterbalance this momentary loss of authority, Mahathir had taken refuge in a joint ASEAN appeal to the USA, the EC, Japan and the IMF to recognise the global context of the crisis and take action to stabilise the region's currencies.[136] However, now playing up the ersatz nature of liberalisation in Malaysia, the IMF and Western finance ministers prepared to 'set the terms' of recovery through demands for more transparent business conditions.

The 'IMF Debate'

At the same time, the crisis in Southeast Asia also sparked a more 'searching' debate on the interventionist policies of the IMF.[137] In particular, many observers asked whether its standard austerity package of public spending cuts and tighter monetary and fiscal policies were really appropriate to the region. Unlike the South American debt crises of the 1980s and 1990s, these economies had been relatively stable. The generic remedial approach not only negated the diverse nature of each country's particular problems, but, more critically, threatened to plunge them into deep recession by cutting off the stimulus to investment. Thus analysts began to warn of the serious knock-on effect for the West should financial confidence deteriorate in the region.

However, this discourse was still built around the agenda-setting issue of 'crony capitalism', thus missing the more structural sense in which the Fund acts in the hegemonic interests of global capital. Thus, while Thailand may have fallen due to an excessive frenzy of credit and out-of-control debt, the debt itself was stimulated by Western banks and global finance capital in particular seeking a slice of this speculative activity. The key issue here is deregulation and free access to financial markets, a principal the IMF has consistently urged upon all countries. And when the inexorable cycle of boom gives way to bust, the belt-tightening prescription is presented with very little variation.

In South America, economies were now just emerging from this 'rehabilitation', though the ensuing crisis of the real in Brazil by 1998 illustrated the ongoing nature of the boom–bust–bail-out cycle. Thus, in one sense, this was a form of old-fashioned capitalist shake-out and shedding of unproductive forces. However, the circumstances within which the cycle comes to crisis point was also being determined by the increasingly complex gyrations of speculative capital and non-productive accumulation. Thailand had accumulated a mountain of bad debt, thus presaging a failure of confidence, but it was the collapse of the baht and the associated panic triggered by currency speculation in the region that helped spread and intensify the crisis. In Malaysia, fears of overheating were evident before 1997, for example, in the property price spiral and high levels of domestic bank lending towards consumer and other non-productive outlets. Yet was it conceivable that foreign fund managers, with the most complex array of market indicators and analysts at their disposal, could have been so 'unaware' of the looming problems?[138] Thus the Asian crisis needed ready scapegoats:

> In the wake of the crisis, what annoyed the free-marketeers, neoliberals, or bearers of the 'IMF–Washington consensus' was the hubris of a historical form of economic nationalism which, having achieved 'East Asian competitiveness', wanted globalization, but still wanted to 'govern the market'.[139]

Those hailed by the IMF–Washington nexus were now chastised as errant and profligate offenders. Intrinsic to the Fund's approach here was to:

> promote the idea that the crisis represented the well-warranted punishment of Asian economies by international financial markets for the governments' gross mismanagement. As First Deputy Managing Director Stanley Fischer kept repeating, the crisis was due to homegrown causes that became, in the words of other commentators, 'Asian crony capitalism'. This was propounded by an organisation that, until September 1997, lavished praise on these countries' economic performance and attributed it in good part to their financial liberalization.[140]

Yet it also served the broad interests of capital to resolve the crisis. The world's stock managers had watched the panic sweep like a whirlwind through Thailand, Malaysia, Indonesia, Singapore, Hong Kong and Japan, fearing it would strike China and spread outwards to the West, plunging the global economy into a 1930s-type depression. The initial legs of the crisis had fed a voracious bout of speculation, particularly as the crisis hit Hong Kong – with the Malaysian authorities indulging in a spot of *schadenfreude* as George Soros himself took a US$2 billion loss during the assault on the Hang Seng.[141] But as Wall Street and the other global bourses felt the downward impact of the Hong Kong wipe-out on their share indexes, a more concentrated agenda for regional assistance began to emerge.

Some signals of a potential recovery in Malaysia had become evident by January 1998. As noted, international investors had shown cautious optimism over Anwar's 'revised budget'. Bill Clinton had also sent a message of 'support' for continued investment in Malaysia.[142] By early February, the World Bank president, James Wolfensohn, had expressed confidence in Malaysia's recovery efforts, echoing a previous visit and assessment by the IMF managing director, Michel Camdessus.[143] Alongside quieter 'advice' to tone down the rhetoric, the main message from both was that while reduced spending and increased interest rates were needed to restrict credit growth, Malaysia's structural problems could be seen as distinct from Thailand, Indonesia and South Korea. Responding to these developments and other bullish regional stock markets (buoyed by these three countries' 'positive reactions' to IMF aid), the KLSE rallied by an impressive 23% on the first day of trading following the five-day Chinese New Year and Aidil Fitri holidays.[144] The KLSE had also fined the UEM in an apparent effort to appear more even-handed to the foreign business community.[145]

Managing the Crisis: Policy Schism and the Anwar Factor

While resisting the indignity of a direct IMF bail-out, Mahathir still *appeared* to accept, for the moment, Anwar's reform agenda. Thus, despite Mahathir's ongoing offensive, the case for fuller liberalisation being pushed by Camdessus from without and Anwar from within was still being 'endorsed' as government policy. In seeking to project the importance of his initiatives, Anwar was to note at this point how the crisis had been a watershed for the country, concluding that it would emerge more confident and committed to greater openness: 'The great lesson we have learned, which is actually a major transformation and a revolution by itself, is that it has called for greater transparency, greater accountability and for greater democracy.'[146]

However, by mid-1998, it was apparent that the country still faced the longer haul to recovery, with economic output contracting by 1.8% (first yearly quarter) and currency and share values still in the doldrums.[147] Neither had export competitiveness been enhanced by the falling ringgit, as the rising price of imported goods now contributed to gathering inflation.[148] Meanwhile, the 'ourselves alone' road to recovery was being invoked, with Mahathir now counselling Malaysian youth on the insidious dangers of 'emerging absolute capitalism'.[149] The government even ran a national public collection to help 'save the country' from economic ruin.[150] With little to show for the austerity package and countenancing global expansion of the crisis, Mahathir began easing up on monetary policy in an attempt to offset looming recession, stimulate growth and save healthy companies – a snub to the high interest rate/tight credit strategy still suggested by the IMF and thought necessary by Anwar and the central bank to limit further attacks on the currency.[151] Other factors such as the worrying fall in the value of big Bumiputera trust funds run by some Malaysian states may also have contributed to Mahathir's reflationary efforts here.[152] With the austerity measures now beginning to bite and the economy heading for recession, Mahathir was also concerned about the erosion of middle-class confidence. With Daim's restoration as chief financial guru, a key policy collision was now looming.

Anwar, the IMF and the UMNO network The wider implications of Anwar's roles within and between these networks will be developed in subsequent chapters. For the moment, it is necessary to note the structural context of these relationships. It is significant, first, that the West by this point saw Anwar, Habibie and Estrada, three close intimates, as the 'new generation' for the region. Like Estrada in the Philippines, Habibie was the Indonesian 'reformer of choice' for the West, someone who, despite his role as co-architect of the Golkar regime and Suharto's cohort, could protect Western interests in the run-up to new elections. If Anwar's case was somewhat more 'respectable', it is, nevertheless, safe to say that he was being 'sponsored' by the IMF–Washington network as the man to do business with; someone who, in the name of 'new civil reform', would, it was hoped, lift restrictive barriers to capital and move business dealings beyond the caustic relationship with Mahathir. Of course, Anwar had other roles here, for example as spokesman for the Southeast Asia Group of developing countries at IMF summits.[153] However, he had also developed close associations with figures such as James Wolfensohn at the World Bank, US Defence Secretary Madeleine Albright and Michel Camdessus at the IMF, with whom he planned to co-author a book on Asian civil reform.

It is too simplistic to say that Anwar was being manipulated here or that he lacked reformist intentions. While the Asian Renaissance image he cultivated as a backdrop was questionable, Anwar did have his own agenda and ideas on economic and intellectual matters, including the development of Islam. Yet he also had his own cronies within the UMNO machine.[154] After 16 years playing the game of heir apparent to Mahathir, it is difficult to accept Anwar as some naive politician unaware of the stakes. Business elites linked to Anwar were also now caught up in a complex scenario of financial bail-outs and judgements over whom to back. As in the mid-1980s, competing corporate interests were seeking to manoeuvre themselves into positions of power. Some of 'Anwar's boys' appeared to believe, *because* of the crisis, that its own ascendancy was imminent. While the naivety of this view was to be revealed in the failure of Anwar ally Zahid Hamidi's (then UMNO Youth leader) anti-corruption platform at the June 1998 UMNO Assembly (see next chapter), Anwar himself had been more muted, realising that any perceived split within UMNO over the crisis might wreck their chances completely. Anwar was also trying to stabilise investor confidence while placating Mahathir and Daim. In the background, corporate elites feared that any practical show of transparency and shake-out would mean a denial of bail-outs. Anwar's ambivalence over rescue packages for Renong and Mahathir's son Mirzan, alongside fears that he was dropping 'big names' to the Anti Corruption Agency (ACA) can be seen as critical here. While it was, seemingly, more prudent to keep Anwar *on the inside*, given what he now knew about internal corruption and nepotism, it was the emerging *policy* differences over crisis management and the *implications* of an IMF scenario *vis-à-vis* bail-outs that may have tipped the balance, prompting Mahathir to use the sodomy allegations and corruption charges as part of a strategy to contain him. Again, the ubiquitous presence of Daim here was not coincidental.

Signalling a key policy impasse, Mahathir was now turning away sharply from a recovery agenda based on IMF adjustments to one built around more immediate domestic interests. In practice, this meant selected bail-outs and continued protection for top corporate elites. But it also pointed to a more fundamental shift in the bloc's relations with international capital. By late 1998, this would be focused around Anwar's incarceration and international calls for liberal reform, a defining moment being Al Gore's speech in support of Anwar and the *reformasi* during the APEC gathering in Kuala Lumpur.[155] However, US and other Western 'concerns' here can be seen as part of a wider liberalisation agenda. In this regard, notions of an external 'conspiracy' to remove Mahathir are not only unverifiable, but diversionary. As revealed by foreign capital's adverse reaction to Mahathir's domestic controls (see following chapters), the key point was that Anwar had been courted as someone more attuned to mediating such tensions between the domestic bloc and Western agencies.

Nevertheless, as finance ministers and bankers sought to stem the global contagion, restoration of confidence in the international financial system was being hindered, albeit marginally, by Mahathir's 'unorthodox' responses and case for capital controls. With most Southeast Asian currencies severely battered, and half the population in Indonesia edging towards poverty, the collapse of the rouble and social dislocation in Russia was being followed by an onslaught on the Brazilian real, threatening to plunge Central America into recession. On Wall Street, the Federal Reserve and an inner cabal of international bankers had launched an emergency $3.5 billion 'lifeboat' to rescue Long-Term Capital Management, a 250 times over-leveraged hedge fund. Without the bail-out, they argued, the whole global system would have faced its worst shock in 50 years.[156]

Yet, while Mahathir could now engage in 'principled' calls for a 'new financial order', this could not conceal the impact of the crisis at the domestic level. By proceeding with expansionist measures to keep domestic business and the middle class on board, Mahathir was trying to steer a consensual course. However, there was still the considerable hazard of the Anwar factor and unknown undercurrents of popular dissent to navigate. With the fear not only of Anwar's influence within the party, but of his first-hand knowledge of corruption within the cabinet and corporate circles, alarm bells had began to sound at the highest levels of the power structure. And it was at this point, with a decisive putsch unfolding against Anwar, that the economic crisis moved towards *political* crisis.

Notes

1. Mahathir (1970), p. 158.

2. Ibid., pp. 166, 167. See also Hooker (1972).

3. Mahathir (1970), p. 31.

4. Mahathir (1986), p. 4.

5. Rodan (1993), pp. 103–4. See also O'Malley (1988) on the relationship between Confucian and Islamic/Malay culture.

6. Mahathir (1986), pp. 57, 59.

7. Ibid., p. 4.

8. Ibid., pp. 54–5.

9. Khoo Boo Teik (1995), p. 64.

10. Ibid., p. 41.

11. Cited in Dixon (1991), p. 183.

12. This fed into a series of brooding diplomatic tensions, leading to Mahathir's Buy British Last policy. See Jomo (1994), pp. 5–6.

13. See Moore (1966) for a historical parallel to the Prussian Junkers' state-bureaucratic control of a dependent bourgeoisie.

14. Khoo Boo Teik (1998), p. 4.

15. See Laothamatas (1997), p. 11.

16. Khoo Boo Teik (1995), p. 127.

17. Gomez and Jomo (1997), pp. 168, 179.

18. Ibid. See also Crouch (1993), pp. 144–5, and 'Great wave of China', *The Australian*, 12 March 1994.

19. Third Malaysia Plan (1976–80), Seventh Malaysia Plan (1996–2000), cited in Gomez and Jomo (1997), p. 168.

20. Gomez and Jomo (1997), p. 166.

21. Crouch (1993), pp. 142–3.

22. Jomo (1999), p. 98.

23. Figures for occupation by ethnic group in 1995, Gomez and Jomo (1997), p. 167. Figures for registered professionals in 1996 (lawyers, 1994), and household income, Malaysia (1998), Department of Statistics, pp. 215, 225.

24. Malaysia (1998), Department of Statistics, p. xxxvi.

25. Malaysia (1998), Ministry of Finance, p. 9.

26. Ibid., pp. lx–lxi, and Moha Asri Abdullah (1999), p. 214.

27. *Tenaganita* (1998), p. 15

28. Wad and Jomo (1994), pp. 217–18.

29. Rodan (1993), p. 82.

30. Malaysian Ministry of Finance (1998), p. 114. Figures for 1970, extracted from Wan Abdul Rahman Wan Abdul Latiff (1999), p. 76.

31. Jomo (1999), pp. 96–7.

32. Malaysian GDP grew at an average 7.8% between 1986 and 1995, *Malaysia Industrial Digest*, October–December 1996.

33. Jomo (1990), pp. 20–1.

34. OECD (1992), p. 259. See also Dixon (1991), p. 222.

35. Munro-Kua (1996), p. 106.

36. Clad (1989), pp. 10–11.

37. Dicken (1991), p. 35.

38. OECD (1992), p. 273.

39. Ali (1994), pp. 112–19.

40. Steven (1991), p. 58.

41. See OECD (1992), pp. 262–3.

42. Munro-Kua (1996), p. 111; Nester (1990), pp. 89–90.

43. Ariff (1991), pp. 88–9.

44. Lee Poh Ping (1990), p. 179; Taylor and Ward (1994), p. 162.

45. Malaysian Ministry of Finance (1998), p. 72, and Malaysian Department of Information (1996), Seventh Malaysian Plan.

46. Malaysian Ministry of Finance (1998), pp. 164, 166.

47. *Tenaganita* (1998), p. 9.

48. Ibid., p. 14.

49. For an informative study of foreign labour and the Penang textile industry, see Rudnick (1996).

50. Rashid (1993), p. 99.

51. Crouch (1990), p. 189. See also *FEER*, 26 May 1994.

52. Jomo (1989), p. 100.

53. Fong Chan Onn (1989).

54. For a critique of the government's selective use of statistics see Kua Kia Soong (1992), p. 26.

55. Gomez and Jomo (1997), p. 167. This figure is for Peninsular Malaysia.

56. Jomo (1990), pp. 6, 10, 26. Crouch (1994), p. 29. Nurizan Yahaya (1991), pp. 212, 220.

57. Halim Salleh (1991), pp. 312–14.

58. See Jomo and Gomez (1997), pp. 117–18, and Chandra Muzaffar (1989a), pp. 498–9.

59. 'Democracy games', *FEER*, 11 February 1993.

60. *The Economist*, 6 November 1993.

61. See Mohd Nor Abdul Ghani (ed.) (1984) for a government and private-sector set of perspectives.

62. *The Economist*, 6 November 1993. Ozay Mehmet (1986), p. 149, also notes how trusteeships, interlocking directorships and cross-ownership help link these networks.

63. See Gomez and Jomo (1997), pp. 98–9, 178.

64. Khoo Boo Teik (1995), p. 132. See also Gomez and Jomo (1997), p. 81.

65. See 'Case study 1: Daim Zainuddin', in Gomez and Jomo (1997), pp. 53–6 and Clad (1989), pp. 49–50.

66. *Aliran Monthly*, 1994; 14: 6.

67. Davis (1986), p. 136, notes that Carter's 'resort to monetarist management' can be viewed as 'the first year of Reaganomics'.

68. The end of the 'post-war consensus' being the culmination of what Cox (1987) terms an 'organic crisis of hegemony', pp. 269–70. Gill and Law (1989) note the main stress points within the global bloc by the late 1970s as: pressure on the dollar within the international monetary system; persistently high US balance of payments deficits; expansionary US monetary and fiscal policies; inflation within other OECD states; the collapse of Bretton Woods, prompted by the 1971 'Nixon shocks'; and the new regime of floating exchange rates. Paul Volcker's appointment to the Federal Reserve in 1979 (following the OPEC oil shocks) saw tighter monetary and fiscal policies in an effort to restore the dollar's credibility. See also Ruggie (1982).

69. This also denotes conflict between competing alignments of state agencies and fractions of capital. Frieden (1988). See, also Strange (1986) and Moran (1990) for accounts of speculative market activity and state responses in the 1980s.

70. Gill and Law (1988), p. 178.

71. Gill and Law (1989), pp. 481, 483.

72. See Jomo, 'Tigers in crisis', Speech to the Asia-Pacific Solidarity Conference, Sydney, 12 April 1998, <http://www.pactok.net/docs/singapore/jomo.htm>. See also Syed Husin Ali, 'Economic and political problems of Asia: with reference to the ASEAN situation', <http://www.pactok.net/docs/singapore/syed.htm>, on the significance of portfolio-based FDI to the crisis in Malaysia.

73. Swift (1994). Italics added.

74. Gill and Law (1989), p. 486. Italics added.

75. Dixon (1991), p. 190; see also *FEER*, 7 August 1986.

76. *New Straits Times*, 26–27 October 1994.

77. Cited in Clad (1989), pp. 68–9.

78. Munro-Kua (1996), p. 107.

79. Khoo Kay Jin (1992), pp. 52, 54.

80. Jomo (1989), p. 27. Crouch (1994), p. 23, notes that the foreign debt level rose from a nominal amount in 1980 to US$51 billion by 1987.

81. Saravanamuttu (1987), p. 59.

82. Jomo (1989), p. 27.

83. As noted in *Aliran Monthly*, 1994; 14: 6.

84. Privatisation Master Plan, cited in Gomez (1994), p. 16.

85. Gomez (1994), p. 17.

86. Ibid., p. 18.

87. Gomez and Jomo (1997), p. 86. The figures are for the period 1983–94.

88. Muzaffar (1989b), p. 147.

89. The *Asian Wall Street Journal* described UEM as a 'financially beleaguered company with scant experience in construction.' Cited in Clad (1989), p. 44.

90. Gomez (1994), p. 17.

91. Gomez and Jomo (1997), pp. 124–9.

92. Jomo (1990), p. 20.

93. See Gomez and Jomo (1997), pp. 137–8.

94. Gomez (1994), pp. 17, 28, 39.

95. Heng Pek Koon (1992), pp. 132, 134, 142.

96. Extracted from Gomez and Jomo (1997).

97. Jomo (1989), p. 65.

98. Jomo (1999), p. 98.

99. Ibid., pp. 97–8.

100. Khoo Boo Teik (1998), p. 9.

101. See 'Malaysia's economic frailties come into focus', *Financial Times*, 6 August 1997.

102. At the end of March 1997, the ringgit was trading at RM2.4790 to the US dollar. Malaysia (1997), Ministry of Finance. By mid-January 1998, it was trading at around RM4.60. *Star*, 13 January 1998.

103. See 'Globalization theory vaults into Reality', *Herald Tribune*, 26 September 1997.

104. *Financial Times*, 29 August 1997.

105. *Independent*, 22 September 1997.

106. For a discussion of the Bank Negara's role in the currency markets, including its RM12 billion loss in 1992 (equivalent to over one-third of Malaysia's foreign exchange reserves) see *Aliran Monthly*, 1997, 17: 6.

107. *Financial Times*, 26 September 1997.

108. Bank Negara, February 1988, pp. 68–9, 72. Malaysia (1998), Ministry of Finance, p. 180. See also Khoo Boo Teik (1998), p. 7.

109. See also Syed Husin Ali, 'Economy in crisis', *Aliran Monthly*, 1998, 18: 3.

110. Jomo, 'Tigers in crisis', Speech to the Asia-Pacific Solidarity Conference, Sydney, 12 April 1998.

111. Bruce Gale, cited in *FEER*, September 1997.

112. *Singapore Business Times*, 30 December 1997.

113. *Sun*, 21 November 1997.

114. See Shroff, *FEER*, 11 December 1997.

115. See 'Bashing for UEM and Renong', *The Edge*, 24–30 November 1997.

116. At this point, the government withdrew the waiver and censured UEM on the instructions of the Registrar of Companies, who found the company to have contravened the Malaysian Code on Takeovers and Mergers by failing to disclose vital information on the deal. *Sun*, 25 November 1997.

117. See ibid. and *Financial Times*, 12 January 1998.

118. See Anil Netto, 'Hey, that's our money', and Lim Kit Siang, 'EPF funds used to save VIPs, tycoons and cronies', in *Aliran Monthly*, June 1998, 18: 5.

119. See, for example, the *FEER* editorials of 11 and 18 September 1997, *Asiaweek*, 'The big slump', 3 October 1997, and the *The Economist*, 'Mahathir's Roasting', 27 September 1997.

120. By September 1997, an increase of 21.7% in export revenue had been recorded, while the construction sector continued to contract. See 'Exports kick in', *The Edge*, 24–30 November 1997.

121. See Khoo Boo Teik (1998), pp. 13–14. In an aside to the 'Asian values' debate, Khoo (1999) notes, p. 5, that this view also reflected a more 'indigenous' reaction against public funds being used to rescue conglomerates at the expense of public welfare.

122. Abstracted from special budget report, *New Straits Times*, 18 October 1997.

123. *New Straits Times*, 18 October 1997.

124. See 'Business', *New Straits Times*, 18 October 1997.

125. Ibid.

126. *Tenaganita* (1998).

127. See 'NEAC will have strong hands and clear mind', *New Sunday Times*, 30 November 1997.

128. See 'Ringgit ends lower in a sceptical market despite tough budget' *Aliran Monthly*, 1997, 17: 9.

129. Reflecting the concerns of domestic capital, *The Edge* noted in its Economic Review, 26 January 1998, that while encouraged by the beneficial effect on commodity prices due to the 40% fall in the ringgit, the overall picture was 'gloomy'.

130. 'Banking system is "solid", says Daim', *Sun*, 26 November 1997.

131. *The Times*, 31 December 1997.

132. *Utusan Malaysia*, 28 January 1998.

133. 'Budget pains', *Aliran Monthly*, 1997, 17: 9. The figures refer to the 1997/98 Budget Report.

134. See *FEER*, 18 December 1997. Further details included an 80% reduction in government-sponsored students going abroad. *Sun*, 8 December 1997.

135. *Star*, 19 December 1997.

136. The appeal was made during ASEAN's 30th Anniversary Commemorative Summit in Kuala Lumpur. *Star*, 16 December 1997.

137. See, for example, 'IMF to the rescue', *Time*, 8 December 1997 and 'One size does not fit all', *Guardian*, 3 July 1998.

138. See Khoo Boo Teik (1998), p. 11.

139. Ibid., p. 17.

140. Wade and Veneroso (1998), p. 18.

141. Mahathir claimed that the Bank Negara had lost RM30 billion in reserves attempting to support the currency. *New Straits Times*, 30 October 1997.

142. The assurance was made to Anwar through Clinton's Deputy Treasury Secretary Lawrence Summers. *Utusan Malaysia*, 14 January 1998.

143. *Star*, 4 February 1998.

144. See 'Investors pour into Malaysia', *Financial Times*, 4 February 1998.

145. UEM were fined RM100,000 for giving 'conflicting information' over the Renong deal. *Financial Times*, 19 February 1998.

146. Interview statement to Greg Sheridan of the *Australian*. Cited in *Utusan Malaysia*, 28 January 1998.

147. *FEER*, 2 July 1998.

148. 'Can anyone save Malaysia?', *Asiaweek*, 20 August 1998.

149. *Utusan Malaysia*, 29 May 1998.

150. *Financial Times*, 20 August 1998.

151. 'Easing the squeeze', *FEER*, 16 July 1998.

152. See 'In units they trust', *FEER* , 11 June 1998.

153. As at the IMF/World Bank 49th annual summit in Madrid. See *New Straits Times*, 4 October 1994.

154. A critical review and list of Anwar associates, such as Kamaruddin Jaafar, Anuar Othman and Nazeri Abdullah, are noted at the Socialist Malaysia site, <members.tripod.com/~socialistmalysia/index.html>, late 1998.

155. See 'Gore speech raises fears of backlash', *Financial Times*, 18 November 1998.

156. See Larry Elliot, 'A tale of two catastrophes', *Guardian*, 7 November 1998.

3

Mahathirism and the Politics of the Power Bloc

Having used the new business climate from the early 1980s to realise a shift in class arrangements, Mahathir needed to embed these changes more concretely within the *political* bloc. Throughout the early phases of post-colonial development, the Alliance state had kept domestic class interests tied to those of international capital.[1] By the 1970s, these *laisser-faire* orientations had given way to greater state regulation, firmer control of labour and the anchoring of political rewards to the NEP. From the mid-1980s, Malaysia Inc. became the new *leitmotif* for such. And by 1997, the project had seen a more conscious propagation of *Bangsa* Malaysia in an attempt to consensualise the Vision.

But while tripartite arrangements between government, business and labour denotes corporatism, it is not *hegemony* in the Gramscian meaning of that term. For a hegemonic order must also be understood in terms of the ensemble of *ideas* a ruling group is able to project as a basis for political legitimacy. In this sense, hegemonic rule transcends what Gramsci calls 'economic–corporate' consensus for one that strives for a 'universalisation' of consent within the bloc and civil society,[2] thus signifying a unity of economic, political and intellectual-moral objectives.[3] Let us consider how Mahathir has sought to build consensus by managing tensions within the political bloc and crafting national–popular support, taking us to an analysis of the political crisis by 1997.

Politics, Conflicts and Institutions: Building the New Consensus

Despite the proclaimed ideals of consensus within the BN, the Mahathir style is not easily given to political consultation. When he assumed office in July 1981, it was clear that Mahathir's approach would be not only proactive and reformist, but highly individualised. Mahathir can be seen as a political motivator of the Thatcher type, his self-initiated assault on civil, administrative and elite institutions reflecting, in many ways, the 'rational populism' of the Thatcherite project. Indeed, an underlying social class parallel might be suggested here. Both figures emerged from non-elite, middle-class environments, unsocialised by, and not easily disposed to, traditional establishment codes, class closure and protocols. While Thatcher, the grocer's daughter, sought to wrest power from the Tory grandees and popularise 'enterprise culture', Mahathir, the first Malaysian leader not educated abroad, brought with him his own middle-class experience and reserved view of privileged institutions. Mahathir also epitomises the proclaimed Thatcherite 'qualities' of diligence, hard work and self-improvement: the ethos of the self-made man inherited from his father, himself a model figure of the colonial *petit bourgeois* Malay schoolmaster.[4] Here, one can observe in Mahathir's relationship to traditional elites a hybrid tone of qualified respect and latent *ressentiment*. Much of this stemmed from an admixture of disdain for the colonial administration and position of the Malay sultans, a privileged detachment that, in the struggle for independence, Mahathir saw as a betrayal of the Malay cause. Thus his assuming power 'from below' means that such 'class prejudice' has never been far from the surface in Mahathir's challenge to elite institutions. Yet it also helped set a rationale for the 'modernist project' in Mahathir's mind through its invocation of hard work and enterprise, qualities perceived as an antidote to Malay 'fatalism' and a stimulant to the new economic growth.

Mahathir was to serve notice of this approach in his early political initiatives. The formative stages of his premiership thus witnessed a systematic rationalisation of the civil service, the streamlining of public sector jobs and the appointment of a select *nomenclature*, reflecting the interdependent sense in which 'modernisation' and the displacement of existing power bases was to be achieved.

Symbolising this process was Mahathir's attempt to check the prerogative powers of the Malay royalty, leading to the first of a series of constitutional confrontations in 1983. In seeking to pass the Constitution (Amendment) Bill, Mahathir wanted to dispense entirely with the Yang di-Pertuan Agong's powers of royal assent. Although no Agong had, in practice, ever refused assent, the proposed amendment (to Article 66) meant that removal of this power could, in theory, lead to the abolition of the monarchy by a parliamentary act after 15 days, a prospect sufficiently alarming for the royals to refuse assent to the amendment itself. While the Agong's supporters invoked deference and tradition, Mahathir, using the BN media, depicted the clash as a modernist challenge to feudal privilege.[5] The subsequent compromise gave Mahathir the right to check royal assent, with the Agong retaining nominal emergency powers. In a further challenge, following the Sultan of Johor's attack on a hockey team coach in 1992, Mahathir alleged that the legality of the rulers' immunity from prosecution. was a colonial legacy, a '"feudal principle" inconsistent with modern development'.[6] Assisted, again, by detailed press coverage of their ostentatious lifestyle,[7] Mahathir was seeking to garner support for populist reform by invoking liberal themes of modern civic nationalism and the sovereign will of the Dewan Rakyat.

In reality, the 1983 skirmish signified an emerging strategy to transfer more power to the centre. Another important, if less obvious, feature of the royal conflict was the attempt to acquire symbolic custodianship over national Islamic interests, traditionally the remit of the sultans through the National Council for Islamic Affairs.[8] In turn, the government proceeded to usher through federal legislation giving it 'the absolute right to interpret Islamic precepts, tenets and *shariah* law'.[9] Backed by the Amendments to the Societies Act (1981), this allowed it overall power to proscribe 'seditious' organisations seeking to challenge the government, Bumiputera rights or Islamic doctrine – legislation used to ban *Al-Arqam* in August 1994.[10]

But while these decrees indicated UMNO's coercive side, Mahathir was also intent on fostering consent through reform of social ideas. An important consideration here was the global Islamic resurgence that had taken root in Malaysia from the early-1980s. Attempting to harness that shift to the project throughout the 1980s, Mahathir had established the Malaysian Institute for Islamic Understanding by 1992. Promoting re-appraisal of Islamic doctrine, Mahathir was seeking a balance 'between spiritual attainment and material development'.[11] More specifically, such fora were now being used as an intellectual counterpoint to PAS in an attempt to keep Malays within UMNO's political constituency.

Likewise, Mahathir was aware of the need to maintain UMNO's support base in the rural environs. But this was not, and never has been, for Mahathir a surface gesture. A deep-rooted part of his own political socialisation lies in the rural experience. Mahathir's own birthplace and parliamentary constituency lies in rural Alor Setar, Kedah. In his early writings (under the pseudonym C. H. E. Det), Mahathir had vented powerful criticism of the colonial *padi kunca* (rice land system) and its exploitative effects upon the Malay peasantry, a view (carried over into his polemics on behalf of the South), which helps explain Mahathir's own long-standing Malay-centred rural populism.[12]

Much of UMNO's own support base has been built at the local level. Significant here has been the practical role played by Village Security and Development Committees, Jawatankuasa Kemajuan dan Keselamatan Kampung (JKKK), in filtering ideas and values. A vital, if low-key, part of the UMNO network, JKKKs provide an integrated system of localised control across each Malaysian state. Appointed, rather than elected (as are local district councillors) in a top-down process via the Chief Minister/Menteri Besar and State Exco Council, local Barisan members control JKKK branches, helping to collect village data, coordinate local development projects and maintain local security by acting as intermediary to the municipal authority. Thus, within each *mukim* (district/ward – comprising lots, or streets), JKKKs build cooperation through, for example, the initiation of new *kampong* road works and local employment projects – although directives issued by planning departments are approved by local councillors and *ex officio* members subject to state policy and federal influence. Increasingly, JKKK activities have been absorbed into Vision development strategies directed by the Rural Development Ministry.[13] In 1997, plans were announced to send committee members on specially designed training courses to help boost growth.[14] At the same time, they play an 'on-the-ground' role as informer by identifying recalcitrant elements and 'providing feedback', thus acting, in Penang CM Dr Koh's words, as the 'Government's eyes and ears' at the state level.[15] In these ways, JKKKs help project the Barisan as the main provider of community services and source of social stability.[16]

There has, nevertheless, been disquiet in the rural hinterlands over UMNO's urban identity and centralised network. Guinness's ethnographic account of social development in the *kampongs* and environs of Mukim Plentong, Johor, for example, demonstrates some of the latent hostility towards local UMNO cadres, despite their provision of social welfare.[17] At the same time, clear patterns of rural–urban migration from the 1980s, typified by the large-scale movement of young Malay women into low-wage employment in the new Free Trade Zones (FTZs) and industrial plants,[18] continued to erode the fabric of *kampong* life and its multi-layered system of village cooperation, or *gotong royong*. Alongside rising drug use, assaults on women, child abuse and increase in Malay divorce relative to other ethnic groups,[19] these new social problems in the major industrial centres have caused a mood of displacement described by one long-term demographic study as a state of 'anomie'.[20]

However, despite the insecurities of the mid-1980s recession, an expanding middle class had also enjoyed the fruits of economic development and upward mobility. It is notable that, to date, market researchers appear to have taken a keener interest than academics in the emerging patterns of middle-class identity in Malaysia.[21] But what both perspectives reveal is the exponential growth of the 'new middle classes' from the 1980s, increasingly segmented by socio-economic position, lifestyle and consumption patterns. It is here, in the new urban landscape of glossy KL and Penang shopping malls and other designer-modish outlets, that 'new middle-classness' has been forged. Yet it is also among a professionalised Malay salariat that the renewal of Islamic consciousness became most prominent, serving to repoliticise Islam as a symbol of ethnic identification. Thus, by the mid-1980s, this 'ethnic–class paradox' and a more fluid middle class were creating new challenges for the Mahathir project. Converging with privatisation and public sector reform, new sectoral divisions were now emerging, bringing underlying tensions within UMNO to the surface.

Internal Conflict and the UMNO Split

The turmoil and eventual split within UMNO by 1988 represented not just an internecine power struggle, but a hegemonic crisis. It signified the political showdown of contending class forces and sectoral interests thrown up by the 1980s deregulatory agenda, revealing, in its aftermath, a fundamental shift in the political basis of the bloc.

In broad terms, the source of the disaffection stemmed from 'traditional' or 'conservative' forces within UMNO. Its most decisive feature involved the failed challenge at the April 1987 UMNO election by former Finance Minister Tengku Razaleigh Hamzah for the post of UMNO president, and Musa Hitam for the post of deputy; positions providing effective accession to the prime ministership and deputy prime ministership. Although Mahathir's and Razaleigh's support bases within the party (respectively, if not very imaginatively, dubbed 'Team A' and 'Team B') represented certain factional and personality-based cleavages, the more substantial source of the conflict can be traced to the broadly different set of policy perspectives held by each grouping in relation to economic development.

Invoking UMNO's 'founding values', the Razaleigh team had campaigned on an anti-corruption platform within the context of UMNO and NEP patronage. However, the source of its grievance lay in its main support base comprising small–medium business fractions and civil servants unhappy at Mahathir's deregulatory ideas. It is worth noting here how these elements had come to constitute the decisive proportion of UMNO delegates – notably at the expense of teachers, UMNO's older base.[22] Thus, Team B's campaign lay in its disquiet over the redistribution of privatisation resources, which, alongside the effects of the 1985–87 recession, had resulted in the more controlled flow of patronage and rewards to new elites.[23] The economic downturn can be seen as the catalyst for a split waiting to happen:

> When Malaysia's economic growth began to falter in the early to mid-1980s, mainstream Malay political and business opinion on the NEP's impact on the economy and its impending end in 1990 started to split between pro-'growth' and pro-'distribution' positions ... [The former] shared a wider concern, traditionally held by non-Malay and foreign capital, that excessive state regulation had led or would lead to a contraction in investment in the

Malaysian economy. [The latter] were committed to the retention of the NEP's restructuring objective.[24]

Thus, while the Razaleigh camp's approach involved a more assertive defence of the NEP state,[25] this perspective conflicted with Mahathir's ambitions to shift the weight of political control away from the state bureaucracy.

Tensions over these policy perspectives had been evident since 1980 when, as deputy prime minister, Mahathir had expressed 'disdain' for the Industrial Coordination Act and the Petroleum Development Act, the latter initiated by Razaleigh in 1974.[26] Under the NEP, a whole plethora of bureaucratic interests had become entrenched within state agencies such as the Treasury Department, the Economic Planning Unit (EPU), the Ministry of Public Enterprises and the Bank Negara.[27] Mahathir's moves to streamline and control them – including the integration of the EPU into an expanded Prime Minister's Department[28] – now brought defenders of those interests, like Razaleigh, into direct confrontation. In turn, Mahathir's deregulatory agenda, a reflection of new state–class priorities, now had to be legitimised in political terms. Thus policy sensitivities that had taken the form of discreet factional positioning within UMNO now took the form of open political conflict.

In defeating Razaleigh's bid, albeit with a marginal 51% of delegate votes, Mahathir had used the UMNO contest as a hegemonic opportunity to remodel the political basis of the party and the power bloc. Again, the modernity argument had been invoked to portray Team B as a repository of anachronistic values. However, Razaleigh, and his Team B ministers had proceeded to challenge the legality of the UMNO election in the courts, a lawsuit being filed by the 'UMNO-11' in June 1987 seeking to nullify the election. In an atmosphere of growing public unease, Mahathir needed to pre-empt any further haemorrhaging of support within UMNO and loss of public confidence in the BN. The party crisis had also coincided with a series of brooding communal tensions between Malay and Chinese in-stitutions over the introduction of Malay-Islamic educational reforms, prompting protests from Chinese guild associations, the MCA, Gerakan and the DAP.[29] Thus, on 27 October 1987, using the spectre of past social and ethnic unrest as an authoritarian populist rationale,[30] Mahathir deployed the ISA to arrest over one hundred opposition figures under Operation Lalang, the detention of academics and intellectuals such as (then) Aliran President Chandra Muzaffar, Kua Kia Soong and Mohd Nasir Hashim being defended as a necessary measure to prevent sedition and civil dis-order.[31] Despite warnings from Tunku Abdul Rahman, Malaysia's elder statesman, that the country was becoming a 'police state', Mahathir used the media to defend the suspension of civil liberties and denounce political dissent as an incentive to social chaos.[32]

The High Court's ruling in February 1988 on the UMNO-11 suit was that illegal UMNO branches had been evident and that while the election itself could not be nullified, UMNO should be deregistered as a party under the Societies Act.[33] With the schism formalised and UMNO technically 'illegal', the registrar, thereafter, allowed Mahathir to reclaim the party title as UMNO Baru (new), with Razaleigh proceeding to found Semangat '46 (S46). As statements of Malay identity, both assignations were instructive. Semangat '46 (the Spirit of '46), referring to the year of UMNO's founding, invoked a 'back to basics' traditionalism; an attempt to repoliticise Malay political culture through an appeal to older values. The concept of *semangat* itself, roughly meaning 'soul' or 'vital substance', derives from the Malays' diverse religious and cultural inheritance, ranging from ancient animism (still prevalent among the Orang Asli aboriginals) to Islam brought by Arab traders. The Malay understands *semangat* as a universal force within man and all other forms of nature.[34] Again, one needs to recognise the significance of Malay *adat* in shaping political consciousness. UMNO Baru, on the other hand, was hailed as a newly 'purified' political force with a revitalised modern vision.[35]

However, the legal impasse now offered an expedient moment to confront the judiciary itself. This followed on from a series of conflicts between the courts and the executive, including the High Court's decision in September 1987 to allow Aliran the right to publish a monthly magazine in the Malay language – overturning an earlier application rejected by the Ministry of Home Affairs.[36] Fearing judicial arbitration on the allocation of privatised contracts, the move to curb the judiciary's powers also came in response to Lim Kit Siang's lawsuit over the legality of the UEM North–South Highway contract. Following protracted legal manoeuvres, Supreme Court President Tun Salleh Abbas was suspended in May 1988 (technically, on the instructions of the Yang di-Pertuan Agong), his dismissal becoming effective on 8 August 1988. The following day, the Supreme Court heard an appeal by the UMNO-11 and dismissed their case.[37]

In the ensuing 1990 general election, coinciding with an economic upturn, Semangat's poor performance within Malaysia's first ever multiracial electoral pact, the Gagasan Rakyat Malaysia (Malaysian People's Front) showed that, while the Barisan had lost ground (losing Sabah and Kelantan), UMNO's political hegemony was still intact. This was evidenced by the steady stream of party personnel returning to the UMNO fold, isolated by the lack of political patronage denied to political bodies outside the Barisan.[38] By late 1996, following Semangat's deteriorating political alliance with PAS in Kelantan, Razaleigh himself returned to UMNO.[39]

By the early 1990s, the dynamics of the split had created a more centralised political bloc, with the Razaleigh–Musa camp's 'protectionist' agenda now checked by a new set of state priorities. But the attendant clampdown had also revealed the limitations of ISA repression as a political strategy.[40] Thus Mahathir required a return to consensus-building to help consolidate the BN's electoral base.

Consolidating the Bloc after 1990

This section considers the attempted consolidation of the political bloc from the period of the split, culminating in the political fallout of the 1997 crisis. Four aspects are addressed here: first, the nature of the political coalition *vis-à-vis* Chinese politics and the other BN parties; second, the *realpolitik* of the 'Anwar succession'; third, the issue of political corruption within UMNO; and, fourth, Mahathir's role on the international political stage. This takes us towards a closer analysis of how these elements fed into the crisis and the UMNO network's emergency attempts to rebuild consent.

Holding the Coalition: Chinese Politics and the Wider Party Alliance

A full analysis of the Barisan parties and their roles within the coalition is beyond the remit of this work.[41] Let us consider, however, some of the principal factors that have continued to hold the coalition together and how Mahathir has sought to fashion a new political base through the Vision project.

Mahathir's charismatic appeal, political judgement and astute handling of the reward structure has been fused with the invocation to work together for growth, helping to keep the MCA, MIC and other junior Barisan partners contained within the political bloc. For the Chinese in particular, the *quid pro quo* for MCA and Gerakan (an offshoot of the MCA from the early 1960s) cooperation has been the consistent promise of material rewards. Indeed, there is an unstated understanding here that this compliant role will enhance the prospects for growth and accumulation for Chinese business.

Thus the extent of the MCA's own political voice has revolved around a rational calculus of what level of business rewards and broader social goods can be secured from working within the Barisan system. As MCA President Ling Liong Sik asserts, the Chinese community: 'want a society where the rules are conducive to doing business, where they can educate their children. And they have it here. This is a land of tremendous opportunity.'[42] From this perspective, one can see the connection between Ling's avid enthusiasm for the Vision project on the one hand and the compliant nature of MCA politics on the other.[43] In this and other senses, the party acts as a controlling mechanism within the coalition, helping to filter government objectives down to the broader Chinese community.

As noted, this compliance has its roots in the politics of decolonisation, the Emergency and Alliance consociationalism. Having supported British attempts to contain the MCP's base of Chinese workers, left-wing Malay nationalists and other rural elements,[44] the MCA had been formed by conservative Chinese elites as a bulwark to class-based ethnic demands from below. In the immediate post-Merdeka period, this allowed the MCA a relatively strategic position within the Alliance. Yet despite a more assertive and intellectual profile in the 1960s and 1970s, under leaders like Tan Siew Sin, party objectives have become more parochial. Despite the benefits accruing from Bangsa Malaysia, the MCA's political trade-off for economic rewards has diminished its status for many Chinese, who see it as a passive appendage to UMNO. In response, the party has made some efforts to reassert its credibility – for example, through its promotion of the Thought Reform Campaign, via Hua Zong, the lobby-based Federation of Chinese Associations. However, this agenda, coinciding with perceived attempts to water down basic Chinese nostrums on democracy, culture and education had been strongly resisted by Dongjiaozong (DJZ), the esteemed Chinese educationalist movement, and its academic director Kua Kia Soong.[45] Ling has also sought to rebuild the party by promoting its women's wing, Wanita MCA.[46] Yet, reflecting the difference between the latter and its Malay counterpart, Wanita UMNO, the MCA's political credentials remain subsidiary to UMNO.

Similarly, Gerakan's influence has been mainly confined to the domestic issues of Penang politics. In defeating the Penang Alliance at the 1969 general election, under the charismatic leadership of Lim Chong Eu (Penang chief minister 1969–90), the party could claim a significant multi-ethnic and social democratic support base. But by the mid-1980s, these had been sacrificed for a passive role within the BN.[47] As Loh concludes, Chinese political discourse has become, in essence, 'the politics of developmentalism ... [a means of] ensuring that the Chinese get a fair share of the cake'.[48] Accordingly, issues of corruption and repressive acts have become taboo subjects for the Chinese BN.[49]

Perhaps more worrying for the MCA and Gerakan is the apparent long-term diffusion of its support base. Neither party has ever been able to nullify the appeal of the DAP opposition within the Chinese community. And while it recorded its best-ever results in the 1995 general election, the BN's best since 1974, much of this can be seen as an endorsement of

Mahathir's economic liberalisation, growth and financial prosperity rather than specific support for the MCA and Gerakan.[50] Here, Mahathir has also taken a more conciliatory view of Chinese education, culture and Confucian–Islamic dialogue.[51]

Internal to the Barisan's support base has been the 'political voice' of Chinese business agencies, most notably the Malaysian Chinese Chamber of Commerce (MCCC). Although it is the principal representative of small–medium Chinese business, this body can be seen as an important part of the UMNO network through its close connections with the MCA and in its efforts to maintain stable relations with local political elites. A good example of this is the role played by the Penang Chinese Chamber of Commerce (PCCC), a particularly significant branch of the MCCC given Penang's large Chinese business community.[52] While it is a professed independent organisation, it acts as a key intermediary between the Penang business sector and the Penang State Assembly. The PCCC has also worked closely with Gerakan, the state's governing party, and its chief minister, Dr Koh Tsu Koon.[53] Likewise, with other regional branches, it engages in more in-depth 'consultation exercises' with government through national AGMs. As intimated in the PCCC's own profile statement, this links it into the broader business–political network:

> The Chamber has great rapport with the Government at regional as well as national level through its direct affiliation to the Associated Chinese Chambers of Commerce and Industry of Malaysia and indirect connection with the National Chamber of Commerce and Industry of Malaysia.[54]

While such dialogue is not in itself unusual, it signifies the channels through which the Chinese business class is absorbed into the political network. Another key factor in the PCCC's support for Mahathir was the benefits derived for the Penang business class through Anwar's political association with the state. The careful attention paid by Anwar to developing such relations could be seen in the MCCC's key pre-election endorsement of Mahathir and the Vision agenda in 1995.[55]

This suggested an important shift in UMNO's electoral base by the mid-1990s. While still concerned with containing PAS influence over rural Malays, UMNO seemed prepared to risk concessions to the non-Malays in order to build a broader multi-racial support base – a strategy, perhaps, consistent with the demographic realities of an increasingly urbanised, consumer-driven electorate. The poor response to the DAP's main 1995 electoral theme of greater democratisation also reinforced the suspicion that Chinese voters attach relatively greater importance to economic rather than political rights.[56] This does not imply any simple disregard for the latter. Rather, the distinction is more nuanced, with Chinese 'political consciousness' inclined towards a more rational assessment of how political rights help safeguard economic opportunities. This is also evident in Kelantan where, despite its Islamic agenda, PAS has consciously sought to protect Chinese political and economic rights. Nevertheless, in the absence of any more mainstream political alternative, small–medium Chinese business has remained tied to the MCA and Gerakan, while big Chinese capital has become linked more directly to UMNO itself. The Chinese BN has thus played a key role in locking these elements into the prevailing structure. By late 1998, Chinese business support for Mahathir was more precarious, given his handling of the crisis, though still tempered by rational considerations.

Very similar parallels can be drawn in relation to the MIC under the leadership of Samy Vellu.[57] Indeed, the MIC's compliant role within the BN structure is in many ways more pronounced than that of the Chinese BN parties. Much of this, however, can be traced to the historical vulnerability and marginalisation of the Indian working class, particularly its rural component, and its need to find a secure channel of political expression within the system.[58] Again, though, the relative increase of middle-class rewards and patronage, dispensed through the MIC, has served to neutralise potential dissent within the Indian community.

In the East Malaysian states of Sabah and Sarawak, a more complex set of political relationships prevail. In Sarawak, the main BN Parti Pesaka Bumiputera Bersatu, (United Bumiputera Party) presiding over a diverse amalgam of ethnic groups (Chinese, Malays, Melanaus and Dayaks – including Christian Iban, Orang Ulu and Bidayuh peoples), pursues a more autonomous and distinct agenda suited to its particular configuration of ethnic politics. UMNO, thus, adopts a more restrained form of influence here. Yet, despite Sarawak's lower level of economic development relative to Peninsular Malaysia, the managed distribution of wealth across the ethnic strata, and acceptance of Mahathir's modernising endeavours at the national level, has helped the Barisan maintain control in the state.[59]

In Sabah, relations between UMNO and the Parti Bersatu Sabah (PBS, United Sabah Party) have been more strained. Though based principally around the indigene Kadazans, the PBS, as a nominally multi-communal party, also draw significant support from the Chinese. In 1990, the PBS left the BN (which it had joined in 1986) to contest the 1990 general election alongside the Razaleigh opposition grouping. However, by 1994, following the co-optation of key PBS figures, Mahathir had re-established control within Sabah through an UMNO-led state coalition government.[60] Nevertheless, despite the BN's victory in Sabah in 1995, strong anti-federal sentiment remains, notably over central government control of development funds.[61] By managing the flow of state government resources, both directly and indirectly, Kuala Lumpur has been able to impose what Sabahans term 'political recessions' in order to delegitimise internal opposition, thus paving the way for federal intervention and UMNO control.[62] Consistently fearful of demands for independence, UMNO have used other various back-door strategies to keep the political class in Sabah and Sarawak divided and tied into the coalition, such as the regular secondment of their state officials to federal posts and the award of scholarships to students for study in other states.[63] During the 1999 state elections in Sabah, the BN poured money in to fund major road projects and other infrastructural inducements. But while tacit support is given to Mahathir's economic agenda, perceptions of centralised interference and political bribery remain a source of ongoing resentment.

Beyond these state–federal conflicts, Mahathir's political acumen was also still needed to maintain control within UMNO and temper aspiring factions within the party hierarchy.

Consolidation and the Succession Issue

The stability of the power bloc by the mid-1990s had come to depend very largely upon the positioning of senior figures within the party, most notably that of Anwar Ibrahim. As Mahathir's 'heir apparent', Anwar had made a long journey from radical Muslim activist and ABIM leader to a position of political accommodation within UMNO. In many regards, the conservatism and prestige of high office seem starkly at odds with Anwar's previous activism and ideas on civil reform. In *Two Faces*, a personal account of the PRM leader Syed Husin Ali's detention under the ISA (1974–80), we get an insightful view of the young radical Anwar, jailed alongside Syed at Kamunting during Tun Abdul Razak's clampdown on social activists, academics and other 'communist agents'.[64] Husin Ali talks admiringly of Anwar the Muslim and social idealist with a vision of society far removed from the oppression of the Barisan state. Yet, by 1981, Anwar had become absorbed into that very system.

In an illuminating article, Zafar Bangash tells how this 'marriage of convenience' was set up by Anwar's former teacher and mentor, the late Ismail Faruqi.[65] Acting as intermediary, Faruqi had managed to persuade Anwar that Mahathir was 'well-disposed towards the Islamic Movement' and could work with Anwar in 'pursuing an Islamic goal'. However, Mahathir had insisted on three preconditions for Anwar's entry into UMNO: that ABIM revoke all associations with PAS, including standing on PAS tickets at elections; that it discard its view of the NEP as un-Islamic and support the promotion of Bumiputera rights; and that it should not condemn the Malay educational policy. In presenting these terms of entry, Faruqi argued that the Islamic movement in Malaysia (and elsewhere) had to participate in the prevailing power structure in order to effect 'change from within', a view subsequently endorsed by Anwar, paving the way for his and ABIM's co-optation. Again, both Faruqi's and Anwar's compliance here can be viewed as the practical application of insiderism and intellectual assimilation by the UMNO network.

Having effectively purged serious dissent within UMNO by the late 1980s, Mahathir appeared to be laying the groundwork for a smooth, if very gradual, succession. Despite other 'contenders', Anwar remained the clear favourite. The question was not if, but when. Yet, while supporting Anwar's eventual succession, Mahathir refused to give a timetable for it, claiming that to do so would make him a 'lame duck' leader.[66] Despite gathering speculation that he would use the 1999 UMNO presidential election as an uncontested event and valedictory for 'the handover', Mahathir, buoyed by an unprecedented level of popular support, had remained circumspect about relinquishing power. Meanwhile elements within the Anwar camp had begun to express open impatience at the process – though not Anwar himself who, recognising the dangers of an outright challenge, proceeded to develop his political profile as a trusted minister and a 'liberal intellectual' with evolving ideas on Islamic modernity and civil reform.

However, this studious persona could not disguise the emerging tensions between Mahathir and Anwar's camp. In a prelude to Mahathir's 1998 purge, Anwar had received a stark reminder of the prime minister's guile and resilience at the October 1996 (triennial) UMNO party elections, with Mahathir allies winning 80% of Supreme Council seats over Anwar's associates. While some Anwar allies remained, many of the 'new team' from the 1993 elections were displaced, including Muhyiddin Yassin, one of Anwar's main loyalists.[67] In a series of deft pre-election manoeuvres, Mahathir had also brought restless party elements in Sabah into line, overcome resistance from UMNO assemblymen in Kedah in his bid to replace Menteri Besar Osman Aroff with Mahathir loyalist Sanusi Junid, and, in a personal *coup de grâce*, had secured a Supreme Council ruling that no contest should be held for the top two party posts until 1999.[68] In effect, Mahathir was blocking any possibility of UMNO divisional delegates nominating Anwar for president. Alongside Zahid Hamidi, Anwar still had the nominal support of 'dark horse' Education Minister Najib Razak at this point. [69]

Yet, despite careful endeavours not to provoke disunity, deep sensitivities remained between Anwar and key Mahathir loyalists Sanusi Junid, Foreign Minister Abdullah Badawi and UMNO Treasurer Daim Zainuddin. Again, much of this has to be seen in the context of privatisation and the strategic placement of business elites by political figures. With lucrative resources becoming more scarce, the conflict for control of the remaining prime assets had intensified. In particular, there had been continuous acrimony between Anwar and Daim at the scale of privatised benefits handed out by Daim to privileged business figures, including the Bakun Dam project in Sarawak (Malaysia's biggest-ever privatisation) to Ting Pek Khing and the contract for the second Malaysia-Singapore causeway to close business associate Halim Saad, head of Renong.[70] Against this, Anwar had secured considerable corporate and editorial influence through the *New Straits Times* and *Utusan Malaysia* groups.

Nevertheless, having shown consummate skill in counterbalancing these elements, Mahathir was still firmly in charge, his supporters asserting that Anwar would assume the leadership only when he was seen to represent UMNO as a whole, rather than a faction within it. It is significant, then, that as the 1997 crisis unfolded, an apparent *rapprochement* between Anwar and Daim could be observed (see below), with both 'working closely' to restore economic confidence. At the same time, Mahathir, playing down media speculation, dismissed serious differences between himself and Anwar, casting their relationship as akin to father and son.[71]

A more critical aspect of their relationship, though, was Anwar's intellectual qualities. As a key insight for the policy differences and crisis to follow, Gomez had noted the particular relevance of Anwar's leadership abilities with regard to moral issues and Islam:

> if the Islamic rhetoric propagated by PAS continues to gather momentum, UMNO will probably have to depend more on Anwar, rather than Mahathir to stem the tide. Unlike Mahathir, Anwar is still respected in Islamic circles for his knowledge of Islam and his attempts to inculcate more Islamic values within the government. Anwar's moderate stand on issues and his promotion of modernist Islamic views may also help him retain the support of the urban electorate, while curbing PAS's influence in the rural Malay heartland. If the need arises for a vision of politics that must be articulated on essentially moral positions ... Anwar would appear to be one of the very few leaders in UMNO who can respond persuasively.[72]

But alongside fears of Anwar's 'moral authority' within UMNO, a more malevolent campaign against his succession was emerging. The first serious indication of such was the circulation of a *surat layang*, or poison pen letter, in August 1997 claiming that Anwar had engaged in homosexual and adulterous liaisons. Although subsequently dismissed by Mahathir, such smears signified the beginning of a concerted campaign to discredit him in the run-up to the 1999 UMNO elections.

A further element here had been Anwar's attempts to foster a more qualitative dialogue on civil society. In many ways, it was Anwar's, rather than Mahathir's, engagement of 'democratic reform' and a more expansive conception of civil society that had informed the political and intellectual aspects of the Vision. Indeed, in the wake of the crisis, Anwar had come to pose this as a critical issue for the rehabilitation of the region as a whole. Thus, in a speech in June 1998, he argued that the crisis had 'unleashed a gale of creative destruction' that would 'cleanse society of collusion, cronyism and nepotism',[73] a theme adopted by Anwar allies to prepare a coded assault on Mahathir during the 1998 UMNO gathering. Anwar also used his close ties with Habibie – whom he had supported openly following Suharto's fall – to promote a redefinition of civil society 'appropriate' to the region. Alongside a tolerant interpretation of Islam, Anwar and Habibie had been instrumental in sponsoring such ideas through think tanks like the Institute for Policy Research in Malaysia and the Centre for Information and Development Studies in Indonesia.[74] In the short term, this did not presage any qualitative reform or 'opening up' of civil society. But it did expose more seriously the underlying tensions between Mahathir's brand of 'restrained liberal development' and Anwar's more enthusiastic, if still guarded, shift towards free-market liberal reforms. Thus, as in 1987, latent tensions within UMNO, hitherto kept at bay by economic optimism, were once more ready to erupt as conflicting policy ideas and expressions of state–class interests.

Addressing Corruption

While Mahathir's political dexterity had helped realise a factional *détente* within UMNO, the integrity of the Barisan by the late 1990s was now deeply tainted by the association of corrupt practices. Despite much self-righteous use of the term by Western elites, 'crony capitalism' does exhibit certain features in the Malaysian system of money politics. In contrast to the familial and military-based structure used by Suharto, UMNO patronage has operated through a more party-based system of political–corporate closure.[75] Openly critical of UMNO's part in major financial scandals, Chandra Muzaffar has, for example, long argued for a clearer separation between business and politics, claiming that Mahathir's consistent calls for greater 'moral values' cannot disguise the deeper malaise.[76]

Three basic factors lie at the heart of the corruption issue in Malaysia: institutionalisation, centralisation and privatisation. The first refers to the ways in which business and politics became enmeshed through the institutional circumstances of the NEP state, drawing not only Bumiputeras, Malay business elites and UMNO, but also the MCA, MIC and their political–corporate functionaries, into the network of state-based money politics. The second concerns the greater centralisation of executive power under Mahathir from the early 1980s, including closer control of the judicial process (through, for example, the 1988 legislation to make the judiciary subservient to Parliament and controls over bodies like the Electoral Commission) and the absence of fully independent investigative status for the Anti Corruption Agency. The third involves the massive opportunities of wealth that privatisation and the sale of public services came to offer, making what had gone before seem like a drop in the ocean. By the mid-1990s, all these elements had created a 'corruption epidemic'.[77]

The legitimacy of the power bloc depends on the ability of its state managers to maintain political cohesion. Thus, in crisis scenarios, political–corporate networks will, ultimately, 'sacrifice' their senior executives (Nixon, Thatcher, Suharto), in order to protect the bloc itself. In this regard, Mahathir and the party hierarchy had become increasingly sensitive to the spectre of corruption within UMNO/BN.

A graphic, if somewhat theatrical, indication of such came during the 1996 Party Assembly. Here, Mahathir wept openly during his speech on the dangers of money politics, warning how it could 'destroy' UMNO.[78] In April 1997, following a highly emotional Supreme Council meeting, Mahathir sent a definitive signal of intent by securing the resignation of Muhammad Taib, chief minister of Selangor, in connection with alleged currency irregularities and false declarations to customs officials at Brisbane airport.[79] As in the case of Kedah, the subsequent appointment of Abu Hassan to the Selangor post was instructive: a Mahathir loyalist, pledged to root out corrupt practices, and in a vital location to administer the proposed MSC project in Putrajaya.[80]

Alongside a more 'assertive' role for the government's Anti-Corruption Agency,[81] the image portrayed here was of Anwar and Mahathir working closely on this issue – signifying a congenial atmosphere and a 'united resolve' within the party. In May 1997, Mahathir left Anwar in charge as acting prime minister before departing on a two-month vacation to Europe – his longest official break in 16 years. Within days, Anwar had signalled his own authority by calling to account two senior government officials over the questionable disbursement of public money.[82] By December 1997, Mahathir's appointee Abu Hassan was himself under suspicion, breaking down as he tried to explain the circumstances of a RM5 million renovation plan for his official residence to the State Assembly.[83] Meanwhile, Abdul Rahman, a top official in the Prime Minister's Department, was charged over a RM260 million fraud involving false documents showing plans for a government award to two construction companies.[84]

Against this backdrop, the corruption and nepotism issue was introduced at the 1998 UMNO Assembly by UMNO Youth chief Zahid Hamidi. While reflecting broader concerns within UMNO Youth, this suggested a concerted attempt by Anwar proxies to raise the temperature in the leadership issue. Again, though, Mahathir had shown political prowess in silencing his critics, firstly in an open rebuke to Zahid for raising the issue publicly, rather than within UMNO, and then, in an 'act of transparency', by publishing for the first time a list of the many companies and individuals – including Zahid – who had benefited from privatisation and government awards.[85]

While such acts only revealed the tip of the political–corporate iceberg, it now signified the political dangers of the corruption problem for key elements within UMNO, particularly with allegations of crisis bail-outs mounting.

Playing the International Stage: Politics and Diplomacy

While Mahathir's attempts to build political consensus had been conducted against a background of domestic reforms, recessionary fears and party splits, the project also had become more globally focused by the early 1990s. Here, Mahathir has crafted a prestigious persona for the international stage. A key aspect here has been his role as 'chief executive' of Malaysia Inc., leading business delegations around the world in pursuit of inward capital and new investment sites – Proton's penetration of the Western car market being emblematic of the new confidence. Mahathir's achievement, in this regard, has been his ability to portray Malaysia's foreign dependence in nationalist–economic terms. Thus the proclaimed challenge of Vision development offers a populist *raison d'être* for growth while 'camouflaging' its fragile base.

A second, interacting, aspect involves his role as 'emissary' for the South, offering a post-Bandung discourse of Malaysian-style 'economic nationalism' for peripheral states to follow. Fashioned around themes of political solidarity with poor and developing countries, this has seen, for example, emerging ties between Malaysia and South Africa, with Mandela, pre-crisis, endorsing Mahathir's growth-led strategy as a model of socio-economic development.[86] Indeed, even as the Malaysian economy fell into critical recession by mid-1998, Mahathir's decision to 'break ranks' and enforce capital controls (see following chapters) represented an alternative to Western orthodoxy for such countries.

A further measure of this confidence was Malaysia's determination to proceed with Burma's controversial admission to ASEAN.[87] Mahathir has been rigid in seeking to present sensitive regional issues such as trade with Rangoon, Indonesian repression in East Timor, or the various claims of ownership to the Spratley Islands, as *internal* ASEAN affairs. On top of other diplomatic problems, the formal decision in May 1997 to grant admission to Burma had created some friction between ASEAN and the West.[88] A more sensitive factor for Mahathir here was that many Malaysian-based NGOs had opposed Burma's membership, notably ABIM, who had criticised the harsh treatment of Muslims by the ruling State Law and Order Restoration Council. However, as the regime's sixth largest foreign investor, Malaysia's bilateral and intra-regional trade agenda now took precedence over its previously stated concerns.[89]

Mahathir also continued to look East for other political props. Most notable here was his vocal promotion of a regional East Asian Economic Caucus (EAEC) over the broader Asia-Pacific Economic Cooperation (APEC) countries. This included persistent attempts, most prominently at the APEC Jakarta summit in November 1994, to stall moves towards a more open trading regime with the USA and other Pacific countries by 2020. Besides appropriating Mahathir's 2020 slogan, the fear expressed here was that any such trading order would allow the USA unequal advantage in the region, thus compromising Malaysia's development schedule. Against this, Mahathir had played upon the troubled US–Japan trade relationship as a way of encouraging a closer Japanese identification with the EAEC. Part of this discourse included Mahathir's co-authorship of *The Asia That Can Say No* with the controversial Japanese politician Shintaro Ishahara (an adaptation of the latter's now infamous *The Japan That Can Say No*), a strident appeal to Japanese sensitivities proclaiming 'an anti-American front on the issue of values'.[90]

Behind this polemic, Malaysia has always maintained a practical foreign policy stance towards the USA, both in bilateral terms and through ASEAN, formed in 1967 partly as a bulwark to communist Vietnam. While ASEAN member states have not always shared a common outlook *vis-à-vis* the superpowers, Malaysia's pragmatic support for US security arrangements in the region have been evident in, for example, the ASEAN Regional Forum (ARF), set up in 1993 in response to the rising power of China.[91] This essentially pro-US security position should be borne in mind when considering the circumstances of Mahathir's anti-Western rhetoric, particularly at the height of the Anwar crisis.

For some time, Western diplomats had been content to 'note' Mahathir's polemics. But as the 1997 crisis unfolded, the implications of his attacks on Western capitalist institutions were beginning to create more serious disquiet at home and abroad.

Political Pressures and Crisis Management: 1997

The ways in which the UMNO network deployed its resources to manage public anxieties during the economic crisis and the Anwar situation will be dealt with in the following chapters. For the moment, let us focus here on the more immediate *political* implications of the crisis leading to the Anwar purge and the impact of this within the bloc.[92]

As Mahathir's attack on Soros and the USA reached its critical peak, the perennial question of its content was once again posed by Malaysia watchers: populist diatribe or Asian values? Perhaps in Mahathir's own mind it was a mixture of both. Although one can recognise the familiar accoutrements of gesture politics played out for the domestic audience, this does not invalidate the sense of conviction or enigmatic purpose behind such discourse. Indeed, an intrinsic part of Mahathir's political style lies in this very ability to present himself as an enigma.

The more important aspect here, however, concerns its *hegemonic* content. While Anwar's budgetary interventions were being used to ameliorate market fears, the worry for BN elites was that the economic crisis would deteriorate into political and ideological ones – an organic crisis of hegemony. Here, the dominant group may use selective hegemonic strategies – economic, political or ideological – at expedient points to protect the bloc. Thus, while hegemony is always a three-fronted affair, a crisis at any one level may be offset at another. With the economic crisis deepening, Mahathir was, therefore, seeking to shore up the political bloc and use the ideological network (see Chapter 4) to maintain control.

At the centre of this confidence-building exercise lay two particularly sensitive issues. The first involved threats from within the US State Department to impose punitive measures on Malaysia over the activities of its national oil company Petronas. Following its Iran–Libya sanctions policy, the US wanted to 'investigate' Petronas investments in Iran to evaluate the grounds for punitive action.[93] The second issue involved a draft resolution by 34 US Congressmen led by Robert Wexler calling on Mahathir to apologise, or else resign, for alleged anti-Semitic remarks directed at George Soros over his role in the financial crisis.[94] The resolution called upon Mahathir to repudiate his 'claim' that Soros's speculative activities formed part of a 'Jewish conspiracy' against Malaysia as a Muslim state.

Although they are ostensibly separate, it is not difficult to see how both issues became entangled in the political hubris of emerging events. With economic tension escalating, Mahathir insisted that his comments had been taken out of context and that he had merely noted the 'coincidence' that Soros, a Jew, had been involved in speculative activity detrimental to a Muslim country.[95] Despite other prejudices, there is little in Mahathir's make-up to cast him as a racist. Nevertheless, it is difficult to imagine that he could not have foreseen the political impact of such a sensitive remark. If there was an element of calculation in its delivery, it may have involved Mahathir's willingness to trade the wrath of the US 'Jewish political establishment' in order to galvanise political support at home. Moreover, with Clinton keeping a pragmatic distance from the resolution, Mahathir may have thought it possible to defy the Congressional grouping without damaging bilateral relations with Washington. Thus what emerged as the focal issue was not the alleged anti-Semitic element but the heady politics of US aggrandizement and claims of an unwarranted intrusion in a sovereign country's affairs.

With the media reporting a nationwide upsurge in anti-US sentiment and the receipt of death threats to the US Embassy, Mahathir was compelled to reassure US citizens in Malaysia.[96] Particularly evident at this point were the 'shock-troop' activities of UMNO Youth.[97] While Mahathir had sought to raise the political stakes by encouraging public shows of nationalist support, there was also the danger of too much anti-US provocation endangering the economic recovery. In a further attempt to calm emotions, the American Ambassador to Malaysia, John Mallot, intervened to describe the Wexler resignation demands as 'inappropriate' and announce the arrival of a key US state official to 'explain the law' over the sanctions issue.[98] Nevertheless, support for Mahathir had been a reminder to those within the BN, quietly anxious about the impact of the crisis, not to go against the grain of public feeling. More importantly, it served to concentrate minds within UMNO of the dangers of factionalism. Thus, rejecting allegations of ill feeling towards any racial or religious group, an expression of solidarity for Mahathir was confirmed at a special Supreme Council meeting of the 14-member Barisan.[99]

Having initiated the BN vote of confidence, Anwar proceeded to table a more substantive motion of support in the Dewan Rakyat. Anwar's enthusiasm at this point also suggested a pragmatic attempt to demonstrate loyalty as a counterbalance to his own rising status. The vote of confidence in Mahathir and, *ipso facto*, his handling of the economic crisis was included as an internal part of the motion rejecting the Wexler resolution and the US Petronas investigation. Denouncing foreign interference, the DAP leader had supported the government on the Petronas and Wexler points, but wanted a separate motion, debate and vote on Mahathir's specific handling of the crisis,[100] a call rejected by the Speaker, Ong Tee Keat. Despite DAP and PAS opposition, the five-point motion of confidence in Mahathir was passed by the Speaker as a unanimous vote.[101]

While the Barisan were never likely to refuse their support, Mahathir had displayed impressive judgement in cultivating political capital from economic adversity. Yet, while factional splits were avoided, underlying tensions remained. An indication of this was the outcomes of two key by-elections at Sungai Bakap and Changkat Jering, held eleven days before the Dewan Rakyat motion of confidence. Although the Barisan, with the considerable support of the media, won both, it did so with substantially reduced majorities. Indeed, at Sungai Bakap, the Gerakan-BN candidate Lai Chew Hock could muster only 47% of the total vote, with the rest going to the DAP and the independent candidate.[102] More significant, though, was the swing of Malay votes from the BN to the Independent Malay candidate Abu Harith, a shift acknowledged in Dr Koh's admission that the BN needed to learn lessons from the result.[103] Allowing for by-election dissent in the midst of economic crisis, these results now pointed to new electoral fluidity and an erosion of UMNO's Malay support base.

The bloc was also vulnerable at this point to the fallout from other regional crises. The economic contagion had caused political turmoil and undermined the authority of powerful regimes. In South Korea, the damage to the once-mighty *chaebol* system, the IMF bail-out and severe retrenchment had sparked student and civilian riots. Amidst rising anger at the corrupt practices of Kim Young Sam's government, a humbled political elite were forced to acknowledge their mistakes in customary public fashion as the country elected Kim Dae Jung, its first left-of-centre leader in 50 years.[104] Facing harsher retrenchment and poverty, the Thai electorate placed their faith in the more humble figure of Chuan Leekpai after popular protest had secured the resignation of Chavalit Yongchaiyudh. In Indonesia, rampant inflation, including a 400% increase in staple food prices, had given rise to major civil unrest, intensive ethnic purges against small-scale Chinese traders, an emergency military crackdown and an unprecedented crisis for the Suharto family. Suharto had sought to link the collapsing rupiah to a $US currency board in a desperate effort to stave off further financial crisis and insulate the regime from political attack, a strategy that had jeopardised the terms and conditions of the IMF's $US33 billion bail-out.[105] With the rupiah's downward effect on the ringgit, the returning smog crisis over Borneo and the spectre of mass immigration into Malaysia threatening to hold back economic recovery, Mahathir moved to repatriate thousands of Indonesian workers in March 1998, leading to riots at four detention camps, including the deaths of three Indonesians and a guard at Kajang.[106]

Nevertheless, reflecting other assistance to Suharto, Malaysia has viewed internal cohesion in Indonesia and good relations with Jakarta since the Konfrontasi (1963–66) as strategic to its own political stability.[107] A related aspect of this for Mahathir has been the need to control the spread of Islamic-based politics, a force that, despite diverse opposition groupings in Indonesia, had shown its ability to capitalise on the crisis.[108] More ominously, Suharto's fall and ongoing pressure on Habibie threatened to erode at least the *idea* of Barisan invulnerability in the minds of Malaysians.

Much of the crisis management now centred around the National

Economic Action Council (NEAC). In its conception, it looked little more than token neo-corporatism drawing together political, business and public support. But as the scale of collapse and indebtedness, particularly within the banking sector, became more apparent, the NEAC looked set to undertake a more far-reaching appraisal of financial institutions.

It was exquisitely fitting that Mahathir should appoint the architect of Malaysia Inc. and privatisation, Daim Zainuddin, as an executive director. While Anwar, as finance minister, would 'oversee' its remit, it was Daim and Mahathir, as chairman, who came to make the key proposals. As Mahathir's closest confidant, suspicions were, not unreasonably, expressed that having overseen and benefited from, the new privatised wealth flows,[109] Daim was precisely the wrong person for the job. Yet, while the immediate task for Daim was the bailing out of favoured corporate figures and former protégés, the NEAC was also being used, as in the 1980s crisis, as a medium of hegemonic readjustment.

One of the most politically sensitive issues to be addressed, in this regard, was that of Bumiputera equity rights. Here, the crisis had brought into focus the problem of financially unviable industries hitherto controlled through Bumiputera share trusts. The 'solution' was to allow Chinese capital greater access to struggling Malay businesses in order to save and rebuild them. By waiving certain equity rights and encouraging takeovers, firms within the major sectors such as banking, transport and telecommunications would emerge leaner and more competitive. All standard capitalist principles. Yet, even in the harsh landscape of economic crisis, the political dangers of such a strategy were considerable. Thus, as merger plans for the country's biggest finance companies and the splitting up of government-backed conglomerates such as Renong began to emerge, so too did political tensions over the threat to Bumiputera business privileges.[110]

Symptomatic of this tension was the contrasting press responses of the UMNO Youth leader Zahid Hamidi ('Give priority to bumi firms') and MCA leader Ling Liong Sik ('Ling lauds move on bumi equity').[111] Once again, it was Mahathir who played the role of allaying Malay fears and arbitrating political tensions. In seeking to balance these interpretations, Mahathir argued that while such steps were necessary for the survival of many Bumiputera companies, this did not signify any specific threat since many Bumiputeras had themselves already bought into non-Bumiputera firms, many of which were also facing problems: 'So on an aggregate, the amount of Bumiputera [ownership in the economy] will not change.'[112] To some extent, though, Chinese capital had been strengthened. For while the crisis had led to bankruptcy and losses for Chinese firms, it had also given impetus to new policy ideas based on a further negation of Bumiputeraism and a more level playing-field for Chinese business.

While Daim, as veteran fixer, appeared to have formed a 'new partnership' with Anwar,[113] the tensions between them were becoming more apparent by mid-1998. Having dispensed with veiled political attacks on his leadership at the UMNO 1998 Assembly, Mahathir was now manoeuvring to focus attention on the economic recovery process. It was also evident that Mahathir had no intention of relinquishing overall control here. With some justification, Mahathir was by now arguing strongly that the domestic crisis (by this point registering a 6.8% contraction in GDP for the second quarter of 1998)[114] was part of a protracted global problem, as evidenced by the collapse of the rouble and political crisis in Russia by late August – an episode again, as in the Far East, featuring the predatory activities of Soros's Quantum Fund. Having followed tight monetary policy and IMF prescriptions, the country was no nearer recovery. Indeed, with the ringgit still falling and the country now in recession, this had intensified the problem. Mahathir's consequent turn to monetary expansion now saw Anwar's free-market position marginalised as a recovery strategy, a message confirmed by Daim's promotion to the Cabinet as special functions minister and his launching of the National Economic Recovery Plan (NERP).[115] With Mahathir reverting once more to the 'old partnership', Anwar's response was to adopt a more vocal line on currency speculators,[116] although this cannot simply be read as cynical manoeuvring on Anwar's part.

Nevertheless, despite Anwar's protestations of loyalty, the crisis had revealed essential policy differences with Mahathir, differences that under less critical circumstances may not have led Mahathir to the conclusion that Anwar was attempting to undermine him. Part of Mahathir's fears here can also be traced to Anwar's apparent reluctance to support some of the major corporate bail-outs. Yet Mahathir was not clinging to power for reasons of mere nepotism. There was simply no parallel here between Mahathir and Suharto in terms of the latter's massive family stake in the economy. However, with Mahathir's position under threat, there was the concern that an Anwar ascendancy might not provide the requisite guarantees of protection Mahathir was seeking.

But there may have been a much more fundamental issue at play here. Mahathir had given 17 years of sustained effort to building economic prosperity, Vision modernity and UMNO hegemony, none of which he intended to see sacrificed ignominiously in a moment of domestic uncertainty, albeit a critical one. Not only was Anwar taking the economy in a direction that, for Mahathir, threatened to undo those achievements, but his relationship with the IMF nexus suggested a wider strategy to replace him. As noted, while he was not a 'Trojan horse', it was apparent that Anwar was being groomed by Western interests as the most favoured free-market reformer within the government. Neither before nor after Anwar's dismissal was the significance of these liaisons adequately addressed in mainstream analyses. For Mahathir, the threat had become all too apparent.

The Purge

The purge was, thus, under way. In a pre-emptive curb on Anwar's media base, Mahathir, already unhappy over 'negative' reporting of the crisis, had secured the resignations of key Anwar allies Johan Jaafar and Nazri Abdullah, respective editors of *Utusan Malaysia* and *Berita Harian*. The character attacks on Anwar had also gained momentum at the June 1998 Assembly with the circulation of a *surat layang*-type book entitled *50 Reasons Why Anwar Can't Become Prime Minister*. Mahathir's initial response to the book had, as with the previous defamatory material, been dismissive. Nevertheless, despite the arrest of its author, Khalid Jafri, and a court injunction banning it,[117] the book's contents, including allegations of corruption, adultery, unnatural sex, complicity to murder and acting on behalf of foreign powers, had now become widespread.[118] With the Inspector-General of Police (IGP) Rahim Noor investigating Anwar and others 'implicated' in the text, notably Anwar's friend S. Nallakaruppin (Nalla),[119] a smear campaign at the higher level of the network was now apparent. At this point, it was unclear to what extent anti-Anwar elements had convinced Mahathir of the possible veracity of the allegations. Either way, Mahathir was now using it as a ready instrument for ruining Anwar.

With calculated timing, Mahathir made his move, beginning with Anwar's allies at the Bank Negara. On 28 August 1998, the Bank's governor and deputy, Ahmad Mohamed Don and Fong Weng Phak, resigned their posts, citing 'policy differences' over the impending currency measures. On 1 September, the Bank announced the immediate imposition of exchange controls, the adoption of a fixed exchange system for the ringgit (to be pegged at RM3.80 to the US dollar) and restrictions in Malaysian stock dealings on the KLSE. The following day, Anwar was dismissed from his duties as deputy prime minister, finance minister and executive director of the NEAC. He was formally expelled from the party early on 4 September after a late-night showdown meeting of the UMNO Supreme Council.

By initiating both Anwar's removal and the emergency currency measures, Mahathir had staked the political legitimacy of the bloc on saving the economy. While the IMF, foreign capital and other Western agencies condemned the abandonment of free-market reforms, Mahathir's case was that the country, by now already devastated, mainly by external forces, had nothing to lose – a claim given some credence by the immediate strengthening of the ringgit and welcoming signs from domestic business.[120]

Meanwhile, the UMNO and BN hierarchy closed ranks, defending Anwar's removal as a prerogative power of the prime minister and a necessary part of the recovery process.[121]

As protesters took to the streets, Anwar, calling for calm, went public, reaffirming his loyalty to Mahathir, his patriotism and his readiness to tackle the economic, political and social turmoil now facing the country:

> The time to launch a reformation has arrived ... The reformation is demanded from within, not due to external pressure ... Therefore let there not be groups who are accusing it of being an external conspiracy ... Don't be fooled and deceived by those who are afraid of the wave of reformation. They are void of ideas, repeatedly playing old songs ... I trust in the wisdom of the UMNO members.[122]

Even at this point, Anwar's criticism of Mahathir remained relatively tempered. Warning that the conspiracy to topple him would lead not only to his own arrest, but hundreds of others, Anwar claimed that Mahathir had become 'paranoid' and fearful of suspected challengers, increasingly so, he had noted, since the fall of Suharto.[123] But with the full extent of the purge and trial now confronting him, this language now gave way to a more detailed and ferocious denunciation of Mahathir and his acolytes.

As the trial got under way, Anwar's prison letter 'From the halls of power to the labyrinths of incarceration'[124] set out for the first time the 'inside story' of corruption, nepotism and abuse of power within the UMNO system. Mahathir, Anwar alleged, was now a 'despised dictator'. He, his family and his cronies had 'siphoned off billions'. He had turned politics into a 'sordid occupation and politicians into a bunch of immoral sycophants'. Struggling to conceal his 'revulsion' at the level of corruption (a restraint advised by friends seeking to protect his political career), Anwar had attempted to strengthen the ACA and pursue key players in the Perwaja scandal (such as corporate elites Eric Chia and V.K. Lingam), much to the discomfort of the attorney-general, Mohtar Abdullah. More critically, Anwar had informed Mahathir of reports that Daim had taken between RM700 million and RM1 billion out of the country and had attempted 'to abscond with RM800 million worth of UMNO shares'. Mahathir, Anwar alleged, had concealed his alarm at this news, as he had his annoyance over Anwar's attempts to limit Ting Pek Khing's compensation for the stalled Bakun project. Less hidden was his displeasure at the RM1.7 billion (rather than RM2.2 billion) eventually paid by Petronas for his son Mirzan's Konsortium – Anwar (and Petronas) having argued for settlement through an international shipping valuer. While Anwar 'promoted civil society' through the *Asian Renaissance* and other fora, Mahathir 'disparaged it', showing 'contempt for my relatively liberal ideas'. Anwar also defends his position within the IMF as part of an attempt to introduce transparency. In 'furious' response to Zahid Hamidi's corruption speech at the 1998 Assembly, Mahathir had used the privatisation list as a 'cheap trick' to discredit Anwar and his family, none of whom, Anwar insists, had been issued 'one share or awarded a single contract' in his six years as finance minister. Anwar also notes at this point the frequent visits of the IGP Rahim Noor to Mahathir's office, the targeting of Nalla and Anwar's adopted brother Sukma Darmawan and the close involvement of Daim in the whole affair. According to Anwar, the eventual showdown in Mahathir's office was deeply acrimonious. Anwar would not 'resign or be sacked with grave consequences'. Rejecting Mahathir's 'perverted understanding of Asian values', where a subordinate goes quietly in deference to his leader, Anwar vowed to follow 'the dictates of my conscience' and seek to expose the conspiracy, even though the unfolding events would be 'beyond my worst expectations'. Anwar goes on to talk about the manoeuvrings of Daim, his sycophants, such as 'side-kick' Ahmad Sebi (a businessman and former journalist), the latter's power over *New Straits Times* editor Kadir Jasin and the corruptibility of many High Court judges – although he tells the many morally upright judges to 'be patient'. He berates those in UMNO who betrayed him, such as Deputy Information Minister Tajol Rosli, who, at the UMNO Council meeting to dismiss Anwar, had re- marked: '"My philosophy in politics is, the boss is always right".' Finally, invoking the *reformasi* (see following chapters), Anwar thanks his loyal friends in UMNO and acknowledges the support of NGOs, Muslim scholars, low-income groups and others. The last word, though, is for Mahathir: 'Are the people expected to continue indefinitely to endure the ranting and raving of a senile, power-drunk tyrant?'

Before addressing these claims, let us consider, for the moment, Anwar's own role within UMNO. First, we have to ask precisely why Anwar had chosen to stay silent on the above during all his time in office. Even if he had decided to play the long-term game of securing control, could this excuse him from complicity in the inner affairs of the UMNO hierarchy? For years Anwar's refrain had been: 'There is no policy difference between myself and Mahathir'; 'I support the PM'; 'He is like a father.' Now the 'true picture' had been revealed, was it not pertinent to ask why Anwar had, effectively, misled the Malaysian public? For example, in relation to Mahathir's conflict with the Malay rulers, Anwar notes: 'Of course we supported him in the constitutional amendment issue, thinking rather naively that the powers taken from the Rulers would revert to the people and not go to him alone. How blind we were then not to see through his vile plan.'[125]

But was such support for Mahathir's centralisation of power mere naivety, as Anwar claims? Again, this brings us back to the culture of insiderism within UMNO. Certainly, Anwar had understood the necessity of playing by Mahathir's rules, even if, as noted, 'Anwar's boys' had shown an ultimate failure of judgement in these matters. During his tenure, Anwar had taken a relatively strong stance on social policy, for example in his promotion of low-cost housing. There were also genuine indications of an attempt to push a reform agenda from within. But this had made him neither an innocent bystander nor a champion of the poor. While Anwar did not enjoy the wealth and power of Daim and his corporate circle, neither did he lack cronies or seem averse to UMNO operating as a corporate entity.

On the other hand, Anwar had never been accepted into the political establishment. His previous radical Muslim/ABIM connections had not endeared him to many in the party. His imprisonment in support of such had placed him at a different 'moral level' from other party apparatchiks. For this and other reasons, Anwar's relations with Abdullah Badawi had never been easy, while Razaleigh saw Anwar as having usurped his position within UMNO. Najib, on the other hand, had been 'closer' to Anwar on policy matters and outlook. However, there was to be no show of sympathy as he too closed ranks behind Mahathir. Most of all, Anwar was feared by Daim.

In the aftermath of the Anwar purge, Mahathir had to decide on a deputy and, in effect, successor from among these main contenders. His initial tactic had been to leave the position open, declaring that the post would be determined by UMNO members at the June 1999 Assembly. Part of the reason for this was to allow Mahathir a free hand in dealing with the crisis. Another was a reluctance to be seen endorsing a favoured candidate (possibly, at this point, Najib) for fear of 'tainting' him with the crisis. Yet another was a more basic uncertainty over whom to trust. In particular, Mahathir feared giving it to someone who would strike a deal with Anwar or Anwarites within UMNO, thus endangering both his policy view and private interests. It is not without significance that Najib had himself started to appropriate some of the reformist themes in an attempt to court Anwar people within and beyond the party. In lieu of the 'Assembly poll', a special meeting of UMNO was convened in December 1998 to amend parts of the party's constitution in order to limit the pro-Anwar faction.[126] Following this, Mahathir was quoted as saying that he wanted his next deputy to be an 'exact replica of myself' (spawning a plethora of 'cloning' jokes among the opposition) with regard to policy direction: 'The main thing is that the policies are followed ... not so much the personalities.'[127] Again, this emphasis was indicative of the policy issues, rather than the personal nature of Mahathir's dismissal of Anwar. However, alongside growing concerns over Mahathir's health, there were gathering fears that such prevarication would be read as signs of fumbling and disunity within UMNO. Mahathir had managed to avoid an outright split. But deep down, the party had been riven by serious, if still contained, factionalism, particularly at the divisional levels.

In January 1999, Mahathir moved to ameliorate this situation by appointing Abdullah Badawi as his deputy. However, while this helped ease short-term speculation about a 'timetable' for the 'handover', it was, in reality, a cosmetic move; part of an unfolding PR initiative by the UMNO network. Thus, there was no certainty that 'Mr Clean', as he would come to be packaged (inadvertently casting a stain over the rest), would ever succeed Mahathir. In seeking to stem dissent, around four hundred known Anwar sympathisers had been expelled from UMNO by mid-1999.[128] However, this could not disguise the growing gulf with UMNO's 2.7 million members. Another worrying indicator for UMNO at this point was the by-election loss of the BN stronghold Arau seat (Perlis) to PAS.[129]

In response, clampdowns on DAP and PAS *ceramahs* and police harassment of civil gatherings were now increasing. The police had also disrupted a civil rights convention of concerned Malaysian lawyers, the 'Gathering of Legal Eagles', in May 1998.[130] Another such dinner gathering in Negri Sembilan was permitted to take place on condition that no speeches were made, prompting a media statement from Lim Kit Siang entitled: 'Is Mahathir's Vision 2020 nothing more than Vision 'Animal Farm' where the people can eat but cannot talk?'[131]

In a sharper reminder of the network's coercive capacities, the Court of Appeal increased DAP MP Lim Kit Siang's RM15,000 fine for 'criticising the judiciary' and 'spreading false news' to a three-year prison sentence (two 18-month sentences to run concurrently). Lim, the DAP leader's son, had been found guilty in April 1997 of offences under 8A(1) of the Printing Presses and Publications Act (1984) and Section 4(1)(b) of the Sedition Act (1948) following his criticism of the decision not to prosecute UMNO politician and former Malacca Chief Minister Rahim Tamby Chik on under-age sex and statutory rape charges. Lim, who had supported the girl in question, had been fined for publishing a critical pamphlet (*True Story Talk*) and for making a critical speech on the issue at a Malacca hotel in 1995. Under Article 48 of the Federal Constitution, Lim was also disqualified from office as an MP.[132]

While public concern was growing over these abuses of power, open dissent had been limited. However, the Anwar purge now provided the catalyst for a new 'moral politics'. In particular, a mood was emerging that Mahathir had transgressed Malay cultural sensitivities by seeking to shame and humiliate Anwar. As one key *Aliran* piece put it in early 1999:

When Anwar Ibrahim was dismissed on moral grounds, the party president (being too much of a moderniser) was out of touch with the existence of an ancient Malay social covenant: a ruler should never resort to the ploy of shaming a subject (*memberi áib*) ... Not once in the history of UMNO has any prominent dissident been so publicly humiliated ... and removed on moral grounds ... The removal of Anwar Ibrahim is the one single political event that has been responsible for unleashing the many facets of Malay resentment.[133]

Here, in effect, was one 'Asian value' that Mahathir could not invoke to legitimise his actions. In this sense, the crisis had created new political uncertainties.

Thus, the political bloc had been reshaped in significant ways by the time of the 1997 crisis. While the Razaleigh challenge had been contained, Anwar's ascendancy had seen a new power faction within UMNO competing for control of key political–corporate sites. Here, Mahathir had shown consummate skill in managing internal dissent, protecting his own position and holding the bloc together. While using the political process to divert attention *from* the economy in the early phase of the crisis, he had skilfully refocused attention *towards* it during the emergency phase in order to rationalise the Anwar purge. But while support *within* the political bloc had held, UMNO had been badly damaged as a party and at the national–popular level. Moreover, an 1987-style clampdown now appeared a less viable option given the severity of the crisis and the futility of that strategy in Indonesia. Thus, with a cross-ethnic middle class badly hurt and 'moral concern' building within the wider Malay community, UMNO was now seriously detached from its populist moorings. This takes us, more specifically, to the *ideological* dimension of the Vision project, the network's management of the crisis and the implications of the Anwar affair.

Notes

1. Gomez and Jomo (1997), pp. 16–17.
2. Forgacs (1988), p. 421.
3. Buci Glucksmann (1982), p. 120.
4. See Khoo Boo Teik (1995), pp. 183–6.
5. Means (1991), pp. 113–17.
6. 'The die is cast', *FEER*, 28 January 1993.
7. 'Tit for tat', *FEER*, 4 February 1993.
8. See Munro-Kua (1996), p. 120.
9. Ibid., p. 125.
10. *New Straits Times*, 26 August 1994.

11. 'Hearts and minds: new think tank seeks to modernise Islam', *FEER*, 20 May 1993.

12. Khoo Boo Teik (1995), p. 199. Mahathir wrote under the pseudonym C. H. E. Det from the late 1940s to the early 1950s. See pp. 81–8 for discussion of this output.

13. See 'Masterplans for villages to check urban migration', *New Straits Times*, 25 June 1996.

14. 'Training for all village panels to boost growth', *Star*, 1 January 1997.

15. 'Koh: provide feedback', *Star*, 29 March 1996.

16. My thanks to Encik Talib Bin Ahmad, assistant district officer of Penang Municipal Council (MPPP) for information on JKKKs. Any observations on their ideological functions belong, of course, to the present writer.

17. Guinness (1992), pp. 200–3.

18. Between 1970 and 1990, female employment in the manufacturing sector increased from 28.1% to 46.4%. Kling (1995), p. 63.

19. Ibid.

20. Ariffin (1995).

21. Kahn (1996), pp. 12–13.

22. In 1981, teachers accounted for 40% of UMNO delegates, falling to 32% by 1984; Khoo Kay Jin (1992), p. 68.

23. Khoo Boo Teik (1995), p. 106.

24. Ibid., p. 63.

25. Khoo Kay Jin (1992), pp. 47, 48.

26. Khoo Boo Teik (1995), p. 137

27. Khoo Kay Jin (1992), p. 64.

28. Munro-Kua (1996), p. 113.

29. Khoo Boo Teik (1995), pp. 280–2.

30. For a further discussion of 'authoritarian populism', see Hall and Jacques (1989).

31. Khoo Boo Teik (1995), p. 284

32. Munro-Kua (1996), p. 134.

33. Khoo Boo Teik (1995), pp. 278–9, 290.

34. Yousof (1991), p. 1.

35. Khoo Kay Jin (1992), p. 46.

36. Khoo Boo Teik (1995), p. 277.

37. Ibid., p. 293. Munro-Kua (1996), pp. 134, 139.

38. Gomez (1994), p. 64.

39. A process that began in April 1996 following Mahathir's first meeting with Razaleigh in seven years.

40. Munro-Kua (1996), p. 105.

41. For a comprehensive account of the MCA, see Heng Pek Koon (1988).

42. Cited in 'Unwritten rule': *FEER*, 17 March 1996.

43. See Ling Liong Sik (1995).

44. Khoo Boo Teik (1997a), pp. 51–3.

45. See Joceline Tan, 'MCA thought reform plan mired in controversy', *New Sunday Times*, 9 November 1997.

46. Joceline Tan, 'Chinese women heading for new heights in politics', *New Sunday Times*, 30 November 1997. For an account of the UMNO, MCA and MIC women's affiliates see V. H. Dancz (1982).

47. Khoo Boo Teik (1997b), p. 166.

48. Loh Kok Wah, cited *FEER*, 17 March 1996.

49. Kua Kia Soong (1992), p. 69.

50. Gomez (1994), p. 35.

51. Ibid.

52. My thanks here to Lee Kok Cheong, executive director (press secretary) of the PCCC. Any observations on the roles of the PCCC and MCCC belong to the present writer.

53. See, for example, details of 'Talk and dialog [*sic*] with the chief minister', noted in Penang Chinese Chamber of Commerce, *Annual Report, 1996*, p. 41.

54. PCCC, *Directors Handbook 1996–1997*.

55. Gomez (1994), p. 36.

56. Ibid., p. 37.

57. Disparagingly referred to in some political circles as 'semi-value'.

58. Crouch (1996), p. 49.

59. Taib Mahmud, Sarawak's chief minister, and a Melanau, has held this political base by accommodating the state's 29 separate ethnic communities.

60. See Crouch (1996), pp. 51–2.

61. For an incisive analysis of state–federal tensions in Sabah, Sarawak and Kelantan, see Chin (1997).

62. Ibid., pp. 106, 118, note 30.

63. Ibid., p. 112.

64. As a then lecturer at the University of Malaya, Syed Husin Ali's own detention followed on from his involvement in the Baling peasant protests in November 1974.

65. See Zafar Bangash, 'America's kiss of death and some crucial issues in the Islamic movement', *Harakah* (Internet edition), 7 December 1998. The author is director of the Institute for Contemporary Thought (ICIT), London. The article draws on correspondence between Professor Faruqi and Dr Mahathir, *Harakah*, 12 October 1998.

66. 'Tough talk': interview with Mahathir, *FEER*, 24 October 1996.

67. Zahid Hamida beat Rahim Tamby Chik for UMNO's Youth wing, and Siti Zaharah Sulaiman took the women's wing from Rafidah Aziz. 'Succession saga', *FEER*, 24 October 1996.

68. See 'Showing who's boss', *FEER*, 16 May 1996.

69. Zahid had become a significant figure through the backing of Anwar and Najib.

70. Gomez (1994), p. 12.

71. Mahathir comments in this regard: 'He sees me almost every morning if he is in the country. Even when I was in Harare, he sent me letters asking me about certain things, things which he couldn't decide for himself.' 'Tough talk': interview with Mahathir, *FEER*, 24 October 1996.

72. Gomez (1994), p. 56.

73. 'Read the signs', *FEER*, 18 June 1998.

74. 'Helping each other', *FEER*, 25 June 1998.

75. The structure of UMNO's corporate affairs are critically assessed by Gomez (1990).

76. Muzaffar, *Aliran* (compiled articles) (1988), pp. 186–8, 272–3.

77. See 'The way forward', *Aliran Monthly*, 1997, 17: 5.

78. 'On the spot', *FEER*, 24 April 1997.

79. Ibid. The amount involved 2.4 million ringgit in cash.

80. 'Selangor's broom', *FEER*, 15 May 1997.

81. The increased powers of this body derive from a new Parliamentary Act on corruption passed in 1997. Alongside a special section investigating corruption at the higher levels, each state in Malaysia has its own ACA. My thanks to an Officer from the Penang ACA for details on its role.

82. *Financial Times*, 3 July 1997.

83. *Utusan Malaysia*, 4 December 1997.

84. *Sun*, 4 December 1997.

85. *FEER*, 2 July 1998.

86. Southall (1997) notes here the respective problems faced by the African National Congress and UMNO in seeking to redress black inequalities and Bumiputera rights. Mahathir and Mandela carried out reciprocal state visits in 1997.

87. Burma, Laos and Cambodia were admitted at the 30th Anniversary meeting of ASEAN (May 1997) in Malaysia.

88. *Financial Times*, 2 July 1997.

89. 'Seeing red', *FEER*, 12 August 1996.

90. Cited in *The Australian*, 12 November 1994.

91. See Yahuda (1996), pp. 5, 13.

92. The analysis here draws upon media resources and discussions with academics, opposition party figures, NGO activists, media personnel and other sources. My thanks also to Mahyiddin bin Wan Wawang, secretary for research/information, UMNO HQ, Kuala Lumpur, Mr Azmi, head of Penang UMNO and staff at the Penang State Assembly for information conveyed.

93. Under the Iran–Libya Sanctions Act (1996), action may be taken against any company with total oil or gas assets of more than US$40 million in either country.

94. The remarks were made on 10 October 1997 at a Kuala Terengganu rally in support of Mahathir. *New Straits Times*, 11 October 1997.

95. 'I did not say it was a Jewish conspiracy. I said it was by coincidence that this person … is a Jew and that by coincidence we are Muslims.' Mahathir, cited in *New Straits Times*, 12 October 1997.

96. 'Mahathir reassures American citizens', *Sun*, 14 November 1997.

97. Note, for example, how a rally in support of Mahathir by Malaysia Pos (national post) employees (with a banner proclaiming 'Pos Malaysia supports our beloved Prime Minister') contrasted with the more threatening message of UMNO Youth ('Go to Hell America') during its protest outside the Kapitan Keling Mosque in Penang. *Utusan Malaysia*, 15 November 1997.

98. *Sun*, 18 November 1997. Despite assurances by William Ramsay of the US Energy Sanctions and Commodities department that any action could only be applied unilaterally by the USA, a Malaysian official insisted that Petronas would continue to extract gas in the South Pars Field in Iran. *Sun*, 21 November 1997.

99. *New Straits Times*, 19 November 1997.

100. 'Kit Siang calls for amendments', *Sun*, 20 November 1997.

101. The Speaker ruled that: 'As there are no MPs here who stated they opposed the motion, it is then unanimously passed.' Cited in 'The politics of the confidence motion', *Sunday*, 30 November 1997.

102. The by-election results were: Sungai Bakap (Penang), Lai Chew Hock (Gerakan-BN) 5,010, Goh Kheng Huat (DAP) 3,570, Abu Harith Ahmad (Ind) 1,758 – majority, 1,440 (1995 general election, 5,327); Changkat Jering (Perak), Mat Isa Ismail (UMNO–BN) 7,221, Idris Ahmad (PAS) 3,677— majority, 3,544 (1995 general election, 6,402). *New Sunday Times*, 9 November 1997.

103. See 'Independent's good showing is food for thought', *Sun*, 10 November 1997. Malays comprised 47.9% of the Sungai Bakap constituency.

104. See 'Blown away', *FEER*, 25 December 1997 and 1 January 1998.

105. See 'Double or nothing', *FEER*, 26 February 1998.

106. *Star*, 26 March 1998.

107. The Konfrontasi represented Indonesia's critical response to the formation of the Malaysian Federation in 1963, a development that the Sukarno leadership denounced as a neo-colonialist construction. See Yahuda (1996), pp. 70–1.

108. See '"Us" and "Them"', *FEER*, 12 February 1998.

109. See 'Consummate insider', *FEER*, 19 February 1998.

110. See 'Pull together', *FEER*, 15 January 1998.

111. *Star*, 26 February 1998.

112. Ibid.

113. See 'Calling Doctor Daim', *FEER*, 19 February 1998.

114. An announcement described by Lim Kit Siang as 'the greatest shocker in the past 14 months of the economic crisis'. DAP Homepage, 28 August 1998.

115. 'Easing the squeeze', *FEER*, 16 July 1998.

116. See, for example, 'Anwar: market forces betrayed our trust', *Star*, 25 August 1998.

117. Khalid Jafri was subsequently charged with 'spreading false news' over one of the allegations in the book that Anwar had fathered an illegitimate child.

118. With some understatement, Anwar noted: 'I believe it is a conspiracy to smear my image and topple me.' 'Press pressure' and 'Smear campaign', *FEER*, 30 July 1998.

119. This involved Anwar's businessman friend S. Nallakaruppan ('Nalla'), who had, allegedly, organised sexual encounters on Anwar's behalf and had been caught with a stockpile of illegal bullets at his house.

120. 'Ringgit pegged at RM3.80 to dollar', *Star*, 3 September 1998.

121. 'MBs back Mahathir action', ibid.

122. From Anwar's Text Statement, *Reuters*, 3 September 1998.

123. *BBC Online*, 4 September 1998.

124. Published, 3 November 1998, at *Anwar Online*: <http://members.xoom.com/anwar98/prometheus.htm>.

125. Ibid.

126. Mahathir secured a ruling that candidates for president and deputy president achieve, respectively, 30% and 20% thresholds for nomination, thus replacing the existing scheme of ten bonus points given to candidates nominated by any of UMNO's 165

divisions. The new arrangement, in effect, minimised the voting power of any pro-Anwar grouping. See *Asiaweek*, 4 December 1998.

127. *AFP*, 13 December 1998.

128. *AFP*, 6 July 1999.

129. PAS took the Arau seat on 4 July 1998 by 1,323 votes, overturning a 6,929 BN majority at the 1995 general election. *Utusan Malaysia*, 5 July 1998. This followed other by-election defeats for the BN to PAS at Bagan in 1995 and Teluk Intan in 1997.

130. Held at the Federal Hotel, Kuala Lumpur, 31 May 1998.

131. See DAP Homepage, 14 July 1998.

132. Lim Guan Eng's appeal was rejected on 24 August 1998, his two concurrent 18-month jail sentences beginning, thereafter, in Kajang jail.

133. Maznah Mohamad, 'Can UMNO survive?', *Aliran Monthly*, February 1999, 19: 1. See also 'The social contract', *Aliran Monthly*, May 1999, 19: 4, a reproduction of the ancient compact from *Sejarah Melayu*.

4

Organic Intellectuals: Ideological Production and the UMNO Network

We are living through a revolutionary period in the history of mass communications, with profound implications for the organisation of states and societies. As political and social identities become less uniform, the medium of communications becomes more crucial. The more fluid the reward system, the more vigilant the state must be in managing the evolving social outcomes. Social control and ideological persuasion are thus being fashioned through a new complex of information sites and emerging technologies. Combining these developments with the view that hegemony is an ongoing enterprise, the production and dissemination of information, entertainment and populist iconography has come to represent an increasingly vital element of class control and political legitimation.

Malaysia's 'passage to modernity' has created new social expectations, economic divisions and cultural uncertainties, complicated by the conflicting claims of Islam and consumer ideology. In response, Mahathir has sought to fashion hybrid forms of capitalist modernity, Islamic morality and ethnic collectivism. Such shifts invite consideration of the ways in which Vision discourse and other ideological production has helped sustain the bloc, notably through the mass media. This takes us, in the following chapter, to a closer analysis of the media during the Anwar affair.

Civil Society, Organicity and the UMNO Network

One of Gramsci's most prescient insights was his attempt to show the importance of cultural production as an evolving feature of capitalist society. Here, intellectuals play a central role in the construction of ideas, the very organisation of hegemony, across state and civil institutions. As a party apparatus, UMNO embodies this idea of organic integration between these spheres. The principal axis of the network is the UMNO/BN political alliance. But it extends outwards and beyond conventional party arrangements, with chains of influence ranging from corporate elites to the BN media, from party affiliates to Islamic fora, voluntary bodies and a panoply of NGOs.

This is not to suggest uniformity of thought or absence of discrete agendas. Rather, 'hegemonic networking' denotes fluidity, interaction and accommodation, wherein particular actors and institutions may have particular sectoral interests to protect or advance, but also hold to a 'shared outlook' on the maintenance of the broader power structure. Such bodies perform a commonly focused support role, helping to reproduce dominant interests and ideas through diverse processes of political, corporate and ideological exchange. At the same time, there is always room for the incorporation of new interest groups and alliances.

It is not difficult to see liberal objections to such a view. Here, the state is viewed, *a priori*, as a potentially pluralist realm distinct from civil society, with generic models of state authoritarianism used to explain how civil freedoms are curtailed. Understandably, liberal and left-leaning reformers in Malaysia are reluctant to move beyond this paradigm as they witness the deployment of the ISA and other repressive instruments. Yet, while recognising this apparatus, one can also see how coercion and consent have been blended as variable forms of authoritarian populism in the West, a form of state–civil control comprehensively utilised by Thatcherism.[1] Also crafted around populist discourse, 'Thatcherism was ... defined, to a large extent, not in specialist journals or elite forums but in newspaper columns and in well publicised reports and position papers; it represented a well thought-out (and effective) use of the media by intellectuals.'[2]

Alongside the more overt threat of coercive mechanisms in Malaysia, Mahathirism and the Vision project have also been built around intellectual populism and the need to win in civil society. In this sense, social control in Malaysia was becoming organised around a more nuanced mix of state coercion *and* civil persuasion by the mid-1990s, indicating the growing importance of civil society as a contested space.

Some recent findings on rising levels of civil consciousness in Malaysia would appear to corroborate this view. For example, the major national study *Caring Civil Society* found high rates of civil awareness across a wide range of social, political and cultural issues.[3] Noticeable here was the absence of any significant variation across the three sample states studied, Penang, Kedah and Kelantan. Measured against sampled questions to 5,000 respondents, a Civil Consciousness Index (CCI) showed high levels of civil awareness on four out of five main indices:

- *Ethnic tolerance* (attitudinal orientation toward other ethnic groups including affinity to accept differences and interaction with other ethnic groups) 69.7%

- *Political efficacy* (willingness to use formal–institutional as well as non-formal processes to affect political outcomes) 76.5%
- *Civil rights awareness* (concern for basic human rights as well as awareness of these rights) 45%
- *Public spiritedness* (willingness to contribute to the public good through various responsible public acts) 78.3%
- *Ecological awareness* (concern for the preservation of the natural environment and willingness to act to preserve or not to destroy the natural environment) 79.9%

The main exception here, the low level of civil rights awareness, indicates the still rather conservative nature of the Malaysian electorate and a certain ambivalence over political rights. Other responses reveal concerns over the erosion of social institutions and the spectre of overconsumption. While the family was upheld as the main provider of moral values, the overwhelming majority believed that the state should maintain a central role in ensuring public welfare such as education and the main health services. Likewise, with regard to the Vision, most felt the need to participate in issues of national development, having benefited from the process, although the limiting of individual rights was not seen as necessary to this.

Thus, if such indices suggest growing levels of civil awareness in Malaysia, the task of controlling the civil space is becoming more significant for the UMNO network. A key feature of that enterprise is the articulation of its ideas through the mass media.

Networks of Influence: The Media in Malaysia

The main aim here is to identify the ways in which news, information and cultural output in Malaysia are structured and presented, not only as overt state propaganda, but as a more subtle vector of civil values. Again, this invites assessment of how civil persuasion and coercive interventions are being used as variable tools to maintain the leading group's ideas. In this regard, Loh Kok Wah and Mustafa K. Anuar have noted three main instruments of press control in Malaysia (each broadly applicable to the electronic media): 'coercive legislations'; 'ownership and control of the major publications'; and the practice of 'responsible development journalism'.[4] Here, we are mainly concerned with the latter, as a conceptual indicator of Vision discourse. However, let us first note the significance of the other two elements as complementary to this process.

The foremost state mechanism of press control is the Printing Presses and Publications Act (1984). The main corresponding legislation for the electronic media is the Broadcasting Act (1988). With regard to the press, all publications are required to apply for an annual publishing permit, which can be revoked where the applicant has been deemed to have negated certain 'national interests'. This was the *Star*'s fate in 1987 during Operation Lalang. Since the return of its permit in March 1988, the *Star* has never regained its previous 'liberal flavour'. With similar intent, the home affairs minister ruled in 1991 that distribution of the respective DAP and PAS papers the *Rocket* and *Harakah* be limited to party members. Despite this, *Harakah* has been widely available on many news-stands, although, as we shall see, it was subject to more serious restrictions as the crisis developed.

At the same time, the proliferation of new media forms had created more sensitive problems over the control of public information and entertainment. Much of this stems from the deregulatory process and gathering corporatisation of the press and electronic media from the 1980s. Thus, while the Ministry of Information sought to promote competition by issuing more publishing permits for new daily newspapers such as *The Edge* (a business-based title 'reflecting the higher demographic profile of the "new Malay", who is increasingly urban, middle-class and professional'[5]) it also continued issuing cautious reminders. For example, the three Chinese-language papers *China Press*, *Sin Chew Jit Poh* and *Nanyang Siang Pau* all received warnings that their licences would be revoked if they published articles undermining government attempts to create a multiracial society.[6]

Under the Broadcasting Act, similar stringent conditions and powers apply. The 1988 Act, notes Zaharom Nain, was introduced:

> in anticipation of the further commercialisation of broadcasting, especially television. Indeed, in the midst of the supposed 'deregulation' of broadcasting [it] now gives the Minister of Information virtually total powers to determine who will, and who will not broadcast, and to determine the nature of the broadcast material ... On paper, this means one individual has the power to decide.[7]

Control of media output has also been used to contain the social consequences of economic development. In 1995, the information minister, Mohamed Rahmat, directed the Film Censorship Board to enforce a clampdown on sex, violence and consumer imagery on TV, afraid that, among other things, it would leave the government open to charges of moral relativism from PAS.[8] Other reactions, such as an anti-vice crackdown on the entertainment industry and early closing of fashionable Kuala Lumpur nightspots, reflect the added concern that the disproportionate share of such activity involves Malays rather than other ethnic groups.[9] Indeed, the emergent crisis had intensified these concerns. In the first three months of 1998, overall crime figures, most notably armed robbery and property-related crime, rose by 53%,[10] indicating a direct correlation between economic instability and social dislocation. In this regard, coercive media control has been used as a reactive strategy, allowing the state an expanded rationale for further censorship.

The second form of media consolidation has been through corporate ownership. The central point to be noted here is the tight concentration of media control in Malaysia, whether through state ownership, political patronage or trustee proxies. Comprising a complex web of interlocking companies, the bulk of media equity in Malaysia is controlled by a minority circle of UMNO, MCA and MIC holding companies alongside other business elites aligned to the Barisan. For example, through trustee companies tied to the UMNO investment arm Fleet Holdings and Renong Bhd, UMNO has control over the two main publishing groups, New Straits Times Press (NSTP) and Utusan Melayu.[11] In the field of electronic media, the state retains direct control over the two Radio Televisyen Malaysia (RTM) channels, TV1 and TV2. However, with the shift towards privatised delivery of public services from the 1980s, new commercial media franchises signalled a corporate bonanza for well-placed business clients. Beginning with the launch of TV3 in 1984, Sistem Televisyen Malaysia Bhd (STMB), another holding company closely linked to UMNO, was awarded the first commercial contract by the government. In 1994, the Utusan Group became part of a four-company consortium awarded the tender to operate the second new commercial TV station Metro Vision. Sistem Television also attained a majority 40% share of Mega TV, the country's first subscription channel launched in 1995, the other major shareholder being the Ministry of Finance with 30%.[12] In March 1998, another commercial station Natseven (NTV7) began broadcasting. Owned by Effendi Norwawi, vice-president of the PBBB, part of the BN coalition in Sarawak, it has sought to position itself as a main challenger to TV3, offering a more 'feelgood' and 'risk-taking' output.

The Utusan Group, one of the two major national newspaper publishers, also produces one of the leading Malay dailies, *Utusan Malaysia*. Its main competitor, the New Straits Times Group, latterly controlled by business executives linked to Anwar, publishes the country's two main English and Malay titles, the *New Straits Times* and *Berita Harian*.[13] The major controlling stake in Star Publications Sdn Bhd, publisher of the English daily *Star* is held by Huaren Holdings, an investment arm of the MCA.

The newest major English-speaking daily, the *Sun*, owned by Vincent Tan Chee Yioun, multi-millionaire head of the lucrative Berjaya Group, has positioned itself as a fresh contender, notably to the *Star*.[14] Tan's acquisition of Sports Toto in 1985, a key privatisation facilitated by Daim, was the main impetus for the rapid expansion of the Berjaya empire, Tan's wealth reflecting close relations with prominent UMNO elites.[15] However, 'quiet warnings' over content have been issued on occasion to the *Sun* by the Ministry of Information. In part, this reflected attempts to market the paper as a more innovative and 'critical' alternative to the other dailies (see below).

Media ownership and editorial influence had also become part of the political manoeuvring for control within UMNO – as key Anwar people within the Utusan Group and TV3 would soon discover to their cost. However, while these power games continued behind the scenes, mainstream press output continued, for the most part, to reflect the overall Barisan view rather than particular elements within UMNO. And yet, despite this compliance and failure to cover key issues,[17] a nominally more 'liberal' press had emerged by the mid-1990s. This was because proprietors and journalists now understood, more fully, the *boundaries* of critical output.

The third aspect of media control, invoking 'responsible development journalism', offers a helpful gateway here. The promotion of such, through a populist ideology of growth, has helped cast UMNO as beneficent provider, while concealing the contradictions and weaknesses of the development process itself. Thus the Malaysian media is constantly awash

TABLE 4.1 Selected Peninsular Malaysia (daily) newspaper circulation figures (1996–99)[16]

	July 96– June 97	July 97– June 98	July 98– Dec 98	Jan 99– June 99
Bahasa-language newspapers				
Utusan Malaysia	253,680	267,765	265,515	229,133
Berita Harian	272,615	249,756	245,445	208,559
Harian Metro	85,540	77,036	65,111	62,404
English-language newspapers				
New Straits Times	163,287	155,977	143,110	134,812
Star	206,832	220,493	231,573	239,789
Sun	77,328		82,247	82,705
Malay Mail	54,234	48,569	44,406	38,376
The Edge		11,862	12,092	12,280
Chinese-language newspapers				
Sin Chew Jit Poh	237,604	264,283		
Nanyang Siang Pau	184,279	175,339		
Guan Ming Daily	91,602	100,475		
China Press	171,636			

with photo opportunities, messages, slogans, soundbites, nationalist songs and jingles, editorials and corporate advertising all extolling the common challenge of onward industrial development. The messages are both overt and subliminal, whether it be Mahathir's almost daily appearances on the front page of the *New Straits Times*, *Star* or *Utusan Malaysia* opening another industrial plant, or the *Telefakta* information adverts (TV2) displaying (over catchy music) simplified statistics of improved industrial output. As noted below, responsible development journalism is also implicit in the content of TV news and current affairs output. Thus both media seek to limit critical analysis and adversarial commentary by utilising developmentalism as a routine context for the filtering of news.[18]

This agenda is particularly evident during general elections. Here, the mass media play a pivotal role in framing ideas and issues, camouflaging news, creating punchy political adverts, humanising coalition candidates, demonising others, and promoting a sense of 'naturalised' affinity between the Barisan and the electorate through images of ethnic harmony, nation-building and other Vision emotionalism.[19] During the 1995 general election, the media frequently misrepresented opposition messages, lampooned opposition leaders and alleged underhand dealings between DAP and PAS. *Utusan Malaysia*, the *New Straits Times* and the three main TV channels also refused, at this point, to cover the story of Razaleigh's victory in Hong Kong's High Court, clearing him of any blame over the RM1.5 billion loss incurred by Bumiputra Malaysia Finance in 1983.[20] The effectiveness of the UMNO media was also evident during Mahathir's bid to replace Kedah Chief Minister Osman Aroff with Sanusi Junid. Here, without openly supporting the PM, the media ran detrimental stories about Osman, criticised his leadership and speculated consistently on whether he would resign.[21]

A further variation of responsible journalism could be seen in the media's self-imposed news blackout during the Kampung Rawa mosque-temple disturbances in March 1998. This was followed by praising reports of Anwar's public arbitration between the contending parties.[22] Despite the understandable vigilance over alarmist coverage, the incident characterised the way in which UMNO/BN seek to monopolise the moral high ground on ethnic relations. Here, for instance, Mahathir had 'appealed' to DAP and PAS not to make political capital from the incident, a statement carrying an overtone of moral authority and an undertone of suggested distrust, provoking Lim Kit Siang, in defence-like manner, to restate his own commitment to ethnic harmony.[23]

This message is also evident in the coverage of the annual Merdeka Day. Here, the Barisan become synonymous with the 'hegemonic triangle' of moral harmony, economic achievement and political benevolence, a blended imagery captured at the height of Mahathirism in the *New Straits Times* 1994 National Day Special. The thematic headline 'Towards a Caring Society' is proclaimed along the page top. Below this is an attractively designed feature on the Malaysian car industry, with the upbeat heading: 'Proton car best symbol of growth.' Completing the page is the ebullient figure of Anwar pictured at the controls of a tractor and a detailed article announcing his plans for a major low-cost housing package. Other pages contain a similar array of pictures, graphics and features projecting messages of social cohesion, technological advancement and caring government. Such ideals are also reflected in the full-page corporate adverts, such as Telekom Malaysia's Merdeka Day message: 'As We Race To The Vision, Let's Not Leave Our Values Behind'.[24] Thus, both here and beyond the coverage of popular events, the 'national' becomes merged into the political. As Kua notes: 'the most serious aspect of the press is its failure to point out the clear line between the "interests of the nation" and the interests of the government'.[25]

The anodyne nature of mainstream media content can also be seen in the process of film and television production. Here, Nain notes how 'the media as a whole in Malaysia dulls the senses of the audience, virtually never inviting us to question the status quo'. Noting the profusion of locally produced films and TV series which 'unashamedly aim at legitimating the existence of the state apparatus', and the reluctance to offer critical reviews of such output, the source of the malaise, he argues, lies in a passive acceptance of the social order. The problem expresses itself at the levels of cultural production *and* intellectual enquiry, creating an insularity of thought and a lack of stimuli to think the unconventional:

> the activity of film making ... cannot divorce [itself] from the prevailing political, economic and cultural circumstances. Ours is an extraordinarily 'sensitive' society – or at least has been made to become that way by powerful social and political forces. It is a society where even a tender kissing scene between two consenting adults in a movie is deemed sufficient to corrupt us ... What we need to understand is that religion – in its narrowest sense – has become firmly entangled with our political and cultural circumstances ... [Thus,] we risk creating ... 'a society emotionally lobotomised by the loss of its freedom to dream and fantasise on the dark, as well as the light, side of the imagination.'[26]

But the Malaysian media was also being conditioned by the 'Murdoch effect' in the 1990s,[27] with corporatisation and privatisation of the press and TV denoting new accommodations to transnational interests. Thus:

> what may ... initially have been a convenient and, perhaps, necessary

compromise in terms of programming is becoming an unholy alliance between transnational media companies and the local media elites. In their seemingly relentless quest to get as much revenue as possible from television, the policy makers, consciously or otherwise, have aligned themselves with the transnational actors, leading Malaysian television even further into the international marketplace, not so much as a producer but as an insatiable consumer.[28]

Despite Mahathir's own warning that the profit motive was undermining the responsibility of local television stations to produce varied programmes, Malaysian television has continued to offer a diet of cheap imported soaps, movies and sport, with locally produced sit-coms, drama and current affairs formats appearing as essentially 'sub-standard copies of mainly western genres'.[29]

Of course, it would be facile to suggest that all such media representations are accepted uncritically by Malaysians. Beneath the veneer of conformity, there is an underlying capacity for critical reflection, iconoclastic humour and political repartee.[30] Yet this is still confined mainly to alternative publishing forms and quietly tolerated urbane satire. For example, favoured within the convivial circle of Kuala Lumpur's smart set, the comedy group Instant Café Theatre have engaged in a somewhat *risqué* routine of underhand social commentary and political parody. Though tame by Western standards, their jabs at UMNO authority and the party elite have touched sensitive political nerves. However, it is still a contained middle-class outlet, rarely subversive or capable of mainstream dissent. Indeed, having amused Mahathir and Anwar, the group became *de rigeur* at the big fashionable dinner parties of top corporate elites like Ananda Krishnan.[31]

Middle-class perceptions of 'press freedom' and political dissent have, likewise, been qualified by this internalised view of authority, a view acknowledged and rationalised by the writer Rehman Rashid:

> It's not done in Malaysia, it's not your fundamental right to stand up [as in] Hyde Park corner or London [*sic*] and say your piece. We don't have that here. So ... dissent is not encouraged in this country ... it's neither encouraged or discouraged. If you've got something to say, you can say it, but you have to think it through and you have to be prepared to be argued down very sternly, even maybe not argued down, maybe taken away and told to shut up. You know. But that's the price. And, God bless us, Malaysians have not been cowed to the point of total silence.[32]

This careful middle-class consciousness permeates Malaysian society. In turn, it has allowed the political elite, notably in times of economic boom, to adopt a relatively relaxed attitude towards 'middle-class expression', even the occasional lampooning of government policy. As such, one of the more significant features of changing press styles in Malaysia has been a growing propensity towards would-be middle-class issues, consumer concerns, identity and lifestyle. The *New Straits Times* can be seen as something of a forerunner in this respect with its major revamp and introduction of a new *Lifestyle* – now *Life and Times* – section in 1991. This was followed by similar stylistic changes at the *Star, Utusan Malaysia, Berita Harian* (sister paper to the *New Straits Times*) and the main Chinese-language dailies *Sin Chew* and *Nanyang*. What energised all the mainstream press here was the realisation of how economic expansion had created vibrant new middle- and service-class sectors, with new stimuli for consumer-style features, 'middle-class social formats' and, of course, increased advertising revenue.

Few of these 'bourgeois concerns' have any immediate resonance in the poor rural *kampongs* or the impoverished working-class housing sprawls of Kuala Lumpur, Penang and Johor. Yet 'middle-classness' in Malaysia has become not only a social identifier of the middle classes, but a cultural reference point for an aspirational working class. Here, a new blend of middle-class media discourse has emerged, acting, simultaneously, as a cultural filter and as an arbiter of social values.

At the first of these levels, stylised representations of upward mobility and consumer gratification are being projected as new forms of 'cross-class' consumer culture. Among the profusion of new retail sites in Malaysia, the fast-expanding Looking Good chain of grand shopping malls illustrates this semiotic synthesis of 'new individualism' and 'Vision prosperity' – although, with some concession to postmodern irony, things were looking not so good for Looking Good, the consumer or the Vision as the economic crisis unfolded. Nevertheless, the 'crisis of consumption' has not seriously weakened middle-classness as an influence over the wider cultural *milieu*.

At the second level, new media discourse has also come to reflect a more specific middle-class *social* agenda. Indeed, middle-class response to the economic crisis has involved a relatively serious 're-examination' of middle-class consumerist values. *Life and Times*-type features, in this sense, encourage a certain form of 'responsible' civil dialogue. Criticism is permitted. But only in the sense that it forms part of a collective, problem-solving agenda, akin to the received values of responsible journalism. Moral panic and economic fears prevail as classic symptoms of middle-class insecurity. But the crisis has also given rise to a relatively more informed type of middle-class sociological debate within the mainstream press and other media,[33] encouraging intellectual analysis and observation to be expressed *from the inside*. Here, Malaysian editors and proprietors appear increasingly receptive to this type of internalised exchange among academics, policy intellectuals and others, thus allowing 'social problems' and 'government problems' to be expressed and 'debated' as generalised 'us' problems.[34]

More challenging forms of the discourse can sometimes be allowed. For example, in the *New Straits Times* Perforated Sheets article 'The return of the Vision Squad', Amir Muhammad, in whimsical fashion, takes Mahathir to task for the questionable reality of his much-vaunted Vision adjectives: 'psychologically liberated, secure, self confident, mature, democratic, scientific, liberal and tolerant'.[35] In this instance, the author feigns his right to critical comment by citing Mahathir's apparent defence of social critics (as necessary to national progress) made in the foreword to a book by his daughter Marina. Prompted by the gagging order restricting Malaysian academics from talking to the media about the haze crisis, the piece goes on, in mildly subversive tones, to cast doubt on the actual scope for social criticism, the 'democratic' purpose of the ISA and the government's commitments to civil freedom. The Perforated Sheets column was, ultimately, thought too underhand, with Amir moving into online journalism.

The tenor of middle-class media discourse is thus guided by a 'permitted' subtext of 'reasoned liberalism', 'shared dialogue' and the need to solve social anomalies together *on our way to the Vision*. Here, Marina Mahathir has been projected as a role model of liberal Vision-speak, combining 'reasoned' criticism with a public media profile on social issues such as AIDS.[36] The Anwar crisis would, of course, be the real test of Marina's liberalism. However, in her fortnightly *Star* column and elsewhere, the seriousness of the reform movement is played down, while her criticism of the foreign media becomes an extension of Mahathir's own 'us–them' dichotomy and an encoded apology for the system.[37]

Of course, this is not to claim that there is always outright endorsement of such media messages at the popular level. As one past content analysis of the *Star* notes, the press have come to convey a particular view of social reality where:

> the *Barisan* is moderate while the opposition is extremist; the *Barisan* can guarantee harmony between ethnic groups while an opposition government would unleash the forces of ethnic conflict ... Implicit [here] is the power of the *Barisan* as natural and wise as the power of a parent. This vision is rendered so often in the mainstream papers that its very redundancy seems to lessen its persuasiveness.[38]

However, the potency of such discourse should not be underestimated, particularly where it involves prolonged articulations of 'the other'. This is one of the main insights captured by Kershaw in analysing the Malaysian media's coverage of the Pergau Dam affair. Not only are the media themselves already primed for anti-Western propaganda, so too is there a certain 'readiness' amongst intellectuals, part of which becomes distilled through the media at the populist level:

> The opportunity to take advantage of a certain 'them/us' perception of the structure or the modern world is inherent not only in the presence of a media equal to the task, but also in the evolving cognitions of a Malaysian minor elite and the people generally. Eye-catching theorising of the Huntington kind quickly finds its way, in summary, to the more literate groups through international news agency features printed in the Malaysian press. This creates a certain expectancy of international conflict, especially among Muslim intelligentsia. Moreover, it is possible to assert after prolonged acquaintance with 'ordinary Malaysians' that when an anti-Western media campaign does take place, it fosters a popular receptiveness towards such actions – indeed an expectation of more of them as confirmation of Malaysia's 'international credibility' on the very terms defined by Mahathir himself.[39]

Thus, in Kershaw's view, Malaysians do absorb, through the filter of 'them/us' media projections, a certain sense of 'national identification' with the Barisan. Indeed, this latter view is much closer to the present writer's own evaluation of how 'ordinary Malaysians' had come to interpret the message of Vision development. These and other perceptions of the social order may also be informed by resignation, apathy or cynicism. Yet similar feelings prevail in the West.

However, the crisis had also now prompted a more serious examination of the media's role, creating new pressures for proprietors and the political class. Thus, while key elites within the UMNO network have secured the power and resources to control the media and influence output, it is still important to view this as a *contested* space. That is, one in which political–corporate power is concentrated, but where intellectual enterprise is always required to confront economic crises, political pressure and social disaffection.

Hegemony is thus a managed affair. Legitimacy does not depend upon consistent adherence to a particular ruling party or open endorsement of partisan media representations. Rather it is about persuading people, more generally, of the 'moral authority' of the prevailing *system* – a more flexible mode of control, which allows, and, indeed, encourages, the view that dissatisfaction can be expressed, so long as it can be contained within acceptable boundaries of 'democratic participation'. Thus, the key point is to keep critical journalism within a peripheral, manageable space. What matters, in particular, is effective control over *mainstream* media content. Here, intellectuals help fill designated spaces for problem-solving, social observation and 'soft dissent' through agenda-setting discourse. This does not mean uniformity of thought. Rather, it is part of a more subtle appeal to 'insider reason'; a more refined process of co-optive persuasion where policy-planners and media critics are encouraged to internalise the *terms of debate* and argue within acceptable parameters. This suggests a more expansive form of social, political and cultural assimilation, wherein people come to regard the existing order as somehow 'natural'. Thus, while salient, the Boulanger view is too narrowly focused on the 'media-as-messenger' rather than the ways in which the media, alongside other system-reinforcing agencies, help mould perceptions of social reality in the longer-term. At the same time, it understates the more nuanced forms of popular ideology emerging within the Malaysian mass media, in particular, that of 'role-model' middle-class discourse and Vision-type problem-solving. The Malaysian media is, indeed, biased towards the Barisan. But it is important to see the more complex forms of consensus-building within that process.

Vision Discourse and National Culture

To contextualise this shift, it is helpful to note the gradual re-emphasis in 'cultural policy' by the late 1990s. Under the NEP, the control of social debate through the media had encouraged not only political quiescence, but a more profound sense of intellectual conformity. This frustration of critical expression can be identified with the 1971 National Cultural Policy (NCP). Framed by a select group of Malay policy intellectuals, it went beyond the ideals of the Rukunegara to embrace an assimilationist view of culture, education and vernacular language. Resisted in particular by the Chinese community, the NCP held to three main principles:

1. The National Culture must be based on the indigenous culture of the region.
2. Suitable elements from other cultures can be accepted as part of the NCP.
3. Islam is an important component of the National Culture.[40]

In seeking to 'fix' culture to nascent Bumiputeraism and the NEP, the NCP was at odds with the complex aesthetics of custom, religion and belief in Malaysia, a diversity evident in the festival ambience of Hari Raya, Deepavali and Chinese New Year, the ceremonial of Mak Yong dance, Thaipusam and Hungry Ghost, the mystique of *bomoh* ritual, *kavadi* devotees and *datuk kong* spirits. While still recognising the right to cultural expression, and the social significance of daily mosque and temple activity, the NCP represented an artificial attempt to synchronise and incorporate these disparate energies, rather than acknowledge their rich interaction.

Mahathir had also been a key exponent of such cultural ordering. As part of his attack on archaic institutions, he sought to define the symbols of the present by invoking constructed images of the past. Following themes in *The Invention of Tradition*,[41] Kessler shows how this mystification of convention helps reinforce legitimacy, noting how traditional political culture has been blended into a modern context in the Malaysian case.[42] Symptomatic of this 'need of a serviceable past' was Mahathir's commissioning of the party anthem *Lagu Setia* ('The Loyalty Song') in an attempt to turn Bumiputera loyalty from one of archaic deference for the traditional order to one of modern loyalty for UMNO. The song 're-imagined and reinvented loyalty as something modern, subtle, low key ... [Capturing the] quintessence of traditional Malay legitimacy ... [it] modernised the traditional and archaised the modern'.[43]

Again, though, cultural meaning is complex here. The cachet of Malay tradition, from consumer products to theme park culture, remains a general feature of middle-class lifestyle.[44] Yet, as Tan Sooi Beng notes, government endeavours to influence this cultural field by the late 1980s – notably its attempts 'to centralise and control the performing arts' – were being met with increasing 'resistance' from a more independently minded middle class.[45] Thus, for Loh and Kahn, middle-class 'cultural visions' were becoming both 'particularistic' *and* 'fragmented', suggesting a more equivocal view of culture and the modernity process.[46]

Nevertheless, the NCP had allowed given 'cultural priorities' to become 'defined' and naturalised within the society through civil organisations, educational bodies and the prism of the mass media. Throughout the 1970s, the Malaysian state sponsored an ethno-cultural ideology which viewed any criticism of the NEP, Bumiputeraism and 'cultural assimilation' as somehow deviant. State controls and censorship were invoked to protect the special status of Malay rights and cultural expression, an agenda 'inherited' by Mahathir to cultivate Malay support. However, alongside the NEP, the idea of cultural uniformity remained inimical to a non-Malay community denied the same social and economic opportunities as Malays. Not only was this a source of ongoing ethnic resentment, it was also a growing obstruction to the modernity project. By the period of the NEP–NDP transition in 1991, the validity of Bumiputeraism and its cultural accoutrements were becoming increasingly tested. Thus, Mahathir needed a more consensual ideology to complement the post-NEP agenda.

Vision 2020: The New Context of Communication

From the early 1980s, the ideals of Malay economic development had become statements of political nationalism, with Mahathir's own charismatic leadership and unifying image providing the focal point for a rising mood of national euphoria.[47] Khoo notes in this regard that, unlike his predecessors, Mahathir has always presented himself as a 'plebeian leader', rather than a 'patrician ruler', building support around 'his total identification with the Malay masses'.[48] However, the traditions, customs and conventions of 'the nation' – or 'imagined communities'[49] – do not evolve in isolation from other cultural influences. By the early 1990s, Mahathir was beginning to promote a less exclusive type of communal ideology from that of the NEP. In contrast to the Malay Dilemma and its attempt to reassert an imagined Malay community, the Vision invoked a more inclusive concept of community, allowing greater cultural diversity in the process.

But this more expansive view of community was also consistent with the new realities of globalisation. Bumiputeraism was becoming an anachronism in a country experiencing not only major social adjustment, but exposure to the dynamic forces of global capital and information technology. In turn, these forces required new intellectual responses from within. For Mahathir, the Vision offered a new millennial context within which to address and manage these changes: a new type of nationalist project for a new international age.

The crystallisation of Vision ideology was coincident with the gathering deregulation of the media and the arrival of satellite technology by the early 1990s. Their emergence promised not only enhanced growth, but a vast source of wealth for corporate elites close to UMNO. In appealing for sensible censorship and controls, Mahathir saw that advanced technology was outpacing policies and laws to control global communications. But rather than resist these new technologies, Mahathir, recognising their inevitable momentum, 'embraced' the media revolution, seeking to promote it as an intrinsic part of the Vision project. Reflecting the pre-crisis prosperity, there were also indications of a more relaxed approach towards media output. But 'more open' media still came with a reminder that broadcasters had to 'act responsibly'. State sanctions remained. Yet Mahathir was also seeking to present these changes as part of a new consensual process, a maturing form of 'balanced' democratic expression and cooperation within the context of Vision collectivism.

As the government considered the potentialities of the new privatised channels and subscription networks,[50] there was a growing realisation of the need to control the allocation of licences. Mahathir was also anxious at this point to resist the encroaching influence of the Murdoch network, by now establishing itself in the region through pragmatic overtures to Singapore and Beijing.[51] In response, Mahathir had overseen the launching of the Malaysia East Asian Satellite (MEASAT), Malaysia's first satellite system, which, by 1996, was offering multi-channel TV and radio services to Malaysia and other countries in the region.[52] With the additional private stations (TV3 and Metrovision) competing with TV1 and TV2, the government had also come to realise the massive market in airtime advertising space.[53]

Vision 2020 had also become identified, symbiotically, with the opportunities and ideologies of multimedia technology. By the late 1990s, the new media technologies were being closely linked to the integrative possibilities of 'cyber-vision' services such as teleconferencing.[54] However, in seeking to take advantage of these sites as generators of growth, Mahathir needed new media populist ideology to give it meaning.

'Oh IT ... Guna IT'

On the evening of Saturday 11 October 1997, the prime minister informed the nation that the integration and use of information technology (IT) was the most urgent task facing all Malaysians. For two and a half hours, all the main TV stations in Malaysia were given over to Mahathir's Live Telecast speech and forum on the challenge of IT for the Malaysian economy and society at large. Although it was a platform for the Barisan, the tone of the broadcast was seminarial and 'consultative', the technical content wide-ranging for mass audience television. In essence, argued Mahathir, the widespread expansion of IT would be critical to the realisation of future economic development, national integration and enhanced prosperity for all sections of Malaysian society.

Launched by Mahathir during the Infotech Malaysia '96 Conference, the National IT Agenda (NITA) calls on all sectors of the economy to work in an integrated effort towards technological innovation and ideas that will transform Malaysia into a global IT hub and information-rich society. Under the aegis of the National Information Technology Council (NITC), set up in 1993, it envisions the development of a National Information Infrastructure (NII). Broadly speaking, this foresees rapid advancements in the fields of national telecommunications, computer networks, hardware systems, software services and database holdings, alongside new human resource training, educational packages and management applications – all helping to generate the technical skills and labour pool needed for such infrastructure.

At the centre of this Vision-based construct lies Mahathir's most grandiose development, the Multimedia Super Corridor (MSC). Despite the crisis and cancellation of other mega-projects, Mahathir had managed to maintain the MSC, claiming that it would lift Malaysia beyond the conventional stage of industrial development into a new landscape of 'intelligent administration', electronic government and global production webs.[55] Stretching south from the existing business heartland of Kuala Lumpur City Centre through a 50 by 15 kilometre corridor to the new KL International Airport, the project involves the ongoing construction of Putrajaya, the new seat of electronic government, and Cyberjaya, an adjoining Smart City comprising multimedia industries, R&D facilities and other advanced infrastructure.[56] As the first part of a three-phased plan set out by the Multimedia Development Corporation (MDC) over 20 years, the aim of the MSC is to offer multinationals a suitable cyber locale within which to expand their technological capacities, investment potential and broader global interests. By 1997, Mahathir had assembled, under his chairmanship, an MSC International Advisory Panel comprising 44 of the world's multimedia corporate luminaries, most notably Bill Gates of Microsoft.[57] By late 1998, the Anwar affair and Mahathir's restrictions on foreign capital had created major uncertainties over the project's viability. Yet, with the formal opening of Cyberjaya by July 1999, the first phase of the MSC would be an enduring testament to Mahathir. In marking its completion and relocation of the Prime Minister's Office to Putrajaya, Mahathir was still extolling IT-led growth as the motor of middle-class prosperity.

Beyond its 'testimonial' status, the MSC suggests an ambitious attempt to circumvent conventional industrial development through the 'spin-off' benefits of information-led investment, as proclaimed in the new 'Vision-speak':

> Malaysia has embarked on an ambitious plan to leapfrog into the Information Age by providing intellectual and strategic leadership ... As a first step, Malaysia has created the Multimedia Super Corridor – a world-first, world-class act – to help companies of the world test the limits of technology and prepare themselves for the future. The MSC will also accelerate Malaysia's entry into the Information Age, and through it, help actualise Vision 2020.[58]

Through its delivery of special business and lifestyle features, the MSC will be:

> A Multimedia Utopia offering a productive, intelligent environment within which a multimedia value chain of goods and services will be produced and delivered across the globe.

> An island of excellence with multimedia-specific capabilities, technologies, infrastructure, legislation, policies and systems for competitive advantage.

A test bed for invention, research and other groundbreaking multimedia developments spearheaded by seven multimedia applications.

A global community living on the leading-edge of the Information Society.

A world of Smart Homes, Smart Cities, Smart Schools, Smart Cards and Smart Partnerships.[59]

'Smart Partnerships' can be seen as a key term in the lexicon of Vision-speak, informing middle-class media discourse and MSC marketing language alike. In a message applicable to both, Mahathir's basic claim is that 'in enriching the other, you enrich yourself'.[60] The term had also been adapted as an axiom of economic development for the South. Thus, as argued by Mahathir at the First Southern Africa International Dialogue in May 1997, Smart Partnership – between the civil service, private sector, political leaders and trade unions – had given Malaysia consistent growth rates and an alternative development strategy.[61] Later that month, at a London gathering of European IT business figures, Mahathir offered similar partnership promises in the Ten Point Multimedia Bill of Guar-antees to prospective MSC companies, including free capital movement, full company ownership, tax incentives, intellectual property rights, no internet censorship, competitive telecom tariffs, prioritised MSC contracts and a 'high-powered' coordinating agency.[62]

This, of course, suggests a number of critical questions. For example, why would cutting-edge IT corporations such as Microsoft centre their key operations and R&D installations in Malaysia? Certainly, transnationals, by their very nature, are no longer confined to a 'home base'. Indeed, Bill Gates has been a keen advocate of global IT networks, exemplified by Microsoft's rapid expansion into India, with its abundant reserves of trained software professionals. In contrast, Malaysia has an acute shortage of trained IT personnel.[63] So why should IT transnationals see Malaysia as anything more than an information version of branch-assembly pro-duction – a low-labour-cost 'cyber-service sector'? By early 2000, a steady number of companies had signed up for MSC status, but these were still mainly small-scale outfits. Thus, the special MSC provisions indicate an ongoing struggle to secure a niche role within an increasingly crowded sector of the 'new economy'.

In pushing DAP's *IT for All* agenda, Lim Kit Siang has also criticised the government's specific promotion of the MSC as the jewel of its National IT Plan as a 'project-centred' rather than 'people-centred' strat-egy.[64] However, it is not only the 'value' of technological innovation, or its economic potential, that is significant here, but the way in which IT has come to be used as a new dimensional means of production and ideological resource. Missing from Lim's analysis is any critique of who controls such capabilities, how their diffusion empowers capital, and to what extent this constrains, rather than enhances, social development. Here, 'IT discourse', serving private-sector ideas, has been reproduced for *agenda-setting* purposes, providing the MSC and National IT Agenda with a synonymous identity. In this regard, the NITA offers an ideological rationale for the MSC, allowing the government to promote its populist elements while the private sector and UMNO proxies derive the key benefits.

Nevertheless, DAP's alternative *IT For All* has demonstrated an impressive grasp of potential IT applications, their extended use within education, commerce and government, problems of computer illiteracy within the Dewan Rakyat and the technical issues underlying the new 'cyberbills', such as the Computer Crimes Bill and the Digital Signature Bill. Reflecting criticism that none of the country's first cyberbills by 1997 was allowed proper legislative debate or public scrutiny, the DAP posted all four on their homepage.[65] Thus, while the government has idealised information technology, it remains highly circumspect about its actual use as an instrument for debating information technology itself.

In effect, awareness *of* IT has been promoted more vigorously than IT awareness. At the heart of this agenda has been a massive media campaign to 'inform' the public *about* IT and its imperative place within Vision development. The Ministry of Information's IT Awareness Campaign has mass produced leaflets and other literature explaining the objectives of the NITA and IT programmes. Linking IT development with social development, it also proclaims: 'The objective of NITA is to build a continuous learning culture on IT to enhance the quality of work of individuals, performance of organisations and quality of life towards the creation of a Civil Society.'[66]

The campaign has also seen the proliferation of stylish TV adverts extolling IT and the MSC. The frequent airing and close juxtaposition of these adverts is intended to distil their commonality in the public mind. Thus, invoking themes of cross-ethnic harmony and Bangsa Malaysia, a group of smiling Malaysians give happy-voice to the nation's catchy sing-along: 'Kenal IT ... Suka IT ... Pelajari setiam hari ... IT terkini ... Oh IT ... Guna IT ... Tingkafkan ilmu IT ... Malaysia bistari ... Terima IT ... Belejar IT ... Sayang IT ... Guna IT ... IT.'[67] In more dynamic mood, another fast-moving collage of high-tech graphics and multimedia images conveys the IT message and its part in Malaysia's master development plan, with key features of the MSC flashing across interchanging images of computer technologies, KL tower blocks, and young 'on-line' Malaysians:

> With the realisation of Vision 2020, the Multimedia Super Corridor was born ... In the era of the information age, multimedia will be used in every

aspect of our everyday lives. With IT comes development to take us into the next millennium. Now we can stand tall with the rest of the world. Tomorrow's Technology for Today's Living.

In a subsequent advert, a beautifully crafted landscape of swirling colours and alluring music draws the viewer into the exotic world of Putrajaya, the residential hub of the MSC, a new experiment in living and 'virtual' home for the new generation of environmentally friendly, IT-aware middle classes.

As with most clever adverts, the impact is subliminal, intended to naturalise an image, an impression, an association, a sense of what Malaysia and Malaysians might aspire to. A plethora of other upbeat glossy ads enticing Malaysians into a consumerist dreamworld of smart homes, Mastercards, mobile phones, Sega City virtual reality theme parks and 'happy banking' deliver a message of onward development where the national and the personal become merged into one idealised vision of 'social mobility'. Yet with real economic prospects declining by the day, the relevance of this and all other mass-media output was becoming increasingly tested.

Managing the Crisis: The UMNO Network and Media Coverage

At the onset of the crisis, it was apparent that the language and terms employed by the press and electronic media to describe the unfolding events were being carefully controlled. Initially, the term 'crisis' itself had been routinely avoided, and reference was made, instead, to 'the situation'. However, the selective use of language was not the only means of managing popular consciousness. People still recognised the situation as a crisis. More important was the attempt to contextualise it: that is, to make the crisis a 'collective problem', a shared situation of national adversity. Yet, while the broad media adopted this agenda on behalf of the Barisan, there was also some significant variations within mainstream newspaper output. Thus, while the following is concerned to show the compliant role played by the media, it also seeks to highlight some of the more nuanced interpretations, meanings and underlying tensions within that reportage.[68]

TV News and Current Affairs

Of all the main news media outlets in Malaysia, mainstream TV news can be seen as the most heavily sanitised. Its general purpose during the crisis appears to have been one of 'normalising' the situation by providing a 'calm exterior' in a situation of gathering uncertainty. Four main elements of TV news output were discernible here:

- to project positive headline images of Dr Mahathir and other Barisan figures;
- to condense, simplify and talk-up government measures for dealing with the crisis;
- to provide a rationale for the falling value of the ringgit and the KLSE – mainly by citing regional or global factors affecting the Malaysian markets; and
- to provide populist report slots and upbeat features on the crisis.

Of course, the content and presentation of TV news output at this point was part of an already well-established format. Neither are there any substantive differences in content or style between the main English news (TV3 *News Hour, News on 2* and TV2 *News Scan*) and vernacular news (*Berita Perdana*, on TV1 and Metrovision, TV3's *Buletin Utama* and *Berita Mandarin* on TV2), each projecting positive impressions of the Barisan. The key subtext of TV news generally, though, masking any overt propagandist purpose, lay in the careful pronunciation of news as 'public service information', thus providing a means of 'receiving' the crisis and rationalising the emerging social situation. This was integral to the way in which news items were prioritised, structured and delivered, as the following selections illustrate:

* TV3 News Hour (11pm) (28/11/97) *Main item*: expansive coverage of Datuk Sri Dr. Mahathir's (hereafter Dr. M) deliberations on the crisis. *Dr. M making the case for an 'Asian Fund' rather than IMF assistance. *Dr. M on the dangers of any IMF package leading to bank closures and higher interest rates. *Dr. M on the need for tighter banking regulations to curb speculators. *Dr. M criticising the WTO's apathy over speculators' attacks on poor nations. *Dr. M on reports of falling foreign investment, explaining that many of his statements have been 'misunderstood or misinterpreted, in some cases, quite deliberately.' *Anwar: interest rates need to be kept 'firm', but not excessively high. *Upbeat film report on national publisher's decision not to increase price of school textbooks, despite feared paper shortages. *Similar report on Kentucky Fried Chicken (Malaysia Bhd) decision to hold prices, as announced at a KFC scholarship award ceremony officiated by Education Minister Najib Abdul Razak. *Interview with chief medical official on the need for random health checks on foreign workers. *Feature on Malaysian designers' efforts to develop a cosmetics industry. *On the markets: various stock indexes shown (to catchy music) and upbeat report on the KLSE, citing Daim Zainuddin: 'There's never been a better time to buy local stocks at bargain-basement prices.' *On the FOREX markets: 'The *ringgit* closed lower against the US dollar today. This is due to jitters over the regional currency turmoil that continues to depress sentiment on the

local currency.' *Report on TV3's 20% increased turnover for the year: TV3 will 'continue to emphasise news-based and informative programming, particularly in-house productions.' *Positive financial statements (played-over high-tech film sequences) on other major corporations. *Brief foreign news.

* News on 2 (TV2, 8pm, 30/11/97) *Main item*: Dr M speaking about traders (notably cooking oil manufacturers) raising the price of goods, comparing them to unpatriotic saboteurs, no better than the currency speculators. *Dr M filmed during his launching of Family Day. *Report on agenda for next day's ASEAN meeting of Finance Ministers. Anwar speaking on the nature of a standby-fund and the need to work 'in close collaboration' with the IMF. *Foreign Minister Abdullah Badawi (pictured addressing a teachers' conference) urging Malaysians to become more knowledgeable about international politics to help 'overcome issues which are negative to the country.' *Education Minister Najib (at a 'meet the people' session) advising school-leavers 'not to be choosy about jobs', but to 'enter the workforce to help reduce the country's dependence on foreign workers.' *Deputy Education Minister Fong Chan Onn (opening a kindergarten) on the government's efforts to bring textbook prices down. *Information Minister Mohamed Rahman (speaking at an Islamic forum) calling on all Muslim countries to co-operate on IT in order to portray 'the true form of Islam.' *11 more cholera cases confirmed. *Business news: KLSE Securities Commission assurances that trading restrictions on five stockbroking houses do not signify default. *Stock indexes and Forex (to catchy music) *Foreign news, weather and sport.

Malaysian TV also has a number of social, business and consumer-type programmes,[69] constituting the basis of 'current affairs'. Overall, the content and tone here was more expansive, though still ordered around 'positive' interpretations of the crisis, rather than any critical analysis of government policy. Here again, academics and other commentators were encouraged to partake in 'policy-planner'-type discussions on how to arrest the decline. The following synopsis of an edition of *Money Matters*, TV3's 'flagship' business affairs format, is representative of such output:

* Money Matters (TV3) (28/11/97) Introducing the main item, 'Road ahead for local manufacturing industry', presenter Melissa Goh's film considered ways for Malaysian firms to adapt to the crisis. Noting fears over high interest rates, the weaker *ringgit*, she suggested, now offered export oriented industries (EOIs) such as the semiconductor and textile sectors the opportunity to enhance their market position.

During the subsequent panel discussion with Paul Low, President of the Federation of Malaysian Manufacturers, and P. Arunasalam, Deputy

Secretary-General of the Malaysian Trade Union Congress (MTUC), Goh asked the latter: 'How do you think the trade unions will help [ensure] that these opportunities are tapped to the fullest?' Noting the MTUC's good intentions, he replied, echoing Mr Low, that they would continue to work towards 'increasing productivity in order to sustain competitiveness.' However, a linked comment on the government's use of non-union labour in the electronics sector was brought back quickly to the theme of productivity and union-management co-operation.

In the 'phone-in' component, 'constructive questions' were being encouraged, such as that addressed to Mr Low asking how domestic manufacturers could help develop the MSC, 'the brainchild' of Dr. Mahathir. Mr. Low responded with an endorsement of the MSC and the need to develop IT and R&D clusters. Noting the low level of strikes, Mr. Arunasalam also commended the government's role in human resource development, while calling for more education in the workplace as a stimulus to 'responsible' industrial relations.

Preceded by an upbeat feature on a young pizza-chain entrepreneur, Goh moved to a discussion with R. V. Ravaratnam, Advisor to the Sungei Way Group. Asked for his comments on the points raised, he noted the need for unions and employers to 'have the same objectives' based around Dr. Mahathir's 'concept of smart partnership.' Stressing the need for 'confidence-building', he welcomed the NEAC, but warned that it must address macro-issues, be transparent and (acknowledging Chandra Muzaffar) help 'eradicate' the 'denial factor.' At this point, Goh asked: 'What is your comment with regard to the so-called political bail-out that has been much talked about?' Ravaratnam (smiling): 'How do you mean political bail-out?' Goh: 'For example ... the issue of UEM ... ' Ravaratnam: 'I think there were some mistakes made ... however well intentioned ...' The programme ended on an upbeat story about the Malaysian music industry's efforts to promote its export market.

With growth-driven development curtailed, the crisis had also brought 'sustainable development' to 'closer attention' as a media issue. In Penang, for example, rapid growth, unchecked planning, road construction, hillside reclamation, high-rise development, a booming population (1.28 million) and increased pollution have all combined to threaten the quality of daily life and Penang's fragile ecosystem. As one advertising hoarding next to a lone *kampong* in the now booming south of the island proclaimed: 'Watch this space and see how things develop.' The crisis had given added impetus to projects such as the Sustainable Penang Initiative, under the aegis of the Socio-Economic and Environmental Research Institute (SERI).[70] But while government and state officials appear to be supportive of such projects, and sustainable planning generally, this cannot disguise the political–corporate interests underwriting the physical development process in Malaysia. This can be gleaned in output such as *Property Watch*, a relatively questioning format of concerned, but safe, middle-class discourse.

• Property Watch (TV3) (30/11/97) The feature reports, introduced by Karen Ho, combined consumer-based concerns with broader issues of social development. For example, the main report centred on the need for a 'total planning doctrine' to tackle the gathering problems of Western-style urban development in Malaysian cities. The perennial problem of traffic jams, air quality and lack of houses for the poor were among a number of policy issues raised. Professor of Environmental Design, Ismawi Zen noted that policy planners have been too-focused on building beautiful mega-cities rather than trying to understand 'the complexity of the social problem.' (Pictures of police questioning '*lepak*' youths at amusement arcade.) However, this promising line of enquiry gives way to the case for Putrajaya as the model solution, the presenter noting that 'the 67,000 homes in Putrajaya will cater to all income groups.' She also commends the new guidelines on balanced development noted by the Director General of Town and Country Planning. On a less sanguine note, questions are raised about the private-sector's willingness to follow this model due to cost. However, private-sector 'acknowledgement' of the total planning concept is re-affirmed by Zaiton Md Noh, a Senior Development Manager who agrees that 'we cannot think of profit 100%.' Following a feature on *feng shui*, a further report weighs-up the case for property rental as property prices fall.

Overall, the purpose of TV and current affairs output was to normalise, rationalise and, ultimately, depoliticise the crisis. Such coverage did not, indeed, could not, disguise the actual impact the crisis was beginning to have on ordinary Malaysians' lives. Rather, its function was to provide an appropriate *context* and filter for receiving the crisis and measures to contain it. In this, the slavish regularity of pro-government TV news was slightly mitigated by the more 'discursive' approach of current affairs output. Thus, while the former was a sanitised version of events offering no alternative viewpoint whatsoever, the latter was built more subtly around a 'problem-solving' axiom, whether in its 'policy-planner' play to academics, business figures and trade unionists or in its appeal to the Malaysian consumer.

Turning more specifically to the domestic press, we find a variation of these approaches. That is, the 'Dr Mahathir says' variety and the 'encouraged dialogue' version. Essentially, the objective is the same as that assumed by the electronic media: the normalisation of news and the neutralisation of dissent. However, the print media, generally, can still be regarded as a relatively more 'expansive' format in terms of critical commentary, popular polemic and nuanced reportage – at least, potentially so. As noted above, gathering competition, feature revamps, the play for middle-class readership and a certain liberalisation by the mid-1990s had increased the scope for a more expanded press product. To what extent, then, were any of the mainstream dailies attempting to move beyond the 'standard text' of responsible development journalism as the crisis unfolded? As an emerging daily with a 'claim' to this mantle, let us consider the particular output of the *Sun* at this point. An analysis of other Malaysian press output in relation to the Anwar issue follows below.

The *Sun*: Pushing the Boundaries?

From its launch in 1994, the *Sun* had sought to fill a significant niche market occupied by the *Star*. Part of the impetus for this had arisen from a certain disenchantment amongst some *Star* journalists and others over the paper's passivity after 1987. More particularly, the *Sun*'s Berjaya group owners appeared to have identified a promising new market for a younger, 'more discerning' readership seeking less 'staid' news, more foreign features and a better produced magazine section. Thus the *Sun*'s content and approach at this point may be measured against three indicators relevant to the crisis and the issue of civil expression:

1. headline coverage of Mahathir and the Barisan;
2. reporting opposition opinion and ISA detentions; and
3. critical features on civil issues.

Headline coverage of Mahathir and the Barisan In general, the *Sun*'s reporting of Mahathir's pronouncements and the Barisan message was consistent with the responsible journalism found elsewhere in the Malaysian press. What differentiated it, marginally, from other dailies was the relatively less slavish tone of its reporting. This corresponds, to some extent, with a view within the *Sun* that the paper was attempting to express its 'adversarial' voice in a more 'alternative' manner by *not* engaging in the type of hyped-up exposure so apparent at that point in the *Star*, *New Straits Times* and *Utusan Malaysia*. However, this supposed 'subtle criticism' can be seen more as a difference of style rather than one of substance.

For example, while front-page headlines in the above appeared as overt Barisan announcements,[71] the *Sun* used relatively more abbreviated headline forms, as in 'Trust us: PM' – on Mahathir's resistance to the IMF (2/12/97). But while the *Sun*'s headline reports were somewhat less 'proclamatory' than the other press, the main 'Mahathir said' format was still employed in most lead stories. Similarly, throughout the Wexler/anti-American affair, the press in general adopted a safe pro-Mahathir position. In essence: no foreign interference. However, in its headline treatment, the *Sun*'s output was generally more moderate in tone, as in 'Envoy: enough' – US Ambassador Mallot calling for an end to the bickering (18/11/97). This slightly more 'equivocal' view of Mahathir's anti-US posture reflected, perhaps, a deeper undercurrent of concern amongst the Chinese business class. Likewise, the *Sun*'s coverage of the proposed investigation into Petronas – 'Sanctions, if imposed, will apply within US only' (18/11/97) and 'Ramsay: I'm here to explain, not investigate' (21/11/97) – was also more informative than other output. Again, though, much of the *Sun*'s information fitted the PM's own agenda by this point, as in 'Mahathir reassures American citizens' (14/11/97), and was being reproduced by the *Sun* and other press via the Bernama news agency. Thus, while using more restrained language, this did not detract from the essential content of headline reports, which was generally favourable to the Barisan.

Reporting opposition opinion and ISA detentions Opposition views are rarely aired as main stories in the press, except where they reflect support for the Barisan, a convention practiced also by the *Sun*, as in 'Set aside differences, be united: Nik Aziz' (17/11/97). More obvious differences can be found between the *Sun* and the *New Straits Times* in their respective 'At the Dewan Rakyat yesterday' features. In general, the former offered more space for DAP opinion, as in 'Opposition men walk out to protest cut in debate time' (5/11/97) and 'People have right to foreign news: Lim' (27/11/97), in contrast to the latter's more typical, '"PM has proven to the world he was right all along"' (30/10/97).

More revealing, though, was the *Sun*'s coverage of restrictions on academics and ISA detentions at this point. In another civil curb, the government had placed a gag order on academics discussing the haze problem. In response, the *Sun*'s front-page headline 'Dumbstruck' (7/11/97) led on the strong criticism by NGOs, the Bar Council's Cecil Rajendra and Universiti Malaya academics Adnan Nawang and Chandra Muzaffar. The paper's Home page also had 'Public have a right to know, says lawyer' and 'Gag order adds insult to injury, says EPSM'.[72]

With regard to the ISA, the *Sun* report 'Eight held under ISA for deviationist activities' (7/11/97) carried the standard government line on the 'threat' to national security from Islamic groups. But it also noted PRM President Syed Husin Ali's concerns that their actions be met with dialogue rather than ISA detention. Here, the *Sun* has expressed tacit support for the government's purge on 'Shi'ite activism' and 'deviationist teaching' in the universities, as indicated in its main headline, 'Student targets – deviant groups zero in on undergraduates' (*Sunday*, 9/11/97). In this regard, 'public fear' of 'deviant Islam' has been part of a long-standing media agenda aimed at both Chinese and Malay sensitivities. However, there appeared to be something of a line being drawn here between the Islamic issue and the wider concern over civil restrictions. There were also a number of statement pieces, albeit small, from Aliran on this and other issues, as in 'Aliran: charge the 10 detained under ISA' (10/11/97) and 'Clean up own backyard before advertising: Aliran' (19/11/97) – in response to the information minister's moves to obtain advertising space on CNN and other foreign media. In another (letter) article, 'Encourage students to be more conscious politically' (24/11/97), Aliran Exco member Mustafa Anuar was given space, albeit nominal, to rebut calls for government scholarships to be withdrawn from students supporting PAS.[73] This complemented other small pieces, such as 'Human rights talks', noting a HAKAM civil forum (30/11/97).[74]

Critical features on civil issues The related issue therefore was whether such alternative opinion could be translated into more ranging forms of critical commentary. We might note, in this regard, the propensity for 'wider' media expression in English, rather than Malay – even if still balanced somewhat by the more elliptical, less direct, style of critical address common to literary and media forms in Malaysia. Yet, whether in English or vernacular, the general dearth of critical features within the Malaysian press cannot be disguised. It was somewhat refreshing to observe the *Sun*'s output here. For while much of it was similar to the sort of middle-class 'lifestyle genre' noted above, one could also discern a more qualitative vein of critical features on a range of civil and intellectual concerns, as noted in the following sample:[75]

Rusdi Mustapha (Megazine Retrospect) 'Beware the propaganda campaign' (12/10/97) This informed article makes legitimate criticisms about the covert roles of MI6, the CIA and other intelligence agencies' manipulation of the media for propagandist purposes. Is it too fanciful, he asks, to see a connection between current US interests in the region and foreign media attacks on Mahathir? The author also notes that Malaysians must be mature and harmonious in their responses if they want the country to be treated as a serious world player.

Akbar Ali (Focus) 'Newsgroup delivers it piping hot' (22/10/97) This full-page piece discusses in more depth the need for greater media freedom and civil awareness. While noting the wider social context of Mahathir's IT vision, it leads on expressions of admiration for journalists like Bala

Pillai, founder of Sangkancil, Malaysia's most 'vibrant' and 'dynamic' newsgroup. Recognising the malaise within the domestic press, the author notes in one prophetic passage:

> The newspapers in this country should pay close attention to *Sangkancil* newsgroup because the news and the news analysis plus the gossip that goes on in *Sangkancil* is light years ahead of what the newspapers print in the morning. With *Sangkancil* leading the way it is a matter of time before more newsgroups or Malaysian discussion groups appear on the Internet. And where will that place the bland reporting or lacklustre news analysis that goes on in most of our printed media?

Nooraini Mydin (Focus) 'A long, long way from utopia' (27/10/97) This (full-page) piece on civil society in Malaysia took as its departure point a seminar on the 'Media and Civil Society' at Institut Teknologi Mara. Reflecting many of the academic contributions, the author feels that Malaysia has some distance to travel. Having identified what a civil society might look like, he notes that there is general consensus on the need for NGOs as a check on government and the private sector, greater freedom of speech within the media and an understanding of how uncontrolled capitalism was giving rise to corruption, greed and a loss of social values.

W. G. Mansor (Megazine Special Issue) 'A well-aimed shot at poverty' (27/11/97) This feature is fairly typical of the *Sun*'s coverage of acute social issues. Here, the problem of rural poverty is addressed, taking as its cue the work of the *kampong*-based 'credit bank' Amanah Ikhtiar (AIM).[76] Run by villagers, the scheme has been widely successful (covering 2,659 villages) in providing manageable loans to poor rural people with no access to conventional banks, while helping to generate a sense of solidarity and something of an independent voice for women, the main recipients of AIM loans.

In more enquiring mood, three extensive features on the intellectual and the want of intellectual discourse in Malaysia denote a more basic set of concerns lurking as critical commentary.

Akbar Ali (Focus) 'Filling the intellectual vacuum' (3/10/97) In this thought-provoking piece, the author laments the lack of any meaningful intellectual community as the country moves towards 2020:

> Looking at the lack of intellectual discourse in our country, one wonders if we will at all remember Vision 2020 when we finally get there ... Whether

it is academia, religion, social activism or writing books and articles, there is a dearth of intellectual discussion. Even the level of discourse on our TV talk shows is mild. There are rarely any probing questions about anything and the discussions are rarely to the point ... [The] lack of intellectual discussion has led us to establish a norm that to say anything intelligent or controversial means that one is anti-establishment.

This is a revealing indictment, even though it never makes the connection between Vision ideology as intellectual discourse in itself, notably via the media. However, the link becomes more apparent in the following five-page special on intellectuals.

W. G. Mansor (Megazine Special Issue) 'I think, therefore I am' (9/11/ 97) In the first three-page section, Mansor reviews the thoughts and standing of some key intellectuals of the modern age, such as Bertrand Russell, Julien Benda and Noam Chomsky, before elaborating the crisis of the intellectual in Malaysia through critical voices like Jomo and Syed Hussein Alatas. In the first instance, though, he notes the formative contribution of Gramsci and the connection between media production and the intellectual. Thus, in contrast to Benda's intellectuals as a select band of moral philosophers:

Gramsci's representation of the intellectual as a person who fulfils a particular set of functions in society is probably closer to present-day reality ... Today, everyone who works in any field connected with the production or distribution of knowledge is an intellectual in the Gramscian sense.

The article goes on to explore some of the anti-establishment positions adopted by pre-Merdeka Malay intellectuals, the stance taken by Ungku Aziz on land reform, before helping to draft the NEP, and the determination of writers and poets such as Keris Mas, Usman Awang and Samad Ismail to reveal the plight of the lower classes. However, this confrontation by artists and intellectuals against early capitalist materialism has much deeper roots in the Western tradition, notes Mansor. Invoking Alatas, Malay intellectuals had also been pacified by the smooth transfer of colonial power and the lack of an Indonesian-type struggle for independence. Today, he notes, the West has adversarial intellectuals such as Chomsky, an 'articulator of dissent' who 'argues that the major newspapers and TV networks connive with the elites of government and big business to restrict the range of information and opinion available to ordinary citizens'. In contrast, Malaysian intellectuals generally hold to a culture of passive pragmatism:

In fact, it would appear that only a handful of Malaysian intellectuals conceive their role to be that of the classical intelligentsia, critical of excesses and errors of whatever regime is in power ... One can say that, with notable exceptions, the political ideas of Malaysian intellectuals are marked by run-of-the-millness rather than extraordinariness. In the sense that their views mirror all the ambiguities of society at large, they are more Malaysian than 'intellectual'. On the whole, they do not constitute a vanguard community with a radically different image of the political future.

The result of this, notes Mansor, is a pervasive anti-intellectualism from above. This, he argues, has reified a culture of silence and an absence of intellectual enquiry:

> We can judge this by the paucity of published materials, and the absence of a sustained collective discussion on vital issues. The intellectual output from our universities, the institutes and the press has not been that impressive. There has been little contribution towards a critical discussion of the real issues.

Moreover, without a market for in-depth books, few are published in *Bahasa*, critical discourse thus remaining the preserve of an Anglophone world. As the author concludes:

> A government practising a policy of accommodation, it seems, can tolerate apathy but not ideology from its intellectuals. Thus, the government stands to gain most from a depoliticised intellectual stratum without binding ideological commitments.

Yusoff Ahmad (Megazine Special Issue) 'Who's a clever boy now?' (9/ 11/97) These themes are developed in a further two-page feature. Here, the author takes up Syed Husin Ali's view that: 'In order to think, write and be critical of society, the intellectual must be close to society.' In effect, real intellectual engagement comes not from books alone, but from direct observation and involvement with people. Abdul Razak Abdullah Baginda of the Malaysian Strategic Research Centre (MSRC) acknowledges that intellectuals do operate outwith the university, but must also be respected in this domain. He also sees a more particular need for harnessing local intellectuals. More directly, Syed Husin Ali specifies a number of reasons for intellectual passivity in Malaysia, such as the lack of democratic space within the media, the inability of intellectuals to escape their ethnic trap and the economic lifestyle enjoyed by Malaysian intellectuals in contrast to some of their regional counterparts.

In sum, the *Sun* had pushed the boundaries a little, partly because of a more relaxed press by the mid-1990s, partly because of a market strategy to displace the *Star* and partly as an (apparently genuine) acknowledgement of a more discerning readership. But this in itself was allowed only because proprietors, editors and journalists had come to understand the lessons of the 1980s. In the main, the *Sun*'s editorial approach appeared to be one of pragmatic support for the status quo. At no time did its editorials or lead articles question the wider power *structure*. Nonetheless, the paper's output at this point could be regarded as more 'enquiring' than the other dailies, certainly the *New Straits Times* and *Utusan Malaysia*, even allowing for the *impression* of impartiality cultivated, a reportage presented as 'critical journalism' through selective coverage of opposition opinion. Again, much of the lifestyle features, letters and 'critical commentaries' played up the same basic appeal to middle-class insiderism. Yet, in its cursory examination of the intellectual face of Malaysia, it also appeared cognisant of a deeper seam of civil concern, something it felt able to excavate without undermining the elite structure above it. These articles suggest a wider potential for critical reflection and intellectual engagement. If this has been done in recognition of a more enquiring public, it may indicate, at least, the nucleus of a more assertive press, something which might surface should Malaysians come to reject, wholesale, routine media adherence to the Barisan. As the Anwar crisis unravelled, there were signs of such disenchantment. But it was also apparent that the *Sun*, like the rest of the press, had not diverged in any meaningful way from the practice of responsible development journalism.

Notes

1. A key example here being Thatcher's orchestrated plan to break the National Union of Mineworkers' strike in 1984 through anti-union legislation, the courts, biased media images and an MI5 smear campaign.

2. Frith and Savage (1993), p. 111.

3. Saravanamutta et al. (1996), pp. 12–32.

4. Loh Kok Wah and Mustafa K. Anuar, (1996), p. 100.

5. *FEER*, 6 October 1994.

6. *FEER*, 2 March 1995.

7. Nain (1996).

8. *FEER*, 2 March 1995.

9. *FEER*, 6 March 1997.

10. *Straits Times*, 18 April 1998.

11. Loh Kok Wah and Anuar (1996), pp. 101–2.

12. Nain (1996).

13. The main publications of the NSTP and *Utusan Melayu* groups are as follows: NSTP: (dailies) *New Straits Times, Berita Harian, Malay Mail, Business Times, Shin Min Daily News, Harian Metro*; (weeklies) *New Sunday Times, Berita Minggu, Sunday Mail*; (magazines) *Malaysia Business, Investors Digest, Her World, Jelita*. Utusan Melayu:

(dailies) *Utusan Malaysia, Utusan Melayu, Leader*; (weeklies) *Mingguan Malaysia, Utusan Zaman*; (magazines) *Dunia Sukan, Mastika, URTV, Utusan Pelajar, Wanita, Utusan Qiblat/Al Islam*.

14. Gomez and Jomo (1997), p. 155.

15. Ibid., p. 158.

16. Audited *circulation* figures, *ABC News* (Audited Bureau of Circulation – Malaysia), June 1999, Vol. 16, No. 2; October 1999, Vol. 16, No. 3. The circulation figures for the main Sunday editions (1 July 1997–30 June 1998) were: *Mingguan Malaysia* (522,857); *Berita Minggu* (391,813); *Sunday Star* (252,565); *New Sunday Times* (179,143). The respective *readership* (rather than circulation) figures for *Utusan Malaysia, New Straits Times, Berita Harian* and the *Star* for the year 1997 was: 1,401,000; 628,000; 1,656,000; and 812,000. *SRM Media Index*, Malaysia, 1997.

17. See 'Hard pressed', by Spiked, *Aliran Monthly*, 1998, 18: 6.

18. See also Munro-Kua (1996), p. 125.

19. Anuar (1990); Munro-Kua (1996), p. 140.

20. *FEER*, 13 April 1995.

21. *FEER*, 16 May 1996.

22. The fighting at Jalan Patani, Kampung Rawa, Penang on 27 March 1998 centred on plans to extend the site of the Indian Raja-Raja Maduraiveeran temple and objections from local Malays over its proximity to the local mosque. Police deployed 600 members of the Federal Reserve Unit (FRU) and General Operations Force (GOF) to control the rioters (mainly youths) and made 150 arrests. See 'Temple-next-to mosque issue settled, says Anwar', *Utusan Malaysia*, 28 March 1998.

23. See Media Statement by Lim Kit Siang, DAP Homepage, 29 March 1998, <http://www.malaysia.net/dap>.

24. *New Straits Times* (32-page colour edition), 31 August 1994.

25. Kua Kia Soong (1990), pp. 216–17.

26. Nain (1993). The cited words are those of *Financial Times* film critic Nigel Andrews.

27. The 'Murdoch effect' in Britain, notes Pilger (1998), has seen a competitive 'dumbing-down' of the mainstream tabloids (notably, the *Mirror*'s descent against the *Sun*), a decline in serious journalism amongst the 'qualities' and, contrary to its 'Reithian ethics', the emergence of new free-market imperatives at the BBC.

28. Nain (1996).

29. Ibid.

30. See, for example, Provenchar (1990).

31. See 'National lampoon', *FEER*, 24 April 1997.

32. Quoted from Julian Pettifer's report on Malaysia, *Assignment*, BBC2, UK, 18 November 1995.

33. See, for example, the *New Straits Times* special *Life and Times* articles, 'Social ills part of growing pains' by Rose Ismail, and 'The "Malay dilemma" revisited' by Hisham Harun, 5 March 1997.

34. See, for example, Chandra Muzaffar's *New Straits Times* letter 'Global currency coalition can curb manipulation', 29 October 1997.

35. *New Straits Times*, 15 November 1997.

36. An example of such was Marina's appearance on *Global*, (TV2), 30 November 1997, in her role as president of the Malaysian Aids Council.

37. See 'In liberal poses', a lengthy critique of Marina Mahathir's views and position, posted on the *Saksi* reform site <http://www.saksi.com/sohsawlee.htm>, 1998.

38. Boulanger (1993), pp. 54, 61.

39. Kershaw (1997), p. 4.

40. Cited in Munro-Kua (1996), p. 77.

41. Hobsbawm (1983). See also Nairn (1988) on the monarchy's use of archaic traditions in Britain for such purposes.

42. Kessler (1992), p. 135.

43. Ibid., pp. 149, 155.

44. Kahn (1992), pp. 168, 173.

45. Tan Sooi Beng (1992), p. 303.

46. Loh Kok Wah and Kahn (1992), pp. 5, 6, 11, 15.

47. See Chandra Jeshurun (1993), p. 220. For a further discussion of the new generation of UMNO leadership at this point, notably Anwar, see Ho Khai Leong (1994).

48. Khoo Boo Teik (1995), pp. 300, 301.

49. B. Anderson (1983).

50. See *Malaysian Business*, 16 August 1994, on the implications at this point for the domestic television network.

51. In an overture to Beijing, Murdoch's Star TV dropped the BBC World Service News from its schedule.

52. The channels are delivered through the All Asia Television and Radio Company (ASTRO), a subsidiary of Measat Broadcast Network System. *Malaysia Industrial Digest*, October–December 1996.

53. 'Selling to salesmen': *FEER*, 6 February 1997.

54. 'Future shock': *FEER*, 27 February 1997.

55. See, for example, 'Super drive status for Cyberjaya development', *New Straits Times*, 18 March 1997.

56. The first phase of Cyberjaya, a 750-hectare site at Bukit Damar, Sepang, Selangor, was officially launched by Mahathir on 17 May 1997, with a total completion date of 2005. See 'Cyberjaya, the intelligent city', a speech by Mahathir at the ground-breaking ceremony, Malaysian Information Department, June 1997.

57. See the MSC webpage: <http://www.mdc.com.my/msc/>.

58. Ibid.

59. Ibid.

60. 'PM: Smart Partnership must benefit all parties', *New Sunday Times*, 16 November 1997.

61. See 'Smart Partnership. Towards Successful and Prosperous Nations', speech to the First Southern Africa International Dialogue, Kasne Botswana, 5 May 1997. *Jabatan Penerangan Malaysia*, July 1997.

62. 'MSC: A global bridge from Europe to Asia for the world century', Dr Mahathir's address to the Imperial College, London, 20 May 1997. *Jabatan Penerangan Malaysia*, August 1997.

63. As part of his argument for a better-trained IT workforce in Malaysia, Lim Kit

Siang (1997), pp. 12–13, notes how India became one of the top three countries for Microsoft investment in 1996–97.

64. Ibid.

65. The other two were the Telemedicine Bill and the Copyright (Amendment) Bill. Lim Kit Siang (1997). Many of these criticisms were developed in Lim's address to the Infotech Malaysia '98 Conference. Note: the Digital Signature Bill refers to legislation designed to regulate the proposed MSC 'paperless government' project, within which online administrative databases can be accessed using key-encryption technology to view, send and sign legally binding documents.

66. From the IT Awareness Campaign leaflet, Information Department, Ministry of Information, October 1997.

67. Broadly translated: Know/recognise IT. Enjoy IT. Students every day ... use/ take advantage of IT ... the science of IT. Malaysia skilled/accomplished. Embrace IT. Learn IT. Love/have affection for IT. Use/benefit from IT.

68. The following is a selected content analysis of media output during the crisis period early October to mid-December 1997. My thanks to the *Sun* regional editor (Penang) Jackson Ng Kee Seng, Mr Chiew, assistant editor of the *Star* in Penang and to a number of academics and working journalists for their insightful discussions. All observations here belong, of course, to the present author.

69. Including, at this point, TV3's *Face to Face* and *What's Right*.

70. The SPI is funded by the Institute on Governance (Canada), with other input from UN-based bodies. SERI, based in Penang, has also worked with Dr Koh Tsu Koon and the Penang state government on this issue. See SERI Homepage.

71. As in 'A confidence boosting national budget for 1998', *New Straits Times*, 18 October 1997.

72. The article refers to statements by R. Senthirajah of the Environmental Protection Society of Malaysia (EPSM) condemning the government's intervention.

73. This was in response to veiled threats made to opposition student activists by Backbenchers Club president Ruhanie Ahmad.

74. This gathering took place in Kuala Lumpur on 7 December 1997.

75. Feature titles here are in brackets; 'Special Issue' features are taken from the *Sun* and *Sunday Megazine* (magazine) sections.

76. AIM is based on the ideas of the Grameen Bank scheme in Bangladesh founded by Professor Mohamad Yunus. Its only main difference is the use of an administrative fee rather than credit, in accordance with Islamic law. The scheme was developed by Professor David Gibbons and Sukor Kasim of Universiti Sains Malaysia's Centre for Policy Research.

5

The Anwar Crisis and the Media

Anwar's removal, arrest and character assassination provides a graphic picture of the Malaysian media's interacting role within the UMNO network.

Such enterprise had already been evident prior to his downfall in the funding, publication and distribution of the *50 Reasons* book. Anwar was later to claim that the book 'was funded by very senior people in the government and corporate sector. Tens of millions of dollars were spent on several print runs and it was distributed widely. I have a tape to substantiate that.'[1] Another example of the network's response was the way in which affidavits issued against Nalla on the morning of Anwar's dismissal were allowed into the public domain without a full court hearing, their contents being made public on TV3 and in a special edition of the *Malay Mail* rushed out that afternoon.[2]

His arrest forestalled by the Commonwealth Games, Anwar's home became the focal point for mass *reformasi* gatherings, while the 'Anwar roadshow' started to build support across the country. With Queen Elizabeth in Kuala Lumpur to close the games, the international media were serving to highlight the crisis and the movement's ideals. Following a march by thirty thousand demonstrators from the National Mosque to Merdeka Square to hear Anwar's call for reform, rioting and pitched battles with the Federal Reserve Unit (FRU) had broken out, alongside disturbances at UMNO HQ and Mahathir's home.[3] With tension increasing, the IGP, Rahim Noor, took the decision to send in an elite snatch-squad to arrest Anwar (under the ISA) as he addressed a press conference, an open declaration that the authorities would not be cowed by the presence of the foreign media. Large-scale protests continued, met forcefully again by riot police. In an extension of the purge on Anwar's media associates, various pro-Anwar intellectuals were arrested, including Siddiq Baba and Kamaruddin Jaffar (of the Institute of Policy Research), Zahid Hamidi and the top four officials of ABIM.[4]

While the *reformasi* lacked clear objectives at this point, Anwar's Permatang Pauh Declaration had received broad support,[5] helping to bring about two new coalition forums: the Malaysian People's Movement for Justice (GERAK), headed by Fadzil Noor of PAS, and the Coalition for People's Democracy (GAGASAN), led by Tian Chua of Suaram.[6] While both bodies, comprising DAP, PAS, PRM and most reformist NGOs, remained distanced from the *reformasi* as a proto-party at this point, the movement had helped foster a new form of cooperation between the major opposition parties and a working relationship with Anwar's followers, symbolised by Anwar's now open declaration of support for Lim Guan Eng. Meanwhile, Anwar's wife Wan Azizah Wan Ismail had taken-up Anwar's place as a rallying figure.[7] By December 1998, she had formed the Pergerakan Keadilan Sosial (Movement for Social Justice), to be known as ADIL (with Chandra Muzaffar acting as vice-president) in an effort to give the *reformasi* a clearer organisational structure. In effect, ADIL and Wan Azizah, now acting in Anwar's name, were working alongside GERAK and GAGASAN in an effort to build a broad political alignment.[8]

Alongside the 'roadshow effect', fears were now growing over the sensitive information Anwar had become privy to through his party positions and corporate links. The release of two letters from Anwar to Mahathir, one preceding and one following his dismissal, suggested a more serious catalogue of corruption and nepotism than that alleged even by outside observers.[9] Anwar had also claimed not to have been instrumental in ordering 'unwarranted investigations' into key government departments, including the offices of the IGP. Appealing for recognition of his unease, he had noted to Mahathir: 'Lately, some people have become uncomfortable with me because it seems I was the one who directed the Anti-Corruption Agency to investigate the Director-General of the Economic Planning Unit.'[10]

Again, it is difficult to accept Anwar's part here as 'passive victim'. As Khoo was to note: 'Let us not be naive. Anwar is not your innocent bystander ... He is a seasoned political *gajah* [elephant/big figure] who played for the highest stakes in the political game, and lost.'[11] Yet, whether one accepts his version of events or not, the more crucial issue was whether Mahathir believed him at this stage. It is also possible that Daim would have been the first major 'casualty' of any such revelations had Anwar come to power. As noted, what may have precipitated Anwar's removal was his apparent reluctance to participate in the planned bail-out of the corporate giant Renong, understood to be the main conduit for UMNO funding.[12] In a statement circulated prior to his arrest, Anwar (fearing the possibility of being injected with drugs while in jail – even HIV to 'prove' his 'illicit affairs') specified the main reason for the campaign against him:

The reason they are so afraid of me is that I know too many of their secrets.

I know how many billions of ringgit of UMNO money they have stolen to benefit a few people. I know how much money – one billion in October (1997?) [sic] – they took out of the country to deposit in bank [sic] in the vicinity of Zurich. I reported this to Dr Mahathir, thinking I could trust him as leader. As it turns out he kept the information to himself, and I cannot but come to the conclusion that there is a secret pact between him and a few well-known people. I know how many projects were used to benefit a few friends and his relatives. They are terrified because I have this information.[13]

Thus, while Mahathir had begun to 'address corruption' as a legitimation problem, he appears to have become more concerned about the particular charges of nepotism at this point. As Jomo noted, in relation to the 'anti-KKN' challenge in Indonesia, it may have been the 'Suharto factor' that proved the 'last straw' for Mahathir: 'I don't think Dr. Mahathir minded attacking *korupse* and *kronisme*, but *nepotisme* came too close to the bone.'[14]

Yet, despite concerns about the political and private fallout of an Anwar succession, Mahathir also appears to have been motivated by a more fundamental belief in his sole ability to lead the country out of crisis. Allowing for the usual delusions of many long-serving leaders, this view was not without reasonable support amongst the Malaysian public, given Mahathir's past 'successes' in the face of adversity. For this and other reasons, notes Jomo, Mahathir, unlike Suharto, was more likely to 'go with his boots on'.[15]

One of the most critical factors, therefore, was how this strategy would be played out through the media. To what extent could Mahathir sell the Anwar purge and civil crackdown as a popular rationale for political order and economic recovery? At the outset, Mahathir had been under extreme pressure, even within UMNO, to provide a convincing explanation for Anwar's removal, arrest and persecution. For the case alleged not only abuse of political office, but sodomy, a gross violation of Islamic law. As the pressure increased, Rahim's own 'generalissimo' tone towards 'impertinent' members of the foreign media (see below) had only exacerbated the situation.[16] On top of this, both Anwar's adopted brother Sukma Darmawan Sasmitaat and his former speech-writer Munawar Ahmad Anees had now withdrawn their (apparently forced) statements confessing to have been sodomised by Anwar. Both had received six-month jail sentences after pleading guilty to charges of gross indecency. The problem became more acute when, after nine days incommunicado, Anwar finally appeared in court, showing a swollen eye and other injuries, to hear the corruption and sodomy charges against him.[17] As the pictures and account of his alleged mistreatment in custody flashed around the world, Mahathir was now dealing with Anwar the martyr as well as Anwar the reformer.

Precisely how or why all this was allowed to happen, given the adverse reaction it was bound to evoke, remains unclear.[18] Mahathir, reported to have been 'angry' about Anwar's treatment,[19] had sought to ameliorate the situation by suggesting that the injuries may have been self-inflicted, a calculated play for public sympathy. However, a subsequent doctor's report, obtained and distributed by Reuters, concluded that Anwar had, indeed, been beaten and left unconscious – allegedly, claimed Anwar's political secretary, by Rahim Noor himself.[20] The IGP had also tried to suppress the medical report through the Malaysian news agency Bernama, which had sent out the immediate message:

> URGENT NOTE TO EDITORS: The Bukit Aman federal police request the media not to use/publish the medical examination report dated Sept 30th 1998, on former Deputy Prime Minister Datuk Seri Anwar Ibrahim by Datuk Dr Haji Ahmad Shukir Mohamed of Shukri Hardeev eye specialists. A police spokesman said the medical report is only meant for the prosecution and defence in the Anwar case.[21]

On the same day, Mahathir had called a 'consultative' meeting with Malaysian media editors after the local press had splashed the Anwar black-eye picture on their front pages. As a result, the medical report was duly suppressed, the injuries reported as a series of unsubstantiated allegations and the emphasis now placed more specifically on Mahathir's investigation into the complaint – as directed through the attorney-general, rather than the Special Branch, to ensure its 'independence'.[22] Despite assurances that the rule of law would be upheld, calls for the IGP's suspension for the duration of the inquiry went unheeded.

Meanwhile, messages of concern from notable international figures such as James Wolfensohn and Kofi Annan began to mount. Anwar's close relationships with Habibie and Estrada had also put a strain on regional relations, threatening the ASEAN convention of non-interference in each others' affairs. Reflecting this tension, the *Jakarta Post* accused Mahathir of having 'sown the seeds of his own downfall. He has created a martyr.'[23] Paradoxically, while much of the Malaysian media had helped imply Anwar's guilt, it was Justice Augustine Paul's order prohibiting media discussion of the case, after fixing Anwar's trial date, that allowed Mahathir some respite from its adverse publicity at this point.[24]

However, US and Western pressure on Mahathir also reflected growing tensions at the *global* level. With the domestic economy already battered by free-market adjustments – a painful experiment now being attributed to Anwar – Mahathir was seeking to keep public attention focused on the new measures for domestic-led recovery: exchange controls, interest rate cuts, expanded credit and looser fiscal policy. But, like Mahathir, capitalist institutions were also engaged in their own version of the 'denial syndrome'. With key financial figures led by Alan Greenspan at the US Federal Reserve engaged in emergency measures to contain the Asian fall-out and its contagion effect on Russia and South America, this had seen a crisis of neo-liberalism itself. Plans for reform of the global financial architecture ('historical innovations' likened to a new Bretton Woods, though greeted with little enthusiasm by the markets) included new regulatory codes to promote monetary transparency and allow a clearer surveillance role for the IMF,[25] a belated 'acknowledgement' of the Fund's failure to foresee the crisis. What could not be encouraged were the protectionist strategies now being adopted by Mahathir – domestic controls now finding favour in crisis-torn Russia. In effect, Mahathir and other countries now threatened to expose the fallacies of free-market capitalist development. As John Gray was to note at this point:

> The global free-market is falling apart. In a move that is certain to be emulated by other developing countries, Malaysia has introduced old fashioned exchange controls. Hong Kong has torn up the free-market rule-book and provided government support for the stock market. Above all, Russia has rejected the policies imposed on it by the western economic consensus. Russia's crisis is no longer primarily economic. By now it is a crisis of the state [and] neoliberal economic policies demanded by the West.[26]

Thus, perversely, Mahathir's decision to remove the ringgit's convertibility, given credibility by Russia's action over the rouble, had given him 'new standing' as a supposed champion of financial reform.

As the immediate furore of the Anwar issue subsided, Mahathir's use of capital controls had offered some breathing-space to rebuild economic confidence. According to Daim, Mahathir had discussed this option at length with the other five NEAC members (Daim, Anwar, Noordin Sopiee, Oh Siew Nam and Ali Abul Hassan) from January 1998, eventually overcoming their list of 42 concerns, notably the fear of undermining foreign investor confidence.[27] Capital controls were also a legitimate 'window of opportunity', as the US economic 'guru' Paul Krugman had put it in an open address to Mahathir, provided they were used for systematic financial reform rather than the bailing out of more cronies.[28] It may be noted here that Krugman was speaking not as a Mahathir apologist or 'born-again Keynesian', but as a critic of the IMF's monitoring capacities.[29] Nevertheless, Mahathir was now using Krugman's 'validation', the growing consensus against IMF intervention amongst Malaysian policy analysts and the permissive dangers of hedge-funds to relaunch himself as a leading crusader against IMF orthodoxy. But behind this protectionism, Mahathir was also seeking to reassure a middle-class generation who, gilded by years of prosperity, had seen their assets and spending power disrupted by the stock market crash, currency crisis and collapse of property prices.

In October 1998, as finance minister (a post thereafter given to Daim), Mahathir unveiled an expansionary budget of wide-ranging tax and spend measures, signalling a clear break with IMF remedies and raising the ante with foreign capital. Besides a raft of fiscal measures to assist domestic business, notably the service sector, a number of more populist incentives were included, such as the waiving of income tax on earnings for the forthcoming year[30] and attempts to stimulate local demand through new forms of assistance to SMIs. By early 1999, the provision and administration of funds to SMIs via Bank Negara was being pushed by the bank itself and various business organisations.[31] However, it is important to note here that Anwar had also instituted a number of such stimulus policies before being sacked, interventions not noted in the White Paper on the crisis presented to Parliament in April 1999.[32] Moreover, the government 'debt resolution' agencies Danaharta, Danamodal and the Corporate Debt Restructuring Committee (CDRC), charged with recapitalising ailing banks/financial institutions and absorbing bad debt, were actually set up under Anwar's direction in 1998.[33] While using these agencies as a discreet bail-out arrangement, Daim was also trying to reassure concerned foreign fund managers that the exit tax now levied on investments would not adversely affect their holdings.[34] Mahathir also used the budget speech to connect Anwar with the damaging effect of IMF-type policies on the economy.[35]

One year on from Anwar's austerity package, Mahathir's budget, capital controls and case for a new trading order had helped placate domestic capital and a wavering middle class. Mahathir's anti-IMF doctrine had also found 'support' in Japanese Finance Minister Eisuke Sakakibara's denunciation of the Fund as the 'Washington consensus [of] free markets and sound money ... [a] blind application of the universal model of emerging economies' – allowing the *Sun* headline: 'IMF is US dominated says Mr Yen'.[36] By January 1999, Mahathir's bravura calls for exchange controls were finding resonance at the World Economic Forum in Switzerland,[37] helping to restore some of his global prestige. Thus, for all its rhetorical content, Mahathir's attacks on the IMF may be seen as an important point in the 'revision' of neo-Keynesian ideas.

Yet, while Mahathir cultivated populist recovery discourse, there was still the populist backlash of the *reformasi* to contend with. Mahathir's authoritarian crackdown had given rise to serious civil unrest, pressure that had been met, often brutally, by riot police, although, in contrast to Indonesia, no one had been shot or killed. During the protests, Special Branch (SB) officers and *agents provocateurs* had been deployed to 'isolate' the organisers and 'direct' the more gullible protesters. More academics and activists associated with Anwar, ABIM, GERAK and other pro-*reformasi* agencies had been detained.[38] Some made formal complaints of being beaten in prison, including the GERAK leader Tian Chua, now twice arrested. Mass weekly gatherings continued, notably around the Jalan Tunku Abdul Rahman (Jalan TAR) area of Kuala Lumpur, with exuberant crowds (varying between 10,000 and 30,000) chanting 'RE-FOR-MA-SI' and waving pro-Anwar banners.[39] While seeking to present a more restrained, even, by some accounts, friendly, profile during the early gatherings, it was evident that the FRU had adopted specialised chase and dispersal tactics, using *rotans* and water cannons laced with chemicals. Many *reformasi* supporters had also been attacked and detained during the 17 October rally when a section of the crowd moved towards the Istana Negara to hand in a memorandum to the *Yang di-Pertuan Agong*.[40] Similar treatment had been meted out around the Parliament building following the budget speech. The following evening, over 250 arrests were made in and around the Malay Kampung Baru district of KL, the FRU's excessive force being condemned by Amnesty International.[41] (Ironically, these concerns coincided with the release of a major Amnesty report detailing the systematic abuse of prisoners in US prisons.)[42] Scene of the 1969 riots, Kampung Baru was to become a focal point for many such protests during the trial.

However, unlike the Indonesian crisis, these and other demonstrations never looked likely to bring Mahathir down. Permits for opposition *ceramahs* were still being blocked, but so too were proposed UMNO gatherings in the interests of 'public order', allowing claims of 'even-handedness.' Meanwhile, having been quietly eased out by the UMNO Youth leadership, Zahid was now planning to tour the country to 'help allay public fears', UMNO-speak for co-optation. While street protests continued, much of daily life went on as normal.

The Malaysian Press: 'Let's Work Together'

Part of the reason for this lies in the nature of legitimacy that had come to prevail in Malaysia, in contrast to Indonesia. This reflected middle-class sensitivities and a general aversion to violence. But it can also be linked to the encouragement of 'insiderist' dialogue within the media. This is an important point missed by many external observers of the Anwar situation. Despite the irregularities of the electoral process, Mahathir was still an elected leader with a mandate to secure. The threat of state coercion remained – as it does in Western states, only in more attenuated forms. But social control was also being mediated through processes of popular persuasion. Again, one may note here the particularised nature of press content: 'There's a dichotomy in press coverage in Malaysia ... On political issues, there is no critical reporting or open discussion of different sides. But in the non-political areas – such as society and the environment – there is very open debate.'[43] This, notes Syed Husin Ali, was particularly so in the post-1995 election euphoria: 'There was not much to worry about and the economy was doing well. With allegations that the press had been controlled and not fair, they wanted to show it was democratic.'[44] Hence, while many Malaysians were now reacting to overt propaganda by boycotting *Utusan Malaysia* (the paper's 'reformist' ideas on the crisis having been stifled by Johan Jaafar's removal), middle-class 'social debate' was still helping to distil a palliative language of middle-class moderation and support for national recovery, even where that included deep unease over the Anwar issue.

The role of the domestic press in the Anwar affair thus comprised two discrete, yet complementary, elements.[45] The first involved 'verbatim reporting' of Barisan press statements as 'breaking news'. In effect, the Barisan's version of unfolding events, unaccompanied by critical commentary, *became* the news in itself. This did not preclude statements from Anwar, opposition opinions or coverage of *reformasi ceramahs* across the country, giving the semblance of objective news gathering. But this was always treated as marginal in relation to the 'more authoritative' pronouncements of leading Barisan figures. The following headlines and quotes are indicative of this biased form of 'they said' reportage: [46]

> *MBs back Mahathir's action* (Perak Mentri Besar Tan Sri Ramli Ngah Talib said he was confident that Dr Mahathir had 'weighed and studied at length' [*sic*] before taking action against Anwar ... His sentiments were shared by several mentris besar.)

> *Yusof Nor: UMNO Supreme council acted to safeguard party* ('the prime Minister was faced with statements and disclosures which he found difficult to ignore and to safeguard the image of the party, race and country, he had to act with great reluctance against his deputy whom he had trusted,' he said.)

> *Anwar tried to interfere in police investigations* (Asked about this, Anwar, who has described all the allegations against him as fabrications, said: 'I wouldn't be surprised if they add 20 more ... ')

> *Anwar hopes capital control measures will work* ('As a Malaysian and a former member of the cabinet, I really wish that the move announced on Sept 1 will work in the interests of our people,' Anwar said.)

> *PM to give explanation on Anwar's expulsion soon* (UMNO Secretary-General Datuk Sabbaruddin Chik said the explanation is necessary in order

to remove the existing confusion among those who are directly affected by the decision taken.)

PM: Anwar 'arrested' by followers (Dr Mahathir Mohamad said ... Anwar is 'being put under house arrest' by his own followers who are out to create problems.)

PM: Ceramahs show we are democratic (The nightly ceramahs at [Anwar's house] in Bukit Damansara will be allowed to go on because Malaysia is a democratic country ... Dr Mahathir Mohamad said if the public speeches and gatherings were stopped, then the media, especially the foreign media, would brand the country as repressive ... 'It's something one has to submit to if one believes in democracy' [he] said yesterday.)

Anwar encouraged by show of support at talks (Anwar said a multiracial effort was needed to ensure the success of reformasi (reform) for the country. 'It must be a multiracial effort. If not, we will not win,' he said at a public gathering in conjunction with the Free Guan Eng Marathon fast at Sungai Chua.)

Greater sin if Mahathir had not exposed Anwar's sin - Mohamed (Sept 27 [BN Secretary-General] Datuk Seri Mohamed Rahmat today said the Prime Minister could not bear to harbour the greater sin of not exposing the sinful activities of ... Anwar.)

UMNO Divisions used to topple Dr Mahathir – Mohamed Rahmat (Leaders at divisional levels had been paid monthly allowances ... and some divisions had been allocated with RM1 million to RM2 million to carry out subversive activities in UMNO, he said. 'We can identify the divisions involved.')

Anwar 'plotted to oust Dr M' (Aziz Shamsudin, political-secretary to Dr Mahathir, claimed it was Anwar's plan to topple the [PM] by 'killing off people surrounding Dr Mahathir first.' 'Anwar is the biggest conspirator. That is why he wanted to implicate me as a conspirator,' he said.)

Malaysia on road to recovery, says ISIS Chief (as the capital control measures are showing great success, the chairman of the Institute for Strategic and International Studies (ISIS), Tan Sri Dr Noordin Sopiee, said today ... 'I think the recession of 1998 will end in 1998 and that we will have positive growth for 1999,' he said at a press conference to announce the National Congress on Economic Recovery entitled, 'The Way Forward', which will be organised by ISIS and the ASEAN Strategic and Leadership Institute (ASLI) ...)

Anwar attempted to initiate a revolution, not a reformation, says Najib ('He has rejected everything ... whether it be Umno, the government, the police force, the judiciary ... everything,' he said ...)

Court Fixes Nov 2–14 for Anwar's trial (and ordered a gag on public discussion of the case. Justice [Augustine Paul] ... said: 'Justice must not only be done but seen to be done ... ')

Of course, the pro-government bias did not cease with the Judge's prohibition. Indeed, as noted, the gag may even have been a welcome diversion for Mahathir and editors under daily pressure from the foreign media. This allowed attention to be turned again to more familiar forms of 'they said' reportage on the opposition, including, by now, GERAK – for example, in the *Star*'s 'PAS out to exploit, says Ghafar'.[47] Anwar had also rejected the implications of a picture published in *Utusan Malaysia* purporting to show him having a sumptuous meal inside Bukit Aman jail.[48] In an attempt to play the UMNO network at its own game, Anwar also issued a RM100 million writ against the *Sun* for publishing statements by Mahathir in which he described Anwar's 'sexual conduct' as 'despicable'.[49] However, this seemed likely to be a long-drawn-out and difficult action to pursue.

The second element of press output here involved the amelioration of middle-class concerns. Encompassing the 'lifestyle' genre noted above, this was more 'consultative' and 'open-ended' in tone and content. Very noticeable here was the extensive space given to 'educating' about and 'fostering understanding' of the Anwar affair and the economic situation. An example of how such agenda-setting discourse permeates key civil and cultural institutions can be seen in a piece carried by *Utusan Malaysia* entitled 'Najib urges teachers to attend briefings on Anwar's sacking':

> Education Minister [Najib] said today it is important for teachers to attend information sessions on the sacking of [Anwar] to erase confusion among them ... The Education Ministry is briefing the teachers at every meeting, but then all 200,000 teachers nationwide cannot attend such meetings at the same time, he said. 'Groups organising such information at state and district levels are asked to invite teachers to attend such sessions in view of their important function in society,' he told reporters after opening the inaugural meeting of the Congregation of National Language and Cultural Activists Malaysia.[50]

The significance of such 'reports' lay not so much in their 'they said' value, but in their attempt to set the Anwar issue within a prescribed context of national recovery through an appeal for reasoned middle-class debate. The 'restrained polemic' apparent in the talkback features, letters and columns at this point was also being 'guided' by editorials and comment pieces appealing for balanced discussion. The *New Straits Times* editor Kadir Jasin's 'Other Thots' article, 'Treat Anwar's trial like any other', is a case in point, taking to task those 'deliberately trying to politicise the matter':

Even if the [medical] report is true, the fact that Dr Mahathir had no prior knowledge of Anwar's injury shows that he does not interfere with the work of the police. Of course, it is not to the advantage of the critics to acknowledge that under section 73 of the [ISA] which is being used against Anwar, the police do not have to inform the Home Minister of every stage of the investigation nor of actions against detainees.[51]

Again, whether Mahathir was being informed about Anwar's treatment or not remains a matter of conjecture. Certainly, his public appearance in this condition served no purpose for Mahathir, as he himself had pointed out. Yet, allowing for this confusion, it is equally illogical to extrapolate from this Mahathir's non-involvement in the broader Anwar affair, as implied in Kadir's article.

This is not to say that such output lacked genuine concern for Anwar's own predicament. Some seditious tones were even being adopted to get the message across. Reflecting upon *Joseph K*, for example, Amir Muhammad's Perforated Sheets essay, 'The beginning of The Trial', used Kafkaesque allegory to suggest nightmarish processes of state victimisation and political mendacity against Anwar.[52] But while stimulating a certain reaction, most other 'political commentary' here had helped keep middle-class reaction ambivalent, contained and, for the most part, off the streets. Indeed, with the *reformasi* now gaining momentum through GERAK and other political alignments, these media appeals for calm reflection pointed up the real dilemma for the middle class: whether to sit tight in the hope of an economic upturn – and, perhaps, even some internally led reform by an anguished elite – or risk further instability by embracing wholesale reform. Although they were still incensed by Anwar's treatment, the repeated TV scenes and press coverage of Anwar supporters clashing with riot police had only intensified middle-class fears, amplifying an aversion to mob violence among the Malaysian public at large. However, hostility towards the domestic media was also growing, with the *reformasi* message finding new expression through a range of alternative organs, including the Malay-language publications *Eksklusif, Detik, Wasilah, Tamadun* and, more notably, *Harakah* (see Chapter 7).

The domestic press were also now experiencing serious circulation problems, though not yet critical. Alongside increased publishing costs and a decline in advertising revenue, circulation of Malaysia's 39 daily newspapers fell by 11% in 1997 and a further 6% in the first half of 1998 (from a peak of 3.9 million in 1996), a key reason being the younger generation's increased use of the Internet.[53] While media managers were still talking up the prospects for the industry, this development was indicative of a slow, but worrying, trend for the authorities, this being exacerbated by an emerging boycott of the BN press. In a subsequent relaunch, the *Sun*, for example, appeared to be adapting to the new public mood.[54] However, while recognising slanted editorial lines as a key reason for the decline, many editors continued to castigate foreign coverage of the crisis.[55]

Reporting the Media: Foreign Coverage and Competing Ideologies

This brings us, more specifically, to the relationship between the domestic press and foreign media. Much of the Anwar affair was being presented in the mainstream Western media as the final call for yet another autocratic Asian leader: the 'genie was out of the bottle', as Anwar, the adopted symbol of civil freedoms and democratic reform, lay beaten and bruised on 'Mahathir's prison floor'.[56] Yet, while the foreign media had played a key role in highlighting Anwar's persecution and local media bias – all welcome publicity for the *reformasi* – there had been much sensationalist language and simplification of the issues. As one commentator was to note at this point in an article posted on the *reformasi* site, *Saksi*: 'A trawl through their offerings to the world illustrates not just bad journalism but distortion, caricature and a trivialisation of Malaysia's political crisis.'[57]

Examples of narrow reporting and common stereotypes noted were: the depiction of peaceful protests as riots and anarchic situations (BBC, *New York Times*, *Guardian*, *Bangkok Post*); the trivialisation of opposition gatherings (*South China Morning Post*, *Far Eastern Economic Review*); personalisation of the crisis, the 'lionising of Anwar' and free use of caricatures – 'Anwar the freedom lover and Dr M as the James Bond villain' (*Telegraph*, *New York Times*); the lack of reports outside Kuala Lumpur; the play on 'PAS fundamentalism' and implied 'gulf' between middle-class liberals and Muslims – as if a Muslim cannot be a liberal (*Reuters*, *Newsweek*, *Christian Science Monitor*); the intonation of Malaysia as a 'backward' country having failed its 'coming-of-age' – 'we are modern, you are not' (*Newsweek*, Matt Frei for the BBC and *Telegraph*); and the 'fearless liberal hack' performance – the 'ego prize' here going to the *Observer*'s John Sweeney for hamming up his 'threatening encounter' with Rahim Noor.

Meanwhile, trivialised 'reports', more akin to 'travel journalism' than political analysis, continued to be churned out, as in Matt Frei's BBC piece 'Political benefits of sin' on the spectre of 'PAS fundamentalism' in Kelantan. Here, rather than the vital significance of the Anwar affair on PAS politics and the Kelantanese electorate, we find a series of hackneyed phrases and images of the 'Islamic threat'. For example, in Kelantan: 'The genders have to stand in separate queues at the supermarket – just in case they should be overcome by passion while waiting to pay for their frozen peas.'[58]

More significant, though, was the lack of scrutiny given by the foreign media to Anwar's own UMNO record, recovery agenda and relationship with Michel Camdessus and others. By October 1998, the inadequacy of deflationary measures in Malaysia and elsewhere had given rise to G7 emergency talks on IMF/World Bank restructuring.[59] Yet there was little discussion of these power relationships *vis-à-vis* the Anwar issue in *mainstream* foreign analysis, denoting how 'standard liberal journalism' works within accepted parameters of critical enquiry.[60]

Nevertheless, many of the political and social aspects of the crisis were being highlighted through this medium. Noting middle-class concern, the *Far Eastern Economic Review* piece 'Prime mover', for example, illustrated how Malaysians were now confused and polarised in their attitude towards Mahathir. Citing surveys carried out for UMNO (there being no major independent opinion-poll agencies in Malaysia) and other 'anecdotal' evidence, it showed that while most Malays saw him as a nation-builder, a majority (seven out of ten according to an earlier *Review* article) were now unhappy with Mahathir.[61] However, it also indicated a higher level of support for Mahathir in the Chinese community, particularly business people alarmed at the impact of Anwar's high interest rate policy. One Chinese journalist in the piece also pointed to Anwar's cronies and lack of reform while in office. With the Indian community also split, the key point here was that all Malaysians were now part of the debate, a shift linked mainly with Mahathir's own efforts in making non-Malays believe they have a meaningful stake in the country.[62] Endorsing this view, an *Asiaweek* article, 'The Chinese connection', also noted that 80% of letters to local newspapers supporting Mahathir at this point were from Chinese Malaysians.[63]

This reflected, primarily, the concerns of established business and upper middle-class Chinese. Generally older and more conservative, this element saw Mahathir as the only means of averting instability and financial loss. The related question was whether the privatisation *towkays*, the MCA, Gerakan and Chinese business institutions could keep the other Chinese classes tied into this support base.

Here, other foreign reports tended towards a more stereotypical reportage of the Chinese factor. For example, Michael Sheridan's piece 'Anwar in "coward" gibe' (reproduced in *Harakah* from a *Sunday Times* article) had this summation:

Anwar's cause has also attracted support from opposition politicians in the commercially powerful Chinese community. That is unusual in a country where tensions between the 27% of the population who are Chinese and the majority Muslim Malays have spilt over into race riots in the past.[64]

One problem here is the reference to the Malay–Chinese 'conflict', as though it had happened recently rather than 30 years previously, giving the generalised and false impression that the situation was akin to Indonesia. Another is the author's blanket allusion to opposition Chinese politicians and Chinese business. Despite DAP support for the *reformasi* and Chinese business concern over Mahathir's early handling of the crisis, there had been no significant support for Anwar from within the Chinese business sector at this point.[65] Quite simply, Anwar was now unable to convey their concerns to the political hierarchy. Thus, in Penang, for example, many Chinese had abandoned Anwar, his replacement with Abdullah, another Penang-based figure, perhaps being significant.

On the other hand, lower-middle- and working-class Chinese with less to lose had been relatively more disposed towards the *reformasi*. Although still cautious about a 'PAS dividend', many now saw support for Anwar as a way of shaking off the last vestiges of the NEP system. Concern within the BN over this shift can be seen in Gerakan's attempts (notably in Penang) to incorporate elements of the reform agenda. But it had also been Mahathir's own Bangsa Malaysia project which had, paradoxically, galvanised the *reformasi* (see Chapter 8), leaving the ruling elite less able, though still attempting, to play the race card. Thus, for the first time since Merdeka, meaningful cross-ethnic alignments and a putative 'class politics' were now threatening traditional power arrangements.

Meanwhile, the government intensified their attack on the foreign media as purveyors of distorted news, as in this message carried by *Utusan Malaysia* following Anwar's arrest:

> The local media should give a more accurate picture of the situation within and outside the country because the foreign media cannot be relied upon to do so, Information Minister Datuk Moha med Rahmat said today ... 'I call on the local media to play their role in explaining the true situation' ... he told reporters after attending a mass circumcision in Kampung Paya ... Mohamed said the ministry will extend the Information Action Plan nationwide to explain the situation to the people.[66]

While propagandist news reports were being used to depict external news reports *as* propaganda, not all press coverage of the situation was couched in slavish monotones. Following the media's 'postmodern trend' of reporting itself, the press even found itself covering both its own and the foreign media's coverage of the encampment outside Anwar's home. In

'No let-up to political drama at Bt Damansara', the *Star's* Wong Chun Wai offers this acerbic, if still loaded, view of the scene:

> The garden at [Anwar's] residence has become a field of mud as a result of heavy rain and the big crowd over the past few days ... Inside, Anwar's privacy is now confined to the kitchen and the bedroom upstairs ... A few enterprising young men, selling mineral water and burgers, have defied City Hall's order to leave. One has proclaimed his product as air reformasi, while cassettes of Anwar's speeches are being sold at RM5 each ... A university student, sporting gold-rimmed glasses and a goatee – trademarks of Anwarites – complained: 'It's all fabricated, where is the evidence?' His friends nod in agreement, telling the foreign reporters that 'it is a big conspiracy ... '
> ... After more than a week, the strain [on Anwar] has begun to show ... Fatigue has also set in among the local and foreign reporters ... Still, no reporter is willing to miss Anwar's arrest, should it happen. The job is particularly tough for the reporters of a private TV station. They have been heckled and criticised for purported biased coverage. Ironically, this same station was also attacked by Anwar's political foes in Umno just a few months back. The station was then said to be controlled by Anwar's allies and had supposedly blacked out his Umno rivals.[67]

To some extent, what was already being projected by the media as a 'shared *national* experience' was also now being filtered as a 'shared *media* experience'. Having turned the Anwar affair into a media event, the media itself were now subject to, and subjecting themselves to, almost as much attention as Anwar.

All of this might be viewed as just more postmodern irony were it not for the ideological power-play underlying it. Malaysian editors had played a central role in helping to fabricate populist conceptions of a 'foreign agenda'. Yet it was not unreasonable to make the link between certain unfavourable reporting of Mahathir's new policy measures and the free-market concerns of the IMF and other Western agencies. To a significant extent, what was being portrayed in *Time*, *Asiaweek*, *The Economist*, CNN and other such outlets was a business media version of the 'policy view' within these bodies, even where that involved 'critical' debate about the shifting nature of multilateral responses to the crisis and the need for a more 'social developmentalist' approach.[68]

For example, much of the 'crisis analysis' by now appearing in World Bank/International Finance Corporation (IFC) literature pointed specifically to internally created problems within Asian countries, such as 'lack of international standards in regulation', 'directed credit and administered interest rates' and 'poor and non-transparent supervision',[69] an agenda-setting perspective offered by the business media on Mahathir's policy measures. As one *Far Eastern Economic Review* article itself put it:

> [Mahathir's] decision to adopt currency controls to tackle Malaysia's economic crisis has left him in the cold with many Western financial institutions. Privately, American diplomats around the region can barely contain their anger at the man they see as undermining adherence to the International Monetary Fund's orthodoxy of high interest rates and open markets.[70]

In response, the domestic press had begun to target specific news agencies. On the day of Anwar's trial-fixing court appearance, the *New Straits Times* carried an editorial calling for 'errant' foreign reporters to be detained under the ISA if found to be sensationalising the situation. In particular, it singled out the Singapore-based CNBC network and the Hong Kong-based *Asian Wall Street Journal*, both part of the Dow Jones corporation in the USA (which also owns the *Far Eastern Economic Review*). The editorial, carried as a 'breaking news' story by many of the foreign media services, urged them to 'stop being prejudiced and be fair to Dr. Mahathir':

> What Malaysians are basically saying to foreign media companies is this – be fair and truthful in your reporting … As a matter of fact, you will discover that many Malaysians … believe Dr. Mahathir has acted responsibly as a gentleman and a statesman … Local media of Asian countries do not have the circulation and audience to influence global opinion. Even so, the media in this country are generally careful and responsible in their commentaries on the affairs of our neighbours and their leaders … This is very much part of the Asian culture where we are sensitive, tolerant and respectful of the interests of others.[71]

As the staunchest voice of government, the *New Straits Times* editorial may not have been representative of the domestic press, particularly the Chinese press, which had been relatively more graphic in its portrayal of the *reformasi*, inviting possible curbs on their publishing permits. The editorial had also been attacked by other regional newspapers.[72] But the pronouncement was now symptomatic of the discredited status of journalism as a 'profession' in Malaysia. For Nain, structural controls and conservative socialisation within the media had now brought journalists into critical disrepute – unable and unwilling to confront the unfolding issues with any degree of integrity:

> Journalism in Malaysia is no longer – if it ever was – a profession in its true sense, imbued with a mission to seek out truths and to convey them to the public. Instead, journalism, like any other job, is about *cari makan* [seeking a living]. Many journalists evidently believe that, like the *roti canai*

[Malaysian 'street food'] maker who sells *roti canai* for a profit, theirs is a job of producing (and reproducing) news to be sold on the market, like any economic commodity.[73]

Reflecting this passivity, it was fitting that the unease of even senior Gerakan and MCA figures at this point was being aired in the regional, rather than the local, press – as in a *South China Morning Post* report of Penang CM Koh Tsu Koon urging the government to consider the Bar Council's concerns over the justice system.[74]

Although conspicuously few in number, some within the local press were, nevertheless, still trying to push the boundaries of 'critical reporting'. In an incisive piece, written on the Saksi site and reproduced in *Harakah*, a 'local journalist' offers some insight into the difficulties of their task. Disillusioned by the media clampdown in 1987, though still part of the media system, the writer chides those who, in blanket form, denounce all local journalists as 'prostitutes'. Noting the large number of 'critical' stories that *have* been aired over the years (such as the plight of the urban poor, the Bakun Dam issue and illegal land deals), the writer believes that:

> The democratic space is always in a state of flux as far as the local media is concerned ... *The space to express dissent has to be constantly negotiated* ... Still there are those who are determined to believe that the foreign media is fair and the local media is biased. Can people accept the fact that both are equally biased in that they have their own agenda? ... All said and done, there are editors and journalists who are constantly testing and pushing the boundaries. We may be small in number but there is hope yet. And remember this: news and feature contents within the same paper may not necessarily have the same stand.[75]

Acknowledging the discomfort of many journalists within the profession, the prominent local journalist and academic Rustam A. Sani points more specifically to the institutional bias within the domestic media. In one of many critical articles by now appearing in *Harakah* (see Chapter 6), he notes that while during elections and the Anwar crisis, 'the conspiratorial nature of the local media could hardly be concealed', media manipulation during periods of political calm is hardly discernible:

> I have never accused the Malaysian government of exercising stark media censorship. But through a complex network of corporate control of media companies by political parties and through manipulate selection of editorial executives, the media has been subjected not so much to direct control but *more to self and subtle censorship*.[76]

Rustam had stopped writing for *Utusan* at election times, finding 'being a participant in such an unacceptable form of journalism too revolting personally'.[77] Yet, despite this bias and his campaign for an extensive public boycott of the local media, the object of his criticism is the media as institution rather than the journalists inside it:

> Indeed, I believe that a majority of journalists in the country are unhappy with the situation that their profession has to endure and consider themselves the victim rather than the promoter of the kind of media that has developed in this country.[78]

Rustam also sees a distinction here between foreign and local reporting of the crisis. Inaccuracies in foreign coverage were, he believes:

> not caused by a conscious effort to mislead or to conspire against anyone, but merely by the ignorance of the reporters [who were] totally unfamiliar with Malaysia and its political terrain ... [In contrast,] the fault of the local media lies in their conscious participation in a conspiracy ... [Here, a] number of political has-beens, totally unsuitable for the task, were given exposure in the media to talk about subjects such as morality of leaders, the new global economic order and neo-colonialism. Suddenly there was an unexplained and unprecedented editorial interest in certain subjects such as homosexual behaviour.[79]

While Rustam rather glosses over the 'understandable incompetence' aspect of the foreign media here, and the apparent absence of any agenda, it is worth noting his view, as with the previous writer, that media production in Malaysia is of a more subtle nature than that generally allowed for. Such representations of a 'straightforwardly controlled' Malaysian media are, in this sense, part of an external media discourse in itself, as is the view of an openly biased *foreign* media a domestic media construct. Again, this is not to negate the particular institutional controls within the Malaysian media, but to acknowledge the hegemonic interactions and conflicts at both these levels.

Dateline Malaysia: 'Seizing the Moment'

A good example of this interplay during the Anwar crisis could be seen in the NTV7 *Dateline Malaysia* programme. Launched in November 1998 by the newly formed Asian News Broadcasting company, this new 'hard-hitting' current affairs format had shown commercial initiative by producing shows about the crisis and using a new 'bolder' reporting style to allow opposition figures more than the usual space for 'dissent'. Another intention of the show, claimed one of its producers, was to 'heal some divisions through open debate'.[80] As noted by Jomo and other participants, the taping, editing and rapid-style presentation of the show tended to limit, rather than allow, meaningful argument.[81] However, its more immediate function was to satisfy the need for an *apparent* expansion of media discussion, civil participation and objective reporting.

In one notable edition on the media,[82] Khairy Jamaludin, *Dateline*'s bright, precocious presenter, brought together the *Star* editor Wong Chun Wai and Ahmed Rejad Arbeel, group editor of *Berita Harian*, to voice allegations of foreign media bias against Associated Press (AP) correspondent Ranjan Roy, the BBC's David Willis and Chris Blackwell of CNBC. While the programme allowed a frank exchange of views, giving it an air of 'controversial credibility', debate was still directed around the 'problem-solving' theme of 'concerned Malaysians confront distorted coverage of our country', as the following extracts indicate:

Following Ahmed's complaint that the foreign media saw themselves as 'self-appointed guardians of fair play', Khairy asked David Willis whether their coverage had been too sensationalist. In a rather apologetic manner, Willis noted that he did 'have some sympathy' for Dr. Mahathir. How, then, asked Khairy, could he defend the BBC's website story, 'Mahathir: strongman under siege' and the stereotypical view of Malaysians as 'uncivilised pygmies'? Willis, rather disingenuously, deferred comment here, noting that he had not seen the website item but would draw the BBC's attention to it if it was offensive. Asked by Khairy if CNBC was guilty of 'hit-and-run journalism', Chris Blackwell replied 'no', denying also that CNBC were overly-influenced by their owners Dow Jones. However, he thought they had to be careful about over-use of library re-run pictures. Wong noted here that CNBC had been very 'judgmental' and 'speculative' in their coverage of the Anwar affair. Rejecting this, Blackwell insisted that they only wanted to get the other side of the story – there was 'no agenda.' Ahmed countered that the foreign media only show an interest when things are bad. Blackwell accepted this as 'valid' criticism, that the foreign media constantly had to police itself. Khairy asked Blackwell if he thought Malaysians were 'too sensitive?' 'No', he thought, 'Malaysians love their country'. In a further response to Ahmed's claim that the domestic media were not speaking for the government, Blackwell asked, 'are there not some stories you would not touch?' Both Wong and Ahmed noted that they would not cover stories deemed too sensitive with regard to race and religion. Khairy followed this up with the suggestion to Blackwell that the foreign media did not carry the responsibilities of the local press. Rejecting this, Blackwell noted that, 'as a Black man' in America, he was well aware of the need to be careful about reporting racial issues.

Allan Friedman of the *International Herald Tribune* appeared at this point

and was asked by Khairy if the foreign press 'have a cultural agenda?' Noting
that it was 'hard to generalise these things', he conceded that some of the
right-wing press may have. In essence, there were three types of reporters,
he thought: 'local, old timers', 'global economic' (like himself) and 'hit-and-
run' types. Wong insisted here that 'we are more straightforward', placing
'emphasis on the facts ... We are not so judgmental.' Didn't Wong take this
line, asked Khairy, because 'you are not allowed to say certain things?' Noting
also that the most critical output at present is 'Life and Times', Khairy also
asked him if this augured well for the press in Malaysia? Wong responded
that it was 'a tested formula that works well'. Ahmed followed this up by
insisting that 'the press is not the fourth estate. Why should it be so?' What,
then, was the role of the press, and what of hit-and-run journalism, asked
Khairy? Ranjan Roy concluded that, while avoiding hit-and-run journalism,
the press should act as a watchdog. The main purpose was to give the news
as accurately as possible.

While debate of this kind suggested a certain expansion of critical opinion,
it also served a hegemonic purpose by stretching the boundaries at this
point to help manage public sentiment. It offered open exchange, while
keeping the 'discussible' issues within acceptable limits. As the Anwar trial
progressed, *Dateline Malaysia* stopped producing. Although it coincided
with relaunch plans at NTV7, there were suggestions that it had been
'advised' to take a lower profile.[83] Certainly, this was consistent with the
return to a more anodyne media output by early 1999.

The Media and the Net

For many Malaysians, notably the politically concerned middle class, it
was the Internet that helped fill this journalistic vacuum. The importance
of the Net lay not in its immediate availability for most Malaysians (despite
the professed IT policy), but in its use as a medium for accessing, ex-
changing and spreading information on the crisis. Prior to the crisis, the
DAP had been the only major online opposition party – Lim Kit Siang's
page, in particular, being a focal point for media statements and speeches.
By late 1997, a connecting network of sites and homepages was emerging,
linking all the major opposition parties, most reformist NGOs, opposition
publications and cyber fora such as Sangkancil. With the onset of the
Anwar situation, a whole raft of *reformasi* sites (around sixty by the
beginning of the trial) had become part of this 'cybercommunity' – including the newly formed GERAK homepage.[84] Homepages for ADIL
and its proto-party (see Chapter 8) were also under construction by early
1999. A new group of Internet journalists such as Sabri Zain were also

sending first-hand reports of the protests across the net, providing news of gatherings, information to remote *kampongs* and immediate updates for foreign observers.[85] Anwar Online was now a focal point for information, allowing news and pictures to be downloaded, photocopied and distributed at large. It was here that Anwar's letters to Mahathir and speeches detailing his rejection of the charges were published, including statements smuggled from prison. In addition, a range of videotapes, video compact discs and CD-ROMS with culled foreign and private footage of the street protests, Anwar's speeches and arrest were being sold at street markets and other informal outlets, with a message to reproduce and pass on.[86] In turn, use of the Net as an alternative news source for disenchanted Malaysians became a major story in itself for the major news agencies and journals.[87] With cyber-cafés and Net access in Malaysia spreading, the news government wanted withheld was now in the public domain.

Reacting to this expansion, the authorities had begun monitoring e-mail messages and tracking downloaded material. The main Malaysian Internet service provider MIMOS had intercepted 'suspect' messages, culminating in the arrest of four people under the ISA for spreading false rumours about impending race riots in Kuala Lumpur.[88] Although this was condemned as a malicious practice by opposition groups, these security concerns were given extensive coverage by the domestic media, providing a pretext for the continued monitoring of Internet exchanges. Ironically, Kadir Jasin had raised fears here that the use of 'a Cold War-era security law [the ISA] to punish a cyberspace perpetrator may not jell well with our quest to become a wired and kinder nation'.[89] Nevertheless, Kadir and other editors continued to air government threats. As Deputy Home Minister Tajol Rosli (commenting on downloaded pamphlets alleging unease among senior police officers and UMNO members) warned in the *Star*, 'The police will check every bit of information and leaflet.'[90]

One such net article in early 1999 offered insights from a Special Branch operative into the practices of the 'UMNO dirty tricks department' itself. Proudly claiming inheritance of British colonial expertise in this field and detailing a wide range of underhand strategies from organised vote-buying to stage-managed 'PAS demonstrations' and other black propaganda, the article notes how:

> In every organisation we have our SB boys. We have them among the university students, in every government department, and in many of the private offices as well. Some are operators but many are informers. Informers are paid a monthly retainer and they get paid extra if they bring back any information. In fact, your neighbour or one of your family members could be a Special Branch informer and you would not know it ... We trust no

one, whether they are opposition members or UMNO members, or even Ministers for that matter. In fact, in light of the present Anwar crisis, we trust the UMNO members even less.[91]

Intelligence and Internet surveillance were also creating doubts about the MSC and Mahathir's claim to be leading Malaysia towards a new age of open, information-led development. In his 'From the halls of power' letter, Anwar had criticised Mahathir's 'delusions of grandeur' and obsession with mega-projects as a symptom of his gathering megalomania.[92] Now the multimedia guru Alvin Toffler, an admirer of the MSC and Mahathir's 'information age vision of the future', denounced Anwar's arrest, warning that companies such as Netscape, Hewlett Packard and Compaq might now, along with other potential investors, withdraw their interest.[93]

The Crisis of Containment

With many Malaysians now abandoning the mainstream press altogether in search of alternative news sources, the ability to stem political dissent through conventional media controls and persuasion had been severely tested. Anwar's ouster had also allowed the public new insights into Special Branch practices and crony-type relationships. Thus, as the trial got under way, a damage limitation exercise had begun in an attempt to restore Mahathir's public image.[94] For example, Mahathir began writing his own monthly opinion column in the Japanese newspaper *Mainichi Daily News*, this being reproduced in the *New Straits Times*.[95] In early 1999, the government announced 'plans' for a new TV station to counter foreign media bias. Illustrating the inner workings of the UMNO network, the executive role was to be given to Noordin Sopiee, chairman of the 'independent' think-tank ISIS. Sopiee had previously taken out a full-page advert in the *New Straits Times* castigating foreigners for criticising Mahathir. To a similar end, the UMNO Information Chief Yusof Nor revealed plans to update the party's website more often.[96]

However, these PR efforts could not conceal the damage to the UMNO network. With public anxiety growing, what was being played out here was not only a debate about media freedoms, but a crisis of consent. The economic and political fallout of Anwar's dismissal had now created new ideological stress points, the clash of agendas between the domestic and foreign medias indicating a key intellectual attempt to defend the project and hold popular support. Middle-class dissent still took surrogate forms through the 'lifestyle columns' rather than mass street protest. Yet ongoing antagonism over the BN media's coverage of Anwar's treatment had also helped create new forms of political awareness. As the *reformasi* looked to extend that support, the question was whether this signalled a meaningful coalition and challenge to the BN bloc.

Notes

1. Cited in 'I never threatened the PM', interview with Anwar, *Asiaweek*, 18 September 1998.

2. The affidavits were to be used to oppose Nalla's request for a transfer from the Bukit Aman lock-up to Sungai Buloh prison. Contrary to established practice, the judge had refused to 'embargo' their contents before a court adjournment, arguing that since they had been filed, rather than read, in court, they were now public documents. This and other such abuses were raised in a joint statement by concerned lawyers and academics. See 'The rule of law under threat', JUST Homepage, 15 September 1998, <http://www.jaring.my/just/RuleofLaw.html>.

3. See 'Troops guard Queen amid rioting', *Guardian*, 21 September 1998.

4. See *Aliran* statement, 22 September 1998, <http://www.malaysia.net/aliran>.

5. The seven-point Declaration (named after Anwar's Penang constituency where it was delivered) was endorsed by Lim Kit Siang during a 'Free Guan Eng' speech on 13 September 1998. DAP Homepage <http://www.malaysia.net/dap>.

6. The Coalition for People's Democracy was launched at the Federal Hotel, Kuala Lumpur, 27 September 1998. Although it was a cross-party/NGO forum, its main 'sponsor' was the DAP. The Malaysian People's Movement for Justice, headed by Fadzil Noor of PAS, was formed that same evening at PAS HQ in Kuala Lumpur. See Lim Kit Siang, 'Speech at Free Guan Eng dinner', 27 September 1998, <http://www.malaysia.net/dap> and *Harakah* (Online), 28 September 1998, <http://www.pas.org.my/pas/harakah/>.

7. See 'First Lady of reform', *FEER*, 1 October 1998.

8. See Lim Kit Siang's endorsement of ADIL, 11 December 1998, <http://www.malaysia.net/dap>.

9. The letters were published at <http://Anwar.com.my>.

10. Ibid. Cited in Anwar's 'first letter' to Mahathir, dated 25 August 1998.

11. 'All over? Or all over again?', *Aliran Monthly*, September 1998, 18: 8.

12. By October 1998 a complex 10 billion ringgit plan, prepared by investment bankers Crédit Suisse First Boston, had been unveiled to restructure Renong, allowing it control of major government infrastructure projects. The move was defended as helping to prevent a banking collapse and stimulate economic activity. See 'Renong hopes to restructure with state help to settle debt', *Wall Street Journal*, 9 October 1998.

13. Taken from a transcript of Anwar's speech at <http://members.tripod.com/~Anwar-Ibrahim/main.htm>.

14. Cited in 'Recent developments in Malaysia', *Suaram*, <http://www.geocities.com/CapitolHill/1577>, 2 October 1998.

15. Ibid.

16. See 'Don't act like that in Malaysia', *Guardian*, 25 September 1998.

17. Anwar was charged at the Sessions Court, Kuala Lumpur, 29 September 1998,

on five counts of corruption and four counts of sodomy. He was charged with a further count of sodomy the following day at a court in Petaling Jaya.

18. In a later *FEER* interview, 'I was shocked', 24 June 1999, Mahathir notes: 'In fact, I don't mind telling you, I told the police, no violence, no handcuffs ... and I said to myself this is going to be a problem.'

19. As reported in the *International Herald Tribune*, 1 October 1998.

20. Anwar's political secretary Mohamad Ezam Mohd Nor, writing from Jakarta, claimed to have information that the IGP had been personally responsible for Anwar's beating. Anwar Online, October 1998.

21. Cited, *The Electric New Paper* <http://web3.asia1.com.sg/archive/tnp/4/pages/nploo2.html>, 1 October 1998.

22. See 'Full probe: Independent team to look into assault claim', *Star*, 1 October 1998.

23. 2 October 1998.

24. Wearing a neck brace, Anwar appeared in the High Court, Kuala Lumpur, on 5 October to hear his trial date fixed for 2–14 November 1998. Only four of the five corruption charges were to be heard during these dates, the other and the five sodomy charges being scheduled for 23 November onwards. The adjournment 'coincided' with the APEC summit in Kuala Lumpur.

25. See 'Cool response to crisis code', *Guardian*, 31 October 1998.

26. John Gray, 'Hanging together', *Guardian*, 27 October 1998.

27. See 'Doctor knows best', *FEER*, 24 June 1999.

28. See 'An open letter to Prime Minister Mahathir', published at Paul Krugman's homepage, 1 September 1998, <http://web.mit.edu/krugman/www/mahathir.html>. Krugman is Ford International Professor of Economics at MIT.

29. A 'validation' later clarified by Krugman in arguing that the controls should have been better timed, a temporary expedient and accompanied by political reform. See 'Krugman on Malaysia', at *freeMalaysia* <http://www.freemalaysia.com/krugman_book.htm>.

30. The 1999 budget (23 October 1998) projected an overall deficit of 16.135 million ringgit, a budget shortfall 68% higher than the previous year. Officials claimed that much of this would be financed through government bonds and foreign borrowing, alongside duty increases on tobacco, alcohol and gaming levies. See Malaysia (1998), *The 1999 Budget*, pp. 12, 17, 30–1 and *AFP*, 23 October 1998.

31. See 'Bank Negara: be proactive in spreading information', and 'Malay chamber to help SMIs obtain loans', *New Straits Times*, 13 February 1999.

32. See, 'Laundering Lies', a *freeMalaysia* website article, 2 June 1999, noting how the White Paper presented to Parliament on the crisis (6 April 1999) took no account of Anwar's recovery measures – for example, Anwar's cuts in bank statutory reserve ratios, easing of fiscal restraints and increases in social spending between February and March 1998. Reference is also made here to how the White Paper exaggerated the tightness of Malaysia's monetary position at this point.

33. Ibid.

34. See, for example, 'Of privatisation, transparency and corporate governance', a summary of a question and answer session between Daim and foreign fund managers. *Sun*, 9 February 1999.

35. See ' Malaysian leader hits out at IMF policies in budget speech', *AFP*, 23 October

1998. For details of the new fiscal measures see Malaysia (1998), *The 1999 Budget*, pp. 44–5, 77.

36. *Sun*, 25 January 1999.

37. Mahathir's Forum pronunciations (28–29 January 1999) were given major headline coverage by the Malaysian media.

38. A list of detainees noted at this point by Asian Human Rights Commission (AHRC) included Saari Haji Sungub, president of *Jemaah Islah Malaysia* (JIM), Abdul Malek Hussein, executive secretary of PAS and Negri Sembilan, UMNO Youth chief.

39. See Sabri Zain's two accounts ('I went shopping today' and 'When anger overcame fear') of the *reformasi* mass protests in Kuala Lumpur on 10 and 17 October 1998, published at *Anwar Online*.

40. At the 17 October 1998 gathering, 134 people were arrested. Many were badly beaten by the police, requiring hospital treatment.

41. *AFP*, 27 October 1998. The use of tear gas around the Kampung Baru mosque area followed an apparent decision by police to start making random arrests during the, by now, weekly Saturday afternoon protest in Kuala Lumpur.

42. See 'US in dock for prison cruelty', *Guardian*, 6 October 1998. Here, Amnesty claims that within the US penal system, 'the breakdown in human rights has led to atrocities more commonly associated with authoritarian third world regimes.'

43. Cited in 'How the media have fared' *Asiaweek*, 13 November 1998.

44. Ibid.

45. The analysis here covers the period from Anwar's dismissal to his trial-fixing court appearance on 5 October 1998.

46. Headlines and quotes in order of citation (D/M/Y): *Star*, 3.9.98, *Utusan Malaysia*, 6.9.98, *Utusan Malaysia*, 6.9.98, *Utusan Malaysia*, 6.9.98, *Utusan Malaysia*, 7.9.98, *Star*, 11.9.98, *Star*, 11.9.98, *Star*, 18.9.98, *Utusan Malaysia*, 28.9.98, *Utusan Malaysia*, 29.9.98, *Star*, 29.9.98, *Utusan Malaysia*, 1.10.98, *Utusan Malaysia*, 5.10.98.

47. *Star*, 8 October 1998.

48. *Utusan Malaysia*, 15 October 1998.

49. 'Report on sodomy and masturbation', *Sun*, 28 January 1999. The statements made by Mahathir had been reported in the *Sun* on 23 September 1998.

50. *Utusan Malaysia*, 29 September 1998.

51. *New Sunday Times*, 4 October 1998.

52. *New Straits Times*, 30 September 1998.

53. As noted by Azizi Meor Ngah, executive director of the *Utusan* group and chairman of the Malaysian Newspaper Publishers Association (MNPA), See 'Print at the crossroads', *ABC News* (Audited Bureau of Circulations – Malaysia), November 1998, Vol. 15, No. 4.

54. In the relaunch issue on 8 March 1999, the *Sun*'s 'A new look, a stronger voice' statement noted: 'We will continue to take on issues that concern our daily lives, issues of accountability, fair play and good governance, even as we record the joys, tragedies and successes of Malaysians and the nation.'

55. My thanks here to Andy Ng, editor of the *Sun*, for his personal comments on these matters, 14 December 1998.

56. See, for example: Matt Frei's report for BBC Online, 30 September 1998; Alice Donald, BBC East Asia analyst, 'Opposition emboldened by Anwar saga', BBC Online,

30 September 1998; Richard Lloyd-Parry, 'Anwar "on great form" for trial', *Independent*, 1 October 1998.

57. Tom Wingfield, 'Inside out', *Saksi*, 2 November 1998, <http://www.saksi.com/wingfield.htm>.

58. BBC Online, 8 February 1999.

59. The gathering of G7 ministers (3–4 October 1998) coincided with the US Federal Reserve's bail-out of Long-Term Capital Management, the collapse of which, argued Alan Greenspan, would have threatened the entire international financial system. *Guardian*, 2 October 1998.

60. Having observed some of the practicalities of this process, one could see how information on the *reformasi* appeared to have been 'fitted into' a liberal interpretation of events, much of the more nuanced reality being lost in 'translation'.

61. 'A single spark', *FEER*, 29 October 1998.

62. *FEER*, 12 November 1998.

63. *Asiaweek*, 4 December 1998.

64. *Harakah*, 25 January 1999.

65. My thanks here to a senior member of the Penang Chinese Chamber of Commerce (January 1999), a set of views also reflected in discussions with other Chinese business people.

66. 'Give accurate picture, local media told', *Utusan Malaysia*, 7 September 1998.

67. *Star*, 11 September 1998.

68. To some extent, Wolfensohn had tried to alter the World Bank's image since his appointment in 1995, partly in response to NGO criticisms. Camdessus has also sought to give the IMF a more 'developmentalist' profile by concentrating on emerging economies.

69. International Finance Corporation (1998), ppx–xi. The IFC is an affiliate of the World Bank.

70. 'Friends indeed', *FEER*, 8 October 1998.

71. *New Straits Times*, 5 October 1998.

72. See, for example, 'Malaysian democracy fails in the fine print', Editorial article, *The Nation* (Bangkok), 12 October 1998.

73. 'Pathetic press', *Aliran Monthly*, August 1998, 18: 7.

74. 'Penang CM urges KL to respond to discontent', *South China Morning Post*, 13 October 1998.

75. 'Pushing from within', *Harakah*, 12 February 1999. Italics added.

76. 'Journalists with integrity need not feel hurt by criticisms of the media', *Harakah*, 15 February 1999. Italics added.

77. Ibid.

78. Ibid.

79. Ibid.

80. James Gibbons, *Dateline Malaysia* producer, cited in 'Breaking the news', *FEER*, 11 February 1999.

81. Ibid.

82. 17 January 1999.

83. An interpretation intimated to this writer by a news and current affairs figure.

84. These and many other pages were being closely scrutinised by the authorities, leading correspondents to use assumed names.

85. See, for example, 'Very Urgent Warning!!!!!!! Note: print and distribute widely', <http://members.tripod.com/~Anwarite/WARNING.html>, 15 October 1998. This was intended to alert protesters to the likely use of provocative tactics at a gathering in Kuala Lumpur that weekend.

86. See 'Malaysia unmuzzled Internet ensures information flow in turbulent times', by Bob Paquin for the *Ottawa Citizen*, 19 May 1999, published at the *Gerakan reformasi* site.

87. See, for example, 'Sci/tech Malaysians take to Web with Anwar protest', by Internet correspondent Chris Nuttall, BBC Online <http://news.bbc.co.uk>; and 'Alternative news' *Far Eastern Economic Review*, 8 October 1998. A Channel 4 News report (UK), 2 November 1998, carried on the first day of Anwar's trial, noted that Anwar Online had now taken around 1.5 million 'hits'. One of its webmasters was filmed in a darkened room, fearing a swoop by the authorities.

88. This followed false Internet reports on 7 August 1998 claiming that Indonesian migrants, faced with repatriation, had attacked Chinese and Malays with machetes in Kuala Lumpur. The reports caused temporary alarm and panic buying at supermarkets. Three computer workers and a bank manager were detained under the ISA. See *FEER*, 27 August 1998.

89. Cited ibid.

90. *Star*, 2 October 1998.

91. The article draws on an interview conducted by web journalist Raja Petra with an UMNO 'dirty tricks' agent. See Raja Petra homepage and *Harakah*, 12 July 1999.

92. 'From the halls of power to the labyrinths of incarceration', Anwar Online, 3 November 1998.

93. Alvin Toffler, 'Bad news for high-tech Malaysia' *International Herald Tribune*, 29 October 1998.

94. See 'The ringmaster', *FEER*, 15 October 1998.

95. See 'Dr M: Let developing nations play a part in planning new world financial architecture', *New Straits Times*, 2 March 1999.

96. 'UMNO to update its website regularly', *Star*, 30 January 1999.

6

Traditional Intellectuals: PAS, Islam and the Countervision

We now turn to the issue of counter-hegemony and alternatives to the Vision project. The first main area concerns the Islamic model of development proposed by PAS. This requires us to consider not only the immediate political tensions between UMNO and PAS, but, more specifically, the *intellectual* bases of their respective projects, an approach consistent with Gramsci's understanding of the *organic* and *traditional* intellectual. The aim is to show how the Vision has been used to harness Islamic consciousness through idealised forms of 'modern' Islamic identity, and to set this against the model of Islamic social collectivism being advanced by PAS. These issues are developed within the next chapter in relation to the Anwar affair.

In seeking to build its own project, PAS has faced two key tasks: how to construct a working relationship with other parties and civil institutions as the basis of an alternative bloc; and how to cultivate national–popular support for PAS-Islam, particularly amongst the Chinese. To help contextualise the PAS project, let us consider some of the historical tensions underlying its contestation of Vision-Islam.

Vision Islam and the Management of Traditional Consciousness

Illumination of the present, requires appreciation of the past. One of Gramsci's main contributions, in this respect, involves the recovery within Marxism of a 'voluntarist' dimension which acknowledges subjective consciousness in the historical process. In the *Prison Notebooks*, Gramsci's historicism, situated around a critique of Crocean philosophy, helps redefine 'superstructural relations' and the significance of the historical dialectic.[1] Intrinsic to this process is the sense in which human activity is shaped simultaneously by social structures and is itself a force for creative change, thus indicating a close awareness of historical forms and traditions. As one Gramscian contributor notes:

Marxists who seek to establish universally valid systems of thought, who spend their time building neat, logically consistent formal models, ultimately mystify rather than illuminate history by ignoring the unique configurations that emerge through the variations in socio-political development. They also overlook the crucial fact that intellectual processes themselves – of whatever kind – are part of a complex and unique history that is shaped by particular cultural and political traditions.[2]

The intellectual conflict between Vision-Islam and PAS-Islam is a contemporary manifestation of this evolving process. Implicit in the colonial mindset was a view of Islam as a monolithic obstruction to modernism. But, in its search for a modern Malay identity, the anti-colonial movement also came to challenge the traditionalist impulses of Islam as a dogmatic impediment to nationalist development.

Diverging perceptions of Malay–Islamic consciousness crystallised around the *Kaum Tua – Kaum Muda* (Old Order – New Order) debate in late nineteenth-century Malaya. The former adhered to a traditionalist interpretation of Islamic *shariah* law (God's law), a conservative *adat* consistent with feudal hierarchy and a spiritual universalism of pan-Islamic salvation. The latter, reflecting progressive streams of Middle East / Ottoman intellectual thought, embraced a nationalist modernism based upon the ideals of rational secular knowledge, technology and education.[3]

This progressive stream was by no means a negation of Islam. In challenging a reactionary *ulama* (spiritual leaders) and their fatalistic worldview, the *Kaum Muda* sought to restore the humanitarian and socially progressive values of Islam and fuse them with a new Malay nationalism. By 1906, these modernist Islamic messages were finding populist resonance through the Malay periodical *Al-Imam* (*The Leader*). *Al-Imam* offered an intellectual context for the issue of Malay identity by linking it to the broader problem of orthodox Islamic doctrine. It called upon Malays to recognise the centrality of knowledge and the gift of intelligence as a source of spiritual fulfilment, a realisation of the true teachings of the Prophet Muhammad. Inspired by modernist Islamic groups and publications in Cairo,[4] *Al-Imam* argued for a new form of Islamic education and religious instruction which encouraged open thought, the teaching of Western subjects and the independent study of Islamic ideas. Embracing the spirit of the *Kaum Muda*:

> *Al-Imam* was a radical departure in the field of Malay publications, distinguished by its predecessors both in intellectual stature and intensity of purpose and in its attempts to formulate a coherent philosophy of action for a society faced with the need for rapid social and economic change.[5]

In contrast, the reproduction of traditional *ulama* scholarship by religious elites had helped sustain both a hierarchical social order and an effective system of colonial control. As divide and rule innovators, *par excellence*, the British had also used the racist stereotype of Malay indolence to reinforce this subservience.[6] A more routine feature of the system, notably in Kelantan and Terengganu, was the integration of the local *kadi* (civil functionaries), appointed by the Sultans, and the juridical edicts of the *mufti* or *ulama*.[7] Through its predominant influence within the *pondok* (schools) and village communities, this closely linked network of religious-civil officials represented a vital medium of socialisation and social control. By endorsing ideas of fatalism and a conservative *adat* as integral parts of the socio-religious system, Malay elites, under the colonial order, helped propagate Malay–Islamic passivity and a disdain for rational enquiry:

> there are many Malay values and attributes which impeded the modernisation of the Malays in Southeast Asia, [including] the acceptance of arbitrary notions of power ... the downgrading of ... rationalism and the encouragement of myths which serve the interests of those in power ... As producers of ideas and those who condition the thinking of their society, it is the Malay elite who are responsible for the prevalence of these negative values in society.[8]

However, the ongoing contestation of these values also provides a *context* for addressing social issues in Malaysia. In this regard, questions of Malay–Islamic identity represent not only a socio-historical 'subject', but a form of intellectual perspectivism *sui generis*. Thus, intellectuals have not only influenced the subject through discourse and interpretation, the subject has conditioned the mode of intellectual enquiry itself. Representations of modernity, development and political culture are examined quintessentially against this background consciousness. In this sense, the 'Malay–Islam problem' is invoked, deconstructed and, ultimately, exploited as a key narrative in the projection of hegemony.

Recourse to the Malay–Islam identity problem has been central to the marginalisation of traditional Islamic forces. This is evident in Mahathir's own intellectual reflections in *The Challenge*, a development of the claims expressed in the influential text *Revolusi Mental* which, in similar mode, sought to link perceived flaws in the Malay character with the need for a transcendent modernism.[9]

A related aspect here was Mahathir's attempt to associate the Malays' socio-historical predicament with the socio-psychological notion of *amok*. The precise meaning and causes of *amok* are widely disputed. In essence, though, it refers to a culturally derived psychological condition amongst Malays in which emotions of inner repression give (apparent) rise to sudden outward expressions of uncontrolled violence. Deep-seated feelings of stress and angst arising from the internalisation of the Malays' cultural burdens – obedience, fatalism and adherence to form – are said to invoke inner crises, thus activating latent impulses as a form of cathartic release.[10] For Mahathir, *amok* was a symptom of the Malay identity problem: '*Amok* represents the external physical expression of the conflict within the Malay which his perpetual observation of the rules and regulations of his life causes in him. It is a spilling over, an overflowing of his inner bitterness.'[11]

Yet, as Alatas argues, neither *amok* nor any other form of 'social pathology' attributed to the Malays was, or is, unique to the Malay community. Just as the colonial administrator Clifford had contrived to link the psychopathological state of *latah* to the Malays, so was *amok* a crafted distortion of the Malay character.[12] Against the backdrop of the 13 May riots, it was used to suggest a cultural malady, an emotive symptom of the 'Malay dilemma', out of which a 'new Malayness' could emerge as a complement to the NEP system.

However, the ideology of 'modern' Malay nationalism being spawned here had come to reveal new and more significant tensions within the Malay–Islam relationship.

Islam and Nationalism

If not entirely hostile to the aspirations of Malayan nationalism, 'traditional Islam' in Malaya/Malaysia has been ambivalent about nationalist ideology. In the colonial context, this was not unconnected with the political conservatism of the Malayan *mullahs*. Of wider importance was the disjunction between Western conceptions of the nation-state, based on liberal, secular and positivist ideals, and that of the 'Islamic state', the *umma*, based on the ideal of a universal Islamic community.

Within traditional Islamic scholarship, sovereignty has a solely cosmological significance, wherein God is omnipotent and the Muslim's singular form of identity is that of Islam. A traditional Muslim has no sense of national or communal identification higher than this authority. The ideals of nationalism and nation-state are cosmetic artifices impeding the Muslim's true spiritual membership of the Islamic community, the *umma*.[13] Under the tenets of *shariah* (literally 'path') Islamic law, the world is understood as a division between *dar al-Islam* (the 'abode of peace'; Islamic territory), and *dar al-harb* (the 'abode of warfare'; non-Islamic territory). While the faithful are enjoined to extend the former, the latter is synonymous with conflagration and the false ideologies of nationalism.

Historically, Islamic perceptions of the nation-state reflected broader concerns within Islamic scholarship over the role of rational knowledge.

In antiquity, the flowering of a progressive Islamic consciousness, based upon the sanctity of knowledge and learning, long preceded the age of European Renaissance, Enlightenment and reason. Evoking the teachings of the Quran and other *hadith* (sayings of the Prophet), it gave expression to a vibrant civilisation of scientific, philosophical and cultural enquiry. In no sense was this intellectual energy inconsistent with the ideal of an Islamic *umma*.

However, with the exigencies of war precipitating a conservative shift among the *ulama*, the suppression of rational scholarship saw the long-term decline of Islam as a progressive, dynamic religion. Symbolising this hiatus by the tenth century, the *ulama* 'closed the Gate of *Ijtihad*' (Gate of Knowledge), declaring the key tenets of Islam authoritatively defined. Within the main centres of Islamic civilisation, a clerical establishment tied itself to political alliances with feudal rulers and promoted ideals of theological conformity.[14] Thus the *ulama* had, effectively, downgraded the values of the Islamic polity consecrated at Medina (following the Prophet's *hijra* (migration) from Mecca in AD 622); a religious community founded upon the dual concepts of political citizenship and Islamic faith.[15] Under the various caliphs, sultans and other direct rulers, the *ulama*:

> contented themselves with the privileged position offered them by the ruler or dynasty as guardians of the word of God, as teachers, scholars and judges ... Having produced their massive legal compendia according to their interpretation of the Koran ... they formulated the proposition that obedience to the ruler, good or bad, was better than *fitna* (anarchy, disorder) ... This was tantamount to the formal consecration of quietism in Islam.[16]

The subsequent orthodoxy of received faith, *taqlid*, seen as the sole criterion of knowledge, had epochal implications for Islam as an intellectual force:

> Closing the gates of rational knowledge and independent reasoning has had a disastrous effect on Islamic science and education. Secular science was replaced by theology and dogma, and public education, which had flourished in the first two centuries of the Abbasid dynasty, lost its dynamism and creativity. It became institutionalised around the dysfunctional *taqlid* system of learning by memorising and blind imitation. Gradually, the reactionary *mullahs* and *ulama* assumed a monopoly control of education, morality and opinion, and, in the process, advanced the cause of *jahiliyya* (mass ignorance), fatalism and underdevelopment as effectively as imperialism and colonial exploitation.[17]

Not until the nineteenth century did modernist Islamic figures such as Jamil al-Din al-Afghani, Muhammad Iqbil and Muhammad Abduh (of Persian, Egyptian and Pakistani origin, respectively) challenge traditional conformity through the call for a greater understanding of Western rationalism and scientific knowledge,[18] with later like-minded reformists such as Sayyid Shaykh al-Hadi in the 1930s arguing for a reintegration of Western secular and Islamic education.[19]

Such forces represented a gathering progressive challenge to an entrenched *ulama* in Malaya. The modernist movement here was at once politically hostile to Western ideals of colonial 'development' and intellectually responsive to Western concepts of rational learning. It sought to harmonise the benefits of science, technology and lateral thought with the egalitarian impulses of Islamic social justice as a model for Malay modernisation. And it is within this context that a Malay–Islamic nationalism became co-defined amongst progressive Islamic forces. Nationalism, in this sense, was understood as part of an integral intellectual problem, linking modernity, political independence and an Islamic social consciousness: in effect, nationalism was not only a reactive process, but a proactive statement of the need to reawaken the progressive ideals of the Islamic community.

PAS, Nationalism and the Islamic Resurgence

In the struggle for independence, this moral view of nationalist development, although not a specific guiding force, was implicit in the political ideology of PAS. As Malaysia's 'definitive' Islamic party, formed in 1951 in Penang, PAS has never deviated from its desire to create an Islamic state. However, in contrast to its 'unequivocal rejection of nationalism' today,[20] PAS's identification with Malay nationalism from the 1950s to the 1970s was both explicit and partly motivated by this higher progressive idealism. As its president in the 1950s-1960s, Burhammudin Al-helmy (previously leader of the Malay Nationalist Party PKMM, and other leftist coalitions), asserted: 'PAS and I are in content, character and orientation "Malay nationalists" with "Islamic aspirations".'[21]

However, by 1977–78, PAS was undergoing a radical change in its view of nationalism. Following the entry of former ABIM leaders Fadzil Noor, Nakhaie Ahmad and Abdul Hadi Awang, and the crisis departure of PAS leader Mohammad Asri Muda after the PAS Muktamar (party Assembly) in 1982,[22] the party's new guard, in alliance with the older *ulama* figures (notably Nik Aziz and Yusof Rawa), proceeded to abandon its Malay-nationalist position in pursuit of a more pure and pristine interpretation of Islam. Driven, in large part, by the charismatic religious teacher Hadi Awang in Terengganu, and in reaction to Anwar's co-optation in 1982, PAS had begun to rebuild its Islamic agenda in opposition to UMNO. By the mid-1980s, PAS had established new support bases in Kedah and Perlis while extending into the urban centres and universities by the mid-1980s.[23]

In part, this was an atavistic shift influenced by the Islamic revolution in Iran. But it was also, more specifically, a rejection of 'narrow nationalism', or, as PAS had come to define it, *assabiyah*, loosely translated as ethnic chauvinism. Synonymous with false or contrived sectarian loyalty, the term was extended, notably by Hadi Awang, to include a rejection of the NEP and Bumiputeraism. Indeed, Hadi's assertion that a Chinese could, in principle, become prime minister if he was a pious Muslim, had helped foster new dialogue with the Chinese Consultative Committee (CCC) and other such groups in 1985 and 1986, PAS's first direct overture to explain Islam in depth to the Chinese community.[24]

At the same time, PAS has sought to impose limits, where possible, on the expression of culture it considers inimical to an Islamic worldview. For example, in Kelantan and Kedah this has involved opposition to the performance of Western music by Malaysian groups. In Kelantan it has also seen the attempted banning of the traditional Malay dance drama *mak yong* as it involves men and women performing together and is too focused on Malay, rather than Islamic, elements.[25]

Thus, from the early 1980s, the intricacies of domestic politics and the Islamic resurgence had sharpened the Malay–Islamic identity problem. But it also sponsored a more contemplative reaction within the wider intellectual community. The Islamic indictment of Western values and neo-liberalism (see below) has helped shape intellectual discourse more generally towards critical reflections on capitalism, the free market and its social consequences – acquisitiveness, wealth disparities and social injustice. This, in turn, has created new tensions between UMNO and PAS as capitalist development in Malaysia proceeds. In this sense, PAS intellectuals have resisted Mahathir's attempts to entrench modern nationalist ideas about Islamic development through state and civil institutions.

Emerging contradictions could, thus, be seen within the Mahathir project by the early 1980s. The first was the dialectic of the NEP generation. In facilitating the socio-economic advancement of Malays through enhanced educational opportunities, NEP policies were creating a more politicised middle class, much of it sympathetic to, and involved in, the spread of Islamic revivalism. This could be traced to changes in tertiary education from the early 1970s and the exponential growth of NEP-sponsored students at local and overseas universities. It was within this new environment of Malay assertiveness that many students came to understand the meaning of their 'nationalist identity' in Islamic terms and embrace Islam as a form of religious–political commitment. The campus experience, thus, formed the key source of recruitment for the *dakwah* movement – notably ABIM and the National Association of Muslim Students Malaysia, PKPIM. This was strengthened from the mid- to late

1970s by the gradual return of Malay students from abroad, notably England, many of whom had been influenced by fundamentalist streams of Islamic thought and/or had found cultural security in Islam as a way of channelling their alienating exposure to Western values. Indeed, it was from English campuses that Malay students began to denounce government policies and to indict UMNO itself as 'a secular, Malay nationalist party, thus unIslamic'.[26]

In response, UMNO had moved decisively to neutralise these forces. In 1979, under Tun Hussein Onn, *Al-Arqam* had been forced, in the 'public interest', to relinquish many of its 'deviationist' views. With Anwar now inside UMNO, ABIM had also been badly divided and brought under control by the early 1980s. Potential dissent among ABIM and other Islamic revivalists was being further tempered by their material dependence on, and close surveillance within, the state bureaucracy.[27] Yet, this could not diminish the extreme rivalry now growing between UMNO and PAS by this point. Indeed, the tension became a *cause* for many PAS followers after the deaths and violence resulting from the Memali incident in September 1985 when police tried to arrest the local cleric Ibrahim bin Mahmood in Kampung Memali, Kedah.[28]

This suggests a second contradictory element of the project: that of the *ulama's* own intellectual leanings. Mahathir has sought to consecrate the idea that UMNO speaks not only for Malays, but for Islam. Thus, the enunciations of the *ulama* have an important bearing upon that process. Yet, the problem of winning and maintaining this support is complicated by the nature of *ulama* power. On the one hand, it remains an integral part of the political establishment. On the other, it derives its prestige and social influence as a *traditional intellectual* community (or 'status group', to borrow from Weber) according it a form of civil authority not immediately tied to party politics. Nevertheless, while the *ulama* maintains a pragmatic distance from PAS as a party, it has remained intellectually sympathetic to PAS's pan-Islamic project and a *de facto* part of the intellectual opposition.[29]

This affinity has seen political resistance to UMNO conveyed through PAS. Notable here was the party's consistent denunciation of the NEP as a wealth charter for middle-class privilege, rather than a solution to poverty, indicating a growing intellectual argument over Islam, nationalism and modernity by the early 1990s. In this context, notes Mehmet: 'Islam may reinforce the Malay's sense of ethnicity, but it does not resolve their identity crisis. In fact it gives rise to a new set of challenges of reconciling Islam with nationalism and modernity, [one they have] yet to confront.'[30] Thus, with new forms of Malay–Islamic consciousness and ambivalent nationalism now constraining the modernist project, Mahathir was signalling the Vision not only as an economic challenge, but as a new context for civil-

Islamic development – hegemony being not just the reproduction of elite interests, but of elite ideas through moral leadership.[31]

Contesting the Vision

As organisers of hegemony, the UMNO network has sought to arbitrate and manage religio-cultural sensitivities by framing policy ideas and civil messages within a basic idiom of moderate Islam. The attempt to forge consensus is also conditioned by an 'ethics of community' expressing alternative forms of social order from those of liberal individualism. Within this ideology, coercion is presented as having a 'moral' rationale. Thus, when the state sanctions Islamic sects or courts the consent of dissident figures, this appeal to moral consensus is frequently to the fore. Such 'intellectual assimilation' was evident in the further purge on *Al-Arqam* in October 1994, the 'voluntary' recanting of its leader Ashaari Muhammad on TV being rationalised by this need to uphold an idealised social collectivism. Here, again, Mahathir was seeking to promote a civil–religious polity attuned to the ideals of nationalist modernity *and* traditional Islamic values.

Mahathir's concern to manage Islamic elements is also connected with the rise of Islamic politics elsewhere. This illustrates the dangers for long-standing dominant parties where the elite are seen to be monopolising wealth and engaging in ostentatious displays of privilege. It is this heady cocktail of underclass resentment and Islamic 'welfarism' that has provided the social and political context for the rise of Islamic parties in Turkey, Algeria, Egypt, Sudan and Nigeria. One of Mahathir's (and the West's) fears during the Indonesian crisis was that it would precipitate a surge of support for Islamic parties, a concern partly realised in the subsequent rejection of Habibie and election of Abdurrahman Wahid.

For Mahathir, the aim has been to control such threats by projecting UMNO's Islamic credentials. Yet, as Hussin Mutalib has noted, UMNO's commitment to an Islamic agenda denotes a more ambivalent set of political and ideological positions: 'the UMNO government's attitude towards the Faith can perhaps be described as 'cautious support' ... [UMNO's vigilance in] regulating ... Islamic activities considered potentially dangerous to the country's political stability ... [is] indicative of the stresses and strains that characterise the Malay–Islam dialectic.'[32]

Nevertheless, the government has endeavoured to build an 'educational discourse' for Vision-Islam. This was evident, for example, in the announcement in July 1997 that 'Islamic civilisation' was to be taught as a compulsory course in all Malaysian universities. Although it came during Anwar's two-month stint as acting prime minister, the decision, made through the Islamic Affairs Development Committee and the Islamic Consultative Body, both chaired by Anwar, was consistent with Mahathir's promotion of Islamic institutions.[33]

Terengganu and Wawasan Sihat

Terengganu provides a more concrete example of how material and Islamic elements have been blended into a model of Vision development and used as a bulwark to PAS-Islam. However, as the fall of Terengganu to PAS at the 1999 election would come to show, the challenge to this construct suggests a vital intellectual problem for the Vision project.

The BN model in Terengganu assumes the title Wawasan Sihat – literally, 'healthy vision'. However, there is also a deeper significance to the term:

> in its real meaning, letters in SIHAT embody the very philosophical underpinning of the Terengganu Islamic development vision. S stands for *sihat* (healthy physical and mental), IH for *ilmu yang dihayati* (practised knowledge) and T for *taqwa* (piety). In short, *Wawasan Sihat* carries a value-loaded model of development that aims at establishing the first *mujtama' madani* (*madani* society) in Malaysia, and, in fact, it claims, the first in the world. By *mujtama' madani* the state government of Terengganu means a society that possesses an Islamic lifestyle and cultural pattern, either at the level of the individual, family, organisations and administration.[34]

While the *sihat* element is based avowedly on the Quran and Hadith, the link to the Wawasan component is made by infusing it with the values of *mujtama' madani*. Thus:

> On material and physical development, the state of *mujtama' madani*, according to the vision, would be characterised by a rapid industrial development, sustainable economy, low rate of poverty, emergence of local entrepreneurs and high productivity. It goes in line with the Balanced Development Policy of the state's Second Development Phase (1995–2010) that consists of three aspects: a balance between human and physical development, a balance between sectors and a balance of infrastructural development between areas.[35]

Launched in conjunction, Wawasan Sihat in Terengganu has been intrinsic to Wawasan 2020, operating within the 'mould' of Malay–Islamic tradition while remaining committed to 2020 development ideals, a fusion of Islamic values and Vision aims overseen by BN Chief Minister Wan Mokhtar Wan Ahmad. The *mujtama' madani* notion of civil society, linking ideas of Islamic family development with the application of technology, was also given impetus by Anwar's promotion of the concept from around 1996.[36]

The further point about Wawasan Sihat has been its gradualist evolution towards an Islamic *civil society* rather than an Islamic *state*; a practical model of civil–Islamic development BN-style. Here, UMNO have sought to absorb traditional civil and cultural elements (Malay and Islamic) and graft them onto Bangsa Malaysia. From Mahathir's point of view, this had kept Terengganu from declaring any intention towards an Islamic state — despite the BN state leadership's closer leanings to such. Thus the latter's role in Islamic affairs has been largely confined to incorporating things such as Islamic Trust Fund Units and pawnshops into the existing structure,[37] a directive role in tune with Vision ideas at the Federal level.

Civil Development in Kelantan

Against the BN model, one might suggest a more intensive application of state-determined Islamic practices in the case of Kelantan. Yet this too is questionable. Despite PAS ambitions, there has been a similar process of incremental *civil* Islamic development also unfolding in Kelantan. In this case, much of what passes for state-led Islamic development is in reality an attempt to introduce Islamic modifications to localised practice and culture. For example, revenue derived from *haram* sources, such as dog licences and pig-rearing, are separated from the *halal* ones and used for non-Muslims only. Gambling is banned, as it is elsewhere for Muslims. Though generally not available for non-Muslims, alcohol is not banned by the state government. *Mak yong* dance is actively discouraged, yet still practised in the rural areas. Moreover, the attempted segregation of the sexes, for example in cinemas and hairdressers, has proved difficult to enforce, and is routinely ignored in the case of separate supermarket queues. Concerned at the apparent disruption to family life now being caused by working women, Nik Aziz has also introduced a five-day working week in the state. However, this type of intervention is being rationalised as part of a more generalised concern over industrialisation and its negative impact on the family. Here, the Tok Guru has argued that capitalist development and cheap factory labour are giving rise to exploitation of young female workers and social dislocation within the family and wider community. But his appeal for the preservation of women's dignity outside the home has to be defended against liberal groups such as Sisters in Islam, who seek a more expansive role for Muslim women.[38] In effect, the construction of Islamic practices in Kelantan, as in Terengganu, has been contested, negotiated and fashioned through variegated forms of *civil* exchange and adaptation rather than top-down state intervention.

Ironically, this gradualist evolution of Islamic practices at the civil level may be seen as having a more permeating effect. Here, as elsewhere in Malaysia, Islamic conventions, such as Muslim women wearing the *tudung* (headscarf), are becoming slowly absorbed as mainstream cultural habits. Again, though, even this is still being offset by deep-rooted *Malay*, rather than Islamic, customs. In this regard, Islamic values are being constantly prioritised and reasserted by PAS. Small examples of this would include Nik Aziz's reminders to observe separate shopping queues,[39] and his instruction to prohibit the use of firecrackers during Hari Raya given its 'un-Islamic' connotations.[40] Other cultural forms for Malays are allowed so long as they are in accordance with Islamic principles. And yet Kelantan appears to be a place where Islamic and non-Islamic cultures co-exist amicably, thus limiting the Vision's relevance to non-Malays. In these regards, Kelantan constitutes a key impediment to the project.

Contesting Kelantan: UMNO Enterprise at Work

Led by Nik Aziz, PAS has established a new political and moral status in Kelantan, quite distinct from the chaotic circumstances that ended its only other period in office (1959–78).[41] At the 1990 elections, UMNO lost all 38 state seats here, PAS winning 24 (the other 14 going to S46) and 6 of the 14 Parliamentary seats. Under the Angkatan Perpaduan Ummah – United Islamic Movement (APU) coalition in 1995, PAS and S46 took 36 of the 43 state seats (24 and 12 respectively) and 12 at the Federal level (6 each).[42]

This strengthening mandate has seen ongoing attempts to delegitimise PAS. For example, reflecting his accusation that 'PAS does not struggle for Islam, but strives for political gain',[43] Mahathir has tried, unsuccessfully, to have the party drop the word 'Islam' from its title.[44] The problem here for UMNO is that PAS populism in Kelantan derives not only from traditional Islamic values, but from the party's social welfarism, an appeal expressed in its 1995 manifesto, *Progress with Islam*, a counterpoint to the BN's *Vision, Justice, Efficiency*. Moreover, APU's retention of power in Kelantan in 1995 was due less to the Malay nationalism of Semangat than to PAS's populist presentation of Islam. Razaleigh's status as a Kelantan prince – a legacy of 'old order' relations – had, to some extent, helped draw Malay and Islamic components together. Yet it was the growing respect for PAS's welfare politics and the charisma of Nik Aziz that could be seen as the more important factors here.[45]

It is instructive to recognise the three-fronted strategy used by the UMNO network. At the immediate *political* level, UMNO had worked diligently to exploit the post-1995 election rift between PAS and Semangat in Kelantan. Here, co-optive pre-election overtures had been made through the BN press to undermine Razaleigh's participation in the PAS-led APU coalition.[46] By late 1996 this cleavage had become critically apparent with the expulsion of Razaleigh assemblymen from the state executive by the PAS leadership, much to the displeasure of the state's Sultan, a nephew of Razaleigh.[47] By using his political dexterity to encourage the rift and open the way for Razaleigh's return to the UMNO family, Mahathir was seeking to establish a new political coalition to challenge PAS in Kelantan. In the recrimination over the PAS–Semangat split, the BN media had also played consciously on PAS's political problems. Although unable to question Nik Aziz's probity, one *New Straits Times* feature, for example, used PAS's exclusion of S46 members from municipal and religious posts to claim that: 'for all its outward trappings of piety, something is rotten in the state of Kelantan'.[48] Yet, disappointingly for UMNO, the first test of the post-APU alliance resulted in a PAS by-election victory (in January 1997), indicating that it could still maintain power without Semangat.[49] Razaleigh's own defection back to UMNO was, similarly, viewed by the Kelantanese electorate as a piece of political opportunism.

The UMNO network has also employed forms of *economic* co-optation in Kelantan. For example, Mahathir's visit to Kota Bharu in August 1997, accompanied by 30 of Malaysia's main corporate figures, and first-ever official meeting with Nik Aziz, was calculated to foster a cooperative climate for UMNO-led investment projects. The principal initiative comprised plans for Kelantan's largest-ever industrial project, a petrochemical complex financed by the KUB conglomerate – a major holding controlled by UMNO – with a limited partnership role for the Kelantan-owned Keloil. Mahathir had also offered assistance to other potential investors, including Kelantanese companies with interests in Kuala Lumpur, provided they were seen to align themselves with UMNO rather than PAS.[50]

With per capita income in Kelantan only a quarter that of the national average, and foreign investment one-tenth the size of adjoining Perlis,[51] economic co-optation in the state has been directed through the selective allocation of development funds to Barisan assemblymen. The main vehicle for this disbursement in Kelantan is the Jabatan Pembangunan Persekutuan (JPP), or Federal Development Department. With substantial funds available from Kuala Lumpur, the JPP operates, in effect, as an oppositional development agency to the PAS state government's own development arm. Given their conflicting ideologies, a key purpose of the JPP is to check PAS-based forms of Islamic development.[52] While providing some all-round benefit, in practice most of its funds are targeted towards UMNO/BN groups, thus alienating others dependent on the local development agencies. One illustration of this was the provision of RM8 million to BN and S46 members (post-APU split) by Rural Development Minister Annuar Musa for the implementation of rural projects in their respective constituencies.[53] Thus such initiatives have been devised to exclude PAS by encouraging a view of UMNO as the main provider of economic benefits, while promoting the select interests of the BN business class.

On a third front, UMNO has continued to wage an *ideological* war of position in Kelantan. Some analysts have noted that within UMNO, and perhaps amongst other Islamic countries, only Mahathir has had the standing and self-confidence to question the *ulama* and Islamic *fiqh* (jurisprudence).[54] While a valid observation, it is also important to recognise the role of 'UMNO-friendly' institutions such as IKIM in helping to construct, present and reproduce these messages.[55] In another instance of the network's enterprise, ABIM had offered to 'mediate' between UMNO and PAS in order to 'bring them closer' on Islamic matters, an offer astutely rejected by Nik Aziz.[56] It may also be noted here that in seeking to build its own Islamic project, the PAS leadership had come to distance itself from Arqam by 1991. While Arqam was appearing to assist PAS by engaging in Islamic business enterprises and spreading Islamic practices at the *kampong* level, Ashaari had been critical of PAS's mode of struggle. Echoing PAS President Fadzil Noor's suspicions, Subky Latif, the party's information chief, argued that Arqam had ulterior motives to compete with, undermine and 'confuse' PAS. Thus Mahathir's banning of Arqam in 1994 was actively supported by Nik Aziz. For similar reasons, PAS has consciously resisted help from the Islamic group Jemmah Islah Malaysia (JIM), seeing it as an attempt to infiltrate the party.[57]

Confronting *Hudud*

The most symbolic aspect of the UMNO–PAS contest involves attempts by the political class and traditional elements in Kelantan to introduce *hudud* codes.[58] Although passed in Kelantan as a State Act in 1993, the introduction of *hudud* law requires Federal approval to become constitutionally enshrined, something which Mahathir has fiercely resisted.[59] In the debate over its attempted implementation, Mahathir has sought to portray Nik Aziz and PAS as latter-day exponents of the Kaum Tua. Challenging Nik Aziz's 'benign' assurance that *hudud* does not apply to non-Muslims where conventional legal punishments exist,[60] Mahathir has shown a remarkable flair for presenting the message in *his own* populist terms. The appeal to moderation here is informed not simply by liberal precepts, but by practical reference to the ideals of mercy, forgiveness and social justice contained in the Quran. Thus, in seeking to illustrate the injustice of *hudud*, Mahathir offers the following argument:

A woman who has been raped, and is unable to produce four witnesses, would not be able to have the rapist punished even if she knows who he is ... On the other hand, if she were to have a child as a result, she would be guilty of *zina* [adultery] and could be punished by stoning to death. By no stretch of the imagination can this be considered justice.[61]

While stressing the need for a moderate and innovative Islam, rather than a concern with form, attire and spiritual observance, Mahathir has walked a fine line in his relations with the *mufti* over the interpretation of Islamic teaching and the practice of civil–Islamic law. This was evident, for example, in his brooding stand-off with the Islamic Religious Affairs Department (IRAD) following the Selangor beauty pageant incident in July 1997, where female contestants had been arrested by local clerics for 'violating' Islamic codes on undress. As a consequence, the head Selangor *mufti*, Ishak Baharum, found his position 'unrenewed', illustrating Mahathir's determination to proceed with reform of Islamic administration.[62] Other such responses have included consideration of whether to invoke the specific Sunni form of Islam – the faith of 99% of the country's Muslims – into the Malaysian constitution as a way of marginalising Shia sects and militant Islamic teaching.[63] Implicit here is a vigilant warning to alleged militant Islamic intellectuals within the universities and other civil institutions.

However, the UMNO network has sought to manage the challenge from PAS, IRAD and other Islamic agencies in more consensual ways. An important factor here was Anwar's populist appeal to Islamic moderation, casting him, largely through the media, as a vital part of Mahathir's containment strategy.[64] Another such feature has been the considerable media space given to 'modernist Islamic' dialogue, such as the Sisters in Islam's critique of *hudud* and other aspects of *syariah* law.[65] The key point of this discourse is its agenda-setting purpose in helping to popularise Vision-Islam as the principal discussion site for checking Islamic extremism. This is not to deny the integrity of such discourse or the illumination offered. For one thing, it served to dispel some of the more simplistic interpretations of the PAS/Islamic issue in the Western press, *viz.* the 'dark threat of fundamentalism', during the crisis.[66] The more subtle point, however, is the way in which much of this discussion 'fits into' a discursive media argument about the value of Islamic modernity and, *ipso facto*, Vision-Islam, even where that involves meaningful criticism of Mahathir himself.

An example of such can be gleaned in the press article 'A new form of Islamic revival?'[67] Here, Chandra Muzaffar and ABIM's Ahmad Azam Abdul Rahman both argue, rather convincingly, that what was broadly seen as 'aggressive' action by the IRAD officers in Selangor was in fact a reaction to perceived pressure on them to uphold Islamic codes. Azam even questions Mahathir's intemperate tone towards the *mufti*, in view of the 'high esteem' in which they are still held by Malays. On the other hand, these and other critical qualifications 'help' provide modernist counterpoints to the version of Islam emerging from within the IRAD, an institution that Azam and Chandra identify as the new source of the Islamic revival.

A further variant of this discourse can be seen in Ghani Ismail's columns in the *Sun*, pointing out the many injustices of *syariah* law, such as marital constraints.[68] In another *Sun* piece,[69] Akbar Ali states the message more directly by suggesting that while there is a need to address what constitutes an 'Islamic deviant', this does not diminish the security threat posed by some of these elements, such as *Al-Arqam* and other *shia* groups. Noting that Pusat Islam now has over one hundred groups listed as 'Islamic deviants', the case is made here for the necessary intervention of the Special Branch to help control this threat to 'democracy' and religious harmony. Thus, while debate and opinion range here, it is the 'concerned language' of Vision-Islam, *viz.* the need for moderation, public vigilance and modernity, which provides the contextual framework for its elaboration.

To what extent, then, was PAS offering an alternative discourse as the crisis unfolded?

PAS–Islam, Party Politics and the Crisis (1)

Let us consider, first, some of the arguments for an Islamic society offered by Nik Aziz and Husam Musa in Kelantan,[70] followed by the views of PAS President Fadzil Noor and other PAS leaders on related issues of PAS's political development.

Nik Aziz and the View from Kelantan

In Nik Aziz we find the very model of the engaged traditional intellectual. Evoking a serene demeanour, it is immediately apparent to the observer why he is regarded as Tok Guru (spiritual leader). He is widely acknowledged by all political elements in Malaysia to be untainted by corrupt practices, and there can be little doubt about his moral convictions in seeking to build an Islamic community in Kelantan, ideals seen as the fulfilment of a long spiritual journey and personal experiences in Pakistan and the Indian subcontinent.

Kelantan, he believes, offers a *practical* example of a tolerant community founded on Islamic teachings. This includes a need to promote consensual relations and convey a tolerant image of Islam, notably to the Chinese.

Reflecting the absence of racial conflict in Kelantan in 1969, the Chinese community in the state has come to acknowledge PAS efforts in allowing free cultural expression. Indeed, many Chinese people, he points out, visited him personally in the course of the crisis to offer assurances of support. Whereas the BN in Kelantan once rejected proposals for Chinese cultural projects, PAS has been prepared to approve them on coming to office. The Chinese community, he insists, can be better accommodated under PAS. However, while this should involve free articulation of ethnic concerns, it must also be accompanied by legitimate explanation of how Islam in particular may have undermined such rights. While recognising the inclusive appeal of the Vision, and the problems of overcoming such perceptions, he believes that the Chinese and other ethnic groups can come to accept Islam in a spirit of cooperation and understanding. Thus PAS must not be seen as a coercive force. A Muslim who persecutes another person is acting outwith true Islamic teaching. Rather, the PAS way must allow people to recognise the validity and practicality of Islamic ideas within their own lives.

While Nik Aziz exudes charisma and considerable acumen as a political leader, non-Malay endorsement of the Kelantan model remains problematic. Nevertheless, given the rapid rate of development and support for the BN elsewhere in Malaysia, PAS support here has been highly impressive. Moreover, one is struck by Nik Aziz's intellectual conviction concerning the ethics of community and ideas of the just society. Indeed, much of the populist support for PAS in Kelantan comes from an acknowledgement of his own personal and political practices: he lives in a simple house, gives almost half his monthly allowance to PAS and the State Treasury (40% and 5% respectively), refuses his RM3,000 monthly housing allowance, places similar obligations on State Exco members, disallows them any gratuities and insists on their availability for mosque and teaching activities.[71]

In coming to respect these ideals, notes Husam Musa, the people of Kelantan desire a model of development that is distinct from the Vision. This is not to dismiss the current development process, but to recognise how the party can bring a more spiritual element to it by stressing values of social collectivism, civil justice and redistribution through Islamic practices. Support for this model is all the more remarkable, he feels, given the power of the BN media, UMNO's localised power and Mahathir's success in promoting the Vision elsewhere. Likewise, while Mahathir has gained much mileage in portraying PAS efforts to introduce *hudud* in Kelantan as 'backward-thinking', most Malaysians in Kelantan, he points out, support its introduction. Contrary to the false stereotypes foisted by the West, *hudud*, he insists, is also a *protective* Islamic convention designed to maintain the security of all in society. Moreover, *hudud* punishment applies only to

Muslims and there are many other forms of censure alongside physical retribution.

Here, one can see the difficulty for PAS in promoting Islamic values of community while rejecting claims that *hudud* is helping to import fundamentalist ideas. In this regard, PAS has also been vigilant in denying Shia links or any supposed Shia conspiracy to undermine the government.[72] As part of its consistent denunciation of the ISA, PAS had condemned the arrest of 'Shia activists' during the crisis as a political diversion. However, upholding the Sunni model of Islam, it has been careful to distance itself from *shia* teachings.

There is also the anomaly here that while PAS allows Chinese culture free expression, Malay culture is being suppressed to that of Islam, for example with regard to the banning of Malay dance in Kelantan. Here, Husam and PAS see the dangers of chauvinistic practices which promote ethnic identity over Islamic identity. Much of what is thought of as Malay culture, they argue, is in fact derived from other cultural forms, including animism. Relevant also to the Selangor incident, there is also the issue of *haya*, or modesty, here.[73] Once women reveal themselves in this way, they not only demean themselves, but are forced to assume all the other accoutrements of Western identity. Thus, they argue, the actions of the clerics signify not 'Islamic intolerance', but the protection of Islamic convention. Similarly, there is a requirement here to develop a more creative culture infused with Islamic ideals – hence the 'relegation' of Malay cultural forms. As an example, Dikir Barat music, the popular ethnic sound particular to Kelantan, has been 'modified' to reflect this new awareness. Here, PAS also claims to be promoting 'real Kelantanese heritage' as part of its tourism policy.

While the PAS–Islamic project in Kelantan has been mainly confined to civil and cultural modifications, the economic crisis has created new arguments for alternative financial structures based on Islamic principles. Here, an intellectual case has been made by Husam and others that the international speculators cannot be blamed solely for the crisis. Noting the extent to which the ringgit has been tied into the global capitalist trading order, the more central issue, they contend, is the need for some form of disengagement from the system itself and use of a gold standard in order to control the trade in money, something that is both antithetical to Islamic practice and detrimental to economic development.

The case for such a system follows the Islamic policy-type document *Islamic Trading: A New World Order* by Umar Ibrahim Vadillo. Here, and in related texts,[74] a series of claims are advanced for an *open* Islamic market in order to end monopolies and the practice of financial speculation propagated by Western economics, itself a structural pretext for money trading and usury. The Islamic market proposes an end to the use of paper money – the choice of the modern state – something that, it is argued, has come to limit any free medium of exchange, *real* marketplace activity and open processes of production and entrepreneurship. The case for a return to gold as a more stable and less corruptible form of exchange, through 'trading' of the Islamic dinar in Islamic countries,[75] is complemented by the promotion of other Islamic business practices such as *qirad* (Islamic business loan) and the *waqf* system in preference to conventional taxation. Also integral to the *waqf* is the renewal of guild associations and *imarets*, a civic arrangement with the mosque and market at its centre. At the heart of such practices lies a belief in free and just access to the market, both as a right and as a form of communal service to others. Implicit here is the view that Mahathir's 'Islamic financial reforms', such as 'Islamic banking', are, in reality, a convenient pretext for 'secular' capitalist accumulation.[76]

PAS has also consistently opposed Mahathir's privatisation process, which many Kelantanese associate with clientalism and corruption. While not wholly opposing privatisation in principle, it seeks a return of the utilities to common ownership and opposes corporatisation of the universities. Again, the argument here is that while materialism is valid, it must be fused with ideals of spirituality. Social development must be based on concepts of compassion and social collectivism.

While retaining a critical view of some of these perspectives, they help delineate the nature of the 'Islamic countervision' in Kelantan, suggesting what an expanded PAS agenda might look like in practice. As further illustration of the PAS project, with more particular regard to party politics and the crisis, let us note here some of the views offered by Fadzil Noor and other key PAS figures. This also provides background to PAS's view of Anwar prior to his fall.[77]

Fadzil Noor and the PAS Leadership

Consistent with the above, Fadzil Noor and other PAS leaders do not oppose modernisation and growth, but see the need for a more moral dimension to the development process – the Vision's false nationalism being a contradiction of that higher Islamic ideal. While many Malays still hold to UMNO for social rewards, that identification, they believe, is becoming more fluid. PAS also recognises the strong support for Mahathir among the Chinese, but sees Chinese economic, political and cultural rights as being more secure under PAS than under the BN. This is precisely because Islamic codes insist on other races being protected. Thus, they argue, the Chinese will act rationally in backing the party that best serves Chinese interests.

While recognising the BN's considerable monopoly over the media and other civil institutions, Fadzil Noor and PAS also believe that, quietly and studiously, it can influence the younger generation, notably in the schools and universities. Here, PAS appears increasingly well informed about cultural trends and the use of media technology. Reflecting a growing sense of critical thought among younger Malaysians, it regards this generation as the key players in effecting social change, evidenced by the increasing level of younger PAS members. Noting the crackdown on 'deviationist' Islamic groups and Shia teachings in the universities at this point, Fadzil Noor insists that this 'fear factor' signifiies not paranoia on Mahathir's part, but concerted propaganda to distract attention from the crisis. However, he believes that Malays can distinguish between the UMNO version of Islam and that of 'true Islam' projected by PAS.

Similarly, with regard to Mahathir's 'three-fronted' strategy to undermine PAS in Kelantan, Fadzil Noor believes that UMNO have failed. At the *economic* level, PAS has lasted much longer in Kelantan than anyone predicted, with Mahathir's centralised policies and conditional investment overtures only alienating the people of Kelantan further. In *political* terms, Razaleigh's betrayal led to more popular support for PAS, not less, and more party defections from S46 to PAS. His return to UMNO had also undermined his own credibility and caused increased factionalism within UMNO itself. At the *ideological* level, he maintains, Mahathir's attacks on PAS over *hudud* have not worked, again, given the reality that most people in Kelantan want its implementation.

Against this, one might suggest the more immediate reality that *hudud* law *hasn't* been introduced in Kelantan, illustrating Mahathir's success in engaging PAS and controlling this agenda. Here, Fadzil Noor and PAS agree, very openly, that there is no clear-cut evidence to suggest *national* support for *hudud*. However, they believe it can demonstrate the case for *hudud* through example in Kelantan and possibly Terengganu. Thus, in the longer term, Malaysians, more generally, will come to see *hudud* not simply as a form of public retribution, but as a valued set of social and moral codes. Indeed, PAS argues that *hudud* is needed more than ever to help address the spread of social problems now associated with the development process in Malaysia.

This ties into a number of critical judgements made by the PAS leadership on Mahathir's use of Islam for naked political purposes. For example, alongside the 'deviationist' scare and attempt to implicate PAS by false association, the Islamic 'fear factor' had also been used to suggest possible deinvestment and concern among the international business community, a fabrication rejected by PAS. After all, it notes, an Islamic society does not appear to have discouraged investment in Saudi Arabia.

With the economic crisis intensifying, Fadzil Noor now asserted that meaningful anti-government sentiment was growing, as shown by the increased turnouts at local *ceramahs*. Reflecting the cross-political nature of these platforms, and acknowledging the party's affinity with PRM, PAS also felt comfortable in being described as 'left of centre' on many issues. However, still at a point prior to the *reformasi*, there remained a much wider problem over PAS's ability to reconcile its Islamic ideals with the DAP. Despite PAS's specific 'no' to an alliance at this stage, this could be seen as standard party manoeuvring, as the subsequent *rapprochement* between the parties was to show.

At this point, Mahathir was also still 'backing' Anwar as his successor. Here, Fadzil Noor and the other PAS figures expressed a clear, and apparently long-held, belief that Anwar *would not* succeed Mahathir. All of Mahathir's deputies had fallen by the wayside, they argued. Likewise, Mahathir was engaged in a long-term game-plan to keep Anwar in position, but never allow him to assume office. A corollary view was that, despite his strong Malay and Chinese support bases, Anwar, unlike Mahathir, lacked the political acumen to mediate the competing factions within UMNO and hold the BN together. Moreover, while Anwar still had significant respect as an Islamic figure, neither he, nor UMNO generally, any longer enjoyed the overall confidence of Malays in this regard. Although Fadzil Noor had been close to Anwar during their 'early days' as Islamic activists, Anwar, it was felt, had lost much of his Islamic awareness. Taken together, this suggested, for Fadzil Noor and PAS, a serious deterioration of UMNO's claim to be the voice of the Malays. Once they were genuine upholders of Malay interests, motivated by higher principles. Now they are little more than career individuals.

Again, a noteworthy feature of the PAS leadership here is their intellectual energy – and keen interest in how external observers view the party. While the argument for *hudud* was still problematic to this writer, one could see more clearly the wider context within which the case for its introduction was being made. Also apparent is PAS's own close understanding of how the BN media and UMNO network operates to control PAS–Islam as a project. Another element is the receptiveness of PAS to 'left discourse', suggesting an emerging basis for meaningful cooperation with other parties and NGOs.

At another level, though, PAS's specific Islamic commitments still distinguish it from all other mainstream parties in Malaysia. One can denote this in the sentiments of any active PAS member. For example, in a casual lunchtime conversation with a young party worker in Alor Setar, I learned how he combined his role as a religious teacher in the local school with long hours and minimal pay working for PAS. Without showing a trace of hostility, he said that this was, as he saw it, an expression of his dedication not only to PAS, but to the wider Islamic struggle against Western ideas. Again, it is easy to misinterpret this *jihad* as a belligerent threat rather than a statement of belief. And herein lies the tension and complexity within the PAS–Islamic project. That is, one can be impressed by many of PAS's basic ideas of ethnic tolerance, compassion, political transparency, fair distribution and social justice, while remaining circumspect about whether a PAS–Islamic society would be either acceptable or desirable to a wider Malaysian community. However, in advancing an intellectual alternative to the Vision, PAS also appears to be sincere in building broad ethnic consent for its project at the national–popular level. Whatever other impressions derived of PAS, the image of the coercive Islamic zealot was not one of them.

PAS, Anwar and the *Reformasi*: Setting the Scenario

Before coming to the Anwar crisis and its implications for PAS, let us note here some of the scenarios thought possible for the emergence of an Islamic polity in Malaysia. In *Islam in Malaysia: From Revivalism to Islamic State?* Hussin Mutalib outlines four main scenarios for the emergence of Islam as a political force. Although written before the crisis, it provides a useful basis upon which to develop our analysis of the PAS project and the Anwar issue.

In Hussin's first scenario, an Islamic polity could emerge if PAS were able to capture more states, such as Kedah, Perlis and Terengganu. For PAS to develop in this regard, two conditions would have to be met: (a) PAS would have to reveal itself as a more tolerant/progressive party; and (b) the internal tensions within UMNO would have to degenerate further.

With regard to the first of these conditions, Hussin sees a basis for development, given PAS's record of political integrity in Kelantan and the apparent confidence of the Chinese constituency there. Confirming the above, the author cites assurances given to Lim Kit Siang and a survey in *Berita Harian* showing eight out of nine Chinese in the state happy with PAS, in terms of economic and political security. With regard to the second aspect, Hussin notes that, despite UMNO's apparent control, competition between UMNO and PAS for Malay support remains highly fluid – a situation that could unravel further.

The second scenario posits a possible UMNO–PAS *rapprochement*, there being a precedent for this in PAS's previous membership of the BN. In this scenario, UMNO may also have to find other ways of bringing the Chinese on board, given the increasing liability of the MCA. A merger between UMNO and DAP is not ruled out within this scenario.

The third scenario considers the possibility of an Islamic coup led by Malay generals, concerned that Malay–Islamic interests were being dangerously eroded. Although this is unlikely, the author retains the view that there is no guarantee that the military would not intervene in circumstances of extreme instability.

The fourth scenario, and the one seen most likely by the author, is an Anwar succession. The basic argument here (again, note, pre-crisis) is that with Anwar still committed to the Islamisation process, PAS could rejoin the BN if Anwar became PM. (Extending this scenario, somewhat, one might include here a possible future coalition between Anwar and PAS itself in some post-crisis arrangement.) Hussin backs this view through reference to Anwar's long-standing 'relationship' with some of the PAS leadership, going back, notably, to Anwar's ABIM days. There is the suggestion here of a PAS/Anwar/ABIM triumvarite.

Hussin also considers the nature of an 'Islamic state' in this scenario. If it is defined as a doctrinal state, reflective of an older traditional order, then this would not happen. If it is defined in terms of the permeation of Islamic values, then, yes, there could be such a state, including an amended form of *hudud*. However, the author also sees a number of counterposing elements holding the Islamic process in check, most notably the complex dynamics of Malay *adat* and cultural identity.

Using some of the above-noted thoughts of the PAS leadership (and the benefit of hindsight), let us consider some of the main propositions contained within these scenarios. The third scenario of a military option remains unlikely, as acknowledged by Hussin, although extended forms of policing and political surveillance appear probable. As regards the second scenario, while any future UMNO–PAS merger cannot be discounted, it appears from the above PAS responses, and the increasingly anti-UMNO sentiment now permeating PAS, that this possibility is also highly unlikely.

Let us turn immediately, then, to Hussin's last scenario, the Anwar factor. Leaving aside for the moment the circumstances of Anwar's ouster, two related features of Hussin's scenario need to be qualified: first, Anwar's supposed (pre-crisis) closeness to the PAS leadership; and second, his suitability in carrying forward an Islamisation process suitable to PAS. Although Anwar had maintained a strong Islamic profile and may have been held in some regard by PAS members, his role in pushing Mahathir's Islamic agenda had undermined his Islamic credentials among the PAS leadership. Thus, in the aftermath of his dismissal, a certain *schadenfreude* could be denoted, with Fadzil Noor's own, quieter, 'I told you so' echoing a long-held distrust of the Anwar view that meaningful Islamisation could be effected from *within* the BN.[78] Moreover, while PAS had defended

Anwar immediately after his sacking, this did not simply translate into outright support for him at this point. Not only was Anwar required to explain his conduct while in office, including his support for the repressive acts now being used against him, he also had to renew his Islamic values and acknowledge the fallacy of trying to work within the 'secular' system.[79]

As will be discussed below, PAS support for Anwar was to strengthen considerably as the trial continued, with the party linking itself more closely to the *reformasi*, *viz.* GERAK and ADIL. However, this did not mean that PAS considered Anwar an eventual Islamic leader in waiting. As was intimated to this writer by various PAS people, PAS had been pushing both Islamic values *and* the demand for civil justice long before the Anwar crisis. One can only speculate as to the shape of any Islamic programme initiated by Anwar in any 'post-detention situation'. However, even this extended Anwar scenario seems problematic given the adverse impact of the whole débâcle on Anwar's political career.

So this brings us back to Hussin's first scenario, one that, due to the unforeseen circumstances of the Anwar crisis, has come to look the more likely. In particular, we can say that the two conditions noted as pre-requisites for PAS to emerge as a stronger contender had been partially met. First, there were growing indications of a new progressive, tolerant thinking within PAS in relation to the wider opposition community. Second, despite Mahathir's nominally successful attempts in holding UMNO/BN together, the whole Anwar imbroglio had caused a serious degeneration both within UMNO and its popular support base. On this basis, let us now look more closely at how PAS has been affected as a party by the Anwar crisis and what this signalled by late 1999 in terms of political contestation and the PAS–Islamic project.

Notes

1. For a comprehensive analysis of Gramsci's critique of Croce, see M. Finocchiaro (1988).

2. Boggs (1976), pp. 28–9.

3. Mehmet (1991), p. 103.

4. See Roff (1967), pp. 57–9.

5. Ibid., p. 59.

6. Alatas (1977a), pp. 44, 215.

7. See Gullick (1987), pp. 286–90.

8. Maaruf (1992), p. 260.

9. This text, published by UMNO in 1971, was the product of 14, mostly academic, contributions compiled by UMNO Secretary-General Senu bin Abdul Rahman. In a damning critique, Alatas points to the book's 'inaccuracies … its lack of intellectual depth [and] its ridiculous conclusions', noting that: 'While many British colonial writers

stressed the laziness of the Malays, they did not strip the Malays of so many other qualities [as the] *Revolusi Mental* (1977a), pp. 147, 150.

10. For an informative account of *amok* as a social, cultural and psychological phenomenon, see Winzeler (1990). Media reports in Malaysia also refer to '*amok* attacks' and the assailant as 'the *amok*'.

11. Mahathir bin Mohamad (1970), p. 118.

12. *Latah* refers to a supposed disorder in which: 'elicited by any sudden noise, shock, or a surprising command, the subject appears unable to realize his own identity, or to do anything but imitate, often accompanied by the use of vulgar language … The condition can last for hours until the subject drops down in exhaustion, after which recovery to normal consciousness takes place. Only adults are known to have such a disorder. According to Clifford, any Malay is capable of developing into a typical case of *latah* if he is sufficiently persecuted, teased, and harassed.' Alatas (1977a), pp. 48, 174–7. As Alatas notes, despite having no empirical basis, Clifford's claim served to reinforce another distorted aspect of the Malay character, as did Mahathir's claims regarding *amok*.

13. See Mehmet (1990), p. 57.

14. Muzaffar (1987), p. 75.

15. Esposito (1991), p. 11.

16. Vatikiotis (1987), pp. 58–9.

17. Ibid., p. 61; Ozay Mehmet (1990), pp. 60–1.

18. Ozay Mehmet, ibid., p. 61.

19. Muzaffar (1987), p. 8.

20. Ibid., p. 9.

21. Cited in ibid.

22. Following their entry into PAS in 1978, Fadzil Noor became vice-president, Nakhaie Ahmad secretary-general and Abdul Hadi Awang State liaison head in Terengganu. Nakhaie later resigned in 1988 (as vice-president) to join UMNO. Fadzil Noor's leadership was confirmed at the PAS Muktamar in 1989. Jomo and Cheek (1992), pp. 95, 96, 102.

23. Khoo Boo Teik (1995), pp. 224, 225.

24. Ibid., p. 226. Jomo and Cheek (1992), p. 98.

25. See *Asiaweek*, 24 August 1994.

26. Anwar (1987), p. 30. This account notes how Malay students in England came to embrace the fundamentalist Islamic teachings of the Egyptian *Ikhwan Muslimin* and Pakistan *Jamaati-i-Islami* movements.

27. Hussein (1987), p. 664.

28. As a result of the stand-off and ensuing violence between police and Mahmood's followers, 18 people, including Mahmood and four policemen, died. The government responded by calling Mahmood an Islamic extremist, linking him to PAS. PAS, in turn, condemned the police and declared Mahmood, and the other villagers killed, Islamic martyrs. See Khoo Boo Teik (1995), pp. 227–8. Jomo and Cheek (1992), p. 98also note that it was Deputy Prime Minister Musa Hitam who, effectively, took the blame for this incident among many PAS and UMNO people rather than Mahathir and Anwar.

29. Muzaffar (1987), p. 77.

30. Mehmet (1990), p. 22.

31. See Bellamy and Schecter (1993), pp. 130–1.

32. Mutalib (1990), p. 127.

33. *FEER*, 17 July 1997.

34. Salleh (1999), pp. 185-6.

35. Ibid.

36. Ibid., pp. 186, 189.

37. Ibid., p. 199.

38. See Salmah Osman, 'Tok Guru Nik Aziz: pro-woman, pro-family', *Harakah*, 5 April 1999.

39. See 'Warning on separate shopping queues', *Sun*, 19 January 1999.

40. 'Firecrackers not Islamic', *Sun*, 22 January 1999.

41. See Salleh (1999), p. 178.

42. Gomez (1996), p. 26.

43. *New Straits Times*, 16 February 1995.

44. *New Straits Times*, 11 December 1994.

45. Ibid., p. 40. Of the 14 parliamentary seats in Kelantan at the 1995 general election, PAS won all six it contested, while Semangat lost two of the eight seats contested to the BN. The key trend here was the relatively higher support for APU in PAS, rather than Semangat, contested seats. Ibid., pp. 26, 43-4.

46. Ibid., p. 3.

47. *FEER*, 15 August 1996.

48. 'Rumblings in the pious state', *New Straits Times*, 20 May 1997.

49. PAS won the Pulai Chondong state assembly seat by 118 votes. *FEER*, 16 January 1997.

50. See James Kynge, 'Mahathir sees attractions in opposition territory', *Financial Times*, 4 September 1997.

51. As noted in 'Man of faith', an article on Nik Aziz, *FEER*, 1 July 1999. The per capita income figure for Kelantan (1998) was RM4,067. The foreign investment reference was for the period 1994 to 1999 (1st quarter).

52. Salleh (1999), pp. 190-1.

53. 'Annuar reps to get RM8m for projects', *Business Times*, 1 November 1996.

54. See 'Blunt message', *FEER*, 8 August 1996.

55. One populist outlet for this has been the weekly IKIM column 'IKIM Views' in the *Star*. See also, 'PM: reappraise Islamic rules', a piece on Dr Mahathir opening an IKIM conference, *New Straits Times*, 15 October 1994.

56. See 'Nik Aziz rejects Abim's offer to be mediator', *New Straits Times*, 5 May 1997.

57. Salleh (1999), pp. 194, 195, 207, note 39.

58. *Hudud* law involves public retribution for offences that violate Islamic codes, including standardised punishments and, in certain circumstances, execution. For a detailed reproduction of the Kelantan Syariah Criminal Code (II) Bill 1993, and the various levels of punishment, see Ismail (1995).

59. See 'No hudud laws in UMNO states', *Star*, 3 May 1992, and 'Govt. say no to PAS hudud', *Star*, 17 May 1994.

60. 'Nik Aziz tells when Islamic laws apply to non-Muslims', *New Straits Times*, 5 May 1992.

61. Cited,'Blunt message', *FEER*, 8 August 1996.

62. The stated reason for the termination of Ishak's contract was that, at 70, he was too old. In the heat of the Selangor incident, Ishak had, allegedly, called Mahathir an 'apostate'. *Star*, 2 November 1997.

63. In 1996, the Prime Minister's Department claimed to have identified 400 Shia followers, including 40 leaders with close links to Iran, spreading deviationist teachings in the country's universities. *FEER*, 11 July 1996.

64. See, for example, 'Anwar: enforce Syariah laws wisely', *New Straits Times*, 6 July 1997, and 'Anwar: authorities should be moderate in their actions – don't be overzealous', *New Straits Times*, 29 July 1997.

65. See 'Hudud laws in perspective', *New Straits Times*, 2 September 1995, and 'Organisation launches book on hudud laws', *New Straits Times*, 28 August 1995. See also 'For an in-depth view of hudud', a favourable review of the Rose Ismail/ SIS book *Hudud in Malaysia: The Issues at Stake*, *New Straits Times*, 4 September 1995.

66. As a good example of the genre, see Matthew Chance's 'Islam's grip tightens as Malaysia's boom ends', *Independent*, 22 September 1997.

67. *Sun*, 25 October 1997.

68. See, for example, 'Victims of an outdated system', *Sun*, 16 August 1996.

69. 'When deviants become a security threat', *Sun*, 19 November 1997.

70. My thanks to Hj. Nik Abdul Aziz Bin Hj. Nik Mat, the Menteri Besar of Kelantan, and to Hj. Husam Musa, political secretary to Nik Aziz and Chief of PAS Youth in Kelantan, for their discussions at the Komplek Kota Darulnam (State Building, Kota Bharu), 2 December 1997. Other than their recounted views, all observations belong to the present author.

71. See Salleh (1999), p. 179.

72. See, for example, 'Don't blame PAS for Shi'ite activities: Nik Aziz', *Sun*, 8 November 1997.

73. See 'No *haya* – no life', *Harakah*, 24 November 1997.

74. For a complementary treatise to Vadillo, see also Ibrahim (1999).

75. Although having no practical exchange value on conventional currency markets, the Islamic dinar, a gold coin, is being promoted in Islamic countries as a 'reserve currency' for the world's Muslim population. See <www.users.dircon.co.uk/~netking/murabitn.htm>.

76. Ibrahim (1999), p. 56. This view denotes both the hypocrisy of the Islamic banking system and the amorality of the IMF's imposition of debt interest (usury) on impoverished countries such as Indonesia.

77. My thanks to Hj. Fadzil Mohamad Noor (president of PAS), Hj. Azizan Abdul Razak (PAS Supreme Committee and secretary for Kedah), Dato Hj. Mohamad Muslim Osman (PAS Supreme Committee), Atty Hj. Mohamad Taulan Rasul (PAS treasurer, Kedah) and Hj. Abdul Halim Aishad (PAS secretary-general) for this extensive group interview at the PAS office, Alor Setar, 4 December 1997. The views expressed were a collective PAS viewpoint. Other than their recounted views, all observations belong to the present author.

78. See Zafar Bagash, 'Lessons for the Islamic movement from Anwar's episode in Malaysia', *Harakah*, 15 October 1998.

79. Ibid.

7

PAS, the Anwar Crisis and Counter-hegemony

As the Anwar trial settled into a long litany of sordid testimony, the UMNO network was now engaged in a new PR strategy to soften Mahathir's image and limit adverse public reaction. In January 1999, Mahathir finally announced Abdullah Ahmad Badawi as his new deputy, overturning the plan to hold elections for the post and postponing the UMNO elections till after the general election. Despite the media's laudatory greetings, it was apparent that this was a stop-gap appointment to take the heat off Mahathir. Indeed, Abdullah's very 'dullness' may have served as a useful contrast to the still charismatic Mahathir in the public mind.

That same month, Mahathir ordered an 'independent' inquiry into Anwar's beating, led by the former attorney-general, Abu Talib Othman and the former chief judge of Malaya, Anuar Zainal Abidin. Rahim Noor, the IGP at the centre of the allegations, resigned, although he had not been named as the culpable figure in the immediate police investigation. As acting IGP, Norian Mai also announced a 'major reshuffle' of senior police figures as part of a confidence-restoring 'review' of the force.[1] In February 1999, Rahim finally admitted assaulting Anwar in the lock-up. The media reports here, predictably, played on Rahim's claim that he had been provoked by Anwar's alleged retort: '*Ni, bapa anjing*' (Here's the father of dogs), though there was some variation of this in the press.[2] Rahim's admission and the Inquiry's doubts over Anwar's alleged remark appeared to reveal some 'transparency' within the system. But Mahathir had also come under unprecedented political pressure to institute a royal commission, the first time he had heeded such a call during his tenure. Thus, with efforts to conceal Rahim's guilt now a lost cause, many saw this as a damage limitation exercise with the particular intention of showing that the ex-IGP had acted alone.

These public overtures were also being used to pave the way for a smooth and longer-term handover of power. Having given the Finance Ministry to Daim and the Home Ministry to Abdullah, Mahathir could now offer 'assurances' of such to the public.[3] Meanwhile, the friendly, low-key approach of 'Pak Lah' (Abdullah) was being projected by the media as a valuable asset, complementing his appointment as deputy chairman to the NEAC to work alongside Daim. Razaleigh and Najib were also now being seen to 'close ranks', although, with Mahathir continuing to send conflicting signals about the eventual 'suitability' of his new deputy, both still harboured ambitions of an eventual succession.

PAS, the *Reformasi* and Malay Discontent

While these and other damage limitation efforts had helped neutralise the *reformasi*, they could not disguise brooding Malay resentment. Although economic recovery remained central for most Malaysians, other concerns were now emerging. One was an increasing disregard for the courts, the police and other law enforcement agencies. As central participants in the purging of Anwar, they had brought the judicial system into disrepute. Notwithstanding public support for the BN's 'foreign bias' line, many Malaysians felt aggrieved at the debasement of their legal system in the eyes of the world. The second concern involved, as noted, a more culturally rooted resentment at the 'un-Malay' treatment of Anwar and his family. Whatever the substance of the sexual and corruption allegations, there was a growing feeling that Mahathir had overstepped the bounds of decent conduct, revealing not only a failure of justice, but a lack of social decorum.

A certain ambivalence still prevailed here. Despite Anwar's social in-itiatives, such as low-cost housing, and concern for the poor, many rural Malays had come to see him as part of the UMNO machine, increasingly detached and urban-centred. However, this was being offset by a distaste for the mercenary way in which he and his family had been persecuted, contrary to Malay mores of how to treat 'one of their own'. Even many middle- and low-ranking Malay policemen now felt a sense of shame at Anwar's treatment.[4]

As these feelings spread, PAS emerged as the main beneficiary of Malay discontent. Taking up this new 'moral politics' and linking it to a more 'secular' language of justice, PAS was also now courting other political constituencies, Malay and non-Malay. Through GERAK, GAGASAN and ADIL an understanding almost unthinkable in previous years was now taking shape between PAS and DAP. Alongside stood a large body of displaced Anwarites and other UMNO dissidents looking for a political home. Indeed, notwithstanding his custodial problems, so too was Anwar. Weighing together these groupings, the sensitive issue of Malay rights and the constitutional importance of Islam, the balance still tipped towards a 'Malay agenda', with many Chinese still considering the Anwar crisis a 'Malay affair'. Yet, while still holding to an Islamic worldview, problematic to non-Malays, PAS had also revealed itself as an egalitarian party, engaged in mainstream social issues and receptive to other opposition parties, NGOs and civil organisations.

In populist terms, the Anwar affair had helped reposition PAS as the 'natural' Malay/Islamic party. Yet, far from simply redistributing electoral support across ethnic party lines, Malaysians of all races and persuasions now appeared more receptive to a new kind of non-racial politics. Despite the domestic media's depiction of inter-ethnic violence in Indonesia, the turmoil had not descended into racial scapegoating. In particular, the Chinese community had not been targeted. Even though Anwar had lost Chinese business support, he still appealed to other, mainly younger, Chinese elements, a complement to his main base of young Malay followers, notably within ABIM.

However, it was PAS that stood to gain most from this new political fluidity. The reasons for this were, essentially, twofold: first, because of PAS's party machinery, giving them a greater ability than NGOs or other *ad hoc* bodies to organise and absorb dissent towards UMNO/BN; second, because of their strategic position *vis-à-vis* the Malays. An important factor here concerns the new generation of highly committed members now emerging within PAS. Educated, professional and with extensive links to other Islamic groups, they have come to play a key role in influencing the leadership, explaining Islam's 'non-fundamentalist' side and organising party presentation.[5]

In seeking to redress this, the media were making a conscious effort to highlight Mahathir's Malay and Islamic profiles. For example, during the PM's 1999 Hari Raya open house in Kuala Lumpur, the larger than expected crowds were claimed to be an indication of resilient support for the government,[6] although claims that finance group Mbf had encouraged many of its employees to attend the function suggested other factors at play.[7] Similarly, TV news coverage of the PM's pre-Hari Raya visit to his home town of Kubang Pasu played down the smaller than usual number who had turned out to welcome him, indicating a worrying decline for UMNO in the rural areas.

Aware of rural disenchantment and the Islamic factor, the Barisan were now making political overtures and promises of new development to the Kelantanese. This coincided with Mahathir's pre-Hari Raya visit to Kota Bharu and first ever meeting with Nik Aziz at the state office, Kota Darulnaim. With the limited prospect of winning back Kelantan, the visit and rallying call to the local party could be seen as an attempt to enhance UMNO's rural and Islamic image. However, this was part of a more specific effort to drive a wedge between PAS and other parts of the *reformasi*. The *modus operandi* here can be gleaned from statements made in a press column at this point by Abdullah Ahmad, the government's special envoy to the UN. While reminding Malaysians of Mahathir's free-market development agenda, which has given years of all-round prosperity and growth, he raises the spectre of PAS ambitions as a re-enactment of the 'communist threat' and its use of the *reformasi* as a convenient front:

> The notion that *reformasi* is secular, liberal and democratic is troubling. *Reformasi* is PAS in thinly disguised form. The DAP and the others will have to work out for themselves how they can identify their policies with PAS's rigid *syariah*. Will they ride the 'Islamic tiger' simply on account of their animosity towards Mahathir? The 'Islamic tiger' is as dangerous as the once powerful 'communist tiger' ... The nation continues to need a strong leader, otherwise our efforts to rescue the economy could be stymied by *reformasi* and the Islamists.[8]

Despite this alarmist language, confidence was growing within PAS. Through GERAK, it had raised its political profile significantly in the urban centres, notably Kuala Lumpur. In the Malay heartlands of Perlis, Kedah and Terengganu, anti-Mahathir sentiment was spreading, with well-organised *ceramahs* bringing PAS and other *reformasi* figures together. In this regard, there was some validity in the above claim in that PAS and *reformasi* were becoming synonymous in the public mind. What was driving it, though, was not some dark Islamic agenda, but a more grassroots disillusionment with UMNO.

Again, the PAS party machinery was critical here. For example, along-side the *ceramahs*, PAS and GERAK were distributing videos, cassette tapes, leaflets, pamphlets and downloaded material from Internet sites around local villages. Travelling through Kedah and Perlis in early 1999, the 'flag war' now in progress was also a colourful illustration of PAS support in these areas, the proliferation of green and white circled flags along the rural roadways indicative of the battle to come at the polls. Not to be outdone, the BN had launched a substantive campaign to get their own blue-backed scales of justice flag displayed, the BN in Kedah promising at one point to have 10,000 flags out in response. Excitement was also growing around the Kubang Pasu area, Mahathir's Kedah constituency, where, having addressed a 20,000 crowd, Wan Azizah was considering appeals for her to stand against the PM. Signifying the growing collaboration between PAS and ADIL, Fadzil Noor had made it known that, wherever she stood, PAS would withhold its own candidate and support her campaign.

PAS, the *Reformasi* and *Harakah*

Perhaps the most significant indication of PAS's new surge was the rapid growth of *Harakah* (Movement), its twice-weekly publication.[9] From the start of the Anwar crisis to the end of 1998, its circulation had grown from around 60,000 to around 300,000.[10] By early 1999, *Harakah* had established itself not only as a party organ, but as an open space for opposition opinion and a focal point for the *reformasi*. As the paper's editor Zulkifli Sulong noted with candid satisfaction: 'We try to be an alternative paper for Malaysians, besides being a mouthpiece for the party.'[11] Reflecting this, the paper was allowing critical discourse against PAS within its own pages. One such example included an expansive piece on the subordinate role of women in PAS, something that, as argued, was inconsistent with any true understanding of Islam.[12] In an apparent attempt to reach out to non-Malays, one could also denote in *Harakah* new open discussion of Muslim codes and their place within a multi-ethnic society.[13] In this vein, other pieces were enjoining PAS to expand its English section and build a moderate support base. As one wide-ranging letter to the editor put it:

> Judging by the number of non-Muslims who have managed to get their letters and articles published shows [*sic*] that *Harakah* is being widely accepted by people outside the PAS, Malay and Muslim circles ... [W]e have to realise that a big majority of non-Muslims in this country does not have the faintest idea of what Islam is all about ... PAS through its mouthpiece *Harakah* must remain moderate in its views both in the English and Bahasa Malaysia sections so that its views can gain acceptance by all non-Muslims of this country ...
>
> Moderate Muslim, Ipoh, Perak.[14]

In taking up this task, both PAS and *Harakah* were providing a vital medium of cross-political exchange. To some extent, the appearance of DAP, PRM, JUST and other party/NGO output was part of a reciprocal networking of articles and commentaries between opposition organs and websites. However, as a well-established Malay newspaper with an expanding English section, *Harakah* was in a more significant position to bring together an amalgam of opposition viewpoints. As one *Harakah* editorial comment put it, PAS:

> is an Islamic movement whose lifeblood in this information age is correct information on all aspects of our environment, political and religious, not just propaganda spewed out by the official media. This is good reason for Harakah to allow space for the oppressed of other communities and sections

of the people. The role of media to break down the barriers between peoples cannot be overstated. Harakah being the only alternate news media for PAS members must serve as an open window to the outside world.[15]

The pages of *Harakah* were by this point also a fair reflection of growing PAS support for Anwar. While questions remained, the broad attitude had now shifted significantly from that of 'UMNO foe' to '*Saudara* (brother) Anwar', as shown in the following sentiments in a piece by the regular *Harakah* columnist Sadirah K.:

Having followed closely the events of the last six months, there is increasing disbelief that Saudara Anwar Ibrahim is the man the ruling elite paints him to be. If anything stands against Saudara Anwar it is that he was party to several questionable events which took place during his sixteen years tenure in Government. This he has to seriously reflect upon. One prays that he would be open about collective decisions which have had a negative impact both upon institutions and individuals in the country ... [However, is it] too difficult to accept the view that there were concerted hands behind the scenes? Had Saudara Anwar become a serious threat to people in the higher echelons of power? The economic issues of mid 1997 did cast a shadow on relationships. He was beginning to hold his own and differed from the PM on economic strategies. He took a stance on bailouts hence attracting corporate pressure. Would this not be the best time for anti-Anwar factions to move in, especially at a time when Dr Mahathir was also vulnerable?[16]

The sentiments at the end of this piece are also a telling commentary on Malay resentment:

As a father with daughters myself, I find the allegations an affront to the family. Innocent people are being hurt. Saudara Anwar's innocence is best championed by his wife and children. Many enjoin in their cause 'Justice for Papa'. When political intrigues descend to levels of indecency then people must act, for not to act will be a contradiction to our faith.[17]

As other *Harakah* output showed, the crisis was also exposing the moral and intellectual claims of Vision 2020:

So we end up as a nation with fine slogans and great characters like the *Rukunegara*, Vision 2020 and a host of others ... We see the tremendous chasm between such noble aspirations and the state of our institutions, be it the Police, the Judiciary or the Banking sector. We have the vision, but no examples of how to work it. This breeds cynicism ... We want development, but not the climate of thinking that is integral to this ... The Youth, the flower of our nation are stunted by the University and University Colleges Act. They can neither say nor act but have to be eternally grateful.[18]

As a consequence of all this, PAS now claimed to have increased its membership applications tenfold in the six months leading up to the Anwar crisis, with a record 15,000 applications in October 1998 alone.[19] Pointing to the growing number of PAS members in Kubang Pasu in the wake of Anwar's persecution, Fadzil Noor now asserted that 'the people hate Mahathir. UMNO members who have an independent mind are leaving the party and joining PAS.'[20] The PAS MP Hashim Josin, who, in July 1998, had captured Arau from the BN for the first time, also noted that many civil servants in Perlis were now joining the party and forming new branches.[21]

Despite the partisan claims here, the PAS leadership had largely refrained from over-confident language. Its approach had been more cautious, using the Anwar issue to highlight the iniquities of the BN system and to draw Malay intellectuals closer to the PAS project. Admiring Nik Aziz's model of a corruption-free administration, many middle-class Muslims now saw the PAS alternative as the only way of cleansing the government.[22] Indeed, many key UMNO figures had also quietly conceded PAS's appeal here. Thus, the BN/media stereotype of PAS as a backward, fundamentalist party with little 'secular' support was being eroded, notably by the new intellectual and popular appeal of *Harakah*. At the same time, though, this was being mediated by an ongoing affirmation of Islamic values in the paper, for example through Nik Aziz's regular *Tazkirah* column.

Again, it is necessary to distinguish between party propaganda and the more meaningful subtext of PAS discourse. Much of *Harakah*'s own output certainly belongs to the former – as skilfully directed by Subky Latif, the party's information chief. Yet the party has also been engaged in a more nuanced dialogue with non-Muslim intellectuals and political forces in an effort to bring them into a PAS–Islamic orbit of thought. Here, PAS is, at once, appealing to other ethnic and religious streams to recognise its ideas, while 'subjecting itself' to internal reappraisal and seeking a more mainstream political and civil position. This does not suggest compromise *per se*. Rather, it denotes, *viz*. war of position, a more mature attempt to confront the realities, strategic and intellectual, of building an alternative project to Mahathirism.

In response, the UMNO network, using the communal card and the BN media, was seeking to project the fear factor in two ways. The first was by warning the Chinese, notably via the MCA and Gerakan, not to support PAS for fear of being relegated as second-class citizens. (The irony of this claim *vis-à-vis* Chinese status under the NEP should not be lost here.) In January 1999, with reports now emerging of a possible electoral pact between PAS and DAP, MCA spokesman Lim Si Cheng urged the DAP to state its position on PAS plans for an Islamic state: 'Malaysians, especially the Chinese community, also have a right to know whether DAP supports the policies carried out by the Kelantan PAS government.'[23] The second aspect of the communal message involved warnings that, under PAS, Malays risked losing their existing political rights, the implication here being that PAS's refutation of false nationalism would mean, in practice, a denial of the Malays' special constitutional position.

We need not detain ourselves with the implicit contradiction in this dual message. In a sense, its has its own quintessential 'logic' within Malaysian politics. More significant is PAS's own response to the BN's communal agenda. Allowing for PAS's continued goal of an Islamic state, one may denote a certain candour in its appeals to the Chinese. First, taking basic tenets of faith, PAS argues that Islam and racism cannot coexist – *ergo* PAS cannot be a racist party. One illustration of this is PAS's insistence that it has no problem in sharing top political or cabinet posts with other ethnic party figures or allowing non-Muslim institutions to function both within and outwith government. Second, in the context of the NEP/NDP, PAS's reservations over Bumiputeraism as a framework for socio-economic distribution assume, at least in principle, a more level playing-field for the Chinese. While this still includes a commitment to 'special assistance' for Malays (notably, in the poorer rural locations), it also, as claimed above, offers the Chinese more economic rights than under UMNO/BN. PAS is also attentive to the tension between Malay and Islamic identity – two constructs that, as noted, cannot always be conjoined. But, in claiming to 'represent' all these ethnic–religious currents, the party has sought to extend its presence within the 'secular' political arena without compromising its Islamic agenda.

As the Anwar trial commenced, a *Harakah* comment piece signalled PAS's intent in making it a particular issue of public morality, as captured in the headline 'Are liars and slanderers qualified to lead a Muslim nation?'[24] Here, PAS was focusing on the immediate issue of justice for Anwar (and others such as Lim Guan Eng) rather than dwelling on the 'merits' of the sodomy charges, the alleged details of which represented an affront to Islamic codes. It should be noted here that this was not mere political pragmatism on PAS's part. In the first instance, it reflected a strong feeling amongst Malays that the Islamic *syariah* court was the appropriate place to hear these allegations – a sentiment quietly expressed at the time by many within and around UMNO itself. Second, it was in keeping with the party's long-standing denunciation of the ISA and other repressive instruments, a position that could now be linked into the Anwar affair as a PAS call for wholesale reform of the legal and judicial system.

PAS's careful negotiation of a secular politics via *Harakah* and the *reformasi* had, thus, given it both a mainstream electoral profile and a leading role in building an alternative bloc. This did not mean that Malays and non-Malays were blinkered to PAS's Islamic aims. But it did show that PAS could find common ground within the wider anti-BN community. This was evident in the many joint statements given at this point by Fadzil Noor (for GERAK) and Tian Chua (for GAGASAN) on the Anwar situation. Other networked pieces, such as articles on the Renong bail-out, were also being co-published in *Harakah* and at various *reformasi* sites, providing detailed insights into the specifics of BN money politics.

Against this background, the critical Malaysian journalist MGG Pillai advanced the view that a new type of social/class cleavage was now evident. Noting also the open secret of Cabinet figures' own 'peccadilloes', one could see the emergence of: 'two distinct camps ... that of the amoral corporate bigwigs on the one hand and the moral fundamentalist Muslim on the other. If this hardens, then everyone in between will be neutralised, and the situation set, in the future, for a clash between the two extreme groups.'[25] In this scenario, Mahathir was himself being egged on by big corporate cronies who stood to lose much under Anwar. As this sector pressed for a more repressive use of state instruments to protect their interests, the moral vacuum created was being filled by a new Islamic-centred politics.

In the main, this power cleavage looked a little too neat. It understated the tensions within domestic capital at this point as well as the concerns of foreign capital, while omitting to mention that the 'moral camp' was both Islamic *and* secular. Nevertheless, there was an interesting point to be extrapolated in that PAS was, indeed, now centring itself as the 'vanguard' of that 'new moral order', with support for PAS reflecting not only Malay dissent towards Mahathir, but a more basic antipathy towards the BN *system*.

PAS, the Opposition Bloc and National–Popular Support

In perhaps the most critical impasse since Merdeka, the question for PAS now was how to negotiate this new political fluidity and assume responsibility for building a popular alliance. As one opinion piece in *Harakah* put it: 'If PAS does not read the mood of the people correctly, it will amount to a betrayal of the people.'[26]

Here, PAS had to brook the inevitable question of its relationship with the opposition, and the DAP in particular. As this debate unfolded, one could discern how short-term priorities were now being linked with longer term aims. As one view in *Harakah* put it, PAS should:

focus on leading a government in coalition with other groups ... all the time

> emphasising that such clean government is the result of their being Islamic. They should talk more about a Moral Order which is acceptable to all … [and] open a dialogue with non-Muslim based parties … It is also necessary to re-negotiate with the DAP and other secular groups a definition for 'state religion' and what it exactly means to them … In our opinion this is more important in the long run so that we can take the country out of the communal cul de sac which must be the first step on the long march to an Islamic moral order based on Justice for All.[27]

But while there appeared strong and growing support for a PAS–DAP coalition, both parties remained circumspect about its nature and timing. Of the two, PAS now looked the more positive, its 'needs time' approach indicating a patient game-plan, with a decision being held back for the full party assembly in May 1999.[28] The DAP had also been consistent in its cooperation with GERAK and the other *reformasi* bodies. However, behind the scenes, the DAP leadership were engaged in a more detailed debate over the implications of a coalition with PAS, the issue of Islam and the potential loss of Chinese support. Another concern here was that with PAS likely to dominate any contest in the Northern states, DAP had little to gain from a formal pact. On the other hand, any refusal to enter a coalition would be seen as narrow sectarianism, provoking popular rejection and internal crisis in any event.

By January 1999, these tensions were more evident. One indication was Nik Aziz's statement in a *Star* article noting that PAS would be prepared to form a pact with the DAP, 'even Satan', to oust the BN, although he later clarified this by insisting that he did not intend to make the equation.[29] While acknowledging this, Lim nevertheless suggested that as a political leader in a multicultural society, Nik Aziz had to be 'more careful … in his public statements'.[30] However, alongside the rebuke was Lim's message that, despite their 'great political differences', the DAP would be 'prepared to work with PAS and other political parties, including those in the Barisan Nasional, on common objectives'.[31]

While the 'Satan' remark was readily exploited by the BN media,[32] a less obvious, if still biased, reportage posing as liberal polemic could be seen in Akbar Ali's *Sun* column, 'Premature for opposition parties to fly flags'.[33] Remarking on the proliferation of PAS flags in Kedah, the article asserted that the PAS–DAP relationship was a marriage of convenience flawed by ideological differences: 'turbans, robes and liberal socialist principles do not mix very well'. More important, he thought, was the need to concentrate on 'the more important goal of restoring the economy and maintaining the peace'. Thus, again, we see a perennial language of insiderism at play, with 'critical' opinion expressed through a 'national problem-solving' idiom.

By the end of Hari Raya and the anticipated announcement of the Sabah state elections, the case for an accommodation with the DAP was becoming more urgent. With Mahathir's rural support falling, PAS saw the real prospect of taking the four northern states. Despite refusing it formal registration, ADIL was also building steady support across the country. The sacking of Chandra, ADIL's now active chairman, from his academic position at the University of Malaya had helped galvanise student reaction, a boldness that was beginning to grow with Rahim Noor's admission of guilt over the Anwar beating. The idea of breaking the BN's two-thirds majority was now finding popular resonance, even though more sober evaluations prevailed among PAS and DAP leaders. Yet even if this psychological barrier could not be broken, the prospect of a sizeable number of seats would create the basis for a *working* opposition and a viable alternative to the BN in the public mind. Thus a new set of realities was emerging for the PAS leadership. As Narni Saila put it in four key question themes for a *Harakah* Opinion piece:

1. How prepared is PAS to govern the country?
2. Assuming [Fadzil Noor as] the next PM, who will be in his cabinet? [and will it] attract its own cronies?
3. Will PAS have the wisdom to invite talents from other political parties?
4. [Will PAS] exercise deliberate restraint on other issues?[34]

Responding to the above pointers, and illustrating the new populist tone of debate within *Harakah*, a subsequent piece, rejecting the view that PAS lacked competent people, addressed the crisis of confidence within UMNO and the possible PAS dividend:

> Consider this scenario. UMNO is declining, yet UMNO is the main component of the ruling BN. If UMNO doesn't obtain sufficient support from the Malay Muslims, how can it claim leadership of the BN? And how can the BN survive, or for that matter any other coalition, if it is led by a non-Malay, non-Muslim party? MCA cannot take the lead. This is *realpolitik*. What follows is that BN will cease to exist unless there is another Malay based party ready to fill in UMNO's shoes. In the Malaysian context, one must accept the reality that the Malays cannot accept another alternative besides PAS.[35]

Yet, while support for a PAS–DAP alignment was growing, it remained stalled by restraining voices, notably within DAP. Some of the tension had come to focus on a 'resurrected' remark by the Penang DAP chairman and lawyer Karpal Singh that there would be an Islamic state only 'over my dead body'. Made in an off-the-cuff manner during the 1990 election, and given a 'new airing' by the BN media, the remark was, nevertheless, symptomatic of the PAS–DAP dilemma. To some extent, the acrimony over this statement was to have something of a cathartic effect on PAS–DAP relations. However, before a more contemplative language could emerge, Karpal's view had been subject to critical rebuke, as in this *Harakah* editorial:

> It is a pity that [Karpal] knows very little about Islamic state [*sic*] and must be swallowing all the garbage spewed out by the media about Islam ... Election or no election, it is the religious duty of every Muslim to establish an Islamic state in every land ... But what is an Islamic state? I do not blame Karpal Singh for misunderstanding the concept ... Islam recognises the rights of other religious groups not because Karpal or other human rights activists demand it. It is because the Muslims are bound by a revealed paradigm which enshrines the rights to freedom of religion to all peoples.[36]

In a further example of PAS's adherence to Quranic principles of religious tolerance, the Comment also notes how, in Kelantan, Nik Aziz:

> refused to ban the sale of liquor to the non-Muslims for he could not find sanctions ... under the *Shariah*. Is this not enough guarantee to Karpal Singh that in an Islamic state the Rule of Law will be supreme and justice will be the cornerstone of every move it makes vis-à-vis a non-Muslim community?[37]

By the same token, argued PAS, the Quranic principle can be applied to the constitution and power sharing:

> PAS has already committed itself to power sharing with non-Muslims, not as a political expediency, but [as] sanctioned by the *Shariah*. Since PAS has also committed to democratic means in the struggle for an Islamic state, the issue is actually a non-issue as PAS would never be able to change the constitution as it stands now on its own without the support of its partners in government.[38]

In its inability to manage BN provocation and contain this tension, the 'Karpal affair' showed up a certain naivety on the part of the main opposition. On the other hand, by allowing the issue into the open, a qualitative exchange of views had taken place, signalling a new, if still cautious, understanding. In the spirit of tolerance, both Lim's and Karpal Sing's views were being allowed free and respectful expression in *Harakah*.[39] Karpal was also allowed critical space in *Harakah* to remind PAS of the country's constitutional guarantees with regard to other religions under Article 3.[40] Yet, while reflecting many non-Malay (and Malay) concerns, much of this debate could be seen as academic, given the reality that PAS would need either its own two-thirds parliamentary majority, or considerable coalition support, to initiate an Islamic state, neither scenario seeming likely.

However, it was the growing desire for a new type of non-partisan politics that was now driving the PAS–DAP issue. Alongside Malay disenchantment at Anwar's treatment was a considerable undercurrent of distaste for Mahathir among non-Malays. Building on this, Wan Azizah and ADIL were giving impetus to a new, if still gradual, non-racial politics.[41] While Chinese business remained, for the most part, behind the BN, one could discern from casual conversations a growing unease among professional and middle-class Chinese and Indians, notably within academia. Among 'service-sector' Chinese (such as Penang and KL taxi-drivers), one could also hear political sensitivities ranging from moderate concern to outright condemnation. The more important nuance, however, was that many Chinese were holding back their verdict on the BN for election time. Moreover, while sharing common cause with non-Malays, a growing stream of PAS members and supporters now saw very clearly the more immediate value of a PAS–DAP alignment as a necessary stepping-stone to meaningful political power, and thereafter to some form of Islamic state.

A number of these tensions had come to the surface at a keynote DAP 'Justice For All' forum in Penang.[42] The event was especially significant, being the first time, as an ADIL figure, that Wan Azizah had addressed the more varied ethnic gathering of a Penang crowd. Prior to the gathering, UMNO Youth had called on all Malays not to attend, for fear of 'break[ing] Malay unity in the nation and the state [sic]'.[43] In the event, over four thousand people packed the main auditorium and an overflow hall to hear Wan Azizah, Karpal Singh, Lim Kit Siang, the lawyer Cecil Rajendra and the journalist Rustam A. Sani.[44] Opening the forum, Karpal criticised the boycott call as a symptom of the Barisan's racial politics, calling for closer cooperation between opposition parties and NGOs. In her entrance and speech, Wan Azizah was given an emotional reception by cheering Malays and non-Malays (roughly equal in number) chanting the *reformasi* slogan. Yet, while she and others spoke eloquently of the need for unity, at no point was the DAP–PAS issue addressed directly. It was only following the speeches, from within a now more tense audience, that a self-declared PAS member and Islamic teacher finally raised the matter, challenging Karpal, with courteous argument, to substantiate his 'over my dead body' statement. Following other such questions from Malays – Chinese comments from the floor being noticeably absent – asking why DAP could not join with PAS to break the BN, Karpal, in a principled statement, reiterated (as a Sikh) his belief in free and equal expression for all religions and their progressive ideals. However, while apologising for any false impression given over his regard for Islam (a sentiment warmly applauded by all), in the final analysis all faiths, he insisted, had to be protected under the constitution.[45] In the following Friday edition of *Harakah*, the front-page headline read 'Karpal Minta Maaf' (Karpal apologises).[46]

While Karpal's apology and the gathering itself illustrated the potential for Malays and non-Malays to work together, it also revealed some of the deep-lying sensitivities of religion within Malaysian politics. In another telling moment, one Muslim speaking from the floor had advised Wan Azizah not to shake hands with males, given its un-Islamic association and the fear that it might be used by the media to cast aspersions on her own morality. In a tactful, and well-received, response, she had noted that her duties as a doctor required her to touch the human body – although it was noticeable that Wan Azizah did 'follow this advice', to some extent, by covering her palm when shaking hands.[47] At the same time, other small gestures of good faith were helping to build trust. Karpal, for example, had offered (to wide applause) legal help to an old Muslim man who had never received compensation for being assaulted during the Memali incident. Wan Azizah had expressed empathy with Lim, whose son Lim Guan Eng had been unjustly incarcerated like her husband; recognition of a Chinese sacrificing his liberty to help a Muslim family. Wan Azizah's use of Chinese greetings (as taught by Anwar) was also well received.

In another such gesture, with more chilling implications, Lim Guan Eng had sent Anwar a letter of reply, wishing him well, but regretting to inform him that: 'the prison authorities here in Kajang are making feverish preparations for your cell even though your trial is still continuing. One is curious how they can be so certain of your impending conviction.'[48] Consistent with growing public perceptions (and personal observations of Anwar's testimony)[49], this fuelled speculation that the trial was, indeed, being 'prejudged'.

As the hearing neared its inevitable conclusion, ADIL's promotion of a non-racial front was helping to draw the opposition together. However, while working closely with the DAP, ADIL were now finding voice as a proto-party and alternative to the DAP for non-Malays. At the same time, Wan Azizah was moving closer to PAS, as reflected in the latter's ongoing support of her candidacy.[50]

This had also helped bring about a new relationship between PAS and ABIM. Although having been 'brought in' by the BN, ABIM was being closely monitored at this point.[51] In particular, the BN feared not only that element supportive of Anwar within ABIM, but of more mainstream members and associates now going over to PAS or ADIL, a rapport evident, for example, in Wan Azizah's address to a 10,000-strong crowd at an ABIM Hari Raya gathering in Perak.[52] There was also a growing appeal from PAS to ABIM to realise the futility of their 'courtship' with UMNO. In seeking to build its Islamic base, PAS argued that they should 'close ranks with other Muslims ... to continue the struggle under the true Islamic leadership.'[53] As PAS pointed out, Anwar's predicament now proved the folly of trying to bring about Islamic transformation through UMNO.[54] So, while PAS, DAP, PRM, ADIL, GERAK, GAGASAN and various NGOs continued to build a *de facto* alliance based on broad political goals, another more particularised realignment was occurring as Malay and Islamic elements now de-linked from UMNO and drew closer to PAS.

PAS–Islam, Party Politics and the Crisis (2)

As an ongoing set of pointers to PAS's political collaborations and the Anwar affair by early 1999, let us note here some further observations offered by the PAS President Fadzil Noor.[55]

Fadzil Noor and Anwar's Fall

Prior to Anwar's removal and arrest, Fadzil Noor and the PAS leaders had intimated that he would never be PM and lacked the ability to hold UMNO together. However, while apparently vindicated in that set of views, one could see that the PAS president was averse to pushing the 'I told you so' line, a reticence that, although politically expedient, also seemed motivated by a deeper sense of compassion.

In practice, he argued, it was always going to be difficult for Anwar to become PM, particularly after Mahathir came to see him as a direct challenge. Hence Fadzil's considered belief by this point that there was no chance of an acquittal. Anwar, he predicted, would be convicted and imprisoned, perhaps for two to four years. Barred from office, he would be kept out of the way, his political career conveniently curtailed, possibly for ten years.

Judicial independence, Fadzil lamented, had been usurped by the executive, leaving no effective separation of power. Allied to Mahathir's encroachment of the state was the clique around the PM, who, more 'secular-minded' than Anwar, had come to see him as a threat, particularly after 1993 as Anwar's profile increased. This, Fadzil insists, is when the conspiracy to stop him really began to develop. Maintaining that Mahathir had a hidden agenda all along never to let Anwar become PM, the main basis of Anwar's threat to the clique was his differing economic policy agenda with Mahathir. This, in turn, tied into the *korupse, kronisme, nepotisme* (KKN) issue and the challenge posed on Anwar's behalf by a section of UMNO Youth. However, Fadzil suggests that, having shown little regard for poorer Malaysians, Mahathir also feared Anwar's popularity among the lower-income groups. Moreover, while accepting that there had been general antipathy towards Anwar's recovery agenda and IMF connections, Fadzil saw this as a separate issue from the wider concern over Anwar's treatment.

With regard to Islam, Fadzil argued that while Anwar had moderated his values to 'UMNO secularism', his Islamic background and popularity had been specifically needed by UMNO to oppose PAS. In fact, because of this, he still had many supporters within UMNO. Still, if Anwar was not to be part of UMNO again, Fadzil saw little likelihood of a place for him within PAS. Rather (anticipating events to come), Anwar would probably form a new party, which, Fadzil suggested, PAS could work with, perhaps through a formal coalition.

The PAS president also reiterated at this point the 'needs time to develop' position on the PAS–DAP relationship. While he acknowledged DAP's fears over Islam, its caution, he felt, was bound up with concerns over its Chinese support base. Through GERAK, GAGASAN, ADIL and the pages of *Harakah*, the basis of PAS–DAP relations, he felt, had now shifted to one of 'close understanding'. Fadzil also appeared to accept the sincerity of Karpal Singh's position and apology. With DAP moderating its tone on the Islamic issue, PAS was also endeavouring to present itself as less fundamentalist in image.

While recognising the need for each side to appear less chauvinistic, Fadzil was by now extremely aware of the media's ability to exploit any such pact by claiming a sellout of their respective party principles. Nevertheless, given the BN's strategy to silence Anwar, it was more important that the counter-attack be focused and united in the run-up to the election. With Kelantan providing a model for adjoining states, PAS also hoped for an expanded power base, although, combining political pragmatism with personal modesty, Fadzil still avoided speculative commentary on PAS's electoral prospects or his own role in any post-election scenario. Thus, while observing cautious pre-election language, PAS was now open about using Anwar's cause as a key issue of justice and political development.

Planting the Seed: Party Cooperation and PAS Influence by mid-1999

This careful view could also be discerned in comments made by Nik Aziz at this point. Asked in a newspaper interview about a possible coalition, he stressed that groups such as GERAK were an important 'first step':

> GERAK is the seed which unites DAP and PAS … Maybe one day, the seed sown will grow and bring about co-operation. Our condition is that whoever

wants to co-operate with us, if they don't want to embrace Islam, should at least accept the Islamic concept. It is not impossible that one day, DAP with its concept, and PAS with its concept, will find a common meeting point.[56]

However, like Lim Kit Siang, Nik Aziz was also extending this message to UMNO, or, at least, a disenchanted element within UMNO:

> There is no reason for the rivals to fight PAS ... I use PAS as a bridge to promote Islam. I would like to repeat my statement, if UMNO can act to strengthen Islam in terms of faith, guidance, morals and practice, there is no reason for PAS to fight UMNO.[57]

Yet Nik Aziz also sees in his religious beliefs a political duty to remove UMNO:

> I cannot retire from politics. Muslims cannot retire from politics. Islam came to the world to correct man's being. To correct man's condition is political work. Political work does not mean to find money to put into a politician's pocket. That's wrong. That's why the people hate UMNO.[58]

For Mahathir, this required a restatement of Vision-Islam. In preparing for a main tour of the states before leaving for the *Haj*, Mahathir signalled his intent by attacking Nik Aziz's assertion that UMNO was a 'secular party'.[59] Commencing the tour in Alor Setar, Mahathir launched a scathing attack on the PAS leadership, its view of women, its 'enticement' to rioting and its willingness to 'collaborate with Satan' for political ends. Condemning Wan Azizah, ADIL and Al Gore, Mahathir also gave descriptive examples of 'nauseating' homosexual liaisons (noting a marriage between a Dutch minister and his male partner), an allusion, to Anwar's alleged conduct. Thus, in seeking to 'explain' the current situation to the people, one could see that smear tactics and inference would be a key part of UMNO/BN's forthcoming electoral strategy.[60]

Yet this old politics of fear was becoming increasingly redundant. The 'Islamic issue' had, indeed, now been raised to a new level of political sensitivity. From within the UMNO network, this was still being presented as a straight choice between an imposed Islamic state or a moderate, Vision-led, version of Islamic development. But the issue of political morality and Anwar's persecution was now serving to dismantle this modernist–fundamentalist construct. The artifice of Vision-Islam as a basis for managing traditional Islam had been compromised, principally because UMNO had lost much of its 'moral authority' to speak on behalf of Islam.

By the time of its 45th Annual Muktamar in May 1999, PAS had, effectively, agreed on some, as yet to be finalised, form of party cooperation. Debating this and other issues of development, education, social policy and the role of IT, Fadzil Noor's keynote speech 'Standing Together for Justice' had sought to blend traditional concepts of Islamic collectivism with 'modernist' ideas on electoral partnership, economic reform and social justice.[61] DAP also now signalled its assent to a pact and form of electoral understanding. As Lim was to note shortly after the Muktamar: 'The [only remaining] question to be decided is the final shape and form of such an Opposition.'[62]

So, from these observations of the unfolding situation, we can make the following summary of the 'PAS project' by mid- to late 1999:

In political terms, PAS had emerged as a more mature political outfit, increasingly aware of how the power game with UMNO/BN had to be conducted. Using the crisis and the Anwar affair, it had embraced both Islamic and non-Islamic energies in an attempt to build a new political bloc. While this process had revealed key tensions between PAS and DAP over the Islamic issue, PAS, could now, as the principal Malay alternative to UMNO, assume a leading role within the opposition alignment. In particular, the cultivation of a new 'moral politics' had seen a major expansion of its *national–popular* base. However, the political cohesion of this arrangement still depended on meaningful accommodations with the other parties and the wider *reformasi*.

In class/economic terms, the PAS project was focused on a renewal of the state, greater political–corporate transparency and a set of Islamic alternatives for development, financial practices and social planning. Based mainly on localised forms of development in Kelantan, the PAS model here does not constitute a major structural blueprint. But it does suggest a tentative challenge to the 'hybrid' version of 'Islamic economics', *viz.* 'Islamic banking', promoted by Mahathir in pursuit of Vision-led capitalism. While this was unlikely to gain mainstream support or threaten existing capitalist institutions, it had served, in the wake of the financial crisis, to highlight the abuses of economic power within the BN system.

In ideological terms, the party was now contesting Vision ideas more ably through a range of civil institutions. This reflects the role now being played by a new generation of committed professional party members through political education, media presentation, linkages with wider Islamic groupings and other forms of populist organisation. Again, while PAS–Islam was not acceptable to many Malaysians, its principles were being fused with broader secular concerns about justice, transparency and good-governance. As a proto-project involving wider cross-ethnic support and intellectual streams, this still had to find direction. But it did illustrate the contextual space within which the arguments and ideas for such a project were now located.

Yet, while the PAS project was evidence of an 'integration' of Islamic, non-Islamic and *reformasi* oppositions, it also suggested questions about the status of 'left' politics and ideas within that process, a set of issues to which we now turn.

Notes

1. 'Reshuffle in police force will involve top brass', *Sun*, 31 January 1999.

2. See the more specific *Sun* headline 'Rahim did it', in contrast to the more equivocal *New Straits Times* (front page bottom line) 'Rahim admits hitting Anwar after grave provocation', both 1 March 1999.

3. 'Transfer of power will be smooth: PM', *Sun*, 15 January 1999.

4. See Raja Petra Kamarudin, 'The aftermath of the reformation movement', *Harakah*, 5 October 1998.

5. My thanks to Dr Syed Azman Syed Ahmad, PAS Secretary of International Affairs/Director of R&D and lecturer in politics at University of Malaya for his extensive discussion on party organisation and related issues, PAS HQ, Batu Caves, Kuala Lumpur, 8 March 1999.

6. See '20,000 attend PM's Raya open house' and 'Mahathir gets a huge vote of support', *Sun*, 19 January 1999.

7. TV news and press reports had also carried stories that *Raya* open houses were being used for free food. See, for example, 'Give me more', *Sun*, 22 January 1999.

8. 'UMNO in the new Millennium', *Sun*, 10 January 1999.

9. *Harakah* was launched in 1987.

10. Details of *Harakah*'s circulation figures (not included in the Audit Bureau of Circulations or other indexes for Malaysia) are given by the PAS office. The figure of 300,000 has been generally accepted as valid and is consistent with the surge in PAS support during the crisis. See, for example, 'Pas time', *FEER*, 18 March 1999.

11. 'Anti-Mahathir campaign reaches Malay heartland', *Harakah*, 14 December 1998.

12. 'Why can't Muslim women be *wakil rakyat*?', *Harakah*, 22 February 1999.

13. See, for example, 'Can a Chinese Muslim celebrate the Chinese New Year?', *Harakah*, 19 February 1999. The answer was, basically, yes, provided any celebration was confined to ethnic/cultural, rather than religious, Chinese aspects.

14. 'Some realities that PAS members should know', *Harakah*, 8 March 1999.

15. *Harakah*, 7 September 1998.

16. 'Gratitude - a privilege', *Harakah*, 1 March 1999.

17. Ibid.

18. Sadirah K. 'Ruling elite fear a "thinking public"', *Harakah*, 8 March 1999.

19. See 'The exodus begins' *Harakah*, 14 December 1998.

20. 'Malaysian Moslem opposition strikes deep into Mahathir's rural bastion', *AFP*, 6 December 1998.

21. Ibid.

22. See 'Comment: winds of change', *Harakah*, 9 November 1998.

23. 'State stand on PAS, DAP told', *Sunday Star*, 24 January 1999.

24. *Harakah*, 14 September 1998.

25. Published at 'Malaysia. Net' site, 11 September 1998.

26. 'PAS cannot afford to miss this chance to lead Malaysia to a new era', *Harakah*, 5 October 1999.

27. Ibid.

28. 'Nik Aziz: PAS assembly will discuss poll pacts', *Sun*, 23 January 1999.

29. *Star*, 25 January 1999.

30. Lim Kit Siang, Media Statement, DAP Homepage, 25 January 1999.

31. Ibid.

32. See, for example, 'PAS–DAP link nothing new, says Yusof' (Yusof Noor, UMNO information chief), *Sunday Star*, 24 January 1999.

33. *Sun*, 27 January 1999.

34. Narma Saila, 'Has PAS done its homework? ... we need to know', *Harakah*, 25 January 1999.

35. Ibnu Ibrahim, 'Discard the captive mentality, go for Islam', *Harakah*, 8 February 1999.

36. *Harakah*, 1 February 1999.

37. Ibid.

38. Ibid.

39. See, for example, 'DAP "prepared to work with all parties", asks PAS to "carefully consider" Islamic state', *Harakah*, 1 February 1999.

40. Ibid.

41. See 'Rise of an icon', *FEER*, 18 March 1999.

42. 1 February 1999.

43. 'Don't attend Justice for All forum, Malays urged', *Sunday*, 31 January 1999.

44. The event was reported in a small *Sun* article, 'Large crowd gathers for forum', 3 February 1999.

45. After the meeting had ended, Karpal Singh told this writer that his 'over my dead body' remark had been taken out of context and used in a manipulative fashion by the media.

46. *Harakah*, 2 February 1999.

47. A small point noted during the present writer's own brief exchange with Wan Azizah inside the courtroom during Anwar's first trial.

48. Cited at 'Guan Eng replies to Anwar', Media Statement by Lim Kit Siang, DAP Homepage, 3 February 1999. Guan Eng's actual letter to Anwar was dated 28 January 1999. See also 'Sel Anwar siap di penjara Kajang – Guan Eng' (Anwar's cell being prepared – Guan Eng), *Harakah*, 8 February 1999. This information was also conveyed to the present writer by another authoritative source.

49. As suggested (10 February 1999) by the judge's rulings and substantive constraints on the defence, in contrast to the leeway given to the prosecution.

50. See 'Azizah to take on Mahathir in Kubang Pasu?', *Harakah*, 12 February 1999, and 'The secret of PAS's strength in Kelantan', *Sun*, 11 February 1999.

51. A claim related in discussion with ABIM members and close observers.

52. 'Massive turnout', *Harakah*, 22 February 1999.

53. Comment: 'The obvious choice for ABIM', *Harakah*, 7 September 1998.

54. Ibid.

55. My thanks to the PAS President Fadzil Noor and PAS Supreme Council Member Mohamad Taulan bin Mat Rasul for their lengthy discussion at the PAS Head Office, Alor Setar, 4 February 1999. Other than their recounted views, all observations belong to the present author.

56. 'The secret of PAS's strength in Kelantan', *Sun*, 11 February 1999, reproduced from a two-part article by Baharom Mahsun in *Mingguan Malaysia*.

57. 'Kelantan Menteri Besar speaks his mind', *Sun*, 12 February 1999, from part 2 of above.

58. 'Nik Aziz on life, religion and the future', from linked article, ibid.

59. See 'Nik Aziz tidak faham' (Nik Aziz wrong understanding), *Utusan Malaysia*, 17 February 1999.

60. See 'Fighting words', *Asiaweek*, 2 April 1999, and 'Lies my PM tells me', *Harakah*, 29 March 1999.

61. See 'Standing together for justice', *Harakah*, 4 June 1999, giving excerpts from Fadzil Noor's speech, and 'Bracing for the general elections', *Harakah*, 7 June 1999.

62. Media Statement, Lim Kit Siang Homepage, 6 June 1999.

8

Counter-hegemony: *Reformasi,* Left Politics and the Conditions of Dissent

This chapter makes some assessment of the opposition alignment as it approached the 1999 general election. With new political and intellectual forces coming together under the aegis of the *reformasi*, it also considers the extent to which 'left ideas' were now part of this alternative bloc. Invoking Gramsci's view of intellectual development as historically specific and Said's reflections on the intellectual as 'outsider', this requires us to note four key senses in which a 'left community' has been 'conditioned' in Malaysia: first, with regard to its own definition of what 'left' means; second, in relation to its 'negotiation' of the 'Islamic factor'; third, with respect to cultural–ethnic cleavages; and, fourth, through the co-optive efforts of the UMNO network. However, we are also concerned to show here how left ideas were finding potential new direction through the language and praxes of *reformasi* politics.

The Emerging Bloc and Anwar's *Dénouement*

On 4 April 1999, ten days before the Anwar verdict, and following mounting signals of intent, Wan Azizah and the ADIL leadership announced the formation of Parti Keadilan Nasional (National Justice Party), or KeADILan. A cross-ethnic party open to all Malaysians, KeADILan had 'circumvented' government restrictions by assuming the credentials of a dormant party previously registered in 1900.[1] Held at the appropriately named Renaissance Hotel in Kuala Lumpur, the launch had been a tumultuous affair, with the PAS, DAP and PRM leaders given special invitations to join other *reformasi* activists within the packed hall, while many more exuberant supporters celebrated outside.[2] In her first speech as party leader, Wan Azizah spoke of a historical moment, allaying fears of splits and emphasising the need for all the opposition to work together:

> PKN will not split the Opposition. We will work with all parties that have

justice as the foundation of their struggle. Our party is prepared to sacrifice its own interests in order to achieve the larger goal of forging a credible alternative to the Barisan Nasional, an alternative government that will be accepted by the people.[3]

On his return from exile in Indonesia, Anwar's former political secretary Mohamad Ezam Noor read out a prepared statement on Anwar's behalf noting his endorsement of the party. Significantly, though, Anwar would not be joining KeADILan in a formal capacity, the strategic view, at this point, being that he should act as a unifying figure for all the opposition parties.

Yet, while resolving to work with other parties, KeADILan's arrival now altered the basic configuration of opposition politics. In the first place, it undercut DAP's nominal role as the main opposition party, although, questioning a commentary in *Sin Chew Jit Poh*, Lim Kit Siang noted that KeADILan's real test would be its impact on UMNO's base rather than DAP's.[4] By mid-1999, there was also some tension over the movement of some DAP members to KeADILan,[5] though the extent of this was being played up by the BN media while the opposition parties met to mend the damage. Second, KeADILan's emergence offered a meaningful alternative for mainstream Malaysians uncomfortable with the perceived religio-ethnic options of PAS and DAP. Ezam had noted in an earlier interview that while the *reformasi* would still work with PAS and DAP, 'I sense that certain sectors are more comfortable with having a new party that is more moderate and captures the middle ground.'[6]

The announcement had also been hastened by the extent of the BN's victory in the Sabah state elections (12 and 13 March 1999) which, despite some evidence of electoral chicanery, had seen the BN take 31 of the 48 seats (down from 43 in 1994), the other 17 seats going to the opposition PBS.[7] While the Anwar situation had not been a key issue in the Sabah election, and, thus, not a true test of political feeling in Peninsular Malaysia, it had served as a salutary lesson on the need for opposition unity. In a timely reminder of such, Jomo had warned the opposition not to under-estimate the power and influence of the BN machine on the ground, while pointing out some political realities to DAP:

> the opposition has to get its act together, present a solid united front ... and, very importantly, achieve the co-operation and co-ordination at all levels which is now a BN monopoly ... [T]he DAP must also appreciate that for the Malay-based opposition, especially reformasi, it is crucial to offer a superior alternative to the public, especially the Malay population ... But my emphasis on the problems facing the opposition is mainly due to the naive wishful thinking which is quite widespread among opposition sym-pathizers and well-meaning analysts.[8]

Reinforcing Jomo's point here was the UMNO network's increased offensive against the foreign media and opposition academics. In February 1999, all government agencies were instructed to cancel their subscriptions to the *International Herald Tribune*, *Asiaweek* and *Far Eastern Economic Review*.[9] Earlier that month, Mirzan Mahathir had issued a writ against the Malaysian printers of the *Asian Wall Street Journal* for US$39.5 million, following an account of how his financial success had been linked to favoured deals and money politics. Also pending was a suit against Jomo for 'slandering' Vincent Tan of Berjaya in the *AWSJ* piece. Likewise, a RM60 million action had been raised against the human rights lawyer and UN rapporteur Param Cumaraswamy. The *Far Eastern Economic Review* journalist Murray Hiebert was facing a jail sentence as he prepared to appeal a conviction for writing a 'defamatory' article about the speedy processing of a lawsuit brought by the wife of a prominent Appeals Court judge.[10] And, with an election imminent, the government's anti-slander campaign was stepped up to sue Ruslan Kassim, KeADILan's information chief, over claims that Megat Junid had RM80 million 'stashed away' in Israeli banks.[11] In another warning shot, Chandra had been sacked from his post as director of civilisational dialogue at University Malaya, partly as a move to manage the Centre's influence (including its links with Anwar)[12] and as a more direct response to Chandra's, by now, prominent role in ADIL and the proto-KeADILan.

On 14 April 1999, after 77 days of testimony, Justice Augustine Paul handed down his verdict in the Anwar case. In a 394-page ruling,[13] Anwar was found guilty on the four corruption charges and sentenced to six years on each count (to run concurrently). His seven-month detention was not deducted from the sentence and no bail was allowed pending appeal. The verdict came as little surprise to close observers,[14] Anwar or his defence team, though Wan Azizah was said to be shocked at the length of the sentence. Many foreign governments 'expressed concern', while Amnesty International reconfirmed Anwar as a prisoner of conscience.[15] Street protests and sporadic rioting followed, again met by water cannon and the beating of protesters by a well-prepared deployment of police and FRU. Alongside other activists, Tian Chua was, again, arrested. That evening, *reformasi* figures addressed a mass protest near PAS's Taman Melewar headquarters, Kuala Lumpur. In a damage limitation exercise, the BN issued statements calling for calm, asking the public to respect the verdict and the judicial process. This coincided with the Royal Commission of Inquiry's judgement into Anwar's beating, recommending Rahim Noor's prosecution as the sole offender,[16] this and other such news being timed for release through Bernama.

While there would be no repetition of the September 1998 riots, Anwar's incarceration as a leading political prisoner now offered the *reformasi* a potent new symbol. In this sense, the trial and verdict illustrated the dilemma for Mahathir and the power bloc: whether to allow a fair hearing and risk letting Anwar loose as a political combatant, thus restoring the credibility of the judiciary and wider system; or to ensure Anwar's conviction, risking loss of faith in the legal process, but keeping him under political wraps. As a strategy, Mahathir appeared to have gambled that recourse to the latter might be disguised by the pretence of an impartial trial. However, it was evident that Augustine Paul's handling of the trial was consistent with more critical judgements being made within the UMNO network about the need to protect the power structure itself. There is no space here for a full survey of the trial and its tangled detail, but the following aspects illustrate both the concerns expressed over its conduct and the fears of key elites behind the scenes:[17]

- Justice Augustine Paul's refusal, at the outset, to grant special observer status to human rights groups and other official foreign figures.
- The judge's negation of key evidence from the main prosecution witness, Special Branch director Mohamed Said Awang, admitting in a letter to Dr Mahathir that the sodomy and adultery allegations made by Azizan Abu Bakar (Anwar's wife's driver) and Ummi Hafilda Ali (businesswoman and sister of Anwar's former private secretary Mohamed Azmin Ali) were baseless.[18] Said had also admitted the 'possible existence' of a second police report naming Daim, Consumer Affairs Minister Megat Junid and Mahathir's Political Secretary Aziz Shamsuddin as the main conspirators in a smear campaign against Anwar. Despite 'instructions' to the prosecution to look for the report, it was never produced in court.
- The judge's acceptance of claims made by Said, Amir Junus, the deputy director of Special Branch, and Special Branch officer Abdul Aziz Hussin that Anwar had instructed them to '*gempar*' (frighten) Azizan and Ummi into retracting their 'statements' (concerning Anwar's 'sexual impropriety') to the PM, this being the 'substance' of the prosecution's corruption case. Azizan's own testimony, contradicting his claim (made to Ummi and sent as part of her letter to the PM) to have been sodomised by Anwar, was also allowed to stand despite defence attempts to have it thrown out.
- Said's own admissions that he might, if required, 'lie for Mahathir' and that intense mental pressure and other *menggemparnya* (fear-instilling) police techniques had been used to 'turn over' Azizan and Ummi.
- The judge's acceptance of chief CID officer Musa Hassan's account of

an alleged 'cover-up' discussion he had with Anwar in the presence of the attorney-general (AG) (directing him not to proceed with the investigation) despite Anwar's denial and lack of evidence that Musa was present.[19]

- The judge's disregard for Azmin Ali's testimony that his sister Ummi was a 'compulsive liar' and had been disowned by her family, that Megat Junid had written Ummi's letter to the PM and that Azmin himself had not been sodomised by Anwar despite police threats to confess. Azmin's wife Shamsidar Taharin also denied having an affair with Anwar, as alleged by Ummi.

- The decision to disallow the defence's presentation of taped conversations between Ummi Hafildi and businessman Sng Chee Hua in London. The judge also later barred media reporting of names referred to in telephone conversations made by Ummi from London to Malaysia, taped by businessman Nor Azman Abdullah, as noted in his testimony.[20]

- The decision, at the prosecution's request, to amend the wording of the corruption charges and (having, in effect, failed to prove the sodomy charges) the amendment of the overall charges to include only the corruption charges. The 'evidence' from the sodomy charges (including the production of a semen-stained mattress allegedly linked to an affair with Shamsidar) had been allowed extensive public display, thus serving the intended purpose of casting doubt on Anwar's character.

- The constant blocking of the defence's lines of enquiry – eliciting the considerable skills of its lead counsel Raja Aziz Adrusse. The most critical aspect of this constant 'not relevant' refrain was the ruling that the defence could not pursue examination of the case for 'political conspiracy', despite the defence's attempt to prove that police *malafide* was linked to an orchestrated conspiracy from above.

- The ruling that Mohtar Abdullah, the attorney-general, could take over the role of lead prosecutor from Abdul Ghani Patail at a crucial stage of the trial (Anwar's testimony) despite himself being a potential witness and alleged figure in the conspiracy.

- The decision to embargo key parts of Anwar's testimony in order to maintain the confidentiality of sensitive conversations Anwar had (as related in court) with Mahathir and the IGP Rahim Noor. Reference to discussions with Trade and Industry Secretary Rafidah Aziz were also barred to the media. (Alongside others able to observe Anwar's testimony on this day, one could see the significance of this ruling.)[21]

- The 'not relevant' ruling on defence evidence (by Anwar's former aide Zull Aznam Harun) that Azizan had been paid money to send a letter to the PM containing allegations of sexual misconduct.

- The judge's petty interruptions and slow note-taking during the defence's questioning, stemming the flow and spontaneity of their case, in contrast to that afforded to the prosecution.

- The ruling disallowing the defence from producing ten of its last key witnesses.

- The contempt of court ruling and three-month (suspended) sentence against one of Anwar's defence lawyers Zainar Zakaria for moving to disqualify two public prosecutors.

- Augustine Paul's own rejection of a defence application to have him disqualified on grounds of bias.

While Augustine Paul's embargo had been intended to prevent the damaging content of Anwar's exchanges with Mahathir and Rahim Noor being aired, key aspects of these meetings did find their way into the public domain.[22] The first involved Mahathir's alleged ultimatum to Anwar to resign or be prosecuted, calling into question a number of issues regarding Mahathir's powers of office. Another concerned Rahim Noor's alleged conversation with Anwar during which, holding Anwar's hand, an unusual habit for Rahim, he urged Anwar to sort out the problem with the PM himself. Again, this and related conversation between the two suggests that delicate approaches were being made to Anwar at this point as part of a control strategy from above. What also emerges from the court transcripts is the very close and often cordial relationships Anwar had with the two Special Branch figures, the AG and the IGP prior to his downfall. Another is his close dealings with a number of key business elites.

This indicates two main things: first, the extent to which Anwar had been a privileged part of the power structure, even allowing for Daim's watchful eye and the unfolding plot to oust him; second, the crisis within the power bloc which, when the purge on Anwar was decided upon, saw these and other top figures turn against Anwar. This also gives credence to the defence claim that the police conspiracy formed an internal part of the political conspiracy from above, suggesting, in turn, a necessary, if unpalatable, set of actions taken to protect not only Mahathir but a more concentrated set of political and corporate interests.

By late 1999, the opposition, comprising PAS, DAP, KeADILan and PRM, had gathered itself into the Barisan Alternatif (BA) (Alternative Front), its manifesto, 'Towards a Just Malaysia', pronouncing the party's new cooperative intentions.[23] Despite his ongoing sodomy trial (and new moves by the Anti-Corruption Agency to investigate his financial probity while in office), the Front confirmed Anwar as its nominal leader. Recognising his custodial position, the BA stated that it would appoint an interim leader, based on majority support in the Dewan Rakyat, should it be elected. Thereafter, there would be a full judicial inquiry into the political conspiracy that had led to Anwar's imprisonment, allowing him to take his rightful place as prime minister.

Despite doubts over its imediate electoral abilities, the BA's importance also lay in its potential to establish longer-term structures, alliances and intellectual challenges to the prevailing power bloc. To what extent, then, had the crisis created new space for political mobilisation? In particular, with regard to conceptions of a socialist praxes, what kind of 'left agenda' could be noted within and around the *reformasi* by this point? To address these questions, let us consider four main factors that have served to 'condition' ideas within the 'left intellectual community', beginning with the problem of definition itself.

Situating the Left: Conditions and Legacies

Some of the historical context of 'left politics' in Malaysia has been noted in the preceding chapters. However, it is necessary to offer some kind of defining statement of what we mean by 'the left' in order to situate it *vis-à-vis* the *reformasi*. In particular, it is important to make the distinction between 'left' and 'liberal' ideas within this relationship. With specific reference to the left in Southeast Asia, Hewison and Rodan provide a helpful point of departure:

> The 'Left' is a term which is often used loosely to refer to a variety of reformist movements and ideas. However, we understand the common de-nominator of the 'Left' to be an emphasis on alternatives to the individualism of market relationships and a commitment to values which advance public and collective interests. At one extreme, this involves revolutionary social movements, grounded in class analysis and carrying a vision of an alternative social system, such as socialism or Communism. It can, however, also involve reformism of a social democratic nature which may challenge the pre-rogatives of capital and the market within much tighter limits, and without any serious vision of an alternative social system. Both these variants of the Left can be differentiated from liberal reformism which may champion individual human rights, the rule of law and liberal democracy, for example, without embracing collectivism and challenges to the market.[24]

Assuming this basic definition and distinction, it can be argued that the decisive part of left activity in Malaysia lies somewhere between the 'left-social-democratic' and the 'liberal reformist' variants. Two main points can be made in this regard.

First, the left has *always* been a marginal (and marginalised) political force in Malaysia – certainly if we are to take the outlawed status of the

Malayan Communist Party as a historical indicator. A key reason for this, as noted, has been the BN's use of communal politics as a form of class control. Another is the sense in which neo-liberalism, global accumulation and the search for low-cost investment sites undermined socialism as a strategy for developing countries in the region.[25] To some extent, the BN's practical commitment to basic social spending and rural development has also kept left politics in check. For this and other such reasons, domestic NGOs are less numerous and active than their Indonesian, Thai and Philippine counterparts.[26]

Thus, second, those groups one might associate with holding 'leftist' credentials cannot simply be viewed as such. For example, since its initiation in 1977, *Aliran* has provided a broad forum for reformist discourse among the broad NGO community. Its position on most issues is strongly egalitarian and underwritten by a sincere desire for the just society. This has been informed, in the main, by liberal values and 'spiritual' concerns, particularly under Chandra's presidency. But while reflecting a nominally (middle-class) 'moral-left' politics, this does not denote any particular 'socialist' agenda. Nor has the 'Aliran community' been specifically engaged, in the past, as a direct action group – although, by the time of the crisis, it appeared to be taking a more 'mainstream' role in breaking down ethnic tensions and encouraging new forms of cross-ethnic politicisation.[27]

In contrast to Aliran, Suaram denotes a more grassroots activism, though its main status is that of a human rights organisation. Although politically peripheral, Suaram and other bodies such as the women's grouping Tenaganita, the Community Development Centre and People's Communication Centre have been engaged in on-the-ground activities in support of, for example, plantation labour and other low-paid workers inside the (FTZ) electronics and textile factories. Tenaganita has also taken up diverse issues such as trafficking in women and the impact of the crisis on migrant workers.[28] Through consistent campaigns, opposition seminars, workshops and other gatherings, these groups had provided the nucleus of a small, but active, 'left-democratic' community prior to the *reformasi*.[29] Indeed, alongside other 'politically connected' court actions to come, this had seen Tenaganita's director Irene Fernandez subject to prosecution and trial for highlighting the harsh conditions of illegal migrants in Malaysian detention camps.[30] Thus, while many NGOs are *de facto* government fora, other liberal-reformist groups, through single-issue-type campaigns, have helped build significant support bases within the emerging opposition.[31]

At the formal level of politics, only the PRM, under Syed Husin Ali, has any real credentials as a meaningful socialist party. However, within the context of ethnic party arrangements, it has always been a peripheral part of the opposition, even compelled to guard against alleged communist associations – hence the dropping of the word 'socialist' from its name. As part of the inter-communal Socialist Front (1957–66), the PRM (with the Labour Party) opposed Alliance 'consociationalism', its continued collaboration with British colonial interests and its *laisser-faire* policies. Although 'left-social-democratic', rather than 'far-left', PRM policy objectives are strongly weighted towards meaningful control of capital, social ownership and strong institutions of participative democracy.[32] Perhaps more than any other leader, Syed Husin Ali has been consistent in his denunciation of US foreign policy – a position uncompromised by US support for Anwar in 1998.[33]

The lack of a left agenda is most apparent within the DAP. As, perhaps, its foremost critic, the leftist writer, activist and academic Kua Kia Soong has offered a number of searching assessments of the DAP leadership and the party's lack of a coherent set of socialist policies. A detailed critique can be found in his key *expose*, *Inside the DAP*, based on Kua's, Lee Ban Chen's and other civil rights activists' decision to join the party in 1990 (Kua being appointed head of Political Education), their inside analysis and their decision to leave after 1995. Here, four main indictments can be noted.[34]

The party's failure to offer a democratic socialist alternative Here, notes Kua, there was an absence of any radical alternative to BN policies on public spending, taxation, privatisation and social services. Rather, the DAP leadership pandered to a soft reformism under the (Vision-type) slogans of 'Malaysian Malaysia'. Democratic socialism was rarely used or discussed as a policy basis. Reflecting this, the Central Executive Committee (CEC) had insisted on using 'Full Liberalisation' as a campaign slogan and agenda for the 1995 election, an implicit admission of UMNO/BN's 'partial liberalisation', suggesting that the DAP could complete this task. This 'out and out reformist', rather than socialist, view denotes the sense in which the DAP leadership accept the rules of the game by giving credence to BN reform as an agenda-setting discourse.[35]

The party's 'fixation' on retaining its Chinese electoral base This concerns the DAP leadership's deep-lying ethnic chauvinism in tying Chinese sensibilities to party interests. Many of the aforementioned problems between DAP and PAS can be traced to the internal debates within the CEC after 1990. The decision to withdraw from the Gagasan Rakyat on 'the eve' of the 1995 election, notes Kua, was specifically informed by this fear of being too closely associated with PAS, still seen as 'the main enemy' by some CEC figures. As secretary-general (SG), Lim Kit Siang's eventual decision to withdraw from the coalition was opposed only by Kua and Lee who, maintaining the case for a multi-racial Opposition Front, argued that any differences with PAS and S46 were secondary to that of defeating the real enemy, the BN.[36]

Lim Kit Siang's leadership style, factionalism and absence of democratic procedures Through a 'central faction', the SG has maintained tight authority over the party, as in his monopoly over the candidate selection process, a 'form of patronage' that, in places like Selangor, had given rise to opportunists and local factionalisms. While Kua and Lim sought to democratise the selection process and infuse 'intellectually uninspiring' CEC meetings, Lim Kit Siang's 'top-down' manner could be seen in his lack of empathy for rank and file elements, including women's groupings, an inclination for 'edict-style' press releases, his grooming of Lim Guan Eng as leader and his refusal to stand down after the party's worst ever defeat in 1995.[37]

The party's marginalisation of the PRM During the 1995 election, the DAP leadership refused to give ground to other opposition elements, notably the PRM. Despite Kua's and Lee's interventions on behalf of Syed Husin Ali (and their recognition of the many intellectuals who supported PRM), the hostile and 'non-bargainable' position towards him and other PRM candidates, notes Kua, was indicative of narrow, sectarian party politics and the attempted monopolisation of the opposition space for immediate political and careerist reasons.[38]

However, as part of the so-called 'KOKS' campaign ('Kick Out Kit Siang'), leading party elements were making a bid for party control by the time of the crisis, resulting in the purging of three CEC members in mid-1998. As noted by Kua in a key *Aliran* article,[39] this signified an ironic power struggle, with disaffected '"Old Turks" squaring off against the "Young Guards" of the Kit Siang/Guan Eng status quo.' It also mirrored complaints by the Old Guard that Lim had been less than consistent in relation to past campaigns by giving special promotion to the Guan Eng roadshow to protest his imprisonment. The CEC members' 'failure to support' the campaign (disguised as not having dispensed their duties properly) thus provided a pretext for their removal, a move supported by the new generation 'wanabee' party figures who had backed Lim's grooming of Lim Guan Eng as party leader prior to his imprisonment. Even if, as DAP claims, Kua's 'tirade' was motivated by the need to justify his own past actions,[40] his account fitted with more widely held concerns by this point over DAP policies and internal practices.

Neither did this limit Kua's and other leftists' support for Lim Guan Eng or the *reformasi*. It constituted, rather, a broad coalition of left/liberal-reformist elements based around the persecution of Anwar and others.

While not a 'left movement' in any radical sense, it was allowing new opportunities for left expression, as in Syed Husin Ali's *Harakah* contributions on issues of social justice. This, of course, is intrinsic to most left discourse. But the moral backlash over Anwar was helping to augment a new class-based context for ordinary Malaysians to think more specifically about the abuse of political–corporate power. Thus, while left-intellectual discourse had been 'conditioned' by liberal-reformist language, the *reformasi* was also providing new space for the articulation of left ideas.

Left Intellectuals and the Islamic Condition

Left-intellectual discourse in Malaya/Malaysia has also been deeply conditioned by Islam. As closely interacting forms of religious and social identity, Islamic and Malay codes have had a profound bearing on the values and perspectives of many Malay left intellectuals. Likewise, non-Malay left-intellectuals have been conditioned by their own religio–cultural context, though also by the omnipresent realities of Islamic society. As noted by Clammer, in relation to both cases, it is important to recognise the particular nature of intellectual identity in Southeast Asia:

> in the West the intellectual is associated with secularisation, but in Asia, very much to the contrary, the emancipatory intellectual is more likely to be religious, and to be very much concerned with, as his primary interest, the relationship of religion to society, *including its economic and political dimensions*.[41]

In this regard, the internalisation of religious and cultural identity has created a certain ambivalence and 'introspection' amongst the wider 'left-intellectual community' in Malaysia. As Jomo notes, manipulation from above, through 'fears' of another 13 May, has created an environment in which intellectual ideas are formed as communal messages and received as such by the public. In this sense, 'an idea is often associated with its promoter, and is evaluated in relation to one's own personal or ethical agenda'.[42]

The Quran, of course, offers an explicit statement of compatibility between Islam and a 'left politics' of social justice. Its message is:

> reformist, if not revolutionary ... The socio-economic reforms of the Quran are among its most striking features. Exploitation of the poor, weak, widows, women, orphans and slaves is vividly condemned ... The Quran demands that Muslims pursue a path of social justice, rooted in the recognition that the earth belongs ultimately to God and that human beings are its caretakers. While wealth is seen as good, a sign of hard work and God's pleasure, its

pursuit and accumulation are limited by God's law. Its rewards are subject to social responsibility toward other members of the community, in particular the poor and needy.[43]

Thus, at one level, there is a consistency of thought linking Islam and progressive intellectuals. At another, however, the interpretation of social phenomena by that intellectual community has become internalised with an Islamic ethics to such an extent that it may have served, inadvertently, to constrain radical political energies in Malaysia. This has been due, in part, to the complex task of fusing Islamic jurisprudence and concepts of secular freedoms into a coherent reformist agenda. But it also relates to the idea of a 'benevolent universalism' of Islamic values as a basis for social reconstruction and justice. Allowing for the egalitarian integrity of Islamic civil and political codes, this suggests a more sensitive problem of whether rights, freedoms and justice for the diverse communities within Malaysian society can be built around an Islamic ethics.

A key illustration of this 'ethical vision' is contained in a seminal article by Chandra Muzaffar, 'Quranic universalism, way to fuse diversity', presented as part of a major three-part series in the *New Straits Times* in 1994, and in *Harakah* during the Anwar crisis.[44] Although he is an Indian Malaysian and convert to Islam, the tone and context of Chandra's argument here, and in the related articles, are symptomatic of the 'Islamic condition' as it confronts the issues of Malay identity, the historical compromise of Malay nationhood and the accommodation of non-Malay interests:

> In order to strengthen accommodation, it is imperative that Chinese and Indian Malaysians understand the nature and extent of accommodation that has taken place in our society ... How many non Malay leaders and intellectuals have shown any appreciation at all of the colossal, monumental sacrifice on the part of the Malays – consenting to equal citizenship for the non Malays and thereby surrendering their dream of a Malay nation and becoming a community among communities in a new multi ethnic society? One of the reasons why the magnitude of this sacrifice is not appreciated is because the non Malays as a whole have an external rather than an internal view of Malaysian history.[45]

While *Malay* intellectuals may not express a consistent or homogeneous view of Islam or Islamic universalism, Chandra's argument here represents a central problem for them and left intellectuals generally. Juxtaposing these problems of ethnic accommodation, he posits the need for a new awareness of 'common history' and the values of Quranic universalism:

> In this connection, one cannot help observe with a tinge of sadness that since Merdeka hardly any non Muslim scholar, theologian, journalist, poli-

tician or social activist has made it his mission to reduce the negative perceptions of Islam within the non Muslim communities in the country ... By incorporating genuine Islamic values and principles into public policies which impact upon non Muslims in education, commerce and industry, it is quite conceivable that they will begin to appreciate the religion's commitment to justice and fairness ... What is required is more than the application of the Islamic concept of social justice. The Malay-Muslim leadership has one of those rare opportunities in history to establish a society which embodies the spirit of universalism contained in the Holy Quran in all its manifestations.[46]

Chandra's polemic here shows how an Islamic ethics superimposes itself over Malaysian society and the special context within which progressive Islamic ideas are framed. While the linkages between state, civil society and *shariah* law in Muslim societies may assume a variety of hybrid forms, what is envisaged here is a benign infusion of Islamic values, initiated through policies and institutions that reach across the racial spectrum. It suggests ideals of reciprocity, contract and communal regard for Islam as the principal source and provider of social justice. Yet, while cross-ethnic understandings of social justice may have been stimulated by the *reformasi*, the idea of a 'primary' Islamic value system for non-Muslims appears to negate basic concepts of equal consultation and ethical inputs for other 'contracting' parties. Thus, while Islamic universalism may offer egalitarian pointers for ethnic cooperation, it is not clear that it can provide an actual basis for social integration across the ethnic spectrum.

A related factor for Malay intellectuals has been the attempt to link domestic political ideas with calls from within Islamic scholarship for a 'new self-image for Islam'.[47] Chandra's own defence of Islamic moderation has involved, in this regard, an ongoing critique of PAS–Islam. Yet, in less 'liberal' tones, Chandra, alongside PAS and other Malay intellectuals, has also denounced Salman Rushdie as a blasphemer and *The Satanic Verses* as a debasement of free speech. While repudiating the *fatwah* as lacking spiritual legitimacy and the compassionate essence of Islam, Chandra talked of the way in which characters and events in the book were distorted: 'to suit the author's vile imagination ... The right to free speech should not be used – or rather abused – to propagate malicious lies, to pour filth upon the faith of a people.'[48]

It is not necessary to proceed with any detailed examination of the Rushdie case.[49] The key point is that Chandra's response helps convey the particular *context* within which liberal/left Islamic intellectuals negotiate social issues, a tension evident in the explicit view of Said who, in reference to the Rushdie affair, argues that:

the intellectual must be involved in a lifelong dispute with all the guardians of sacred vision or text ... Uncompromising freedom of opinion and expression is the secular intellectual's main bastion: to abandon its defence or to tolerate tamperings with any of its foundations is in effect to betray the intellectual's calling. This is why the defence of Salman Rushdie's *Satanic Verses* has been so central an issue ... And this is not just an issue for those in the Islamic world, but also in the Jewish and Christian worlds too. Freedom of expression cannot be sought invidiously in one territory, and ignored in another.[50]

Thus, for Said, intellectuals must remain free to explore and dispute *all* forms of social and spiritual convention, all realms of thought.

Of course, what emerges from that process of reflection itself may be seen as a valid contribution to intellectual understanding. In its pursuit of social justice, progressive Islam, in contrast to conservative Islam, is more clearly motivated by the spirit and emotion of Quranic reason rather than textual orthodoxy, much of which denies open reflection and understanding.[51] Intrinsic to Chandra's view, also, is the idea that progressive Islam can act as a catalyst for encouraging egalitarianism among other religions and cultures in Malaysia – Taoism, Hinduism, Sikhism, Confucianism.[52]

Nevertheless, the idea of Islamic universalism as a keystone for the socially just society does highlight the problem of bringing Malay and non-Malay intellectual communities together. If the common aim of both is to achieve cultural accommodation, economic fairness and social justice, the difficulty for many Malay intellectuals lies in how best to fuse that project with Islam, while for non-Malay intellectuals it is how best to realise universal rights based on secular rather than Quranic values.

Left Intellectuals: Ethnic and Cultural Conditions

Intellectual tension between the Malay and non-Malay left has also been evident at the more specific level of culture. In particular, the problem of cultural rights and practices has led to a considerable degree of estrangement among some leftist intellectuals. Thus many left-based organisations in Malaysia have been shaped by communal identity.[53]

What made this aspect so acute for the left was the centrality of Bumiputeraism as a 'defining' issue. This was evident, for example, in debates from the early-1970s over the national culture and the issue of vernacular education, a tension expressed in a series of exchanges between Chandra and Kua Kia Soong. Defending the Chinese school system, Kua argued that just as the ethnic Chinese have adjusted to a 'learning of the Malay literature, language and culture', so too should Malays make a greater 'attempt to understand Chinese and Tamil literature in the vernacular'.[54] Challenging Chandra's contention that some non-Malay grievances were unjustified,[55] he also charged that there had been a conspicuous lack of support under the National Cultural Policy for non-Malay practices. This included the periodic proscription of Chinese signboards, the refusal of police permits for non-Malay cultural performances, the identification of Malay literature as 'national literature' and the absence of non-Malay university chancellors. Thus, for Kua: 'Dr. Chandra's detached position gives cold comfort to the ethnic minorities ... [It is a] sociologism [that] fails to clarify the objective plight and situation that confront the ethnic minorities in Malaysia.'[56]

While Kua's agenda here was informed by leftist universal principles, the case for Chinese cultural rights was also finding expression as latent anti-Bumiputeraism. Throughout the 1980s, other non-Malay resentments were being voiced over the proliferation of Islamic-Malay institutions, such as the Islamic University and Bank Bumiputera. By 1987, Chinese grievances over vernacular education and other cultural tensions had intensified, providing Mahathir with a pretext to detain left intellectuals and academics, including Kua and Chandra, under Operation Lalang.

But while Malay intellectuals may see the issue of Malay identity as a problem for the collective left, a view prevails that non-Malay intellectuals still need to recognise the special symbolism of Malayness as an historical *experience*: that is, not merely as an ethnic category, but as a displaced nationalist community. As Muhammad Ikmail Said argues, in part following Chandra:[57]

> The centrality of the Malay–non Malay conflict is evident from the involvement of the Malay–non Malay left in communal politics and their inability to get out of the 'ethnic trap' ... For Malays, *including the Malay left*, Malaya/Malaysia is not a newly founded social space, over which anyone can determine its character merely on the basis of the modern claim that everyone has a right to citizenship ... In fact, it was a land of the Malays ... On the other hand, the non Malay left asserts that the sovereignty of the people is based upon equal rights.[58]

The potential for left intellectual exchange across ethnic lines has been constrained by other historical factors. The colonial division of labour, founded on class interests, fostered ethnic enmities that found expression in the Malay demands of 1969. But the NEP settlement and Bumiputeraism merely replaced one contradiction with another for the left, allowing ethnic polarities to cut further across class politics. The historical absence of a Malay left-intellectual stratum, notes Alatas, could also be traced to the colonial education system, the promotion of an inert administrative class, a non-revolutionary struggle for independence and the smooth transfer of power to the Alliance, thus ensuring a climate detrimental to radical ideas.[59]

Under the consociational settlement, conservative Chinese forces also constrained left thinking by 'locking' intellectual concerns into a discourse of self-cultural preservation. Despite the vibrancy of an earlier left Chinese community, and latter-day instances of such in the Dongjiaozong (DJZ) educationalist movement, there has been a reluctance among mainstream Chinese intellectuals to challenge the status quo. With the Chinese BN parties now an integrated part of the ruling order, Chinese politics has thus become more reactive than proactive, with ethnic political arrangements inhibiting cross-ethnic/class solidarity. The very proximity between religious and ethnic identity has also served to crystallise the concerns of non-Malays. Thus, in a society deeply conditioned by ethnic psychology, radical thinking for many non-Malay intellectuals has been subordinated to managing the harboured fears of religious and cultural imposition.

And yet here we find a contradiction with significant import for the left. By the early 1990s, Mahathir and Anwar were promoting a more balanced position on cultural policy in accordance with Vision ideology and Bangsa Malaysia. While the BN construct of ethnic politics still prevailed, Mahathir had also embarked on a strategy of 'cultural liberalisation', a process that was serving to fragment the traditional identities and ethnic symbols that had held the structure together. As Loh has shown, this was linked in the 1990s to an intensifying discourse of developmentalism, marketisation, corporatisation (notably of higher education institutions) and the ideology of consumer individualism, providing the impetus for a shift away from the politics of ethnicism.[60] Thus, by the late-1990s, in contrast to the 1970s and 1980s, the issue of 'national culture' had lost much of its acrimony. Reflecting this, a 1996 document on the National Cultural Policy sponsored by the Federation of Chinese Assembly Halls recommended a more conciliatory position in view of the government's more liberal approach towards Chinese education and other cultural practices.[61] With the new market for foreign-sponsored colleges, the use of English was also being encouraged by the Education Ministry. Indeed, despite its stated aims of promoting Bahasa and related cultural institutions, many were now questioning the government's commitment to the national language.[62]

Vision developmentalism has thus helped 'consumerise' Malaysians, reorientate cultural identities and stimulate cross-ethnic middle-classness. Indeed, beyond any semiotic significance, it was fitting that the weekly demonstrations in support of Anwar were taking the form of 'shopping protests'. As the economic crisis deepened, middle-class fears were finding complementary expression alongside the 'moral politics' of the *reformasi*, creating new hybrid forms of social dissent around which left reformers could organise. However, this does not denote a 'left discourse' in any *organic* sense. This is partly because much of this exchange has been absorbed, channelled and articulated through government fora, Islamic and Chinese bodies, policy think-tanks and media discourse – civil institutions mainly serving the intellectual agenda of Mahathirism. Still caught up in the constructed discourse of ethnic politics, the left has lacked an alternative agenda of its own – a set of common ideas around which disparate intellectual communities, institutions and the national–popular element can identify.

Insiderism: the Conditions of Dissent

Intellectual conditioning in Malaysia is also effected through more subtle forms of moral persuasion. Again, the encouragement of insiderism does not in itself eliminate dissent. Rather, it neutralises it by inviting dissent to be expressed from *within*. Conversely, 'insistent outsiders' can be portrayed as recalcitrants and deviants impeding social cohesion.

Here, the government seek to pacify left intellectuals and academics by bringing them into consultative fora, think-tanks and other policy-planning bodies. One such instance was the inclusion of academics in the National Economic Consultative Council (NECC), set up in 1990 to discuss policy options following the end of the Outline Policy Perspective (OPP1). Their participation reflected Mahathir's need for 'consultation' and 'consensus' in the run-up to the NEP–NDP transition, the outcome having already been determined at a higher level.

It is also worth noting here Anwar's own once reproachful view of agencies outside the Barisan fold. For example, during the 1995 general election, Anwar threatened a 'withdrawal' of support for Penang state if it backed DAP, warning that the BN would not work with a party that promoted racial tension.[63] He had also noted that: 'we do not need the Opposition for the so called check and balance [*sic*] in the administration … They only create issues and confuse the people … Instead, the people should support and co-operate with the Government to ensure continuous progress and unity.'[64]

In another such instance in 1987, following various conferences on human rights and the Malaysian constitution organised by Aliran, CAP and the Malaysian Bar Council, both Mahathir and Anwar denounced the organisations concerned as seditious influences, with Anwar condemning Aliran in particular as 'arrogant intellectuals'.[65] Notwithstanding this, the keynote speech at the December 1994 Just World Trust conference on human rights, organised by Chandra, was made by Mahathir, with Chandra speaking out in 'common denunciation' of the West's 'universal standards' and human rights postures. Mahathir's conference address, maintaining the case for a qualified democratic order based on Asian social values, was boycotted by Suaram and many international human rights groups.[66] Chandra has, elsewhere, charged Western governments, business, and media with trying to: 'thwart the dramatic growth and development of certain Asian economies ... The centres of power in the West do not want this to happen – as the Malaysian prime minister so rightly observed at the recent conference on Malaysia–China co-operation.'[67]

Opposition party stances on international issues are also used to foster impressions of national affinity with Mahathir. One such example was the broad condemnation of the US/UK bombing of Iraq in late 1998. Here, PAS, DAP, PRM and many NGOs had all stated their own positions in questioning the legality and morality of the strikes. In a key *Harakah* article, Syed Husin Ali also noted that Mahathir was condemning Western aggression while maintaining a convenient security relationship with the USA.[68] Yet, against the backdrop of Ramadan, what emerged as the agenda-setting message via the mainstream media was 'Malaysian parties united against bombing', allowing the suggestion of support for Mahathir's own anti-Western line.[69] Complicating this, somewhat, PAS had applauded Al Gore in *Harakah* statements for supporting Anwar and the *reformasi*, articles that now appeared, in the wake of the bombing, to compromise PAS's anti-US stance.[70] However, this 'strange bedfellows' scenario also illustrated the new dynamics of the *reformasi* and the more complex set of political interactions now emerging.

The more deep-rooted issue here has been intellectual endorsement of the system. Intrinsic to this, again, is the way in which the language of power becomes accepted as agenda-setting discourse. For example, among 15 crisis-tackling proposals made by Lim Kit Siang in early 1998, one was a call to: 'Implement Vision 2020 concept of *Bangsa* Malaysia.'[71] Concerning the need for economic recovery allocations to be spread fairly and without discrimination, it was instructive to note here that while 'criticism' was being voiced, it was using the accepted idiom of Vision-speak within which to express it.

A slightly different variation on this was the campaign, led by Lim, to free Lim Guan Eng through a pardon petition to the Yang Di Pertuan Agong. Leaving aside the immediate politics of the case, this can be seen as another such instance of insiderism. In effect, it gave credence to a system that had falsely, and without regard for civil liberty, imprisoned him. At the outset, there was minor debate within the NGO community over this strategy. One must also note the forms of custom and tradition behind the request. From a humanistic point of view, Lim's attempts to save his son from the pain of penury was also understandable. But with any such pardon comes an effective admission of one's own guilt, something that was palpably not the case here. Though helping to focus popular opposition, it also tended to undermine all the other people who had been unjustly detained, either under ISA or through the conventional courts. Again, this ties into Kua's critique of the DAP leadership and the party's soft radicalism.

But the incorporation of intellectuals also works at a more socialised level. The increasing disconnection of the new middle class from 'the rest' has complicated the task of constructing any broad populist agenda. Alongside the ethnic conditionalities noted, this is exacerbated by the fact that intellectuals themselves form an intrinsic part of the new middle class. For many, its attendant culture of aspiration forms a mirror image of their own class predicament. In *A Portrait of the Intelligentsia as an Aspiring Class*, Kua paints a vivid picture of this bourgeois paradox:

> Middle class ideology provides an amusing – if exasperating – object of study. Its ideology is the product of the influence of the dominant ideology on the former's own aspirations. This middle class is thus in an ambiguous class position – it aspires to join the upper class and this aspect often takes elitist forms. It is an attitude that is widespread among intellectuals as we see them wear their PhDs and LLBs and other such academic titles ... to demand unjustified privilege and status in the community ... That these intellectuals feel the need to borrow from working class ideology is also seen in the way some mouth 'socialist' slogans ... The devotees of these intellectuals [embrace this] since it provides them comfort in their secure middle class niche ... [I]n every society there are always intellectuals who are clear about their political and ideological (rather than just their economic class) orientation, who preserve their moral integrity ... My advice to aspiring intellectuals is this: don't mystify knowledge even if you do not see the truth.[72]

This suggests a need for critical self-examination *within* the intellectual community. The attraction of academic status and penchant for 'proletarian language' denote instances of intellectual vanity that, in turn, provide a 'lifestyle context' for middle-class dissent. In more subtle ways, intellectual analysis, in itself, may serve to 'desensitise' issues by turning them into 'respectable' areas of investigation, 'specialised policy problems' or 'seminar room dissent'. Thus, by speaking 'of', rather than talking 'with', the social community, discussion becomes institutionalised, a form of insiderism detaching the intellectual from any broader organic relationship. This reflects Gramsci's view of the intellectual's role in translating ideas into popular political consciousness:

The process of development is tied to a dialectic between the intellectual and the masses ... The popular element 'feels' but does not always know or understand; the intellectual element 'knows' but does not always understand and in particular does not always feel ... One cannot make politics-history without this passion, without this connection of feeling between intellectuals and people-nation.[73]

This is not to argue that dialogue with power institutions is an invalid part of intellectual activism. Liberal intellectuals, upholding ideals of 'academic objectivity', may also use such processes to highlight particular issues – the Chandra–Mahathir shared platform on human rights being, perhaps, a case in point. Yet, in a country where the line between 'consultation' and co-optation is so finely drawn, the context and tone of intellectual criticism has been subtly conditioned. Noting the vacillations of many intellectuals during the ISA clampdown of 1987, the social activist Mohd Nasir Hashim (also imprisoned at this point) has called for intellectuals to confront their own bourgeois proclivities:

We often aspire to be open minded when we communicate with the people, but inwardly we are going through a deep process of self reflection ... We must understand that as we work with the people to change this oppressive environment, we get transformed in the process ... [I]t is up to us to break away from any stereotyped relationships that perpetually make one the leader and the other the follower ... [W]e must be able to move tactically and dialectically from one position to the other ... In short, we are the intellectual-activist and not one or the other. Only then a person truly becomes an *organic intellectual* who blends well with society and can effectively organise the people to help themselves.[74]

Nasir's call for intellectual activism through direct confrontation with the state machinery would find some realisation by 1998. Yet integral to this process was his injunction that intellectuals must engage in an ongoing process of self-demystification and fuller involvement in grassroots struggle. To what extent, then, had the Anwar imbroglio galvanised the *reformasi*, the left and the ordinary citizen for such a task?

Hegemonic Crisis, New Conditions: Situating the Left and the *Reformasi*

In his address to the Justice for All forum in Penang, Cecil Rajendra had talked of the need for more collective responsibility. Citing past violations, such as the UMNO Youth's attack on the East Timor conference (Kuala Lumpur 1997) and the persecution of Irene Fernandez, Lim Guan Eng and Anwar, he noted how:

a few of us raised our voices while the vast majority stood back and kept quiet. This was an NGO problem, the law must take its course and never mind about justice ... Are we still going to stand on the sidelines and refuse to make our voices heard? ... What is happening in this country is not [the responsibility] of PAS or DAP or ADIL, but the concern of every ordinary citizen, citizens like you and I.

While political awareness and public activism had been growing, Anwar's ouster had given the process a vital fillip.[75] Yet this also raised questions about how easily many intellectuals and activists had slipped into pro-Anwar mode. Anwar's liberal credentials throughout his period in office can certainly be seen as more pronounced than Mahathir's. Nor was it easy to promote internal change with Mahathir and Daim at the helm. Yet Anwar's 'passive' position in UMNO and Asian Renaissance profile cannot disguise his policy agreements with Mahathir, denunciation of opposition groups and various political–corporate connections. This is not to say that left or liberal reformers could not work with Anwar to help realise Mahathir's removal, but it does illustrate the sense in which some intellectuals had regrouped around Anwar as more than an adopted symbol of the *reformasi*.

This was evident in Chandra's (Just World) declaration of support for Anwar after his arrest, the culmination of an ongoing association between the two. To some extent, this was indicative of Chandra's 'acknowledge-ment' of a 'liberal' stream within UMNO. Chandra reasoned that Anwar had been constrained by his situation and that he had often talked in reformist language with regard to civil society, participatory democracy and the corruption issue. Yet Anwar had also placed his own people in key positions, worked with Daim, the architect of privatisation, and declared his allegiance to Mahathir after being removed from office. Having also denounced the IMF's recovery agenda, there was also the question of how Chandra and others could now rationalise Anwar's own links with it.

However, while indicating how intellectuals become absorbed into new networks of influence, we have to differentiate here between the type of incorporation cultivated by Anwar and his circle while in office and the emergent support for him as part of the new *reformasi* situation. Following his removal, there appeared to be an uneasy recognition of Anwar's 'other sides', a tension evident in some of the output in *Aliran*, *Harakah* and *Saksi*. However, for figures like Chandra and Tian Chua, this was being mediated by wider considerations of injustice and the need to close ranks against the BN. To some extent, Wan Azizah's emergence as a leader and symbol of the *reformasi* now offered a more 'respectable' imagery for many left/liberal intellectuals.

A related issue was the left's inability to develop debate beyond the 'drama' of the Anwar affair itself. As noted by some left-leaning activists and journalists seeking to create a more expansive web output, there had been a distinct absence of intellectual exchange over *secular* political values. Although complementing *reformasi* aims, PAS–Islam was now assuming a contextual role in shaping opposition discourse, raising concerns among writers such as Farish A. Noor that basic secular tenets were being too easily conceded, thus allowing Islamic forces new social and political influence, particularly within the universities. Within GAGASAN too, those attempting to open up this debate had found themselves isolated. While this was being done in the name of unity – as a pragmatic gesture to GERAK and PAS – it illustrated the nature of the new politics unfolding.

Nevertheless, overlapping the party cooperation issue, a more open exchange with PAS intellectuals was now taking place. In prominent new *Harakah* pieces, Chandra's previous critique of 'PAS traditionalism',[76] for example, was giving way to a new stress on 'civilisational dialogue', drawing Islamic elements together while reaching out to the non-Malay intellectual community.[77] Since he was a key political figure within ADIL, KeADILan and the BA, Chandra's intellectual overtures to Malays and non-Malays now suggested a new effort to construct meaningful alliances. Drawing more consciously on the civilisational tenets of Confucianism, as well as the universalising ideals of the Medina polity, here was a more balanced template of what cross-ethnic social collectivism might represent in a modern context.[78] While Mahathir had 'claimed' Islamic modernity for the Vision project, the reformist message being evoked through this 'new modernist' dialogue was finding resonance for PAS traditionalists, mainstream Muslims and non-Muslims alike. In offering a 'new set' of guiding principles for Islam and cross-ethnic unity, Vision-Islam was thus being undermined. In this respect, the removal of Chandra from his UM post can be seen as part of an intellectual response from within the UMNO network to check the institution's influence and its 'new dialogue' with PAS–Islam.

Reformasi, the Left and Mahathirism: the Dialectics of Change

Alongside various forms of intellectual conditioning, left ideas have been marginalised by Vision discourse. Yet taking the more sanguine view, the Mahathir project, exposed by the contradictions of its own 'liberalisation' agenda, has been unravelling from within. Vision capitalism has also created a more 'globally located' middle class,[79] new social mobility and a nascent consumer politics. Reflecting structural shifts in class, political and cultural identity,[80] the crisis has thus accentuated social changes already unfolding. This greater fluidity suggests new opportunities for drawing disparate elements into an opposition alignment. Although taking form through the main parties, the emergence of left-reformist NGOs also denotes a strong basis for intellectual–populist mobilisation – a more open means of popular dissent.

However, much still depends on the ability of this and other mainstream elements to work together as an *organic* entity by thinking strategically and avoiding narrow party interests. As an injunction to the Italian Communist Party (PCI), Gramsci showed how any such party must avoid bureaucratic centralism, detached cadres and careerism. Thus, the party had to be open, democratic and dynamic, with intellectuals who could bridge the feelings of people and their leaders.[81] UMNO itself has sought to maintain the *ideal* of 'popular participation', its past aura as a party in the struggle for Malay independence still permeating popular consciousness. Yet Vision populism has been more synonymous with Mahathirism than 'UMNOism', making the party an inreasingly remote monolith for many Malays.

The cultivation of a looser politics may be seen as a way of breaking down support for the BN parties. One of the main features of New Social Movement politics is the relative absence of hierarchical structures, allowing a fuller sense of participation. This is precisely *because* it lies outside conventional forms of political representation, reflecting a wider phenomenon of popular disengagement from mainstream political parties. To some extent, KeADILan has sought to cultivate this type of NSM-style politics based on intellectual integration and open participation – an approach appropriate to the left's present status in Malaysia and elsewhere.

The opposition has also become more adept at spreading its ideas. Like Gramsci, Anwar had to be removed from the stage by a leader who feared subversive polemic and its threat to the prevailing order.[82] But unlike Gramsci, the *reformasi* has had the Internet, an unprecedented medium through which to transmit Anwar's prison writings, *reformasi* books and a whole raft of 'street literature'.[83] Alongside the success of *Harakah*, this has helped extend social debate and political awareness.

Hegemony is thus a conceptually infinite task – not, in the Fukuyama worldview, an ultimate state of affairs, a historical contest decided.[84] If history illustrates anything, it is that social relations are contingent, ever-evolving and open to human intervention; a dialectic constantly unfolding. Activists and intellectuals may reflect pessimistically on the power of multinationals and state elites or the chasm between rich and poor. But the 'TINA syndrome' – another instance of hegemonic discourse – belies the open realm of human agency and long-term alternatives.[85]

There remains a deep-lying ambivalence among many comfortable Malaysian intellectuals, professionals and other parts of the middle class.[86]

Thus one might invoke the Gramscian maxim: 'pessimism of the intellect, optimism of the will'. Nevertheless, the crisis and Anwar affair has galvanised the Malaysian public in unprecedented ways, from turnouts at *ceramahs* to a new disdain for the media.[87] Indeed, as a gag order was announced for Anwar's sodomy trial,[88] 581 journalists from eleven newspapers submitted a petition to the government calling for repeal of the Printing Presses and Publication Act.[89] Hence, while the UMNO network has sought to extend its control over key institutions, the civil space is still being contested. By late 1999, the *reformasi* did not appear, as yet, strong enough to displace a resilient BN. But it did signal a key shift in popular consciousness, opening up new challenges to Mahathir and the prevailing bloc.

Notes

1. The party in question was the Ikatan Masyarakat Islam Malaysia, registered in Terengganu.

2. Sabri Zain, 'The eye of justice', at <http://members.xoom.com/Gerakan/eye-of-justice.html>.

3. Cited in ibid.

4. Lim Kit Siang Homepage, 30 May 1999.

5. See 'Malaysia's squabbling opposition under attack by Mahathir's forces', *AFP*, 2 June 1999.

6. 'New and more moderate, an Anwar ally on plans for a political party', *Asiaweek*, 2 April 1999. Ezam had been questioned but not charged on his return from Indonesia.

7. However, sitting Chief Minister Bernard Dompok, an ethnic Kadazan, lost his seat. Dompok, who had led his faction within the PBS over to the BN in 1994, was replaced by Osu Sukam, the state UMNO liaison officer. Dompok had served only one year of his turn as CM under a rotation system worked out by Mahathir to placate Kadazans and other ethnic feeling. For a concise set of insights, see 'Patterns of ethnicity and electoral politics', Loh Kok Wah's guide to the March 1999 Sabah election, published at the *Saksi* and *Aliran* websites.

8. 'Jomo on the current situation in Malaysia', *Harakah*, 15 March 1999.

9. 'Malaysia bans 3 foreign publications', *Associated Press (AP)*, 18 February 1999.

10. The suit against Hiebert was issued in relation to the article 'See you in court', *FEER*, 23 January 1999. Addressing the growing level of spurious litigation in the Malaysian courts, Hiebert highlighted the RM6 million damages being sought by the mother of Govind Sri Ram against the International School of Kuala Lumpur for 'unfairly dropping' her son from the school debating team. Noting the student's father as Court of Appeals judge Gopal Sri Ram, Hiebert commented that 'many are surprised at the speed with which the case raced through Malaysia's legal labyrinth'. Awaiting appeal, Hiebert had his Canadian passport held for two years. He was finally given a six-week jail sentence in September 1999.

11. *Straits Times* (weekly), 5 June 1999.

12. See 'Standing up and speaking out', *Aliran Monthly*, April 1999, 19: 3.

13. The judge cited Public Prosecutor vs Nunis (a minor government official who

had been sentenced to two years for abusing his position) as a precedent case for his deliberations.

14. See, for example, 'Anwar's guilty verdict: no big surprise', *Aliran* Media Statement, 14 April 1999.

15. 'Rights groups, foreign critics slam Anwar verdict', *AFP*, 14 April 1999.

16. 'Panel wants Rahim charged for assaulting Anwar', *Star*, 14 April 1999.

17. The following is based on various transcripts of the trial in the domestic and international press, news agency reports and website documents. See also *Justice in Jeopardy: Malaysia 2000*, published at <http://www.ibanet.org/pdf/malaysia.pdf>, an independent report by the International Bar Association and related bodies on the Malaysian judicial system. In reviewing the first Anwar trial, the report helps substantiate the 'legitimate concerns' felt over the initiation, handling and outcome of the case. See, in particular, the eight points specified at p. 48. Featuring critical reviews of other key cases, such as that of Irene Fernandez and Lim Guan Eng, the report also details recommendations for a clearer separation between the executive and judiciary. The report concludes that the overall concerns expressed since 1987 over the independence of the judiciary in Malaysia are 'well founded' (p. 60).

18. A copy of this letter to Dr Mahathir, 'Re: allegations against Dato Seri Anwar Ibrahim' was posted on the *reformasi* site: <http://members.xoom.com/Gerakan/msaid_let1.html>.

19. Anwar claimed that he could find no record in his diary of Musa's presence at this meeting with the AG on 30 August 1997.

20. The circumstances and motives over the production of these tapes remains unclear. They are thought to have found their way to the defence via Anwar himself who had been given them by Sng Chee Hua. Copies of the tapes were being circulated through various *reformasi* channels.

21. Alongside space for the press and Anwar's family, only around twenty members of the public were allowed admittance.

22. See 'Malaysia's Anwar says PM targeted him', *Reuters*, 10 February 1999.

23. See 'Leadership and the Barisan alternatif', *Aliran Monthly*, September 1999, 19: 8. The BA's manifesto was launched on 24 October 1999.

24. Hewison and Rodan (1996), p. 42.

25. Ibid., p. 58.

26. For a particular account of NGO activity and its limitations, see Loh Kok Wah (1997b), 'Development, democracy and ASEAN NGOs', *Aliran Monthly*, 1997, 17: 1.

27. See, in particular, the cover theme of *Aliran Monthly*'s March 1999, 19: 2, edition, 'Bridging the great divide.'

28. See, for example, *Tenaganita* (1995) and (1998).

29. My thanks to Sharaad Kuttan, Kua Kia Soong, Anne Munro Kua and others for their valuable insights during the NGO gathering, 'Celebration of People's Struggle', Kajang, 16 November 1997. Alongside indications of how grassroots activism, albeit marginal, was being organised in factories, plantations and university campuses, a number of ex-ISA detainees and their families talked about their harsh experiences and the vindictive psychology used by the authorities to break their morale.

30. This trial, first initiated in June 1996, was still ongoing in mid-2000 after a number of long postponements.

31. Hewison and Rodan (1996), p. 62.

32. See 'New Malaysia: policies and objectives of the PRM', (1994), PRM *Pusat*.

33. See, for example, 'Al Gore's remarks: how they react' *Harakah*, 23 November 1998.

34. This text (1996) represents a modified draft of events, a more detailed account (naming names) having been 'held back' for publication 'after the actors have ended their political careers' (p. x).

35. Ibid. See pp. 2, 12, 33, 37, 39.

36. Ibid., pp. 2, 26–9, 56.

37. Ibid., pp. 6, 12–13, 20, 54, 67, 73–4.

38. Ibid., pp. 22, 27, 32, 34.

39. Kua Kia Soong, 'DAP's latest purge: another re-run of a bad movie', *Aliran Monthly*, July 1998, 18: 6.

40. See 'Distorted facts', a response to Kua's claims, by M. Kula Segaran, DAP publicity secretary, ibid. Part of the rebuke includes reference to Kua's disqualification as a candidate for the Petaling Jaya Utara seat in 1995 after failing to submit his nomination papers on time. Kua had noted a sanctimonious 'gloating' among key party officials following this embarrassing mishap. As indicated in statements and an appendix in *Inside the DAP* (pp. 45–7, 123–36), Kua had challenged the ruling in court, claiming bias and a failure of procedure by the Returning Officer. The case, defended by Raja Aziz Addrusse, was rejected on a questionable technicality.

41. Clammer (1997), p. 199. Emphasis added.

42. Cited in W. G. Mansor (special issue article), 'I think, therefore I am', *Sun*, 9 November 1998.

43. Esposito (1991), p. 31.

44. *New Straits Times*, 6–8 June 1994. See also *Harakah*, 8, 15 and 22 February 1999.

45. *New Straits Times*, 8 June 1994.

46. Ibid.

47. Montgomery Watt (1988), p. 68. This liberal Islamic agenda has also been advocated by academics in the West such as Fazlur Rahman and Sayyed Hussein Nasr.

48. Muzaffar (1989), pp. 425, 426.

49. See Ahmed (1992), pp. 169–77, for a more balanced view of the Rushdie case and the sensitivities surrounding the issue.

50. Said (1994), pp. 65–6.

51. Muzaffar (1989), pp. 340–1.

52. Ibid., p. 433.

53. See Said (1992).

54. Kua Kia Soong (1985), pp. 147, 154–5.

55. Cited in Kua Kia Soong (1992), p. 74.

56. Ibid., pp. 75–82, 89, 90.

57. Said (1992), pp. 278–9.

58. Ibid., pp. 274–5. Emphasis added.

59. Alatas (1977b), pp. 1–3.

60. Loh Kok Wah (1997a).

61. Ibid. This included the proposed teaching of Chinese and Tamil languages in primary schools. The 1996 Education Act also allowed for the use of English as a main medium of instruction in key subjects such as maths and science. It was also significant that cultural affairs now came under the ambit of the Ministry for Culture, Arts and Tourism.

62. See *New Sunday Times*, 25 September 1994.

63. Anwar's comment was contained in a *Sun* piece, 15 April 1995.

64. 'People can do without the opposition', *New Straits Times*, 18 January 1995.

65. Cited in Means (1991), p. 198.

66. See *FEER*, 'Right behind you: dissident joins Mahathir on Asian values bandwagon', 22 December 1994, and *New Straits Times*, 7 December 1994. The occasion was the 'Re-thinking Human Rights' conference, 7–8 December 1994. Protesting Mahathir's invitation, Suaram had been stopped by organisers from distributing leaflets among the conference participants, this being criticised as a curtailment of human rights.

67. *New Straits Times*, 17 February 1995.

68. 'Stand against US imperialism: deeds not matched by words', *Harakah*, 7 December 1998.

69. See 'Malaysians begin Ramadan with rare show of unity', *AFP*, 20 December 1998.

70. See 'Comment: what's all the fuss about Al Gore?', *Harakah*, 23 November 1998.

71. Lim Kit Siang (1998), p. 5.

72. Kua Kia Soong (1992), pp. 66–9.

73. Gramsci (1971), pp. 332, 418.

74. Mohd Nasir Hashim, *Aliran Monthly*, 1994: 14: 7. Italics added. Detained for 15 months under the ISA, Nasir, a vocal critic of the state, has a long-standing involvement with workers groups, squatters and bodies such as Suaram and Suara Warga Pertiwi.

75. See Anil Netto, 'Unity a little closer for Opposition', *Harakah*, 3 May 1999.

76. Muzaffar (1987).

77. See 'Islam and Confucianism: the need for a sincere dialogue', *Harakah*, 8 March 1999.

78. Ibid.

79. See Reich (1991) for a discussion of the new global middle class as 'symbolic analysts'.

80. Somewhat complementary to the present approach, Cottrell's (1984) tableaux of 'economic class', 'political forces, and 'social collectivities' denote the particular, yet interdependent, nature of these three levels of identity.

81. A. Showstack Sassoon (1987), pp. 162–80.

82. As the prosecuting attorney at Gramsci's trial put it: 'For twenty years we must stop this brain for working.' Cited in D. Forgacs (1988), p. 21.

83. As an example of unfolding events, speeches and media statements in compilation book form, see Fan Yew Teng (1999). See also 'Anwar: Terbiling tapi Terbuang', a magazine-type publication (edited by PAS figures) on the Anwar affair.

84. Fukuyama (1992).

85. See Amin (1997), notably p. 151.

86. As noted by Maznah Mohamad in 'The rot within us', *Aliran Monthly*, May 1999, 19: 4.

87. See Johan Saravanamuttu, 'From crisis to reform', *Aliran Monthly*, May 1999, 19: 4.
88. The trial commenced 7 June 1999.
89. 'Journalists urge repeal of "media gag" laws', cited at Gerakan Reformasi website, 4 May 1999.

9

Fin de Siècle: Mahathirism, Election '99 and the New Political Landscape

We have seen how hegemonic relations delineate a particularised mode of authority based around leading interests, strategic alliances and moral leadership at the national–popular level. In negotiating various class, political and ideological terrains, Mahathir's efforts to advance the Vision has seen radical alterations and ongoing tensions within the power bloc. With the attempt to build consent exposed by the crisis, the nucleus of an alternative bloc was now evident. Thus, in the aftermath of Anwar's trial and imprisonment, to what extent did Mahathirism and the Vision still have *hegemonic* legitimacy? In lieu of a longer-term verdict, let us conclude here with a résumé of the project's evolving elements, an overview of the 1999 election and some analysis of the counter-project by early 2000.

The Project Reviewed

Early Mahathirism (1981–85) We have noted the antecedents of the Mahathir project in the ethnic constructs of the colonial, Alliance and NEP states. In its transition from the latter, Mahathirism emerged as a new, and more complex, project striving to negotiate the tensions between Malay nationalism and economic developmentalism. From the UMNO campaign of 1946 to the 1969 crisis, Mahathir had linked himself to the prevailing idiom of Malay nationalism and Malay populism, his challenge to the Tunku providing a precedent for his attack on the royals by the early 1980s. Yet, while upholding the 'Malay cause' and NEP ideals, the project was being conditioned by the push for capitalist development. The problem of a subordinate Malay bourgeoisie, diagnosed by Mahathir in *The Malay Dilemma*, had re-manifested itself as a new form of state dependency, a tension expressed in Mahathir's struggle with the civil service and NEP bureaucracy for control of state institutions. Thus, in the rush for growth, Mahathir was moving away, albeit cautiously, from NEP principles towards an *apparent* liberalisation of the state and civil society while seeking to consolidate executive power at the centre. The class base of the power bloc was also being widened to allow a more 'inclusive' role for Chinese and transnational capital, while maintaining a select place for Malay capital. In seeking consensus for a new reward structure, Mahathir was also attempting to refashion political culture, notably through an unfolding discourse on capitalist development *vis-à-vis* Islamic modernity.

Mid-Mahathirism (1985–90) In the mid-Mahathir period, neo-liberalism provided the *economic*/class rationale for deregulation and privatisation, hegemonic opportunities used to shift patronage from the state to the more flexible site of UMNO/BN control, thus allowing a new political–corporate network to be built through concessions to strategic interests. The period also saw major expansions in IT and the financial sector/ KLSE as emergent development strategies.

In *political* terms, Operation Lalang and the threat from Razaleigh was symptomatic not just of a factional challenge, but of a critical policy struggle within UMNO by 1987/88. Attempts by the 'NEP class' to check Mahathir's reconstruction of the state had seen internecine conflict, a recourse to authoritarian populism and a purge of those political elements obstructing the project. Following the BN's good showing at the 1990 election, there had been some movement back along the continuum towards hegemonic control, evidenced by a relative 'relaxation' of the media.

At the *ideological* level, Mahathir's ideas on civil reform and Islamic modernity were finding intellectual and popular resonance, much of this being fashioned around the lingua franca of *The Challenge*. Despite the mid-1980s recession and middle-class unrest, Mahathir had also managed to cloak Malaysia's new foreign dependency around the nationalist ideologies of Malaysia Inc. and Look East. Coincident with the NEP–NDP transition, media outlets were now encouraging a more pronounced discourse of developmentalism.

Late Mahathirism (1991–96) In *economic* class terms, late Mahathirism saw both a consolidation within the bloc and the nadir of national–popular support for the project. The social changes effected by rapid development from the 1980s now required a more *inclusive* conception of the project. While ethnic identity remained a perennial part of social consciousness, Malaysians were being urged to make the country more competitive in the new global marketplace. Renewed overtures to foreign capital, political courting of non-Malays and calls for ethnic cooperation were now being fitted more consciously around the Vision and Bangsa Malaysia – a shift away from the old forms of ethnic balancing towards post-ethnic nationalism. As 'spokesman' and 'role model' for the South, Mahathir was also now a major figure on the world stage. However, while many Malaysians basked in 'reflected glory', Mahathir's Vision-linked investment strategies in Kelantan had not undermined PAS's emerging project.

Following a fortuitous turn in the economy, the *political* high point of late Mahathirism was the 1995 election, a key aspect being the now concentrated support of Chinese business and its social community. By now, Mahathir was approaching reverential status. Reflecting insider processes, Mahathir's attempts to drive a wedge between PAS and the coalition in Kelantan had also seen Razaleigh back in the UMNO fold by 1997. However, while Mahathir's management of the 'Anwar succession' had helped keep the political bloc stable, a more intensive campaign against Anwar was now taking shape within UMNO and the political–corporate network.

Nevertheless, the project had found its *ideological* pinnacle by the mid-1990s. With the economy booming, the message behind Vision adverts and Bangsa Malaysia was becoming associated with the not inconsiderable level of social progress now evident. For Mahathir, it was 'Asian values' and 'Malaysia *boleh*' rolled into one. This sense of national–popular confidence also included a tacit admiration for Mahathir among many 'critical' intellectuals. Thus, at its high point, late Mahathirism had provided a system of rewards and incentives sufficient to realise a considerable level of legitimacy in the system.

Crisis Mahathirism (1997–2000) In contrast to late Mahathirism, crisis Mahathirism had seen recourse not only to emergency economic measures, but also to coercive attempts to protect the bloc. Indicating an *organic* crisis of hegemony, a culmination of economic, political and ideological disjunctions now threatened the wider power *system*. In seeking to hold the various social and class alliances together, Mahathir had used political and ideological diversions to disguise the economic element in its early phase, and a reverse emphasis on economic recovery to mask the political and ideological fallout of the Anwar purge. Yet, a catalogue of coercive interventions by mid-1999 had called into question the project's legitimacy. Anwar was in prison, removed from political office and facing ruin through a second sodomy trial, Lim Guan Eng had been imprisoned for spreading 'false news', and a similar prospect was facing Irene Fernandez. Nalla, Sukma and Munawar Anwees had been imprisoned and vilified in the press. Tian Chua and other Orang Kena Tuduh (OKTs) (accused persons) had been arraigned for protesting, Zainar Zakaria had been convicted of contempt for defending Anwar and the UMNO network had pursued a concerted 'anti-slander' campaign to ruin political opponents. While these actions were presented as legally constituted responses, Mahathir's reversion to 1987-style authoritarian populism now revealed a three-fronted crisis of hegemony.

Crisis of hegemony: economic To some extent, populist consent was still apparent by this point, as evidenced in the support for Mahathir's economic recovery measures, a set of adjustments that, for small business in particular, had been necessary to stave off further crisis. Many Chinese businesses, in particular, still supported Mahathir as the main innovator of 'inclusive' economic development. There also remained a general level of support for Mahathir's opposition to the IMF's and Anwar's deflationary agenda on the grounds that it had not delivered recovery and favoured external rather than domestic interests.

By mid- to late 1999, a significant picture of recovery could be noted. Moody's had raised Malaysia's credit rating from 'negative' to 'stable', industrial production was up by 2.6%, exports (in US$ terms) were up by 13%, unemployment had peaked at around 3%, inflation had fallen from a high of 3.85% to 2.8% (February to May 1999), foreign reserves stood at a record US$31 billion, interest rates had fallen again to a pre-crisis base rate of 7% and Merril Lynch had revised Malaysia's growth projection up from 2% to 4.9% for 1999.[1]

On the other hand, small business was still resentful at Mahathir's bail-out of big corporate capital, while foreign capital was now increasingly estranged. With a forthcoming election, artificial attempts had been made to bolster the stock market, as in the Treasury's 'acclaimed' RM1 billion bond issue, which, in reality, was sold at reduced cost to save government face.[2] Moreover, as noted by Jomo, stock market 'improvement' did not necessarily signify healthy recovery.[3] While many analysts now agreed that recovery was on the horizon, there was still deep concern that financial reforms had been piecemeal and that the euphoria of recovery was re-creating the illusion that there had never been anything wrong with the 'Malaysian way' in the first place.[4] While many neo-Keynesians saw Mahathir's capital control policy as a legitimate counterpoint to textbook IMF austerity,[5] others, such as the Nobel Prize-winning economist Merton Miller, argued that it had achieved nothing and that having abandoned convertibility once, the possibility of doing it again had diminished investor confidence.[6]

Many fund managers also remained unhappy over the preferential treatment still being shown by the debt agencies CDRC, Danaharta and Danamodal to well-connected companies. For example, the CDRC had persuaded the banks not to call in Renong and UEM loans, while allowing Halim Saad and other key management figures to maintain control of both companies.[7] As a formal state resolution trust company, Danaharta was also suspected of working out 'favourable debt arrangements' for other smaller companies. Thus easy debt schedules and lack of clear-out procedures were still being used to keep unviable companies afloat and protect politically connected figures. Reflecting foreign business concerns in a survey by Asian Intelligence (March 1999), Jorgen Bornhoft, outgoing president of the Malaysian International Chamber of Commerce, had also noted the failure of debt agencies in rooting out those who had allowed irresponsible borrowing and lending.[8] Another *Far Eastern Economic Review* business panel, surveying the Asian economies, noted that Malaysia was 'hiding a much higher level of bad debt than Thailand or Indonesia'.[9]

Thus, while still Mahathir's strongest card, the recovery measures could not disguise the state's rupture with foreign capital. At the same time, the crisis had been artificially characterised as the latest instalment of liberal transition in the region: Suharto falls, Mahathir is next, a liberal-business view that obscured both the deeper *policy* issues and state–class conflicts at stake here. As one informed source had noted to this writer, it was necessary to look beyond the public gaze of the Anwar drama and its actors to understand the more critical roles of the *directors* behind the scenes.

Crisis of hegemony: political The consensual element realised during the period of late Mahathirism could not be easily dismissed. Indeed, it was largely due to the very real regard for Mahathir, and what he had 'delivered' during this phase, that kept him from meeting the same fate as Suharto.

Yet, while BN incumbency was unlikely to be broken, this could not conceal the crisis within the political bloc. Beneath the surface lay brooding discontent among UMNO members. For these and many more Malaysians, faith in the political institutions, the courts, the police, the media and other parts of the network had been severely damaged. The crisis had alienated a younger generation, notably in the universities, but also beneficiaries of the NEP.[10] While as yet unable to compete with UMNO's party organisation, KeADILan had recruited 150,000 members by mid-1999,[11] although, with around 600,000 members, PAS was now the centrepoint of Malay resentment.[12] Alongside this popular shift from UMNO, PAS was also now recruiting influential figures such as Hasan Mohamad Ali, a leading businessman, popular at *ceramahs*, well regarded in intellectual circles and able to draw others into the party.[13]

Nevertheless, Mahathir was still resolved in leading the BN into the polls.[14] This reflected the lack of any charismatic replacement and a desire to secure his own interests. But it was also due to tensions over who could hold the wider bloc together. As UMNO marshalled its pre-election forces at the 1999 Assembly, former Anwar ally Zahid Hamidi now appeared on television, in an act of insiderism, to declare that he had been manipulated by Anwar.[15] With election fever mounting, a number of personnel changes had been made in a bid to present a new image, notably the replacement

of Mohamed Rahmat with Mohamad Khalil Yaakob as information minister and secretary-general,[16] and the appointment of Razaleigh as head of
Kelantan UMNO. Yet, despite this and a vigorous anti-foreign campaign
of posters, speeches and media messages claiming 'economic recovery in
adversity', PAS and the *reformasi* were now drawing increasing support,
particularly in the rural areas.[17]

Against this, Mahathir appeared resolute and unfazed. As he asserted
in one interview: 'I've gone against the stream many, many times, and it
just so happens that in most instances I have been proved correct.'[18] As the
crisis unfolded as an economic–political–ideological sequence, Mahathir
had, indeed, shown typical assertiveness in tackling it from that direction.
However, having realised progress through economic recovery, the project
was now facing new forms of political pressure, much of it reflecting
ideological dissent.

Crisis of hegemony: ideological The validity of the project requires
accceptance of the leading discourse as internal to the *system*, whether
through passive resignation or common-sense approval. As organic intellectual, the UMNO network assumes this set of agenda-setting, policy-
planning and crisis management roles, serving to filter ideology, incorporate
oppositions and maintain public support. Thus, two essential reasons for
the ideological crisis can be noted.

First, the Vision project was calling for a more sophisticated form of
mediation within the civil space. Although coercion had always been threatened and used, the emphasis during late Mahathirism had been towards
consensuality. Indeed, ideas of an emergent civil society were still being
linked with Vision objectives even as the economic crisis unfolded.[19] Thus,
the lurch away from that ideal had impacted at the national–popular level,
while causing internal disquiet within the political bloc. The PR initiatives
and 'Asia responds'-type discourse (as in Mahathir's treatise *A New Deal
for Asia*, launched in the wake of the Anwar crisis) had seen renewed
contestation of the civil space in a bid to prop up support. Playing on
middle-class 'problem-solving' discourse, much public dissent had been
tempered. However, with undercurrent anger at Anwar's treatment, and
the media's role within it, Vision ideas of civil expression had been brought
to a new point of disrepute.

Secondly, a crisis of ideology was now evident in the loss of *moral*
authority. In persecuting Anwar and his family to protect political–corporate
elites, Mahathir had gone beyond acceptable *realpolitik*. Indeed, the decision
to proceed with a second sodomy trial indicated a last attempt to discredit
Anwar's character to help counteract this earlier transgression. While
expressed initially in street demonstrations and shopping protests, anti-

Mahathir feeling now took quieter forms in the *kampongs* and in middle-class conversation. But it had not disappeared. Even the Literary Laureate Shahnon Ahmad joined in with a bitter satire in the story *Shit*, an allegory of the political system, wherein the leader of the 'faeces world' (a name shortened to PM) refuses to be expelled from within the foul intestine, the putrid region of power where all his coterie reside. After the hero Wiwaran's failed revolt, he is expelled from the intestine's rear end, leaving him to be regenerated by the pure elements of the earth and the warmth of the people.[20] The book sold out its first print run immediately despite condemnation from Mahathir and the BN hierarchy.

Thus, indicating a more *qualified* form of consent, a certain ambivalence now prevailed among Malaysians. Many were tacitly supporting Mahathir on the *economy* while backing Anwar, PAS and the *reformasi* on the *moral* front.

Implications of the 1999 General Election

On 29 November 1999, the Barisan Nasional retained its mandate and long-standing two-thirds majority at the country's tenth general election, thus ensuring Mahathir a fifth successive term in office and his place as longest-serving Asian leader.[21]

Following major tax and spend inducements in the October budget, Mahathir had called a snap poll, allowing only nine days for campaigning. Coinciding with the election call, Anwar's trial had been postponed indefinitely by Judge Arifin Jaka, removing it from the political limelight. Critically, the choice of date also meant that 680,000 new voters (equivalent to around 7% of the existing 9.5 million electorate) would not be eligible to vote on time. Registered the previous April and May, many having reached the requisite voting age of 21, the Electoral Commission insisted it could not process this group until January 2000, a claim dismissed as gross bias by the opposition.

Smear tactics were much in evidence during the campaign. For example, Chandra Muzffar and Aliran were accused of having received money from Anwar while in office, the claim by Abdul Murad, a former Bank Negara assistant governor, being subject to defamation proceedings by the Aliran executive. Videotapes depicting 'pornographic' references to Anwar and a PAS party member were being distributed in public places. BN adverts were also fabricated to insinuate that Wan Azizah did not trust her husband. Election monitors also observed a number of polling irregularities, including the mishandling of postal votes, the circulation of fake identity cards and other gerrymandering, though this was not considered enough to invalidate the overall poll.

TABLE 9.1 General election, 1999: federal and state results

	Parliament	State
Barisan Nasional	148	281
Barisan Alternatif	42	113
Parti Bersatu Sabah	3	

	Parliament			State*		
	BN	BA	Other	BN	BA	Other
Federal Territory	6	4				
Labuan	1					
Johor	20			40		
Kedah	7	8		24	12	
Kelantan	1	13		2	41	
Malacca	4	1		21	4	
Negri Sembilan	7			32		
Pahang	11			30	8	
Penang	6	5		30	3	
Perak	20	3		44	8	
Perlis	3			12	3	
Sabah	17		3			
Sarawak	28					
Selangor	17			42	6	
Terengganu		8		4	28	
Total	148	42	3	281	113	

* Sabah and Sarawak states elected at other times

As part of the UMNO network, the media had played up the ethnic issue, using various images to suggest that a PAS victory would mean a return to racial conflict. This notional threat of an Islamic state was reinforced by indications of BN support from the Malaysian Council of Buddhism, Christianity, Hinduism and Sikhism, a move acknowledged by Lim Kit Siang as a significant blow to the BA. In a timely move, Mahathir had also used the Chinese premier Zhu Rongji's state visit and public statements on new trade deals with Malaysia to send signals of ongoing rewards for the Chinese community under the BN. Campaigning in Kelantan and the other PAS strongholds, Mahathir had sought to depict PAS as a party of devious fanatics bent on using the BA as a front for its own Islamic goals.

TABLE 9.2 General election, 1999: seats by party

	Parliament	State
Barisan Nasional		
UMNO	71	175
MCA	29	69
MIC	7	15
Gerakan	6	21
Other BN	35	
Barisan Alternatif		
PAS	27	98
DAP	10	11
KeADILan	5	5
PRM		
Other opp.		
PBS	3	

Notwithstanding the media bias, campaign chicanery and other network enterprise, the result did signify an ongoing endorsement of Mahathirism. While bringing about a new political challenge, the Anwar factor alone could not make Malaysians revoke completely the practical accomplishments of the Vision project.

However, the result could not disguise the more particular damage done to UMNO/BN. UMNO's own share of parliamentary seats fell from 88 to 72 and from 231 to 175 in the eleven state seats contested. The BN's overall parliamentary seats fell from 162 to 148, while its share of the popular vote dropped from 65% to 56%. Many majorities were drastically reduced, and a number of key government figures removed, signifying, in particular, the Malay electorate's deep disquiet with the UMNO hierarchy. Alongside the loss of six deputy ministers were a number of senior party figures, notably Finance Minister Mustapa Mohamed and Rural Development Minister Annuar Musa, both in Kelantan, in Kedah, Abdul Hamid Othman of the Prime Minister's Department, Domestic Trade and Consumers Minister Megat Junid in Perak and UMNO Information Chief Yusof Nor in Terengganu. The removal of the latter two can be seen as particularly symbolic given their roles in the Anwar affair and the filtering of government information. Another key casualty was Terengganu Menteri Besar Wan Mokhtar Ahmad, while Education Minister Najib Razak held on with a tiny majority. Despite local disenchantment, Mahathir's own Kubang Pasu seat was never seriously threatened, although his 1995 majority was reduced from around 17,000 to 10,000.

At the outset, the four main BA parties had formed an amicable agreement allowing the strongest-chance candidate to contest each seat. In winning Anwar's Permatang Pauh constituency with a 9,000 majority, Wan Azizah was now an iconic part of a new and more organised opposition. However, KeADILan had failed to make serious inroads, picking up only five parliamentary and five state seats, with Chandra, the KeADILan Deputy, failing to make it to parliament. KeADILan's small showing can be linked, in various parts, to political inexperience, the infancy of its party machinery and more general caution among its hoped-for urban middle-class constituency. The PRM did not win a seat, though having slashed BN majorities by critical amounts in its alloted constituencies (including Syed Husin Ali's 20,000 to the BN's 24,000 in PJ Selatan), it was now an integral part of the BA.

More particularly, the election saw a serious crisis for the DAP. Despite winning ten seats, up one from 1995 (three more than in the previous parliament), the DAP leader Lim Kit Siang and its national chairman Karpal Singh were ousted in both their parliamentary and state seats. Lim thereafter resigned as party leader, following Chen Man Hin, the party chairman, who also lost his seat. While the DAP–PAS arrangement had augured well for the emergence of a more mature coalition, it now left the DAP exposed to new political uncertainty, notably over the party's relationship with PAS and its role within the coalition. DAP's poor showing reflected ongoing Chinese fears over DAP's alignment with PAS, the BN's ability to foster images of racial instability and other conservative business concerns. But rejection of DAP can also be attributed to its own unattractiveness as a party, particularly to the young, its internal tensions and Lim's own autocratic style. Yet the DAP failure also indicated a more decisive statement of Chinese support for the BN, a continuation of the pragmatic vote for economic rewards and 'Vision inclusion' seen in 1995.

This made problematic Lim's claim that Chinese support for the BN was specifically motivated to stop a PAS–Islamic state. Here, the outgoing DAP leader warned that DAP exclusion and PAS gains now posed a serious threat to secular politics as UMNO prepared to retake the Islamic ground. However, one could also see here, *vis-à-vis* the Vision factor, the anomaly of UMNO's own shift away from its Malay base, suggesting something of a dilemma over whether to develop this broad ethnic base or seek to reclaim its lost Malay following through a more pronounced religious agenda. On balance, it is not clear that UMNO must follow this latter route in order to hold the Muslim vote. For it is still the case that many, notably urban middle-class, Malays seek more economic prosperity and political reform rather than more Islamisation policies. Nevertheless, the loss of Malay support to PAS is a factor that UMNO cannot ignore. Paradoxically, it is here that Mahathir and UMNO may now reflect on the loss of Anwar as a prized figure in mediating the Islamic dimension.

Reflecting its 'coming of age', PAS now stood as the main opposition, picking up much of the new floating Malay vote, evidenced by its rise in parliamentary seats from eight to 27. The party also lost by slender margins in ten other parliamentary seats. As a newly elected member in Kedah, the much respected Fadzil Noor, an MP after many attempts, was now set to lead the parliamentary opposition. In Kedah itself, PAS had taken one-third of the state seats and more parliamentary seats than the BN. In Kelantan, the PAS victory was almost total, the party taking 13 of the 14 parliamentary seats, the other going to Razaleigh. PAS also took 41 seats in the state to the BN's two.

However, the single most damaging aspect of the election for UMNO, taking the gloss off the BN's victory, was the loss of Terengganu to PAS. Here, 28 of the 32 state seats were won by the PAS-led BA. The BA also won all eight parliamentary seats (PAS, seven, KeADILan, one). Thus, with PAS, under new Menteri Besar Abdul Hadi Awang, now in charge of a second state, and having made substantial new inroads in Kedah and Perlis, the party's presence in the North was now a worrying scenario for Mahathir and the wider power bloc. Another key factor here is the massive oil and gas revenues PAS will derive from Petronas royalties to the Terengganu state. Utilising these resources for purposes other than feeding the UMNO/BN machine, this also 'joins' oil-rich Terengganu to the less prosperous Kelantan, setting up more consolidated trade links, economic crossovers and other mutual state projects; in effect, an expanded PAS-economic region.

But the PAS gains also illustrate the wide cleavage now evident across Malay society. Here we see the prospect of a growing rural–urban/north–south divide, a rejection of Vision developmentalism and new impetus for the PAS–Islamic countervision. Among Hadi's first tasks, with incoming state exco members, were proposals to form a new Islamic advisory council, ban gambling, prohibit alcohol and initiate other measures to cleanse corruption within the state. As MP for Marang, Hadi has also been an assertive proponent of *hudud* law at the Federal level. While offering assurances to the other BA parties, PAS was now extending its version of an Islamic politics beyond Kelantan as a real alternative to the UMNO system. Thus, reflecting these divisions, the *Sun* warned on the morning after the poll that: 'The Malay world is in turmoil, and nothing has made that more evident than this general election.'

The New Political Landscape: 2000

Despite the BN's victory, the crisis for Mahathir and the bloc was still evident. Thus, as Anwar's second trial resumed in January 2000, new coercive strategies were now emerging to stop PAS and the coalition developing its base.

The first involved increased interventions over media organisation and output. Following articles in the *New Straits Times* critical of the UMNO Supreme Council's decision to waive party polls for the top two UMNO places at the May 2000 assembly, its editor and long-time Mahathir apologist Kadir Jasin 'stepped down', a signal of ongoing conflict deep within the UMNO network and an indication of Mahathir's move to reassert control over the BN media.

More directly, a new assault was launched against *Harakah*, beginning with tougher action against newstands selling the paper to non-PAS members. In March 2000, the Home Ministry announced that *Harakah*'s publication was to be cut from twice weekly to twice monthly. Expectations grew that the government would also curb *Harakah*'s new daily Internet edition. However, in a guarded effort to maintain its MSC credentials, this was left untouched. Here, Mahathir's promise not to invoke Internet censorship had held, albeit tenuously, evidenced by the growth of new independent sites, most notably *Malaysiakini*, the country's first critical on-line commercial newspaper. Yet, despite the Net's vital use as an alternative resource for news, debate and diffusion of ideas, the restrictions on *Harakah* and other opposition press could be seen as a major curtailment, given that newspapers, quite simply, provide a more routine and accessible medium for the public.[22] In another statement of intent, the Malay-language publications *Detik*, *Eksklusif*, *Wasilah* and *Tamadun*, all vocal formats for the *reformasi*, had been threatened with removal of their publishing permits.[23]

The second coercive element was an intensified use of the courts to check PAS and the BA. Thus, overseen by Abdullah during Mahathir's vacation, the *Harakah* editor Zulkifli Sulong and printer Chea Lim Thye were arrested and charged under the Sedition Act (1948) for having published 'subversive' articles during the election. Also charged under the Act were Karpal Singh for alleging conspiracy during Anwar's first trial, KeADILan Vice-President Marina Yusoff for accusing UMNO of using racial politics in 1969, and the party's youth leader Mohamed Ezam Mohamed for 'releasing' classified documents on the Anti-Corruption Agency. In March, the ex-IGP Rahim Noor received a two-month prison sentence for assaulting Anwar, a statement of 'even-handedness' rejected by the opposition as token in contrast to that handed down to Anwar and others. In April, a major operation had also seen a number of key

KeADILan leaders detained in the run-up to the first anniversary of Anwar's sentence, this and the rapid dispersal of demonstrators in Kuala Lumpur being rationalised as a 'public order' intervention.

Ongoing tensions within the party and new efforts by the UMNO network to incorporate the opposition had seen a small number of Ke-ADILan personnel defect to UMNO, notably in Selangor, by June 2000.[24] A number of *reformasi* websites, namely *Laman Reformasi*, *Pemantau*, *Komentar*, *Mahafiruan* and *Black 14*, had also called for the resignations of Chandra and party Secretary-General Mohd Anuar Tahir, to make way for others more 'competent, transparent and sincere'.[25] Defending both, and Chandra in particular, as key figures in KeADILan's formation, Anwar called for their retention and for internal party procedures to be observed. Reflecting these organisational deficiencies, and friction over Chandra's role, Marina Yusoff resigned her post in June 2000.

Another indication of the internal debate within KeADILan by this point was the proposed merger with PRM, a move supported by Anwar. Though it was still resisted by a substantial grassroots element of PRM members concerned to preserve the party's long-standing left-leaning traditions,[26] Syed Husin Ali and the PRM leadership were now advocating a route that would maintain such principles while taking the party into a more mainstream position within the BA.

In April 2000, the Court of Appeal upheld Anwar's original conviction for corruption (the defence, thereafter, seeking a further review through the Federal Court of Appeal). That same month, Judge Arifin Jaka rejected a subpoena application by Anwar's defence counsel to have Mahathir testify in the sodomy trial, in effect foreclosing the possibility of further evidence being heard from other alleged conspirators. Attempts to call key witnesses Megat Junid and Aziz Shamsuddin were, consequently, abandoned. After numerous delays, the defence were instructed to close their case. Despite producing an alibi and other corroborating evidence, Anwar, now increasingly dispirited, appeared to accept as inevitable the outcome of the marathon trial. The case ended on 18 July with Anwar giving final submissions in person. On 2 August, Federal Court Judge Eusoff Chin, dismissing an application that he disqualify himself on grounds of bias, refused Anwar's appeal to have Mahathir testify in the sodomy trial. On 8 August, following a postponed verdict and warnings to *reformasi* protesters, Judge Arifin Jaka found both Anwar and Sukma guilty to the charge of 'sodomising Azizan Abu Bakar at Sukma's Tivoli Villas apartment in Bangsar one night at 7.45 between January and March, 1993'. Anwar was imprisoned for nine years, to run consecutively from his six-year sentence. Sukma received two (concurrent) six-year sentences (the second for 'abetting' Anwar) and four strokes of the *rotan*. Reading a prepared mitigation statement before sentencing, Anwar again denounced Mahathir's insatiable lust for power, the conspiratorial clique around him and the court's complicity in his political persecution. The judgment, he asserted, did not disgrace him, it disgraced the judiciary. Finally, he wished the judge well in his conscience and his religious beliefs. Despite widespread shock and condemnation, no serious disturbances followed the verdict.

However, none of this signalled a resolution of the crisis for Mahathir and the bloc. There are four main reasons for this. First, notwithstanding economic recovery and the 1999 victory, UMNO had been seriously damaged, both as a party and in the eyes of a new generation of critical Malaysians. Second, a more visible and coherent opposition had now been established, signifying a credible option to the BN, particularly for the young. This was evident not only in the increased number of opposition MPs and state members, but in the new civil/NGO network now emerging. It is also significant that both government *and* opposition were now Malay-led. While this shifts the weight of Chinese support to the BN, it also breaks the deadlock of UMNO's claim to be the main Malay voice. In the longer term, this may allow for a more proto-class politics as both sides compete for social and sectoral, rather than just ethnic, support. Third, in securing another untouchable mandate, the problems of corruption and cronyism within the system are likely to go unchecked, thus limiting any serious reform or adaptation of the state–class to the new political landscape. This aspect is also likely to foster ongoing tensions with foreign capital, thus limiting the scope of Vision capitalism. And, fourth, UMNO/BN are now faced with a new and more systematic Islamic counter-force in the northern states, a problem now situated around the loss of UMNO's 'model' Islamic state in Terengganu.

Proclaiming a number of economic indicators, Mahathir reaffirmed his claim that the country was still on course for Vision 2020 status. Yet, while buoyed again by renewed growth, the appeal to authoritarian populism now looked an increasingly redundant means of rebuilding political and civil consent for the project.

Opposition and war of position This term, perhaps, best describes the nature of the challenge to the BN bloc by early to mid-2000. While significant new forms of popular dissent had been born, this was not, as yet, enough to break adherence to the prevailing system. Again, it is the tacit acceptance of such that counts, even where that involves considerable levels of popular disaffection and pressure for reform. Thus, while no longer an unthinkable idea, a non-BN Malaysia still required a further shift in Malay support towards PAS and KeADILan and a consolidation of

Chinese support through KeADILan or/and DAP. While PAS still held to an Islamic state and *shariah* law as eventual goals, this was being mitigated by the 'low-key' discussion of these issues and the two-thirds majority needed to effect such changes. PAS could conceivably push, at some future point, for new Islamic laws through an alliance with KeADILan. Yet even this prospect seems problematic given the latter's ongoing need to appeal to urban middle-class Muslims. In these regards, any realistic counter-bloc will have to develop a coherent and *consensual* alternative to the BN's own ethnic politics and the class basis on which they are built. Nevertheless, contestation of the civil space has taken on new significance for the UMNO network and the proto-opposition alike, opening up new possibilities for meaningful challenges to the BN system.

Notes

1. See: *Asiaweek* (country analysis), 7 May 1999; 'Spoiling for a fight', *FEER*, 27 May 1999; 'Merril Lynch revises Malaysia's GDP to 4.9%', *AFP*, 7 July 1999; 'Capital idea?', *FEER*, 1 July 1999; 'Forgive and forget', *FEER*, 24 June 1999.

2. See, for example, 'The name is Bond: Junk Bond', a *freeMalaysia* article published in *Harakah*, 7 June 1999; Shroff, 'Costly lesson', *FEER*, 10 June 1999.

3. Jomo was by now acting as economic adviser to KeADILan. See, for example, 'More economic disinfo', *freeMalaysia*, 10 June 1999.

4. See, for example, Lim Say Boon, 'Malaysia looking good, but ...', *Straits Times* (Weekly), 29 May 1999.

5. See Larry Elliot and Charlotte Denny, 'Asia tiptoes warily back to work', finance feature, *Guardian*, 6 July 1999.

6. See Miller's remarks in 'Malaysian banking remains weak', *Financial Times*, 9 July 1999.

7. See Michael Shari, 'Malaysian clean-up misses a lot of dirt', *Businessweek*, 5 July 1999.

8. 'Foreign investors want reform' (Dow Jones report), published at *freeMalaysia*, 15 June 1999.

9. The comment was made by David Roche, president of International Strategy, one of a select five-member panel assessing the Asian recovery. 'Reduced speed ahead', *FEER*, 8 July 1999.

10. See Chen May Yee, 'UMNO alienates the young', *Asian Wall Street Journal*, 9 June 1999.

11. 'The will to win', *FEER*, 24 June 1999.

12. See 'Sign of the times' *FEER*, 1 July 1999.

13. Ibid. Hasan was a classmate of Anwar's.

14. 'Combative Mahathir vows to lead Malaysia into next millennium', *AFP*, 18 June 1999.

15. See Anil Netto, 'Anwar's shadow looms over UMNO', *Aliran Monthly*, July 1999, 19: 6.

16. Replaced Information Chief Mohamed Rahmat was allowed to retain his position as BN general secretary.

17. See 'Man of faith' and 'Bogeymen beware', *FEER*, 1 July 1999.

18. Cited in 'I was shocked – Mahathir talks about the black eye, and other issues', *FEER*, 24 June 1999.

19. As in Abdullah Badawi's message: 'Civil society will emerge if Vision 2020 objectives met', *New Straits Times*, 11 August 1997.

20. See 'Below the belt', *FEER*, 13 May 1999.

21. The following analysis of the election and its fallout is drawn fom a generalised survey of domestic media reports, internet sites and opposition literature. All votes noted as approximate.

22. See Zaharom Nain, 'Bare knuckles', <www.malaysiakini.com>, 28 March 2000.

23. See Anil Netto, 'A Y2K crackdown', *Aliran Monthly*, 1999, 19:11/12.

24. *AFP*, 9 June 2000.

25. *Malaysiakini* , 9 June 2000.

26. See 'Merger debate charged with emotion', *Malaysiakini*, 15 June 2000.

Appendix: Theoretical Approach, a Gramscian Perspectivism

Avoiding any pretence to a detailed statement on Gramsci's work, this section offers a set of reference points and observations relevant to the Gramscian perspectives employed within this study, followed by some wider illustration of these themes and a short note on methodological approach.

The Historical Bloc, Hegemony and the Intellectual

The historical bloc/power bloc Transcending reductionist Marxism, and what Foucault terms 'grand narratives',[1] Gramsci offers a dynamic framework for examining capitalism as a system of power. Although it is often regarded as complex and 'disjointed', later critical streams, from the Frankfurt School's work on cultural production to Foucault's genealogical view of 'localised' 'power knowledge', have come to reflect much of Gramsci's thinking on politics, statecraft and civil institutions as multiple sites of social control.[2] However, Gramsci also understands the dissemination of ideas as part of a more structured feature of power relations serving long-term class interests, an analysis built around the key constructs of the historical bloc, hegemony and the intellectual.

Developing ideas set out in *Some Aspects of the Southern Question*,[3] Gramsci uses the historical bloc in two related senses: first, as an abstract critique of Marx's economistic and Croce's idealistic understandings of the relationship between 'structure' and 'superstructure'; and, second, at a more concrete level of social reality with regard to actual class formation.[4] The latter also denotes the idea of internal sub-blocs and the sense in which shifts in the *political* bloc may occur without altering the basic configuration of the entire bloc, thus offering a picture of the entire power ensemble over the longer term.[5]

This view of the historical bloc derives from Gramsci's observations on the socio-economic disparities between the industrialised Italian North and the agrarian South. Noting the complex formation of class alliances between these blocs, Gramsci shows that while the agrarian South had provided the Italian state with a strata of bureaucrats, the North had witnessed an expansion of technocrats, managers and other groupings more closely identified with big industrial capital and the urban bourgeoisie.[6] This attempt to locate the interdependence of state–class forces in Italy under the fascists follows on from Gramsci's writings on intellectual currents and the Risorgimento.[7] Here, in contrast to the Jacobin struggle in France, the Italian bourgeoisie and the Moderate Party had initiated a 'passive revolution' *from above* through the mobilisation of the Piedmontese state and the Italian intelligentsia. The problem, argued Gramsci, invoking Marx's *Eighteenth Brumaire*, was that state–class power was of a premature form, based upon transient alliances rather than *national–popular* support – a type of 'Caesarism', which, in maintaining weak liberal–bourgeois institutions, gave rise to fascism.[8] Developing this analysis in the *Prison Notebooks* (notably *Americanism and Fordism*), written during his incarceration from 1926 till his death in 1937, Gramsci draws out the contradictions of the bloc's state–class base *vis-à-vis* the role of corporate syndicalism, the state's alliances with the Catholic Church and rural bourgeoisie, and the persistence of a reactionary intelligentsia.[9] It is this complex of power relations, beyond standard political coalitions, which denotes the historical bloc's construction and the way in which the leading class builds its hegemony.[10]

Hegemony For Gramsci, 'domination' and 'hegemony' represent two antithetical expressions of power. This relates to his distinction between the specifically coercive role of the state, as exemplified by Tsarist Russia in the East, and the consensual bourgeois societies of the West. The former, equated as *political society*, sees the state as the direct agent of coercion, while the latter, equated as *civil society*, suggests a form of power based more specifically on intellectual and moral direction.[11] Alongside related couplets, such as 'force and consent', 'authority and hegemony', 'violence and civilisation', Gramsci, with a penchant for military symbolism, also applies the respective metaphors 'war of manoeuvre' and 'war of position' to represent the nature of contestation within each.[12]

In contrast to outright domination by the coercive state, hegemony, as a specific manifestation of the *modern* state,[13] involves a higher synthesis of power based on two important elements for the dominant class: first, the organisation of strategic alliances and concessions to subsidiary groups; and second, an articulation of the dominant group's interests and values through moral, political and intellectual leadership. While the first may be nominally instrumental in character, the second helps forge both these and the *national–popular* element into a *consensual* form.[14] This involves:

the disarticulation of the ideologies of subordinate groups and rearticulation of the relevant elements into the ideology of the dominant group ... The unity forged is active and direct, resulting from genuine adoption of the interests of the other groups by the dominant group.[15]

Thus, in contrast to neo-realist theory, which reduces hegemony to 'a physical capabilities relationship among states', the Gramscian conception of hegemony 'joins an ideological and intersubjective element to the brute power relationship'.[16] Crucially, though, Gramsci's conception of ideology does not signify 'false consciousness'; that is, hegemony cannot be reduced to a process of domination where class ideology is *imposed*.[17] With this in mind, notes Mouffe:

a class is hegemonic when it has managed to articulate to its discourse the overwhelming majority of ideological elements characteristic of a given social formation, in particular the national–popular elements which allow it to become the class expressing the national interest.[18]

This *ethical–political* dimension in Gramsci's politics is also expressed in the Aristotelian concept that human emancipation and 'the good life' are attainable through the transformation of ethics, ideas and cultural values.[19] As part of this process, economics and the ethical both become, in a specifically Gramscian sense, *political*.[20] However, it is also vital to remember that Gramsci's conception of hegemony is a specific expression of *class* society. Although an apparently obvious point, there has been a tendency to *reduce* Gramsci's insights to a somewhat singular concern with culture and the ethical–political,[21] thus failing to recognise its implicit class analyses *vis-à-vis* state formation and intellectual engagement. As Gramsci insists in the *Prison Notebooks*: 'though hegemony is ethical–political, it must also be economic, must necessarily be based on the decisive function exercised by the leading group in the decisive nucleus of economic activity'.[22]

Conversely, while Gramsci's critique of historical materialism retains the vital significance of economic relations, he avoids the reduction of ideas, culture and human agency to that of economic imperatives.[23] Thus, it is capitalist relations of production *in conjunction* with political and ideological/cultural power that provides a cumulative expression of class control.

This relates to the 'problem' of class analysis in Gramsci's work. Mouffe, for example, has stressed a 'non-essentialist' reading of Gramsci, negating the view that the proletariat/working class constitute the main agents of opposition.[24] This is a most important dimension for present purposes, given the increasingly diverse nature of capitalist development, class formation and 'new middle-class' identity in Malaysia. One might note, in passing, that Gramsci's focus on *proletarian* struggle does not of itself denote an essentialist position. Rather, consistent with his attack on positivist sociology – *viz.* 'Lorianism' and Bukharin's 'scientific materialism'[25] – we find in Gramsci an open, humanist Marxism with prescient understanding of class society as a dynamic and shifting site. Denoting the idea of 'organic crisis', Gramsci sees here the *ever-present* possibility of social challenges and dislocations within the bloc; a constant dialectic of state–class pressures, signifying the sense in which the 'new society' emerges out of the crises points and contradictions of the old.[26]

This also suggests a more specific view of civil society as a site of inequality and contested power. Gramsci's distinctive insight here lies not in any narrow conception of class power *vis-à-vis* the state, but in the specific relationship between the state and civil society. Bobbio emphasises, in this regard, how Gramsci's concept of civil society derives from a critique of Hegel rather than Marx, and that the 'revaluation of civil society is not what links him to Marx, but what distinguishes him from Marx'.[27] Gramsci was critically aware of the rapid expansion of civil institutions as bourgeois society developed, a shift apparent today in the growth of parties, trade unions, NGOs, voluntary bodies, pressure groups, media agencies and other political–cultural outlets. This does not make civil society a realm of liberal activity. Like the state, it is a site of inequality. However, in order to build civil consent, the state has to expand its educative role. In effect: 'its repressive character should diminish and its ethico-political character, its hegemonic function should grow in importance.'[28]

While the related subject of democracy is not well developed in the *Prison Notebooks*, it is intrinsic to Gramsci's exegesis on civil society. Consistent with more recent attempts to theorise Gramsci's ideas on participatory principles as the basis for a new post-liberal democracy,[29] it is also within the civil space that any *alternative* bloc needs to build its own hegemony. Thus it is necessary to remove the term's 'pejorative' label, for, quite clearly, Gramsci saw the construction of a new hegemony as the key to a socialist order – although he envisaged the latter as qualitatively different, in an organic and intellectual sense, from that of bourgeois hegemony.

Intellectuals: the organisers of hegemony The intellectual, thus, has a specific role here as a competing political actor. Gramsci's view of intellectual consciousness derives from a broad stream of Italian thinkers, notably Vico. But while Vico saw intellectual consciousness in narrow terms, Gramsci extends it to all human actors.[30] For Gramsci, this involves a departure from the idea of intellectuals as an exclusive elite or clerisy, to a more *structural* view of intellectual enterprise within capitalist societies. It is within this context that Gramsci discusses the liberal intellectual Croce's efforts in galvanising support in the South for a national bourgeois state.[31] Gramsci's intellectual thus moves towards a new synthesis of understanding, seeing hegemony not only as a set of class circumstances, but as a form of intellectual *praxis*:

> The most widespread error seems to me that of having looked for this criterion of distinction in the intrinsic nature of intellectual activities, *rather than in the ensemble of system of relations* in which these activities (and therefore the intellectual groups who personify them) have their place within the general complex of social relations.[32]

Here, potential intellectual activity and communicative action are conditioned by dominant social relations via state and civil institutions:

> The school as a positive educative function, and the courts as a repressive and negative educative function, are the most important state activities in this sense: but, in reality, a multitude of other so-called private initiatives and activities tend to the same end.[33]

Thus the 'neutral intellectual' within class societies is a liberal myth, an ideology.[34] If all human beings have the potential for intellectual thought and action, not all have the opportunity to use it: 'All men are intellectuals, one could therefore say, but not all men in society have the function of intellectuals.'[35]

Organic intellectuals In this regard, actively aware of their links to a particular social order, the organic intellectual gives coherence to the power structure at the economic, political and cultural levels:

> Every social group, coming into existence on the original terrain of an essential function in the world of economic production, creates together with itself, organically, one or more strata of intellectuals which give it homogeneity and an awareness of its own function not only in the economic but also in the social and political fields.[36]

Hence the organic intellectual performs the key *organisational* function across the mode of production, state apparatus and civil society.[37] For example, Gramsci's schema would perceive managers and technocrats, civil servants and judges, academics and journalists as respective parts of the hegemonic order.[38]

And this takes us to a further point of definition. For Gramsci also saw the organic intellectual in a more particularised context: that of the *party*. In other words, the party, as a manifestation of the 'modern prince' (*pace*

Machiavelli) *was* the organic intellectual writ large, representing the critical mass of intellectual praxes. Here, the: "party" for Gramsci was not the usual vanguardist concept. It was to be understood, first and foremost, as an "organic intellectual" ... able to present ... a world-view ... that would be "directive and organizational, educative, intellectual".[39]

Traditional intellectuals Gramsci's organic intellectual is also defined in relation to the traditional intellectual. Thus, offering an instructive paradigm for present purposes:

> every 'essential' social group which emerges into history out of the preceding economic structure, and as an expression of a development of this structure, has found ... categories of intellectuals already in existence and which seemed indeed to represent an historical continuity uninterrupted even by the most complicated and radical changes in political and social forms.[40]

Typically composed of ecclesiastics, scholars and other status-based types, Gramsci notes how, in contrast to the organic type, traditional intellectuals saw themselves as detached, free-thinking individuals removed from the immediate interests of the dominant class:

> Since these various categories of traditional intellectuals experience through an '*esprit de corps*' their uninterrupted historical continuity and their special qualification, they put themselves forward as autonomous and independent of the dominant social group.[41]

Gramsci is referring mainly here to the pervasive power of the Catholic Church in the areas of philosophy, science, education, morality and culture.[42] In class terms, he also shows how hegemonic ideology becomes analogous to popular religion itself.[43] In a more complex sense, traditional intellectuals may, simultaneously, provide, or aspire to, an organic function – as with Croce's role in keeping radical intellectuals in the South isolated from the peasant classes, thus preventing splits in the agrarian bloc.[44] The key task for organic intellectuals thus becomes the universalisation of its ideas through the *assimilation* of traditional elements, as Gramsci indicates in the following keynote passage:

> One of the most important characteristics of any group that is developing towards dominance is its struggle to *assimilate and to conquer 'ideologically'* *the traditional intellectuals*, but this assimilation and conquest is made quicker and more efficacious the more the group in question succeeds in simultaneously elaborating its own organic intellectuals.[45]

Again, it is the party, through the sphere of civil society, that carries the organisational task of winning over the traditional intellectuals:

The political party ... is precisely the mechanism which carries out in civil society the same function as the State carries out ... in political society. In other words, it is responsible for welding together the organic intellectuals of a given group – the dominant one – and the traditional intellectuals.[46]

Likewise, any *competing* network must build organic support around its own party and civil institutions. Implicit in Gramsci's traditional intellectual is the idea of the critical intellectual whose task is to build a new type of consciousness. Thus, from his own role as writer and editor of the revolutionary publication *L'Ordine Nuovo* to the exhaustive mental efforts of the *Prison Notebooks*, it is the idea of proactive intellectual engagement that energises Gramsci's politics:

The mode of being of the new intellectual can no longer consist in eloquence, which is an exterior and momentary mover of feelings and passions, but in active participation in practical life, as constructor, organiser, 'permanent persuader'.[47]

Hence, while intellectual consciousness is always a subjective and contested process, it is through Gramsci's philosophy of *praxis* that the proactive element finds organic expression.

The Power Bloc, Hegemony and the Intellectual: The Global–Domestic Dialectic

Let us note here the significance of the above themes in relation to global forms of power and the wider implications of these constructs within the study.

The global power bloc The dynamics of a *domestic* historical/power bloc requires consideration of *global* relations of power. This does not imply a reductive role for the domestic bloc/state–class. Rather, it denotes relationships of conflict, mediation and accommodation; a 'state–class complex' of shifting alignments between domestic elites, fractions of capital and capitalist institutions.

The emergence of Gramscian ideas within and *contra* International Relations/neo-realist theory offers a helpful grounding here. For example, in Gill's *Gramsci, Historical Materialism and International Relations*, Gramscian conceptions of the power bloc have been used to trace the structural transformation of the global order from the 1970s to the 1990s.[48] Reflecting the greater diversification of global power and the gathering transnationalisation of the world economy from that period, the post-war

Pax Americana has given way to a more complex set of hegemonic relations. The decisive context of this historic shift has been the new technological capacities available to capital and – to borrow from Castells – the new spatial landscape of 'informational capitalism'.[49]

In particular, the greater autonomy of *financial capital* through the new opportunities of information-led accumulation has allowed this component of capital to set the terms of: (a) the accumulation strategies of other fractions of capital; (b) the political boundaries and policy parameters of the nation-state; (c) a new international division of labour based on stratified national and regional accumulation sites; (d) a new global managerial middle class to oversee this process; and (e) the ideological and cultural signifiers which give reproductive meaning to that amalgam of power relations.

Thus, at the *economic* level of the bloc, the growing disjunction between national and transnational fractions of capital has given the latter, notably in the sphere of financial markets, greater power to shape the global order. As such, the 'internationalisation of production' has become synonymous with the 'internationalisation of the state'.[50] Hence, through international policy networks such as the IMF, World Trade Organisation (WTO), Organisation for Economic Cooperation and Development (OECD), World Bank and Trilateral Commission, a new managerial class has emerged, connecting financiers, production managers and state officials.

The ongoing case for corporate rights proposed under the Multilateral Agreement on Investment (MAI) offers an illustration of these linkages.[51] Negotiated in secret by top global companies and OECD ministers, MAI signatory states were to be subject to litigation through newly formed international courts, where they sought to restrict corporate operations. Following NGO opposition and disputes over the OECD's credentials as a 'venue', proposals to pursue talks through the wider ambit of the WTO were launched in late 1998.[52] Despite major NGO disruption of the WTO's Seattle gathering in November 1999, strategies are being formulated by multinationals and state ministers to ensure a common agenda on corporate rights.[53] As the director-general of the WTO has noted: 'We are writing the constitution of a single global economy.'[54]

The imperatives of transnational capital also shape the *political* configuration of the global bloc more than ever. By narrowing the abilities of political classes to initiate policy objectives, executive functions are being radically transformed. To a considerable extent, the 'crisis response' of the nation-state to the new sovereignty of financial capital is evident in the emergence of supranational political structures – a putative attempt to 'manage' capital flows. Here, we see the paradox of 'globalisation as regionalisation', as NAFTA, the European Union and a Japan-led trade zone in East Asia seek to control specified accumulation sites. Thus, as financial volatilities and wealth differentials intensify, the domestic state's evolving role is becoming one of ameliorating market fallouts and policing the socially marginalised.

Yet, despite this diminution of state sovereignty, the USA remains the key political actor within the bloc. Notwithstanding tensions in the UN Security Council, as evidenced by the 1998 Gulf crisis and 'illegal' bombing of Serbia in 1999 – a shift from hegemony to domination – the USA still directs the principal issues of foreign policy through the UN and NATO, intermediate bodies used to maintain US regional interests, notably in the Middle East. Likewise, geopolitical imperatives in the Asia-Pacific region over Japan and China have formed the basis for US-led security arrangements, which Malaysia has remained tied into via ASEAN.

The *ideological–cultural* complexion of any global bloc is, perhaps, more problematic. This is not only because cultures and ideas in an age of global information and entertainment are fluid and interacting, but also, as Said shows, because ideological forms are always subject to a dialectical process of convergence and resistance. Nevertheless, a key feature of late capitalism has been the hegemonic status of corporate ideology, a *culture of capitalism* denoting the confluence of neo-liberal ideas, 'post-Fordist' consumption and the marketisation of society. Sklair's neo-Gramscian account of 'transnational practices' (economic, political and cultural–ideological) illustrates how transnational corporations have sought to internalise free-market ideology through the reification of consumer imagery and the representation of all social life as a set of bourgeois opportunities, products and desires.[55] For Miliband, the coalescing of corporate values with state control constitutes 'a gigantic enterprise in political socialisation'.[56]

Coinciding with the information revolution, this intersection of forces represents the most dynamic power complex in history. And it is in relation to these new globalised forms of power that hegemonic relations at the *national* level may be understood. In effect, the *domestic* power bloc stands in 'devolved' relationship to the *global* power bloc.

Hegemonic projects The domestic bloc may also be sustained or adapted at different points by a particularised strategy or 'hegemonic project'. Although more amorphous as a global concept, this, again, denotes how state–class arrangements are shaped by external interests, for example in post-apartheid South Africa, where foreign capital still maintains significant influence over the new political bloc.[57]

At the domestic level, the construct has been applied, more notably, by Hall in his analysis of Thatcherism. Although using the concept 'authoritarian populism' to signify the ideological rationale of Thatcherism, Hall has stressed, in answer to Jessop et al., that the project was built around economic political and ideological elements together,[58] as in its pursuit of privatisation, working-class electoral appeals and ideals of enterprise culture. Hall is also faithful to the view of hegemony as an *ongoing* project of state *and* civil engagement:

> the *aim* is to struggle on several fronts at once, not on the economic-corporate one alone; and this is based on the knowledge that, in order really to dominate and restructure a social formation, political, moral and intellectual leadership must be coupled to economic dominance. The Thatcherites know they must 'win' in civil society as well as the state.[59]

New Labour's re-articulation of the Thatcher project also illustrates how the political bloc becomes modified to the wider bloc. The first indication of such is Blair's new liaison with corporate/City interests – the surrender of interest rate policy to the Bank of England indicating the 'new fit' between Blairite economics and global capital. The second concerns a 'renewal' of the middle-class reward structure and centre-ground alliance in an attempt to sublimate class politics to the new 'post-class' language of 'middle-England', a process built around the conscious *presentation* of Blairism as the new site of moderate politics. The third aspect involves the invocation of populist concepts like 'stakeholding', as launched, in a play on 'Asian values', during Blair's visit to Singapore in 1995. While this and other 'big ideas' have been quietly discarded, key intellectuals like Anthony Giddens have provided a 'Third Way' discourse for New Labour, allowing it new scope to absorb private sector-led policy ideas. Likewise, Blair has cultivated a new 'understanding' with the Murdoch press to help entrench its ideas. Thus the Blair project has sought to position itself as more 'corporate-friendly', 'politically modern' and 'tabloid intellectual' than Thatcherism.

Intellectual agencies, agenda-setting discourse and the media In noting the 'massification' of specialised civil–intellectual activity, Said acknowledges the 'reality' of Gramsci's intellectual as: 'a person who fulfils a particular set of functions in the society [particularly when] so many new professions ... and indeed the whole field of modern mass journalism itself – have vindicated Gramsci's vision.'[60] Thus, following Said's related insight that all texts are 'facts of power',[61] one can see how leading ideas are delineated through *agenda-setting* discourse. In *American Hegemony and the Trilateral Commission*,[62] Gill provides background to this process, showing how such fora build *shared understandings* between business figures, policy-makers and academics, thus creating intellectual debate based on, what Holub terms, a 'Western economic, financial and cultural point of view.'[63]

Huntington's *Clash of Civilisations* provides a good example of such.[64] Here we find a post-Cold War language warning of an irreconcilable gulf between the West and contrasting civilisations, most notably Islam. Here, Islam is depicted as a monolithic 'other' and gathering threat to the West, itself viewed as an idealised community requiring renewal of identity.[65] Complementing Huntington's cultural other, Fukuyama also offers an *End of History* in which the 'political project' of the West is realised in the triumph of liberal–capitalist democracy and a transcendent New World Order.[66]

Why, one might ask, have such representations of Islam, 'the East' and post-Cold War relations managed to attain such intellectual gravitas? Part of the reason appears to be the dominant institutions and interests which help sponsor them as texts, creating central discursive paradigms around which *mainstream* academic debate takes place.[67] Thus, symptomatic of a pervasive institutional bias, such discourse negates Islam's inner diversity and contradictions.[68]

For Chomsky, the production of 'necessary illusions' in 'democratic' polities is part of this agenda-setting process:

In the democratic system, the necessary illusions cannot be imposed by force. Rather, they must be instilled in the public mind by more subtle means ... [I]n a democratic political order, there is always the danger that independent thought might be translated into political action, so it is important to eliminate the threat at its root. Debate cannot be stilled, and indeed ... should not be, because it has a system-reinforcing character if constrained within proper bounds. What is essential is to set the bounds firmly. Controversy may rage as long as it adheres to the presuppositions that define the consensus of elites, and it should furthermore be encouraged within these bounds, thus helping to establish these doctrines as the very condition of thinkable thought ... *In short, what is essential is the power to set the agenda.*[69]

Thus, through routine diffusion of 'us' symbols such as the 'free-West', controlled frameworks of meaning allow dominant ideas to be played-out and received, notably through the agenda-setting filter of the 'free media'. This means, notes Chomsky, not that the media slavishly represent, or protect, incumbent state managers, rather that it reflects the consensual interests of the broad state–corporate nexus.[70] In *Television and the Crisis of Democracy*, Kellner offers a complementary view of how powerful interests filter news, information and popular culture. However, taking critical theory as a guide, he sees *hegemony*, rather than *propaganda*, as the appropriate model of analysis. Thus:

Television is best conceptualized ... as the terrain of an ever-shifting and evolving hegemony in which consensus is forged around competing ruling-class positions, values and views of the world ... a complex and open phenomenon, always subject to contestation and upheaval.[71]

Yet, while a contested and enquiring arena, media managers still have the means to select and package 'generic representations' of events, conflicts and oppositions as simplified information. Thus was the Gulf War 'imagined' through a sanitised reportage of 'smart bombs', 'clean strikes' and 'minimum collateral damage'.[72] As a tacit understanding emerges about what constitutes news and analysis, there is partisan political discussion, but limited *mainstream* questioning of the *system* itself – hence the privileged coverage of 'constitutional events' and an articulation of 'the political' as the narrow realm of party politics. Thus, through the filter of 'public service broadcasting',[73] the 'dominant consensus' becomes indivisible from the 'national interest'. Here, media exposure and interrogation of politicians has become an inverted form of information-as-entertainment. Reflecting Chomsky's axiom 'the manufacturing of consent',[74] this suggests a continuity of intellectual enterprise in maintaining standard ideas of 'democratic participation' as national–popular discourse.

In challenging such norms and institutions, the *critical* intellectual's role, for Said, is that of 'the outsider', a conceptually specific space for addressing authority:

> And this role has an edge to it, and cannot be played without a sense of being someone whose place it is publicly to raise embarrassing questions, to confront orthodoxy and dogma (rather than to produce them), to be someone who cannot easily be co-opted by governments or corporations.[75]

Invoking Gramsci, this is not the closeted professional or academic specialist, but someone:

> whose whole being is staked on a critical sense ... of being unwilling to accept easy formulas, or ready made *clichés*, or the smooth, ever so accommodating confirmations of what the powerful or conventional have to say, and what they do. Not just passively unwilling, but actively unwilling to say so in public.[76]

A note on methodology The Gramscian perspectives adopted thus constitute part of the methodological approach *sui generis*. This reflects a pedagogical view in which the 'engaged writer' recognises the specificity of 'discourse as *praxis*', an idea intrinsic to Gramsci's philosophy of *praxis* wherein the educational relationship is 'active and reciprocal so that every teacher is always a pupil and every pupil a teacher.'[77] Thus, our own endeavours as academics and writers are neither detached or neutral, but part of an active, self-reflexive process.[78]

This also signifies the use of such ideas as analytical tools, rather than an attempt to 'apply Gramsci' in a uniform way, a *heuristic* approach consistent with Gramsci's critique of positivist political science and the open-reflexive tenor of his writings. The purpose here has been to highlight the roles of actors and institutions, while seeking to elicit the 'register' and nuance of the language projected in its personalised, media or other discursive forms. Thus, to reveal how academic discourse, media stories or political statement become *text* for national–populist output, it is necessary to locate the *subtext* that gives them *hegemonic* meaning.

In addition, the impressions conveyed have been built around informal discussions with academics, politicians, business figures, media people, political activists and 'ordinary Malaysians' (an unavoidable term) in day-to-day situations. It is only through this interpersonal interaction that one can connect what passes for 'theoretical exposition' with what goes on in the *real* social world.

Notes

1. See Smart (1983), p. 75.

2. Poster (1984), p. 78, Mouffe (1979), pp. 201, 204.

3. This essay, begun in 1926, also forms part of 'Notes on Italian history' in the *Prison Notebooks*.

4. Showstack Sassoon (1980), pp. 120–1.

5. Ibid., pp. xvii, 121.

6. Holub (1992), p. 159.

7. Denoting Italian unification in 1861.

8. Simon (1982), p. 48.

9. Q. Hoare and G. Nowell Smith (eds) (1971), Introduction to 'Americanism and Fordism', pp. 277–8. See also D. Forgacs (1988), pp. 275–6.

10. Showstack Sassoon (1980), p. 121. See also S. Gill and D. Law (1989).

11. For a comprehensive analysis of Gramsci's conceptual antinomies, see Anderson (1977).

12. Ibid., pp. 21–6. Showstack Sassoon (1980), p. 112.

13. Showstack Sassoon (1980), pp. 110, 113.

14. Mouffe (1979), pp. 179, 181.

15. Alagappa (1995), p. 17.

16. Cox (1986), pp. 216–17. For a neo-realist account, see Keohane (1984).

17. Mouffe (1979), pp. 195–6.

18. Ibid., p. 195.

19. Morera (1990a), p. 191.

20. Showstack Sassoon (1980), p. 118.

21. A notion rejected by Showstack Sassoon (1980). See, for example, pp. 14, 116–19, 122.

22. Gramsci (1971), p. 161.

23. Cox (1986), p. 216.

24. Mouffe (1979). See also Morera (1993b).

25. 'Lorianism', denoting the Italian economist Achile Loria, represents, for Gramsci, the adoption of a crude positivist methodology within the social sciences. Together with his criticism of Bukharin's 'scientific materialism' this constitutes the essence of Gramsci's attack on positivist sociology. See J. Buttigieg (1975), pp. 42–64, and (1994), pp. 348–9.

26. Showstack Sassoon (1980), p. xi.

27. Bobbio, (1979), p. 31.

28. Morera (1990b), p. 28.

29. Ibid. See also Golding (1992) and Laclau and Mouffe (1985).

30. Holub (1992), p. 170.

31. See Forgacs (1988), pp. 182–3.

32. Gramsci (1971), p. 6. Italics added.

33. Ibid., p. 258.

34. Showstack Sassoon (1980), p. 254.

35. Gramsci (1971), p. 9.

36. Gramsci (1971), p. 5.

37. Showstack Sassoon (1980), p. 139.

38. Vacca (1982), p. 63.

39. Golding (1992), pp. 111, 112.

40. Gramsci (1971), pp. 6–7.

41. Ibid., p. 7.

42. See Kolakowski (1978), p. 240.

43. See Mouffe (1979), p. 195.

44. Showstack Sassoon (1980), pp. 144–5, 270.

45. Gramsci (1971), p. 10. Italics added.

46. Ibid., p. 15.

47. Ibid., p. 10.

48. Gill (1993). Gill (1995) offers a further, 'post-hegemonic', analysis of global power bloc relationships. See also Alagappa (1995), pp. 16–17.

49. For a succinct overview of informational capitalism, see Castells (1998), Vol. 3, 'Conclusion: Making Sense of our World'.

50. See Cox (1986), p. 230 and J. Frieden (1988), pp. 277–8.

51. The MAI was due to be signed by OECD ministers in Paris in April 1998, but was delayed due to a French boycott and global opposition by trade unions and NGOs. An extensive literature on the MAI as an ongoing issue can be found at various websites. See, for example, the World Development Movement.

52. 'Call for rebirth of moribund MAI', *Guardian*, 13 November 1998.

53. Note also here the role of the Transatlantic Business Dialogue, a powerful forum of US/European corporations and state ministers. One of the key issues debated here

by late 1999 was a bid by the major biotech company Monsanto to secure investment guarantees for its genetically modified organisms (GMOs).

54. Cited in 'Meet the new world government', *Guardian*, 13 February 1998.

55. Sklair (1991), pp. 76–7.

56. Miliband (1989), pp. 145, 147, 151.

57. One may note here the 'historical compromises' granted after 1994 to transnational capital and the World Bank as conditions for South Africa's re-entry into the global business order. See the John Pilger documentary, 'Apartheid Did Not Die'.

58. See Jessop et al. (1989) for the main series of exchanges with Hall on Thatcherism.

59. Hall, cited in ibid., p. 103.

60. Said (1994), p. 7.

61. See, in this regard, Strine (1991), pp. 197–8.

62. Gill (1990a), pp. 159–60.

63. Holub (1992), pp. 180–1.

64. *Foreign Affairs*, Summer, 1993.

65. Henry Kissinger described this as 'the most important book since the cold war'. Cited in *Guardian*, 23 November 1996.

66. Fukuyama (1992). For a critical alternative, see Chomsky (1994).

67. See, in contrast, Halliday's (1995) critique of alarmist views of Islam.

68. Said (1981). See also Ahmed (1996) for a critical account of Huntington's and Fukuyama's views on Islam.

69. Chomsky (1989), p. 48. Italics added.

70. Ibid., p. 149.

71. Kellner (1990), p. 16.

72. See, for example, Pilger (1992), Chapter 3.

73. For a critical discussion of such, *viz.* 'BBC impartiality', see Pilger (1998), notably pp. 521–5.

74. Herman and Chomsky (1988).

75. Said (1994), p. 9.

76. Ibid., p. 17.

77. Gramsci (1971), p. 350.

78. See Harris (1992), p. 29.

Bibliography

Books, Journals and Main Articles

Ahmad Sarji Abdul Hamid (ed.) (1993), *Malaysia's Vision 2020: Understanding the Concept, Implications and Challenges* (Petaling Jaya: Pelanduk Publications).

Ahmed, Akbar S. (1992), *Postmodernism and Islam: Predicament and Promise* (London: Routledge).

— (1996), 'Towards the global millennium: the challenge of Islam', *World Today*, vol. 52, nos 8–9.

Alagappa, Muthiah (1995), *Political Legitimacy in Southeast Asia* (Stanford, CA: Stanford University Press).

Alatas, Syed Hussein (1977a), *The Myth of the Lazy Native* (London: Frank Cass).

— (1977b), *Intellectuals in Developing Societies* (London: Frank Cass).

Ali, Anuwar (1994), 'Japanese industrial investments and technology transfer in Malaysia', in K. S. Jomo (ed.), *Japan and Malaysian Development* (London: Routledge).

Amin, Samir (1997), *Capitalism in the Age of Globalization* (London: Zed Books).

Andaya, Watson B. and L. Y. Andaya (1982), *A History of Malaysia* (London: Macmillan).

Anderson, B. (1983), *Imagined Communities: Reflections on the Origins and Spread of Nationalism* (London: Verso).

Anderson, P. (1977), 'The Antinomies of Antonio Gramsci', *New Left Review*, November 1976–January 1977, no. 100).

Anuar, Mustafa K. (1990), 'The Malaysian 1990 general election: the role of the BN mass media', *Kajian Malaysia: Journal of Malaysian Studies*, vol. 13, no. 2.

Anwar, Zainah (1987), *Islamic Revivalism in Malaysia. Dakwah Among the Students* (Petaling Jaya: Pelanduk).

Ariff, Mohamad (1991), *The Malaysian Economy: Pacific Connections* (Singapore: Oxford University Press).

Ariffin, Jamilah (1995), 'At the crossroads of rapid development: Malaysian society and anomie', *International Journal of Sociology and Social Policy*, vol. 15, nos 8/9/10.

Bagguley, P. (1993), 'Social change, the middle class and the emergence of "New Social Movements": a critical analysis', *New Left Review*, March–April, no. 198.

Bellamy, R. and D. Schecter (1993), *Gramsci and the Italian State* (Manchester: Manchester University Press).

Bobbio, N. (1979), 'Gramsci and the concept of civil society', in C. Mouffe (ed.), *Gramsci and Marxist Theory* (London: Routledge and Kegan Paul).

Boggs, C. (1976), *Gramsci's Marxism* (London: Pluto Press).

Boulanger, C. L. (1993), 'Government and press in Malaysia', *Journal of Asian and African Studies*, 28: 1–2.

Brennan, M. (1985), 'Class, politics and race in modern Malaysia', in R. Higgot and R. Robison (eds), *Southeast Asia: Essays in the Political Economy of Structural Change* (Singapore: Oxford University Press).

Brown, D. (1994), *The State and Ethnic Politics in Southeast Asia* (London/New York: Routledge).

Buci Glucksmann, C. (1982), 'Hegemony and consent: a political strategy', in A. Showstack Sassoon (ed.), *Approaches to Gramsci* (London: Writers and Readers).

Buttigieg, J. (1975), 'Introduction', in Antonio Gramsci, *Prison Notebooks*, vol. 1 (New York: Columbia University Press).

— (1994), review of Gramscian texts by Sue Golding and Renate Holub, *Science and Society*, Fall, vol. 58, no. 3.

Case, W. (1993), 'Malaysia: the semi-democratic paradigm', *Asian Studies Review*, July, vol. 17, no. 1.

Castells, M. (1998), *The Information Age: Economy, Society and Culture* vol. 3, *End of Millennium* (Malden, USA and Oxford: Blackwell).

Chin, J. (1997), 'Politics of federal intervention in Malaysia, with reference to Sarawak, Sabah and Kelantan', *Journal of Commonwealth and Comparative Politics* (July, vol. 35, no. 2).

Chomsky, N. (1989), *Necessary Illusions: Thought Control in Democratic Societies* (London: Pluto Press).

— (1991), *Deterring Democracy* (London: Verso).

— (1994), *World Orders, Old and New* (London: Pluto Press).

Choueiri, Youssef M. (1990), *Islamic Fundamentalism* (London: Pinter).

Clad, J. (1989), *Behind the Myth: Business, Money and Power in Southeast Asia* (London: Unwin Hyman).

Clammer, J. (1996), *Values and Development in Southeast Asia* (Petaling Jaya: Pelanduk).

Cottrell, A. (1984), *Social Classes in Marxist Theory* (London: Routledge and Kegan Paul).

Cox, R. (1986), 'Social forces, states and world orders', in R. Keohane (ed.), *Neorealism and its Critics* (New York: Columbia University Press).

— (1987), *Production, Power and World Order* (New York: Columbia University Press).

Crouch, H. (1990), 'The politics of Islam in the ASEAN countries', in A. Broinowski (ed.), *ASEAN into the 1990s* (London: Macmillan).

— (1993), 'Malaysia: neither authoritarian nor democratic', in K. Hewison et al. (eds), *Southeast Asia in the 1990s: Authoritarianism, Democracy and Capitalism* (St. Leonards, NSW: Allen and Unwin).

— (1994), 'Industrialization and political change', in H. Brookfield (ed.), *Transformation with Industrialization in Peninsular Malaysia* (Kuala Lumpur: Oxford University Press).

Dancz, V. H. (1982), *Women and Party Politics in Peninsular Malaysia* (Singapore: Oxford University Press).

Davidson, A. (1977), *Antonio Gramsci: Towards an Intellectual Biography* (London: Merlin Press).

Davis, M. (1986), *Prisoners of the American Dream* (London: Verso).

Dicken, P. (1991), 'The changing geography of Japanese FDI in manufacturing industry', in J. Morris (ed.), *Japan and the Global Economy* (London: Routledge).

Dixon, C. (1991), *South East Asia in the World Economy* (Cambridge: Cambridge University Press).

Esposito, J. L. (1991), *Islam: The Straight Path* (New York: Oxford University Press).

Esposito, J. L. and J. O. Voll (1996), *Islam and Democracy* (New York: Oxford University Press).

Fan Yew Teng (1999), *Anwar Saga: Malaysia on Trial* (Selangor: Genting Raya).

Finocchiaro, M. (1988), *Gramsci and the History of Dialectical Thought* (Cambridge: Cambridge University Press).

Fong Chan Onn (1989), *The Malaysian Economic Challenge in the 1990s: Transformation for Growth* (Singapore: Longman).

Forgacs, D. (1988), *A Gramsci Reader* (London: Lawrence and Wishart).

Frieden, J. (1988), 'Capital politics: creditors and the international political economy', in *Journal of Public Policy*, 8.

Friedman, E. (1994), 'Democratization: generalizing the East Asian experience', in E. Friedman (ed.), *The Politics of Democratization* (Bouler, CO: Westview Press).

Frith, S. and J. Savage (1993), 'Pearls and swine: the intellectuals and the mass media', in *New Left Review*, March–April, no. 198.

Fukuyama, F. (1992), *The End of History and the Last Man* (New York: Avon Books).

Furnivall, J. S. (1956), *Colonial Policy and Practice* (New York: New York University Press).

Ghani, Mohd Nor Abdul et al. (eds), *Malaysia Incorporated and Privatisation* (Petaling Jaya: Pelanduk).

Gill, S. (1990a), *American Hegemony and the Trilateral Commission* (Cambridge: Cambridge University Press).

— (1990b), 'Intellectuals and transnational capital', in R. Miliband and L. Panitch (eds), *Socialist Register* (London: Merlin Press).

— (ed.) (1993), *Gramsci, Historical Materialism and International Relations* (Cambridge: Cambridge University Press).

— (1995), 'Globalisation, market civilisation, and disciplinary neoliberalism', in *Millennium Journal of International Studies*, vol. 24, no. 3.

Gill, S. and D. Law (1988), *The Global Political Economy* (Baltimore, MD: Johns Hopkins University Press).

— (1989), 'Global hegemony and the structural power of capital', in *International Studies Quarterly*, vol. 33.

Golding, S. (1992), *Gramsci's Democratic Theory: Contributions to a Post-Liberal Democracy* (Toronto: University of Toronto Press).

Goldmann, L. (1973), *Philosophy of the Enlightenment* (London: Routledge and Kegan Paul).

Gomez, E. T. (1990), *UMNO's Corporate Investments* (Kuala Lumpur: Forum).

— (1994), *Political Business: Corporate Involvement of Malaysian Political Parties* (Townsville, Australia: James Cook University of North Queensland).

— (1996), *The 1995 Malaysian General Elections: A Critical Commentary* (Singapore: Institute of Southeast Asian Studies).

Gomez, E. T. and K. S. Jomo (1997), *Malaysia's Political Economy: Politics, Patronage and Profits* (Cambridge: Cambridge University Press).

Gramsci, A. (1971), *Prison Notebooks: Selections From*, ed. Q. Hoare and G. N. Smith (New York: International Publishers).

Guinness, P. (1992), *On the Margin of Capitalism* (Singapore/New York: Oxford University Press).

Gullick, J. M. (1987), *Malay Society in the Late Nineteenth Century* (New York: Oxford University Press

Hall, S. and M. Jacques (eds) (1989), *New Times* (London: Lawrence and Wishart).

Halliday, F. (1995), 'Review article: the politics of "Islam" – a second look', *British Journal of Political Science*, vol. 25, no. 3.

Harris, K. (1992), 'Schooling, democracy and teachers as intellectual vanguard', *New Zealand Journal of Educational Studies*, vol. 27, no. 1.

Harris, L. (1988), *New Perspectives on the Financial System* (London: Croom Helm).

Hashin, Mohd Nasir (1994), 'A long way from home: the struggle of a socialist Activist', *Aliran Monthly*, 14: 7.

Heng Pek Koon (1988), *Chinese Politics in Malaysia: a History of the MCA* (Singapore: Oxford University Press).

(1992), 'The Chinese business elite of Malaysia', in R. McVey (ed.), *Southeast Asian Capitalists* (New York: Southeast Asian Program).

Herman, E. and N. Chomsky (1988), *Manufacturing Consent: the Political Economy of the Mass Media* (New York: Pantheon Books).

Hewison, K. and G. Rodan (1996), 'The ebb and flow of civil society and the decline of the left in Southeast Asia', in G. Rodan (ed.), *Political Oppositions in Industrialising Asia* (London: Routledge).

Hobsbawm, E. (1983), 'Introduction: inventing traditions', in E. Hobsbawm and T. Ranger (eds), *The Invention of Tradition* (Cambridge: Cambridge University Press).

Ho Khai Leong (1994), 'Malaysia: the emergence of a new generation of UMNO leadership', *Southeast Asian Affairs* (annual).

Holub, R. (1992), *Antonio Gramsci: Beyond Marxism and Postmodernism* (London: Routledge).

Hooker, M. B. (1972), *Adat Laws in Modern Malaya* (Kuala Lumpur: Oxford University Press).

Hua Wu Yin (1983), *Class and Communalism in Malaysia* (London: Zed Books).

Huntington, S. (1993), 'The clash of civilizations', *Foreign Affairs*, Summer 1993.

Husin Ali, Syed (1996), *Two Faces: Detention Without Trial* (Petaling Jaya: INSAN).

Hutton, W. (1995), *The State We're In* (London: Jonathan Cape).

Hussein, Syed Ahmad (1987), 'Islam and politics in Malaysia, 1969–1982: the dynamics of competing traditions', PhD thesis, Yale University.

Ibrahim, Mahamad Hakimi (1999), 'The end of capitalism and the waqf thesis', in *Journal of Alternative Political Economy*, January, vol. 1, no. 1.

International Finance Corporation (World Bank; ed., T. Barger) (1998), *Financial Institutions* (Washington, DC: International Finance Corporation).

Ismail, R. (1995), *Hudud in Malaysia* (Kuala Lumpur: SIS Forum, Malaysia Bhd.).

Jeshurun, Chandran (1993), 'Malaysia: the Mahathir supremacy and Vision 2020', in *Southeast Asian Affairs* (annual).

Jessop, B. (1988), *Thatcherism* (Cambridge: Polity Press).

Jesudason, J. V. (1996), 'The syncretic state and the structuring of oppositional politics in Malaysia', in G. Rodan (ed.), *Political Oppositions in Industrialising Asia* (London: Routledge).

Jomo, K. S. (1986), *A Question of Class: Capital, the State and Uneven Development in Malaysia* (Singapore: Oxford University Press).

— (1989), *Beyond 1990: Considerations for a New National Development Strategy* (Kuala Lumpur: Institute for Advanced Studies: University of Malaysia).

— (1990), *Beyond the New Economic Policy?* (Brisbane: Asian Studies Association of Australia).

— (1999), 'Development planning in Malaysia: a critical appraisal', in B. N. Ghosh and Muhammad Syukri Salleh (eds), *Political Economy of Development in Malaysia* (Kuala Lumpur: Utusan Publications).

Jomo, K. S. and Ahmad Shabery Cheek (1992), 'Malaysia's Islamic movements', in J. S. Kahn and F. Loh Kok Wah (eds), *Fragmented Vision*.

— (1994), 'Introduction', in K. S. Jomo (ed.), *Japan and Malaysian Development* (London: Routledge).

Jun, Jong S. (ed.) (1994), *Development in the Asia Pacific* (Berlin/New York: Walter de Gruyter).

Kahn, J. S. (1992), 'Class, ethnicity and diversity: some remarks on Malay culture in Malaysia', in J. S. Kahn and F. Loh Kok Wah (eds), *Fragmented Vision* (Sydney: Asian Studies Association/Allen and Unwin).

— (1996), 'The middle class as a field of ethnological study', in Muhammad Ikmail Said and Zahid Emby (eds), *Malaysia: Critical Perspectives. Essays in Honour of Syed Husin Ali* (Selangor: Persatuan Sains Sosial Malaysia).

Kellner, D. (1990), *Television and the Crisis of Democracy* (Boulder, CO: Westview Press).

Keohane, R. (1984), *After Hegemony: Co-operation and Discord in the World Political Economy* (Princeton, NJ: Princeton University Press).

Kershaw, R. (1987), *Powers of Persuasion: the Malaysian Media in the Pergau Dam Affair* (University of Hull, Centre for Southeast Asian Studies).

Kessler, C. (1992), 'Archaism and modernity: contemporary Malay political culture', in J. S. Kahn and F. Loh Kok Wah (eds), *Fragmented Vision*.

Khoo Boo Teik (1995), *Paradoxes of Mahathirism* (Kuala Lumpur: Oxford University Press).

— (1997a), 'Democracy and authoritarianism in Malaysia since 1957', in A. Laothamatas (ed.), *Democratization in Southeast and East Asia* (Singapore: ISEAS).

— (1997b), 'Malaysia. challenges and upsets in politics and other contestations', in D. Singh (ed.), *Southeast Asian Affairs, 1997* (Singapore: ISEAS).

— (1998), 'Economic nationalism and its discontents: Malaysian political economy after July 1997' presented to conference 'From Miracle to Meltdown: the End of Asian Capitalism', Fremantle, Western Australia.

— (1999), 'Asian values and the economic crisis', paper presented to conference 'Globalization and Asian Civilizations – Implications of the Asian Economic Crisis', Japan Foundation Asia Centre.

Khoo Kay Jin (1992), 'The grand vision', in J. S. Kahn and F. Loh Kok Wah (eds), *Fragmented Vision*.

Kling, Zainal (1995), 'The Malay family: beliefs and realities', *Journal of Comparative Family Studies*, vol. 26, no 1.

Kolakowski, L. (1978), *Main Currents of Marxism* (vol. 3) (Oxford: Oxford University Press).

Kua Kia Soong (1985), *National Culture and Democracy* (Petaling Jaya: Kersani Penerbit Sdn Bhd.).

— (1992), 'The problem with Malaysian statistics', in Kua Kia Soong, *Malaysian Political Realities* (Petaling Jaya: Oriengroup Sdn. Bhd.)

— (1996), *Inside the DAP, 1990–95* (Petaling Jaya: PB).

— (1998), 'DAP's latest purge: another re-run of a bad movie', *Aliran Monthly*, July, 18: 6.

Laclau, E. and C. Mouffe (1985), *Hegemony and Socialist Strategy* (London/New York: Verso).

Laothamatas, A. (1997), 'Development and democratization: a theoretical introduction to the Southeast Asian and East Asian cases', in A. Laothamatas (ed.), *Democratization in Southeast and East Asia* (Singapore: ISEAS).

Lawrence, P. K. (1996), 'Strategy, hegemony and ideology: the role of intellectuals', *Political Studies*, vol. 44, no. 1.

Lee Poh Ping (1990), 'ASEAN and the Japanese role in Southeast Asia', in A. Broinowski (ed.), *ASEAN into the 1990s* (London: Macmillan).

Lim Kit Siang (1997), *IT for All* (Petaling Jaya: DAP Information Technology Committee).

— (1998), *Economic and Financial Crisis* (Petaling Jaya: DAP Economic Committee).

Ling Liong Sik (1995), *The Malaysian Chinese: Towards Vision 2020* (Petaling Jaya: Pelanduk).

Linklater, A. (1989), *Beyond Realism and Marxism* (New York: St. Martin's Press).

Loh Kok Wah, F. (1997a), 'Developmentalism in Malaysia in the 1990s. Is a shift from the politics of ethnicism underway?', research paper for 'Discourses and Practices of Democracy in Southeast Asia', Research and Education for Peace Unit, Universiti Sains Malaysia.

— (1997b), 'Development, democracy and ASEAN NGOs', *Aliran Monthly*, 17: 1.

Loh Kok Wah, F. and J. S. Kahn (1992), 'Introduction: fragmented vision', in J.S. Kahn and F. Loh Kok Wah (eds), *Fragmented Vision*.

Loh Kok Wah, F. and Mustafa K. Anuar (1996), 'The press in Malaysia in the 1990s. Corporatisation, technological innovation and the middle class', in Muhammad Ikmal Said and Zahid Emby (eds), *Malaysia: Critical Perspectives. Essays in Honour of Syed Husin Ali* (Selangor: Persatuan Sains Sosial Malaysia).

Maaruf, Shaharuddin (1992), 'Some theoretical problems concerning tradition and modernization among the Malays of Southeast Asia', in Yong Mun Cheong (ed.), *Asian Traditions and Modernization* (Singapore: Times Academic Press).

McCloud, D. G. (1995), *Southeast Asia, Tradition and Modernity in the Contemporary World* (Boulder, CO: Westview Press).

MacPherson, C. B. (1973), *Democratic Theory: Essays in Retrieval* (Oxford: Clarendon Press).

Mahathir bin Mohamad (1970), *The Malay Dilemma* (Singapore: Times Books International).

— (1986), *The Challenge* (Malaysia: Pelanduk Publications).

— (1993), 'Views and thoughts of the prime minister of Malaysia', in Ahmad Sarji Abdul Hamid (ed.), *Malaysia's Vision 2020: Understanding the Concept, Implications and Challenges* (Petaling Jaya: Pelanduk Publications).

Malaysian Department of Information (1996), *Seventh Malaysia Plan* (Kuala Lumpur: Jabatan Penerangan Malaysia).

Malaysian Ministry of Finance (1997), *Malaysia Economic Report (1997/98)* (Kuala Lumpur: Percetakan Nasional Malaysia Bhd.).

Malaysian Department of Statistics (1998), *Yearbook of Statistics, Malaysia* (Kuala Lumpur: Jabatan Perangkaan Malaysia).

Malaysian Ministry of Finance (1998), *Malaysia Economic Report (1998/99)* (Kuala Lumpur: Percetakan Nasional Malaysia Bhd.).

Malaysia (1998), *The 1999 Budget* (Kuala Lumpur: Jabatan Penerangan Malaysia).

Means, G. (1976), *Malaysian Politics* (London: Hodder and Stoughton).

— (1991), *Malaysian Politics: the Second Generation* (Singapore: Oxford University Press).

Mehmet, Ozay (1986), *Development in Malaysia* (England: Croom Helm).

— (1990), *Islamic Identity and Development* (Kuala Lumpur: Forum).

Miliband, R. (1989), *Divided Societies* (Oxford/New York: Clarendon Press, Oxford University Press).

Milne, R. S. and D. K. Mauzy (1986), *Malaysia: Tradition, Modernity and Islam* (London: Westview Press).

Milne, S. (1994), *The Enemy Within* (London: Pan Books).

Moha Asri Abdullah (1999), 'The inflow of foreign labour to Malaysia: some critical analysis of socio-economic and political implications on the locals', in B. N. Ghosh and Muhammad Syukri Salleh (eds), *Political Economy of Development in Malaysia* (Kuala Lumpur: Utusan Publications).

Mohamad, Maznah (1999), 'The rot within us', *Aliran Monthly*, May, 19: 4.

Montgomery Watt, W. (1988), *Islamic Fundamentalism and Modernity* (London: Routledge).

Moore, Barrington Jnr. (1966), *The Social Origins Of Democracy and Dictatorship* (Boston, MA: Beacon Press).

Moran, M. (1990), 'Financial markets', in J. Simmie and R. King (eds), *The State in Action* (London: Pinter).

Morera, E. (1990a), *Gramsci's Historicism* (London/New York: Routledge).

— (1990b), 'Gramsci and democracy', *Canadian Journal of Political Science*, 23.

Mouffe, C. (1979), 'Hegemony and ideology in Gramsci', in C. Mouffe (ed.), *Gramsci and Marxist Theory* (London: Routledge and Kegan Paul).

Munro-Kua, A. (1996), *Authoritarian Populism in Malaysia* (UK: Macmillan).

Mutalib, Hussin (1990), *Islam and Ethnicity in Malay Politics* (Singapore: Oxford University Press).

— (1993), *Islam in Malaysia: From Revivalism to Islamic State?* (Singapore: Singapore University Press).

Muzaffar, Chandra (1987), *Islamic Resurgence in Malaysia* (Petaling Jaya: Penerbit Fajir Bakti).

— (1988), *Issues of the Mahathir Years* (Penang: Aliran).

— (1989a), *Challenges and Choices in Malaysian Politics and Society* (Penang: Aliran).

— (1989b), *The NEP: Development and Alternative Consciousness* (Penang: Aliran).

Nain, Z. (1993), 'Films and Malaysian society', *Aliran Monthly*, 13: 3.

— (1996), 'Commercialisation with a conscience? restoring the credibility of the Malaysian media', *Aliran Monthly*, 16: 2.

Nairn, T. (1988), *The Enchanted Glass* (London: Radius).

Nagata, J. A. (ed.) (1975), *Pluralism in Malaysia: Myth and Reality* (Leiden: E. J. Brill).

Nester, W. (1990), *Japan's Growing Power over East Asia and the World Economy* (Basingstoke: Macmillan).

Netto, A. (1999), 'Anwar's shadow looms over UMNO', *Aliran Monthly*, July 19: 6.

OECD (1992), *Technology and the Economy: The Key Relationship* (Paris: OECD).

O'Malley, W. (1988), 'Culture and industrialisation', in H. Hughes (ed.), *Achieving Industrialisation in East Asia* (Cambridge/Melbourne: Cambridge University Press).

Pateman, C. (1970), *Participation and Democratic Theory* (Cambridge: Cambridge University Press).

Penang Chinese Chamber of Commerce, (1996), *Directors' Handbook, 1996–1997* (Penang: PCCC).

Pilger, J. (1992), *Distant Voices* (London: Vintage).

— (1998), *Hidden Agendas* (London: Vintage).

Poster, M. (1984), *Foucault, Marxism and History* (Cambridge, New York: Polity Press).

Preston, P. W. (1986), *Making Sense of Development* (New York: Routledge and Kegan Paul).

— (1987), *Rethinking Development: Essays on Development in Southeast Asia* (London: Routledge and Kegan Paul).

— (1998), *Pacific Asia in the Global System* (Oxford: Blackwell).

Provencher, R. (1990), 'Covering Malay humor magazines: satire and parody of Malaysian political dilemmas', *Crossroads/Journal of Southeast Asian Studies*, vol. 5, no. 2.

Rahim, L. (1993), 'Singapore: consent, coercion and constitutional engineering', *Current Affairs Bulletin*, December 1993/January 1994, vol. 70, no. 7.

Rashid, R. (1993), *A Malaysian Journey* (Selangor: Rehman Rashid).

Reich, R. (1991), *The Work of Nations* (London: Simon and Schuster).

Rodan, G. (1993), 'Preserving the one party state in Singapore', in K. Hewison et al., *Southeast Asia in the 1990s* (St. Leonards, NSW: Allen and Unwin).

— (1996), 'Theorising political opposition in East and Southeast Asia', in G. Rodan (ed.), *Political Oppositions in Industrialising Asia* (London: Routledge).

Roff, W. R. (1967), *The Origins of Malay Nationalism* (New Haven, CT and London: Yale University Press).

Rudnick, A. (1996), *Foreign Labour in Malaysian Manufacturing: Bangladeshi Workers in the Textile Industry* (Kuala Lumpur: INSAN).

Ruggie, J. G. (1982), 'International regimes, transactions and change – embedded liberalism in the post war economic order', *International*, vol. 36.

Said, E. (1978), *Orientalism* (London: Routledge and Kegan Paul).

— (1981), *Covering Islam: How the Media and Experts Determine How We See the Rest of the World* (London: Routledge and Kegan Paul).

— (1993), *Culture and Imperialism* (New York: Knopf).

(1994), *Representations of the Intellectual (The 1993 Reith Lectures)* (London: Vintage).

Said, Muhammad Ikmal (1992), 'Ethnic perspectives of the left in Malaysia', in J. S. Kahn and F. Loh Kok Wah (eds), *Fragmented Vision*.

Salleh, Halim (1991), 'State capitalism in Malaysian agriculture', *Journal of Contemporary Asia*, vol. 21, no. 3.

Salleh, Muhammad Syukri (1999), 'Political economy of Islamic development', in B. N. Ghosh and Muhammad Syukri Salleh (eds), *Political Economy of Development in Malaysia* (Kuala Lumpur: Utusan Publications).

Salleh, Muhammad Syukri and Siti Hayati Abdullah (1993), 'Islamisation of state and society', in *Aliran Monthly*, 13: 1.

Saravanamuttu, J. (1987), 'The State, authoritarianism and industrialisation: reflections on the Malaysian case', *Kajian Malaysia: Journal of Malaysian Studies*, vol. 5.

— (1999), 'From crisis to reform', *Aliran Monthly*, May, 19: 4.

— (1999), 'Can the opposition win?', *Aliran Monthly*, June, 19: 5.

Saravanamuttu, J. et al. (1996), 'Caring civil society', in J. Saravanamuttu (ed.), *Final Report of Top-Down IRPA (Intensification of Research in Priority Areas) Social Science Projects 1995)*, (Penang: Universiti Sains Malaysia).